THE TRAUMA OF SEXUAL ASSAULT

Treatment, Prevention and Practice

Edited by

Jenny Petrak
Barts and the London NHS Trust, UK

Barbara Hedge
University of Waikato, New Zealand

JOHN WILEY & SONS, LTD

Other Wiley Editorial Offices

John Wiley & Sons, Inc., 605 Third Avenue,
New York, NY 10158-0012, USA

WILEY-VCH GmbH, Pappelallee 3,
D-69469 Weinheim, Germany

John Wiley & Sons Australia, Ltd, 33 Park Road, Milton,
Queensland 4064, Australia

John Wiley & Sons (Asia) Pte Ltd, 2 Clementi Loop #02-01,
Jin Xing Distripark, Singapore 129809

John Wiley & Sons (Canada) Ltd, 22 Worcester Road,
Rexdale, Ontario M9W 1L1, Canada

British Library Cataloguing in Publication Data
A catalogue record for this book is available from the British Library

ISBN 0-471-62660-0 (cased)
ISBN 0-471-62691-0 (paper)

Project management by Originator, Gt Yarmouth (typeset in 10/12pt Palatino).

This book is printed on acid-free paper responsibly manufactured from sustainable
forestry, in which at least two trees are planted for each one used for paper production.

THE TRAUMA OF SEXUAL ASSAULT

The Wiley Series in

CLINICAL PSYCHOLOGY

Titles published under the series editorship of:

J. Mark G. Williams   *School of Psychology, University of Wales, Bangor, UK*

A list of earlier titles in the series follows the index.

CONTENTS

ABOUT THE EDITORS

Jenny Petrak is currently Head of Clinical Psychology within the Medical Emergency Directorate at Barts & London NHS Trust and Honorary Senior Clinical Lecturer in the Department of Immunology at St Bartholomew's and the Royal London School of Medicine. She has worked in health, infection and immunity, and HIV medicine settings in the NHS for many years and has extensive experience in clinical work with individuals with psychological difficulties related to sexual assault and trauma, sexually transmitted infections including HIV, gynae-cological problems, sexual dysfunction, and other health concerns. Current research interests include: prevention and treatment of sexual assault, abuse and risk behaviours, and HIV and sexually transmitted diseases. She regularly provides teaching to a wide range of professionals on the psychology of health and trauma including forensic medical exam-iners, police, physicians, nurses, and other health professionals.

Barbara Hedge is Director of Clinical Training at the University of Waikato in New Zealand. Previously she ran a Clinical Psychology Training Course at the University of Hertfordshire and was an Honorary Senior Lecturer at St Bartholomew's and the Royal London School of Medicine and Dentistry, University of London. For many years she was a Consul-tant Clinical Psychologist in Barts and the London NHS Trust. She has worked extensively in sexual health centres and HIV clinics in the NHS. Her research interests include the psychological sequelae of sexually transmitted diseases, HIV, sexual assault, and medical interventions and illness management. She has published widely in these areas and has been involved in teaching and training in Africa, Eastern Europe, and Bangladesh.

Imagine constantly relocating your home and business. How do you think Priscilla dealt with this type of lifestyle?

How would you deal with this type of lifestyle?

What lessons can you take from Priscilla's life and apply to your own life?

4word

If you are married, how would you characterize your relationship as compared to Priscilla and Aquila? What can you learn from Priscilla and Aquila's relationship?

NOTES

What is it about work that enables us to really bond? Notice how Priscilla and Aquila bonded with Paul as they worked together. Have you ever experienced this type of relationship with your co-workers?

How can you improve your relationships with your co-workers?

LIST OF CONTRIBUTORS

Ron Acierno *National Crime Victims Research and Treatment Center, Department of Psychiatry and Behavioral Sciences, Medical University of South Carolina, 165 Cannon Street, Charlton, SC 29425, USA*

Jennifer A. Bennice, MA *Center for Trauma Recovery, Department of Psychology, University of Missouri-St Louis, 8001 Natural Bridge Road, St Louis, MO 63121-4499, USA*

Adrian W. Coxell, BSc, MSc DClin Psych, Clinical Psychologist *Academic Unit, Trust Head-quarters, West London Mental Health NHS Trust, Uxbridge Road, Southall, Middlesex UB1 3EU, UK*

Anne-Marie Doyle, BSc, ClinPsyD, Chartered Clinical Psychologist *Psychological Medicine Unit, Chelsea and Westminster Hospital, 1 Nightingale Place, London SW10 9NG, UK*

Christina A. Gidycz, PhD, Associate Professor *Department of Psychology, Ohio University, Athens, OH 45701-2979, USA*

Matt J. Gray, PhD, Postdoctoral Fellow *National Center for PTSD, Boston VAMC/Boston University School of Medicine*

Barbara Hedge, PhD, Chartered Clinical Psychologist, Director of Clinical Training *Department of Psychology, University of Waikato, Hamilton, NZ*

Julia C. Houston, Consultant Clinical Psychologist *Forensic Mental Health Services, Springfield University Hospital, Shaftesbury Clinic, Glenburnie Road, London SW17 7DT, UK*

Helen Kennerley, DPhil, Consultant Clinical Psychologist *Oxford Cognitive Therapy Centre, Warneford Hospital, Oxford OX3 7JX, UK*

Michael B. King, MD, PhD, FRCP, FRCGP, FRCPsych *Department of Psychiatry and Behavioural Sciences, Royal Free and University College Medical School, University of London, Royal Free Campus, Rowland Hill Street, London NW3 2PF, UK*

Nichole L. Marioni, MS *Department of Psychology, Ohio University, Athens, OH 45701-2979, USA*

Amy E. Naugle, PhD, Assistant Professor *Department of Psychology, Western Michigan University, 1903 W. Michigan Avenue, Kalamazoo, MI 49008-5439, USA*

Jenny Petrak, MSc, PsychD, Consultant Clinical Psychologist, Head of Clinical Psychology *Infection and Immunity Specialty Group, Barts and the London NHS Trust, The Ambrose King Centre, The Royal London Hospital, London E1 1BB, UK*

Heidi S. Resnick, PhD, Professor of Psychiatry *National Crime Victims Research and Treatment Center, Department of Psychiatry and Behavioral Sciences, Medical University of South Carolina, 165 Cannon Street, Charlton, SC 29425, USA*

Resick Patricia A., PhD, Curators' Professor of Psychology *Center for Trauma Recovery, Department of Psychology, University of Missouri-St Louis, 8001 Natural Bridge Road, St Louis, MO 63121-4499, USA*

Cindy L. Rich, MS *Department of Psychology, Ohio University, Athens, OH 45701-2979, USA*

Deborah Rogers, MBBS, DCH, DRCOG, MRCGP, DFFP, MMJ, Honorary Senior Lecturer in Forensic Medicine *St George's Hospital Medical School, Cranmer Terrace, London SW17 OAE, UK*

Susan Thornton, BSc, PsychD, Chartered Clinical Psychologist *Psychological Medicine, Chelsea and Westminster Hospital, 1 Nightingale Place, London SW10 9NG, UK*

Lynne Webster, MB, ChB, MSc, FRCPsych, Consultant Psychiatrist *Department of Psychiatry, Manchester Royal Infirmary, Rawnsley Building, Oxford Road, Manchester M13 9WL, UK*

PREFACE

Why another book about rape and sexual assault? As clinical psychologists working in medical and sexual health settings, we found ourselves seeing both men and women who had experienced rape and sexual assault. While we found many interesting books from the 1970s onwards that addressed rape from the feminist, social, and political perspective, we found few texts that addressed the wide-ranging problems we encountered in the clinical setting.

Our motivation in compiling this text is to draw together current theories, research, and clinical practice relating to the management of sexual assault. This is primarily a book for clinical psychologists, psychiatrists, counsellors, support workers, therapists, and clinicians working in settings that provide for sexual assault or who are thinking of setting up such services. It will also prove useful to primary care workers and physicians working in a wider field as well as to voluntary sector agencies. Police, legal, and judicial professionals may also find an understanding of the psychological impact of sexual assault useful in improving the management of complainants.

We deliberated over how to refer to the person who has experienced sexual assault. Many texts use the terms 'victim' or 'survivor' and legal texts frequently refer to the 'complainant'. Each of these terms provides a different insight into the experience of the assaulted person. At different times, any of these terms might be appropriate. We, therefore, decided not to impose any specific terminology on the authors. As a consequence, these terms are used interchangeably throughout the book. Many case examples are used in this book. Each is based on fact but each has been significantly altered in order to protect the identity of the person involved. Cases have also been simplified in order to demonstrate salient points.

Chapter 1 begins with an overview of how rape and sexual assault has been defined in legal and clinical settings. It also introduces readers to background information, epidemiology, and a brief résumé of the way rape and sexual assault has been viewed and managed over time. Chapter 2 reviews common affective, cognitive, and behavioural responses to sexual assault. It also considers factors that affect post-sexual assault trauma. Many texts on sexual assault only consider rape of women. In Chapter 3, Coxell and King familiarize the reader with the differential effects of gender and sexuality on the psychological effects of sexual assault.

Recently, much progress has been made in the development of therapies to address trauma. In Chapter 4, Bennice and Resick critically review a number of models and treatment studies in the field of sexual assault. Doyle and Thornton, in Chapter 5, then provide a basis that should enable the reader to carry out an initial sexual assault interview and psychological assessment. In Chapters 6–8, Naugle *et al.*, Kennerley, and Webster address psychological therapy for different aspects of the outcome of sexual assault. Chapter 9 considers the wide range of medical and physical concerns that may affect adjustment and coping in the aftermath of sexual assault.

A neglected area in the literature has been the evaluation of programmes designed to prevent rape and sexual assault. In Chapter 10, Gidycz *et al.* review the efficacy of single sex and mixed sex prevention programmes.

The first professional contacts that a person encounters after reporting a sexual assault are the police and forensic medical examiner. In Chapter 11, Rogers familiarizes the reader with details of the legal and forensic process. The preceding chapters clearly demonstrate the traumatic impact of sexual assault on the victim. The effects of working with persons who have been sexually assaulted are beginning to be recognized. Chapter 12 considers the impact of working in this area upon health-care workers.

For every person who is raped, there is a rapist. In clinical practice, people who have been assaulted frequently question the motivations of their assailant. In Chapter 13, Houston introduces the reader to theories of rape and the clinical practice of working with offenders.

In conclusion, Chapter 14 draws together relevant themes from previous chapters and highlights the urgent need for an evidence-based health care approach to sexual assault policy, practice, and research.

Finally, we would like to thank the many people whose encouragement and support made this book possible. In particular, we thank the person, who wishes to remain anonymous, who kindly provided her story and illustrations in Chapter 2. We thank the staff and patients of the sexual assault services of Barts and the London NHS Trust who provided us with the inspiration for this text. We are also grateful to our partners and cats who waited patiently for our attention during the preparation of this text.

May 2001

Jenny Petrak
Barbara Hedge

Chapter 1

RAPE: HISTORY, MYTHS, AND REALITY

Jenny Petrak

INTRODUCTION

Rape and sexual assault are common crimes in our society. While few would disagree that the aftermath of sexual assault is traumatic for the individual, it has only been in the past two decades that any systematic description of any psychological consequences has occurred. The advent of feminism in the 1970s led to an increasing focus on the legal, medical, and psychosocial needs of survivors, but, as recently as 1992, the American Medical Association acknowledged the large impact that sexual violence against women has on health care and admits that departments are poorly prepared and researched to deal with this problem (Council on Scientific Affairs, 1992).

Research into sexual assault largely originates from the USA and the applicability of these studies to other populations is not known. However, at least one UK study echoes the above concern and makes clear recommendations for an improvement in medical and psychological services for women, arguing that more specialized support services are needed than what is currently on offer (Lees and Gregory, 1993). The literature on and services for male rape are even more limited. This may be due to the fact that it has only recently been criminalized in the UK (Home Office, 1994) and those rates of reporting are low.

This book will attempt to open the debate on sexual assault by bringing together existing research findings and theoretical perspectives on female and male rape and sexual assault and consider the implications for future practice and policy. Different aspects of male and female sexual assault

The Trauma of Sexual Assault. Edited by Jenny Petrak and Barbara Hedge.
© 2002 John Wiley & Sons Ltd.

will be highlighted throughout, but, since the majority of data available is on women (and it is among women that the majority of those who have been raped are found), the focus will naturally bias towards women. It might, however, be the case that much of the information provided will be applicable to the male survivor. The terms 'sexual assault' and 'rape' are often used interchangeably in the literature. In this text, 'rape' will be used to describe acts meeting the legal definition, and 'sexual assault' to refer to the wide spectrum of assault behaviours (difficulties with these definitions will be discussed on p. 8). The term 'survivor' or 'complainant' will be the preferred terms used, rather than 'victim', to place the individual as having an active role in the experience of survival and recovery from rape and sexual assault. However, it is acknowledged that various debates about nomenclature exist in this area (see Chapter 3) and that much of the available research refers to the 'victim' of sexual assault. The aims of this chapter are to provide a brief overview of how rape has been defined, viewed, and managed over time.

HISTORICAL AND CULTURAL PERSPECTIVES ON RAPE AND SEXUAL ASSAULT

The silence surrounding rape prior to the 1970s has often been commented upon perhaps most notably by Susan Brownmiller, whose classic book *Against Our Will* (Brownmiller, 1975) contributed an analysis of rape which, along with feminist consciousness raising, became a turning point for improvements in social policy and legal and medical care for survivors. Brownmiller (1975) describes how rape and sexual victimization have been part of the subordination of women dating from prehistoric times to present. She cites an example from the Bible with the story of Potiphar's wife (which is an important morality lesson in Hebrew, Christian and Moslem folklore), illustrating what can happen to an upstanding man if a vengeful female cries rape. Judging from recent press coverage of 'date rape' trials in the UK, the impression is given that men continue to be unfairly accused of rape.

Brownmiller (1975) also critiques the beginning of law stating: 'concepts of rape and punishment in early English law are a wondrous maze of contradictory approaches reflecting a gradual humanisation of jurisprudence in general, and in particular, man's eternal confusion, never quite resolved, as to whether the crime was a crime against a woman's body or a crime against his estate.' She was also one of the first commentators on differences in how rape is managed based on social class and race. This work is as relevant today and should continue to be on the 'essential reading' list of those who work with survivors.

In many societies, rape in war became one of the prerogatives of the victor in battle (and news reports from current sites of conflict such as Bosnia and Rwanda suggest this continues to be the case), indicating the totality of defeat and ultimate humiliation of the defeated. This was the case certainly for women but also to some extent for men. In modern times, male rape was considered rare outside the context of incarceration (and this is the only context in which Brownmiller [1975] mentions men being raped). Nevertheless, even in ancient times, there are descriptions of men who, having been raped, 'lose their manhood' and ability to be an effective soldier. A more latter day description of this is found in T.E. Lawrence's *Lawrence of Arabia* who was raped by his Turkish captors during World War I causing much subsequent disruption to his life. Despite the passage of time, myths around loss of masculinity following rape continue to be pervasive.

The origins of research into the social and psychological impact of rape and sexual assault, the Rape Crisis movement, and improvements in care for survivors are found within the social change emanating from the feminist movement in the 1970s. Prior to the 1970s, there was little available information about individuals who had been raped, due to the focus on victimology and characterizing of the offenders often as aberrant and subject to uncontrollable sexual urges. According to Roberts (1989), this focus led to 'the victim' being to some extent irrelevant because the choice of her as victim would be unconnected with her as an individual. She continues 'one fundamental reason why the feminist anti-rape campaigns created such a change in thinking about rape was that they gave space and voice to those who had been silenced' (Roberts, 1989). Accordingly, the first Rape Crisis Centre was set up in the USA in 1970 and in the UK in 1976.

Empirical studies characterizing women's responses to rape also started to appear in the USA around this time. These were essentially descriptive studies conducted without controls and on groups who were seeking help following rape (e.g. Sutherland and Scherl, 1970; Burgess and Holmstrom, 1974; Symonds, 1975). Such studies were nevertheless instrumental in prompting subsequent research and towards improving medical services for survivors of sexual assault. The most well known of these early studies was by Burgess and Holmstrom (1974) who termed the acute traumatic reaction of sexual victimization as the 'Rape Trauma Syndrome'. This syndrome was described based on similarities of response observed in 109 child, adolescent, and adult females who had been subjected to forced sexual penetration presenting to an emergency hospital department. Burgess and Holmstrom (1974, 1979) followed this group longitudinally and noted that approximately one-quarter of women continued to have difficulties consequent on the rape 6 years later. This was one of the few longitudinal studies in this area. Burgess and Holmstrom (1974) emphasized that this syndrome is an acute reaction to an externally imposed situational crisis.

Thus, this early conceptualization of the stress response to sexual assault closely resembles the diagnostic criteria of post-traumatic stress disorder (PTSD; DSM-III-R, APA, 1987; DSM-IV, APA, 1994). Post-traumatic reactions were described for a number of years under various names such as shell shock and combat fatigue, associated with war veterans (Breslau and Davis, 1987), and PTSD did not appear as a diagnostic category within the DSM-III of the American Psychiatric Association (APA) until 1980. PTSD has now largely subsumed the concept of 'rape trauma syndrome' and will be the focus of several chapters in this book. However, studies from the USA suggest that survivors of rape from the largest group of victims of crime affected by PTSD (Steketee and Foa, 1987).

Similar to elsewhere, the way that rape and sexual assault are managed in the UK has been slow to change. Attempts at legal reform began in the 1970s due to the sustained campaigning of groups such as Rights of Women, Women Against Rape, and Rape Crisis. One such legal reform was the amendment to the Sexual Offences Act (1976) which required that the defence should apply for permission from the judge, prior to cross-examining a complainant regarding her sexual history or sexual character. Unfortunately, this seems to continue to have little impact on how rape cases are managed by the legal system in the UK (Lees, 1996). Further notable, early work arising out of the Women Against Rape movement in London was the Women's Safety Survey published as *Ask any woman: A London inquiry into rape and sexual assault* (Hall, 1985). This was the first large-scale UK study providing information about the prevalence and characteristics of sexual offences and the experience of women who reported rape to the police and the legal systems. This study was important in lobbying for social and political reform and increasing sensitivity towards those who had experienced rape. There continues, however, to be a paucity of specialist sexual assault services for women in the UK and funding for Rape Crisis centres has been cut over the years. One pioneering model in the UK has been the Manchester Sexual Assault Referral Centre, which was set up as recently as 1986. There are few other existing specialist services in the UK, although genitourinary medicine clinics are increasingly becoming involved in the care of the sexually assaulted (Bottomley, Sadler, and Welch, 1999). Where the diverse range of legal, medical, and psychological needs that a survivor may present with are best met, however, remains a matter for debate.

While the above has primarily focused on work originating from the UK and USA, it is, however, important to note that prevalence studies suggest that rape and sexual assault are widespread and cut across all socio-economic, ethnic, and cultural groups. That rape, and any other acts of gender-based violence against women including domestic violence, mutilation, and sexual abuse, are a public health issue deserving of international concern and action has in the last decade been adopted by the United Nations Commission on the Status of Women (Heise, Pitanguy, and Germain, 1994) and the World Health Organization (WHO, 1996). The UN Declaration against Violence against Women was stated in 1993 and provided a definition of violence against women which included recognition of both the physical and psychological harm, in both public and private spheres, caused by rape, sexual assault, and a range of other abuses. Increasingly, the very high impact that this abuse has on health is being recognized, and, in industrialized countries, it is reported that rape and domestic violence account for one in every five healthy years of life lost to women aged 15–44 (Heise *et al.*, 1994). It is hoped that by emphasizing that any form of violence against women, including rape, is a violation of basic human rights, pressure can be put on all governments to take action across relevant sectors such as the media, health, education, the legislative, and judiciary system.

Despite these worthwhile efforts, it seems the social change required to end these human rights violations is some way off. Thus, for example, on a more local level, we have had much recent media coverage of the high-profile rape trial of Mike Tyson in the USA and the acquittal of several male university students in the UK for 'date rape'. The impression given in coverage of these trials has often been that men were being unfairly accused of rape as a result of feminist political correctness (Lees, 1996). The media coverage may have contributed to an increase in the number of women reporting to the police and led some to argue that more false allegations are being reported. There is, however, no evidence to support the latter. Public disbelief in the wide prevalence of abuse and sexual stereotypes continue to contribute to the view that spurious complainants are common.

RAPE MYTHS AND STEREOTYPES

There are many rape myths, misconceptions, and stereotypes that impact on how society, and the legal and medical system, approaches the management of sexual assault. Rape myths will also affect the perceptions of the survivor, the availability of social support, and, inevitably, how an individual copes with the emotional and psychological consequences. Attention to rape myths and stereotypes originated in the feminist literature of the 1970s. Susan Brownmiller (1975) identified four fundamental misconceptions (the 'deadly male myths of rape') that *all women want to be raped, no woman can be raped against her will, she was asking for it,* and *if you are going to be raped you might as well enjoy it.*

While virtually every common stereotype existing about rape has been discredited by accumulated knowledge over the past 20 years, there continues to be a persisting image that *rape is a physically violent assault carried out by a psychotic stranger in a dark alleyway at night.* Although this is the reality for some, most rapists do not fit criteria for psychiatric diagnosis, and the majority of rapes take place indoors and by someone known to the survivor (Dunn and Gilchrist, 1993). Terms such as acquaintance or date rape are used to describe the latter which may account for up to 80% of sexual assault reported to rape crisis centres (Warshaw, 1988). Acquaintance rape has been a largely hidden phenomena until recently, but a recent increase in publicity has arisen in the UK due to the finding that such cases are more likely to be dropped and less likely to achieve conviction by the judiciary system (Harris and Grace, 1999). This has led the Home Office to consider the idea of 'grading' the seriousness of sentences attached to rape charges (i.e. less severe sentences for acquaintance or date rape compared with stranger rape) to improve conviction rates. Clearly, there are other routes towards improving conviction rates, but this recent debate is demonstrative of how rape stereotypes are upheld in the law. There is also evidence to suggest that women who are raped by acquaintances are also less likely to report to the police (Lees and Gregory, 1993), are less likely to access medical and psychological care (Koss, Gidycz, and Wisniewski, 1988), and may be seen as more culpable and thereby less deserving of support from partners, family, and friends (Baker, Sholnik, Davis, and Brickman, 1991) than those who are raped by strangers.

Another linked rape stereotype is that *husbands cannot rape their wives*. In fact, marital rape is very common and occurs throughout most cultures (Hall, 1985; Heise *et al.*, 1994). Rape by intimates may also be secondary to other types of ongoing physical abuse. It has, however, been a stereotype upheld in law, and rape within marriage only became a crime as recently as 1992 in the UK (Home Office, 1994). The extent of the problem becomes apparent in a recent review in which it is observed that 'women in the United States are more likely to be assaulted and injured, raped, or killed by a current or ex-male partner than by all other types of assailants combined' (Council on Scientific Affairs, 1992). A further prevalent stereotype is that *woman who are raped must have done something to cause it to happen*. This judgement may be based on behaviour or dress or sexual history (i.e. *nice girls don't get raped*). The idea that someone might choose to be raped is connected to other prevalent myths including the assumption that *rape is motivated by uncontrollable male sexual desire* and accompanying this that *most women secretly desire and enjoy being raped*. Despite accumulated evidence to debunk such myths, this is a prevalent view in the media and literature. Theories of sexual aggression, including those that support rape as a biologically and sexually motivated act, abound and will be discussed in more detail in Chapter 13. However, the argument that sexual urges are the motive are not supported by the fact that most rapists have access to consenting sexual relations at the time of the assault (Dunn and Gilchrist, 1993). Furthermore, the very high level of trauma found post-rape suggests rape is most often a terrorizing, aggressive act, which is carried out with the purpose of controlling, humiliating, and degrading the survivor.

A number of specific stereotypes affect the management of male sexual assault. First, the idea that *a real man cannot be raped* (Groth and Burgess, 1980) has until recently been upheld in the legal system in the UK where 'rape' was specified as forcible vaginal penetration (i.e. only women could be raped). This stereotype also links in with traditional views of masculinity where the expectation is that men should be able to fight back. However, in the few studies which have been carried out in this area, men have reported high levels of shock and fear during these attacks engendering feelings of helplessness and inability to respond (Mezey and King, 1989; Frazier, 1993). Another common myth affecting men is *the presence of erection or ejaculation implies consent on behalf on the survivor.* While this has been disproved in a number of human and animal studies, where it is clear that high levels of physiological arousal can lead to genital response, this myth continues to be used as a legal defence and can also be distressing for survivors (Coxell and King, 1996).

Further myths concern the confusion that a sexual act between two people of the same sex is a homosexual act: *men who rape other men must be gay* and *a man who is raped by another man must be gay or have been acting in a gay manner* (Coxell and King, 1996). Men may be less likely to report sexual assault because they fear being labelled as homosexual, and, for some men, rape may lead to acute confusion over sexuality and sexual roles. Confusion over sexuality may affect men regardless of their sexual orientation (King, 1995). The impact of rape myths on gender and sexuality are elaborated upon in Chapter 3. The above stereotypes also emphasize the sexual component of the assault whereas, similar to studies of female rape, it seems more likely that degradation and domination motivate the crime. These stereotypes have undoubtedly contributed to low reporting of male rape, and it may be particularly difficult for a man to acknowledge his victimization to family or friends, let alone the police. Consequently treatment programmes for men who have been raped are rare.

The pervasive nature of the above stereotypes are upheld in a number of studies of the rape attitudes of various professional groups including lawyers, police, doctors, nurses, and mental health professionals (for a review see Ward, 1995). In general, it seems health care professionals respond more positively to those individuals who fit a stereotypical pattern of sexual violence (Best, Dansky, and Kilpatrick, 1992). Furthermore, these studies often find gender differences such that men tend to be more accepting of rape myths, less supportive of survivors, more tolerant of sexual violence, and more blaming of survivors, compared with women (Ward, 1995).

The above stereotypes are often internalized for survivors and give rise to high levels of self-blame. The negative impact of self-blame (and the blame of others) on post-rape functioning has been demonstrated (Wyatt, Newcomb, and Notgrass, 1991). Although attitude change towards rape has been demonstrated in a limited number of studies primarily in US college settings (Ward, 1995), there are no broader rape prevention strategies incorporating attitude change available to date. It is essential for those working with rape and sexual assault to examine our own attitudes, and misconceptions of this area as summed up in the following saying: 'Judgements are for courtrooms, not consulting and clinic rooms'. The pervasive nature of these stereotypes and their negative impact on survivors suggest a continuing need to educate the public, legal, and medical care system.

DEFINITIONS OF SEXUAL ASSAULT AND RAPE

The terms 'rape' and 'sexual assault' are often used interchangeably in the literature and are synonymous in legal usage (Koss and Harvey, 1991). However, many studies refer to a variety of forms of sexual coercion which may not constitute a legal definition of rape. In addition, legal definitions of rape and sexual assault have also been subject to extensive reform over the past two decades. Definitions of rape and sexual assault, legal or otherwise, reflect wider social movements and cultural practices. It is thus worth reviewing some of these past and present definitions both towards understanding the terminology used in the literature and also towards the complex issue of understanding how sexual assault is socially construed.

In traditional definitions, rape was defined as 'carnal knowledge of a female forcibly and against her will', and was generally restricted to vaginal–penile penetration with a woman who was not the man's wife (Bienen, 1980). Such definitions were criticised as being too narrow and contributing towards prejudicial criminal justice practices in handling rape cases (Berger, Searles, and Neuman, 1995). The feminist movement was instrumental in achieving legal reform and argued traditional rape law regulated women's sexuality and protected male rights to possess women as sexual objects. There is considerable diversity in the reforms that were achieved in rape law. In the USA, some states redefined rape as sexual assault in an attempt to broaden the crime beyond its traditional meaning, vaginal–penile intercourse, to include oral and anal penetration as well as vaginal penetration, sexual penetration with objects, and touching of intimate body parts. Other reforms redefined the crime in gender-neutral terms in order to include male rape and some statutes removed or modified the spousal exemption which has given husbands immunity for rape of their wives (Berger *et al.*, 1995).

Others have sought to provide alternative definitions (e.g., 'non-consenting sexual relations with another person, obtained through physical force, threat or intimidation': Groth and Burgess, 1977) in an attempt to counter earlier definitions which suggested the victim should have been subjected to violence for rape to have happened and to counter the narrowness of definitions based on penile–vaginal penetration only. Many statutes in the USA define rape as the 'nonconsensual sexual penetration of an adolescent or adult obtained by physical force, by threat of bodily harm, or when the victim is incapable of giving consent by virtue of mental illness, mental retardation, or intoxication' (Searles and Berger, 1987). Clearly, this definition is an improvement in broadening the scope for conviction of rape by acknowledging the contribution of vulnerability.

In the UK, rape law reforms resembling some of the above changes have been fairly recent. Rape within marriage was legally recognized as a crime when the law was changed in a House of Lords ruling in 1992. The present legal definition of rape in the UK is presented in Table 1.1. This is the first legal recognition of male rape in the UK. While this law specifies both vaginal or anal penetration where the person does not consent to it as rape, other forms of sexual coercion including attempted rape, oral sex, and penetration by instruments continue to be crimed as 'indecent assault' (Home Office, 1994).

Legal definitions of rape and sexual assault continue to be controversial and subject to criticism due to their narrowness and consequent difficulty in achieving convictions (Lees, 1996).

Rape laws that are prejudicial, particularly against women, are universal. In many countries, the judicial system often treats rape as a crime against public morality, family honour, or 'property' (e.g. African customary law), as opposed to a crime against the individual (Heise *et al.*, 1994). In some countries, laws make it almost impossible to prosecute rape. In Pakistan, for example, the Law of Evidence considers women 'incompetent' as witnesses in cases of rape and would require four male Muslim witnesses

Table 1.1 Sexual offences in the UK: definition of rape (adapted from *Criminal Justice and Public Order Act*, Home Office, 1994)

1. It is an offence for a man to rape a woman or another man.
2. A man commits rape if –
   (a) he has sexual intercourse with a person (whether vaginal or anal) who at the time of the intercourse does not consent to it; and
   (b) at the time he knows that the person does not consent to the intercourse or is reckless as to whether that person consents to it.

A man also commits rape if he induces a married woman to have sexual intercourse with him by impersonating her husband.

to provide corroborative evidence. In several Latin American countries, rape is only defined as a crime if it is committed against 'honest' (e.g. virginal) girls or women, while laws in Chile and Guatemala specifically dismiss the charge if a man agrees to marry the girl or woman he has raped (Heise *et al.*, 1994).

While definitions of rape and sexual assault and accompanying laws have to some extent been reformed over the years in a number of countries, Heise *et al.* (1994) point out that 'such laws are only as good as their enforcement', and it is, unfortunately, in the latter where legal responses to rape and other abuse notably fail. This is not a problem confined to developing countries; recent work in the UK suggests that only 6% of cases of rape being reported to the police actually result in a conviction, which is a decline from 24% in 1985 (Harris and Grace, 1999). Given the difficulty in reaching a consensus in defining rape and sexual assault and the inherent prejudice in many existing definitions and legal systems, it is probably not surprising that incidence and prevalence figures vary widely as described below.

THE INCIDENCE AND PREVALENCE OF SEXUAL ASSAULT

In 1983, Andrea Dworkin wrote: 'we use statistics not to try to quantify the injuries, but to convince the world that those injuries exist.' This statement exemplifies the motivation of researchers who continue to attempt to quantify the scope of rape and sexual assault in our society beyond that reported in crime statistics. The incidence of rape as reported by crime statistics refers to the number of separate criminal incidents that occurred over a fixed time period, usually a 1-year period. Reporting of rape by this method would suggest that it is a relatively infrequent crime,

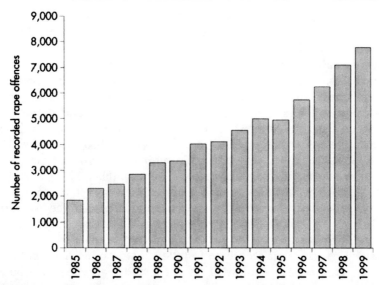

Figure 1.1 Home Office recorded rape offences (female) in the UK 1985–1999 (adapted from Harris and Grace, 1999; and *Crime and Criminal Justice Unit*, Home Office, 2000).

for example, rape represented just 3% of the violent crimes reported to National Crime Statistics (NCS) in the USA in 1985. In contrast to community surveys, according to the NCS, women are more likely to be raped by strangers than by someone they know and weapons are used in a third of rapes reported (Koss and Harvey, 1991).

Figures in the UK also suggest a low (but increasing) incidence of rape. The data available relates to rape of females. Thus, the number of rape offences recorded in England and Wales in 1992 was 4,100 which is over three times the number recorded in 1982. This is explained by both increases in reporting by the public and changes in police practice towards a greater number of cases being recorded as offences. Similarly, there is again an increase in 1994 figures where 5,082 cases of rape were recorded (Home Office, 1993, 1994). The changing incidence of recorded rape offences is shown in Figure 1.1.

Data on the number of cases of rape in men are only just starting to become available in the UK, and, in 1995, 3,142 indecent assaults and 227 rapes were recorded (*Criminal Statistics*, Home Office, 1996). In the USA, crime statistics on male rape are also limited due to the fact that the Federal Bureau of Investigation do not report men as being raped in their crime statistics because of defining rape as something that can only be committed against a woman (Isely, 1998).

The omission of male rape from recorded crime statistics is only one of the problems in this area and, in general, there is agreement in the literature that recorded offences grossly underestimate the incidence of rape and sexual assault in the population. Thus, the NCS method of collecting has been criticised due to the use of questions which require respondents to answer questions which use the term 'rape' and conceptualize it as a violent crime (Koss, 1995). Studies both in the USA and the UK have estimated that only somewhere between 7 and 25% of rape and sexual assault offences are reported to the police (Hall, 1985; Koss *et al.*, 1987; Koss, 1995). This figure may be even lower in cases involving marital rape and where the assailant is known to the survivor (Hall, 1985). In addition, a large problem, identified in a number of studies, is that complaints of rape are not always recorded by the police and if 'crimed' they were more likely to fit the classic stranger rape (Lees and Gregory, 1993). Lees and Gregory (1993) argue that the high rate of complaints of rape which are classified as 'no crime' continue to reflect a strong belief by police that women make false allegations. They cite a study carried out by the New York Crimes Analysis Unit which found that the rate of false allegations for rape and sexual offences was only around 2% (Adler, 1987).

Koss *et al.* (1987) suggest that prevalence data reflecting the cumulative number of women who have been sexually victimized are more relevant to mental health research because of the long-term medical and psychological after-effects of sexual assault. However, prevalence studies are also subject to methodological difficulties, in particular, variability in the definition of sexual assault used (which may be used as a generic term that includes rape as well as other degrees of unwanted and pressured sexual contacts not involving penetration, and incest and child sexual abuse) and the use of select populations. Koss and Harvey (1991) review a number of prevalence studies of sexual assault in the USA and, selecting those using probability sampling methods and a definition of rape resembling legal standards, suggest a 20% rape prevalence for adult women (Kilpatrick, Saunders, Veronen, Best, and Von, 1987; Koss *et al.*, 1987). In the UK, similar figures have been found; a survey questionnaire distributed to 2,000 women in London found that 17% reported completed rape (60% of these were marital rape) and a further 20% had been victims of attempted rape (Hall, 1985). Within genitourinary settings in the UK, prevalence studies of outpatient attendees suggest 28 to 35% of women report a lifetime history of sexual assault (Petrak, Skinner, and Claydon, 1995; Keane, Young, and Boyle, 1996).

Prevalence surveys on rape have typically excluded adult males until more recently (Coxell, King, Mezey, and Gordon, 1999). Early prevalence data on male rape and sexual assault have been of small and atypical samples from, for example, incarcerated populations or from men presenting to medical and psychiatric clinics. In the USA, up to 10% of individuals reporting to treatment centres for rape are men (Kaufman, DiVasto, Kackson, Voorhees, and Christy, 1980). A more recent study in a US prison population reports that up to 22% of men may have had non-consensual sexual contact, of which over half involved anal sex (Struckman-Johnson and Struckman-Johnson, 1994). However, all prevalence figures in such studies are thought to reflect underreporting. One of the main US prevalence studies of male sexual assault carried out in the general community found that 7% of a sample of 1,480 men in Los Angeles had been sexually assaulted since the age of 16 (Sorenson, Stein, Siegel, Golding, and Burnham, 1987). Touching on an area which has received very little attention over the years, due to the assumption that perpetrators are almost always male, this study also reported a higher rate of female perpetrators compared with male perpetrators. This finding has been attributed to how forced sexual contact was defined in the study (i.e., 'In your lifetime, has anyone ever tried to pressure or force you to have sexual contact? By sexual contact I mean their touching your sexual parts, you touching their sexual parts, or sexual intercourse?') leading to respondents precluding anal penetration (Coxell and King, 1996).

In the UK, there has been one large survey reporting the lifetime prevalence of non-consensual sex in men (Coxell et al., 1999). Of 2,474 men recruited through general practices, 71 (3%) reported non-consensual sexual experiences as adults (and 5% of men reported sexual abuse as children). Similar to surveys of women, having a history of child sexual abuse was predictive of non-consensual sexual experiences as an adult (Coxell et al., 1999). Further data is provided in studies detailing prevalence rates of male sexual assault in specific populations. In a sample of 930 homosexual men, Hickson et al. (1994) found that 27.6% had been sexually assaulted at some point in their lives, and that 99 of these men had been raped. In genitourinary medicine settings in the UK, two anonymous surveys report rates of 11 and 14% of male attendees providing histories of sexual assault (Petrak et al., 1995; Keane et al., 1995).

Prevalence data of rape and sexual assault in women (but not men) have now been reported from many other countries; for example, Shim (1992) reports, from a sample of 2,270 women in Korea, a prevalence rate of completed rape of 8% and completed and attempted rape of 22%. In South Africa, it has been reported that a woman is raped every minute and a half, totalling approximately 386,000 women raped each year (Bindel, 1996).

Brutal rapes as part of war have occurred throughout history and are not exclusive to developing countries. The high prevalence of these crimes has only just begun to be recorded and receive wide media coverage; for example, since fighting in Bosnia began in 1992, it is estimated that more than 20,000 Muslim women have been raped. There are reports that women have been held in 'rape camps' where they are raped repeatedly and forced to bear Serbian children as tools of 'ethnic cleansing' (Post, 1993 cited in Heise *et al.*, 1994). A study from the civil war in Liberia reported that 49% of a random sample of 205 girls and women experienced at least one act of sexual or physical violence from soldiers (15% had been raped or subjected to attempted rape) (Swiss *et al.*, 1998). Much less is known about the prevalence of sexual assault on men in war and Carlson (1997) argues this relates to wider social stereotypes denying the possibility of male rape and, perhaps, particularly in military contexts. While beyond the scope of this text, readers are referred to Swiss and Giller (1993) for a recent review of the impact of rape in war.

Precise figures of the incidence and prevalence of rape and sexual assault will remain difficult to assess. All data from which these figures arise are dependent on information given from survivors themselves. Concepts of what constitutes rape vary across cultures and there is no widely accepted universal classification system. There is evidence in the UK to suggest that, in both, women and men, reporting to the police is very low (Lees, 1996). There are no certainties that legal authorities will take appropriate action. In addition, the assaulted person may feel revictimized by the police and judiciary process (Lees, 1996). Disclosure remains problematic due to pervasive negative attitudes towards survivors who may, by acknowledging his or her rape, incur further devaluation and stigmatization.

THE CARE OF SURVIVORS OF RAPE AND SEXUAL ASSAULT

The focus of this book is to bring together much of what is known from existing research findings and theoretical perspectives from clinicians and academics in the field about the mental health care which can be provided for survivors of rape and sexual assault. In doing this, there will always be omissions, and there will always be inherent difficulties in tackling a topic that is infused with social and political values. The above discussion provides a backdrop for some of these difficulties. In attempting to provide care for the survivor, it is, however, important to gain an understanding of the context of rape and sexual assault. It is within this social and political context that the psychological responses of survivors are framed.

Rape and sexual assault are risk factors for physical and mental health difficulties. Not all individuals will need medical and psychological care following rape. For those who do, there is no one established way in which such care should be provided. In many countries, there will not be a health infrastructure to implement rape interventions, and innovative culture specific community based programmes will be needed. It has been argued that the involvement of mental health professionals, with their tendency towards disease models and diagnoses, places emphasis on the pathology of the woman (or man) and diverts attention away from the responsibilities of the perpetrators of rape (usually men). It is also argued that, used with responsibility, diagnoses such as PTSD can be a tool to help individuals understand their behaviour and feelings as long as the underlying violence is acknowledged (WHO, 1996). Thus, this is the challenge to every mental health clinician, counsellor, and researcher who may read this book. As our knowledge expands regarding the impact of rape and sexual assault, we must assume the responsibility of how this knowledge is applied to the lives of individuals affected. As socially ingrained as rape and sexual assault may seem to be, there is evidence from anthropological research that it is not inevitable in all societies (e.g. Levinson, 1989) and evidence that strategic rape prevention interventions can be effective (Hanson and Gidycz, 1993). Our responsibility will also inevitably be to contribute towards the elimination of these crimes from our lives.

REFERENCES

Adler, Z. (1987) *Rape on trial*. London: Routledge and Kegan Paul.

APA. (1987) *Diagnostic and statistical manual of mental disorders* (3rd edn, rev.). Washington, DC: American Psychiatric Association.

APA. (1994) *Diagnostic and statistical manual of mental disorders* (4th edn). Washington, DC: American Psychiatric Association.

Baker, T., Skolnik, L., Davis, R., and Brickman, E. (1991) The social support of survivors of rape: The differences between rape survivors and survivors of other violent crimes and between husbands, boyfriends, and women friends. In A. Burgess (ed.) *Rape and sexual assault III*. New York: Garland Publishing.

Berger, R., Searles, P. and Neuman, W. (1995) Rape-law reform: Its nature, origins, and impact. In P. Searles, and Berger, R. (eds) *Rape and society: Readings on the problem of sexual assault*. Boulder, CO: Westview Press.

Best, C.L., Dansky, B.S., and Kilpatrick, D.G. (1992) Medical students' attitudes about female rape victims. *Journal of Interpersonal Violence*, 7, 175–188.

Bienen, L. (1980) Rape III—National developments in rape reform legislation. *Women's Rights Law Reporter*, 6, 170–213.

Bindel, J. (1996) *Women overcoming violence and abuse* (Research Paper No. 15): Bradford, UK: Research Unit on Violence, Abuse and Gender Relations, University of Bradford.

Bottomley, C., Sadler, T., and Welch, J. (1999) Integrated clinical service for sexual assault victims in a genitourinary setting. *Sexually Transmitted Infections*, **75**, 116–119.

Breslau, N. and Davis, G. (1987) Post-traumatic stress disorder: The stressor criterion. *Journal of Nervous and Mental Disease*, **175**, 255–264.

Brownmiller, S. (1975) *Against our will*. Harmondsworth, UK: Penguin.

Burgess, A. and Holmstrom, L. (1974) Rape Trauma Syndrome. *American Journal of Psychiatry*, **131**, 981–986.

Burgess, A. and Holmstrom, L. (1979) Adaptive strategies and recovery from rape. *American Journal of Psychiatry*, **136**, 1278–1282.

Carlson, E.S. (1997) Sexual assault on men in war. *The Lancet*, **349**(9045), 129.

Council of Scientific Affairs (American Medical Association). (1992) Violence against women. *Journal of the American Medical Association*, **267**, 3184–3189.

Coxell, A.W. and King, M.B. (1996) Male victims of rape and sexual abuse. *Sexual and Marital Therapy*, **11**, 297–308.

Coxell, A., King, M., Mezey, G., and Gordon, D. (1999) Lifetime prevalence, characteristics, and associated problems of non-consensual sex in men: Cross sectional survey. *British Medical Journal*, **318**, 846–850.

Dunn, S.F. and Gilchrist, V.J. (1993) Sexual assault. *Primary Care*, **20**, 359–373.

Dworkin, A. (1983) Cited in: Searles, P. and Berger, R. (eds), *Rape and society: Readings on the problem of sexual assault*. Boulder, CO: Westview Press.

Frazier, P.A. (1993) A comparative study of male and female rape victims seen at hospital-based rape crisis program. *Journal of Interpersonal Violence*, **8**, 65–79.

Groth, A.N. and Burgess, A.W. (1977) *American Journal of Orthopsychiatry*, **47**, 400–406.

Groth, A.N. and Burgess, A.W. (1980) Male rape: Offenders and victims. *American Journal of Psychiatry*, **137**, 806–810.

Hall, R. (1985) *Ask any woman: A London inquiry into rape and sexual assault*. Bristol: Falling Wall Press.

Hanson, K.A. and Gidycz, C.A. (1993) Evaluation of a sexual prevention program. *Journal of Consulting and Clinical Psychology*, **61**, 1046–1052.

Harris, J. and Grace, A. (1999) *A question of evidence? Investigating and prosecuting rape in the 1990s* (Research Study 196). London: Home Office.

Heise, L., Pitanguy, J., and Germain, A. (1994) *Violence against women: The hidden health burden* (World Bank Discussion Paper 255). Washington, DC: The World Bank.

Hickson, F.C.I., Davies, P.M., Hunt, A.J., Weatherburn, P., McManus, T.J., and Coxon, A.P.M. (1994) Gay men as victims of nonconsensual sex. *Archives of Sexual Behaviour*, **23**, 281–294.

Home Office. (1993) *Criminal Statistics—England and Wales*. London: Her Majesty's Stationery Office.

Home Office. (1994) *Criminal Justice and Public Order Act*. London: Blackwell.

Home Office. (1996) *Criminal Statistics—England and Wales*. London: Her Majesty's Stationery Office.

Home Office. (2000) *Crime and Criminal Justice Unit*. London: Her Majesty's Stationery Office.

Isely, P.J. (1998) Sexual assault of men: American research supports studies from the UK. *Medical Science and Law*, **38**, 74–79.

Kaufman, A., DiVasto, P., Kackson, R., Voorhees, H., and Christy, J. (1980) Male rape victims: Non-institutionalised assault. *American Journal of Psychiatry*, **137**, 221–223.

Keane, F., Young, S., Boyle, H., and Curry, K. (1995) Prior sexual assault reported by male attenders at a department of genitourinary medicine. *International Journal of STD and AIDS*, **6**, 95–100.

Keane, F., Young, S., and Boyle, H. (1996) The prevalence of previous sexual assault among routine female attenders at a department of genitourinary medicine. *International Journal of STD and AIDS*, **7**, 480–484.

Kilpatrick, D., Saunders, B., Veronen, L., Best, C., and Von, J. (1987) Criminal victimization: Lifetime prevalence, reporting to police, and psychological impact. *Crime and Delinquency*, **33**, 479–489.

King, M. (1995) Sexual assaults on men: Assessment and management. *British Journal of Hospital Medicine*, **53**, 245–246.

Koss, M. (1995) Hidden rape: Sexual aggression and victimization in a national sample of students in higher education. In P. Searles and R. Berger (eds) *Rape and society: Readings on the problem of sexual assault*. Boulder, CO: Westview Press.

Koss, M. and Harvey, M. (1991) *The rape victim: Clinical and community interventions*. Newbury Park, CA: Sage Publications.

Koss, M., Dinero, T., Seibel, C., and Cox, S. (1988) Stranger, acquaintance, and date rape: Is there a difference in the victim's experience? *Psychology of Women Quarterly*, **12**, 1–24.

Koss, M., Gidycz, C., and Wisniewski, N. (1987) The scope of rape: Incidence and prevalence of sexual aggression in a national sample of higher education students. *Journal of Consulting and Clinical Psychology*, **55**, 162–170.

Lees, S. (1996) *Carnal knowledge. Rape on trial*. London: Hamish Hamilton.

Lees, S. and Gregory, J. (1993) *Rape and sexual assault: A study of attrition*. London: Islington Council.

Levinson, D. (1989) *Violence in cross-cultural perspective*. Newbury Park, CA: Sage Publication.

Mezey, G. and King, M. (1989) The effects of sexual assault on men: A survey of 22 victims. *Psychological Medicine*, **19**, 205–209.

Petrak, J., Skinner, C., and Claydon, E. (1995) The prevalence of sexual assault in a genitourinary medicine clinic: Service implications. *Genitourinary Medicine*, **71**, 98–102.

Post, T. (1993) A pattern of rape. *Newsweek*, 4 January.

Roberts, C. (1989) *Women and rape*. Hertfordshire: Harvester Wheatsheaf.

Searles, P. and Berger, R. (1987) The current status of rape reform legislation: An examination of state statutes. *Women's Rights Law Reporter*, **10**, 25–43.

Shim, Y. (1992) Sexual violence against women in Korea: A victimization survey of Seoul women. Paper presented at Conference on International Perspectives: Crime, Justice and Public Order, St Petersburg, Russia, 21–27 June.

Sorenson, S.B., Stein, J.A., Siegel, J.M., Golding, J.M., and Burnham, M.A. (1987) The prevalence of adult sexual assault: The Los Angeles Epidemiologic Catchment Area Project. *American Journal of Epidemiology*, **126**, 1154–1164.

Steketee, G., and Foa, E. (1987) Rape victims: Post-traumatic stress responses and their treatment: A review of the literature. *Journal of Anxiety Disorders*, **1**, 69–86.

Struckman-Johnson, C.J. and Struckman-Johnson, D. (1994) Men pressured and forced into sexual experience. *Archives of Sexual Behaviour*, **23**, 93–114.

Sutherland, S. and Scherl, D. (1970) Patterns of response among victims of rape. *American Journal of Orthopsychiatry*, **28**, 527–529.

Swiss, S. and Giller, G. (1993) Rape as a crime of war: A medical perspective. *Journal of the American Medical Association*, **270**, 612–615.

Swiss, S., Jennings, P.J., Aryee, G.V., Brown, G.H., Jappah-Samukai, R.M., Kamara, M.S., Schaak, R.D., and Turay-Kanneh, R.S. (1998) Violence against women during the Liberian civil conflict. *Journal of the American Medical Association*, **279**, 625–629.

Symonds, M. (1975) Victims of violence: Psychological effects and aftereffects. *American Journal of Psychoanalysis*, **36**, 27–34.

Ward, C.A. (1995) *Attitudes toward rape*. London: Sage Publications.

Warshaw, R. (1988) *I never called it rape: The MS. report on recognizing, fighting and surviving date and acquaintance rape*. New York: Harper and Row.

WHO. (1996) *Violence against women*. Women's health and development family and reproductive health. Geneva: World Health Organization.

Wyatt, G., Newcomb, M., and Notgrass, C. (1991) Internal and external mediators of women's rape experiences. In A. Burgess (ed.) *Rape and sexual assault III*. New York: Garland Publishing.

Chapter 2

THE PSYCHOLOGICAL IMPACT OF SEXUAL ASSAULT

Jenny Petrak

INTRODUCTION

The medical and psychological consequences of sexual assault are wide-ranging. These may include physical injury, sexually transmitted diseases, risk of pregnancy, gynaecological trauma, medically explained and un-explained somatic symptoms, chronic illness, emotional disturbance, sexual dysfunction, suicide, and substance abuse (Koss and Harvey, 1991; Golding, 1994). While the immediate concern for the person who has been sexually assaulted may be the treatment of any physical injury (and finding evidence of the latter will be a focus for the forensic medical examiner to prove to courts that an assault has occurred; see Chapter 11), the psychological injuries are those that last. With high prevalence rates (see Chapter 1), it is possible to speculate that large numbers of women and men may have unresolved emotional difficulties related to histories of sexual assault. A history of sexual victimization is associated with overall increased health and medical system utilization (Koss *et al.*, 1990). In those sexual assault survivors who do present to emergency clinics, follow-up rates are very low (Holmes *et al.*, 1998). However, since the majority may never access any professional care (with sexual assault being the explicit presenting issue), a major neglected area of understanding is of the par-ticular resilience individuals may demonstrate in coping with trauma in the aftermath of sexual assault. This chapter will provide an overview of the common affective, cognitive, and behavioural responses to sexual assault. The impact of ongoing stressors, vulnerability history, and assault-related variables that may affect post-assault psychological re-sponse will also be considered.

The Trauma of Sexual Assault. Edited by Jenny Petrak and Barbara Hedge.
© 2002 John Wiley & Sons Ltd.

RAPE TRAUMA

Empirical studies of the psychological impact of sexual assault did not appear until the 1970s and were mainly focused on the experience of US women. Even fewer studies examine the psychological impact of sexual assault in men (see Chapter 3 for consideration of gender differences in response to sexual assault), although it is reported that the needs and responses of males are very similar to those of females (Burgess and Holmstrom, 1979). Early conceptualizations of responses to rape were essentially descriptive studies conducted without controls and on groups who were seeking help following rape (e.g. Sutherland and Scherl, 1970; Burgess and Holmstrom, 1974; Symonds, 1975). Such studies were, nevertheless, instrumental in prompting subsequent research and in educating and improving medical services for survivors of sexual assault. The most well known of these early studies was by Burgess and Holmstrom (1974) who termed the acute traumatic reaction of sexual victimization as the 'rape trauma syndrome'. This syndrome was described based on similarities of response observed in 109 child, adolescent, and adult victims who had been subjected to forced sexual penetration presenting to an emergency hospital department. They described the core feature of anxiety in the rape trauma syndrome to be 'a subjective state of terror and overwhelming fear of being killed' (Burgess and Holmstrom, 1974). The syndrome is divided into two phases, which can disrupt the physical, psychological, social, and sexual aspects of an individual's life. The acute or disruptive phase can last from days to weeks and is characterized by general stress response symptoms. The second phase is characterized by a process of reorganization, during which the victim has the task of restoring order and a sense of control in his or her world. This second phase may last from months to years. Burgess and Holmstrom (1974) emphasized that this syndrome is an acute reaction to an externally imposed situational crisis. Thus this early conceptualization of the stress response to sexual assault closely resembles the diagnostic criteria of post-traumatic stress disorder (PTSD) (Burgess, 1995). PTSD has largely subsumed the concept of 'rape trauma syndrome' and will be considered separately on p. 28. Nevertheless, in clinical practice, these early conceptualizations of traumatic responses to sexual assault may provide useful frameworks towards understanding reactions to rape (and are, arguably, more rape-specific with greater ecological validity than broad, conceptual diagnoses such as PTSD) as illustrated in the case example below.

Based on cumulative evidence from early studies of the acute and long-term response to rape, Koss and Harvey (1991) have described these as the 'anticipatory', 'impact', 'reconstitution', and 'resolution' phases.

The 'anticipatory phase': Immediately preceding the sexual assault, a person begins to realize that the situation is potentially dangerous. This, in turn, gives rise to the use of various defence mechanisms including dissociation and rationalization to preserve a sense of safety. Individuals may also, for example, attempt to verbally reason, dissuade, or gain extra time with the offender, remain calm so as not to provoke additional attention (or violence), or think about how to get away (Burgess and Holmstrom, 1979). The following illustrated case example* demonstrates the immediate impact of the rape:

Ms A was walking home at night after having visited friends. This was a built-up city area that was well lit and tended to be busy at all hours; Ms A had walked this route many times before. Three men approached her asking for directions. She felt uneasy but thought if she remained helpful towards them by showing the directions, she would be safe. Two of the men grabbed her arms and steered her towards a nearby parking lot. At this point, thinking they were probably going to rape her, she attempted to dissuade them saying she was menstruating

*These illustrations were central to the therapeutic intervention and, although distressing, will give the reader some insight into the impact upon the individual. Details have been changed to protect confidentiality; the illustrations are shown with permission of the survivor and are her recollection of the rape and her consequent reaction.

and had 'infections'. Throughout she reported feeling 'like it wasn't happening to me or as if it was someone else in a movie' and 'everything seemed to be happening in slow motion'

The 'impact phase': This phase describes the time period of the actual assault and its immediate aftermath. Burgess & Holmstrom (1974) described the intense fear of death or bodily harm experienced by women during rape which in turn gives rise to varying degrees of disintegration and disorganization in the ability to appraise and respond to the situation. This acute stress response may give rise to high levels of physiological and psychological arousal such as shock, numbness, disbelief, and helplessness.

Ms A started to feel very afraid they might harm her. She tried to scream but nothing seemed to come out of her mouth. There no longer seemed to be any people around. At some point, she thought that if she just let them 'get on with it' she might survive. The men pushed her down and pulled up her skirt. Two men raped her, and the third man watched. Immediately afterwards, they inserted an ink pen in her rectum. She recalled thinking about whether or not

her tights had run at that point. She reported feeling 'numb' and recalls having put her clothes together and then wandered in to a local shop where the police were called. She was admitted to hospital for examination. Police officers (in full uniform) came to interview her but she panicked and sent them away. She felt unable to cope with police and court, and also expressed lack of belief in their ability to help her.

When an individual recollects this phase, she may feel intense guilt and self-blame at her perceived inefficient handling of the situation.

The 'reconstitution phase': Koss and Harvey (1991) describe this phase, encompassing the weeks and months following a sexual assault, as an attempt by the individual to attend to basic living considerations; perhaps, changing telephone numbers, moving to a different residence, and turning to others for support. The individual may display an outward appearance of adjustment, although it has also been suggested this may be a form of 'denial' where the person attempts to actively cope with the trauma and restore equilibrium. Koss and Harvey (1991) argue that a major factor in determining the length of reconstitution phase is whether or not the individual decides to press charges, which may prolong and 'reawaken' rape-related trauma, and may inevitably lead to no conviction. The contentious issue of whether or not psychological benefit is increased by seeking police and legal recognition will be considered on p. 37. In continuing the above case example, it can be seen that the 'phase' model may no longer start to apply as her response developed into more prolonged psychological difficulties:

In the weeks after the rape, Ms A went back to work and attempted to get life back to normal. She found herself thinking about the rape every day (even when trying to 'blot it all out' of her mind). Her sleep pattern was disrupted, she experienced nightmares, and at times felt that the rape was happening all over again. She felt humiliated, self-disgusted, and self-blaming at her perceived inability to respond to the situation (e.g. by being too trusting, by not fighting back). She was disgusted with her genitals and had feelings of wanting to 'cut them away'. She felt very anxious, tense, and startled easily. She imagined seeing these men every time she went out on the street;

sometimes she thought she could see them in cars that were passing. This caused her an intense feeling of panic, and, changing her plans, would go home. She could not return to the area where the assault had occurred and changed her travel routes. She became increasingly withdrawn and felt unable to disclose the rape to her family and friends. Her alcohol consumption increased. She attempted suicide 2 weeks after the rape, after which she was referred for psychological therapy.

The 'resolution phase': Koss and Harvey (1991) suggest that, subsequent to the symptomatic phase, many individuals may experience prolonged anger. This may be directed at the assailant, the courts, police, society, or men. Anger may also be directed at the medical and psychological agencies that provided care. Underlying this may be deep feelings of despair, hopelessness, and shame. Following up on their original descriptive study, Burgess and Holmstrom (1979) reported that 4 to 6 years after being raped, 37% of women felt recovered (i.e., 'felt back to normal, that is, the way you felt prior to the rape') within months, 37% felt recovered but the process had taken several years, and 26% continued to not feel recovered. The long-term psychological impact of sexual assault has since been supported using more rigorous methodologies (e.g., Kilpatrick, Saunders, Veronen, Best, and Von, 1987; Rothbaum, Foa, Riggs, Murdock, and Walsh, 1992).

A further contribution from the early studies of Burgess and Holmstrom (1974, 1979) includes the recognition that individuals may present in the acute phase post-rape with different emotional styles. They noted that about half the women presented with an 'expressed style' characterized by visible signs of emotional distress, crying, restlessness, anxious, and tenseness, while others presented with a 'controlled style' characterized by feelings being masked, seemingly calm and subdued, with little evidence of visible affect. As mentioned in Chapter 1, the former emotional style represents a stereotype of how individuals are expected to present following sexual assault. It is important for the clinician to recognize these different styles to help enable disclosure of the rape, and not least to provide evidence when required, because an individual may not present in extreme emotional distress, that does not mean the rape has not occurred (Petrak, pers. comm.). One further observation noted by Burgess and Holmstrom (1974) was that some of the women presented with a 'compounded reaction' post-rape. This referred to the impact of past or current history of physical, psychiatric, or social difficulties upon rape trauma, and they noted that these individuals might require more specialized intervention than crisis counselling. The impact of factors which may compound psychological response to sexual assault will be considered in more detail on p. 35.

POST-TRAUMATIC STRESS DISORDER

Survivors of rape may constitute the largest group of victims of crime affected by PTSD (Steketee and Foa, 1987). The event of completed rape appears to pose a greater risk for the development of PTSD than other crime events (Norris and Kaniasty, 1994; Resnick, Kilpatrick, Danskey, Saunders, and Best, 1993). Some studies suggest a lifetime prevalence of PTSD in the region of 80% associated with rape (Kilpatrick et al., 1989; Breslau, Davis, Andreski, and Peterson, 1991).

Post-traumatic reactions have been described for a number of years under various names such as shell shock, combat fatigue, catastrophic stress reaction primarily associated with war veterans (Breslau and Davis, 1987). PTSD did not appear in the DSM-III of the American Psychiatric Association (APA) within the major category of anxiety disorders until 1980 and the diagnostic criteria has since undergone several revisions (DSM-III-R, APA, 1987; DSM-IV, APA, 1994). It is essentially a hypothetical concept to describe persisting clusters of symptoms that are observed to co-occur in the aftermath of trauma including re-experiencing phenomena, avoidance of trauma-related stimuli, and high levels of increased arousal. The assessment and treatment of stress disorder diagnoses following sexual assault is the focus of several chapters in this book and will not be described in detail here (see Chapters 4–6).

Studies assessing PTSD using DSM-III criteria with sexual assault survivors are relatively recent. Some workers have argued that the criteria is biased towards re-experiencing symptoms, and, since individuals often cope through denial especially at younger ages, the prevalence of PTSD is likely to be underestimated in this group (Koss and Harvey, 1991). Others have questioned the heterogeneity of the criteria for PTSD and commented that two people could receive the diagnosis having no common symptoms (Foa, Riggs, and Gershuny, 1995). Foa *et al.* (1995) suggest, based on a study combining sexual and non-sexual assault victims, that the current criteria for PTSD may not be sufficient to explain the patterns of post-trauma symptoms observed. Symptoms of emotional numbing (e.g., restricted affect, detachment, and loss of interest in activities) are grouped with symptoms of avoidance of trauma-related situations and thoughts under 'persistent avoidance' according to current criteria. Foa *et al.* (1995) present results of a factor analysis of the symptom clusters of PTSD by DSM-III-R criteria and a distinct factor characterizing a phobic reaction including the above symptoms of numbing. Nevertheless, despite this recent questioning of the concept, studies consistently report significant current and lifetime prevalence figures for PTSD in survivors of rape and sexual assault.

In a retrospective study, Kilpatrick *et al.* (1987) reported a lifetime prevalence of PTSD in a community sample of female rape victims as 57%, and in the same study PTSD criteria was met by 16.5% of victims, on average, 17 years post-rape. In a further retrospective study, Kilpatrick and Resnick (1993) report the lifetime prevalence of PTSD after rape as 35% and the current prevalence as 13%. In the same study, the lifetime prevalence of PTSD after aggravated assault was 39% and current prevalence was 12%. A few prospective studies have charted the development and course of PTSD in assault victims. Rothbaum *et al.* (1992) found that, within the first few weeks after the assault, 94% of rape survivors ($n = 95$) met symptomatic criteria for PTSD, this decreased to 65% at approximately 1 month, and, 3 months after the assault, 47% of survivors continued to experience PTSD and related psychopathology. They suggested those that recovered showed steady improvement over the times of assessment whereas those developing more chronic PTSD did not show improvement after fourth assessment at 1 month. Among the same group of researchers, a further study charted PTSD in non-sexual assault survivors and found that 70% met the symptom criteria within 2 weeks and 25% continued to meet this criteria at 3 months (Riggs, Dancu, Gershuny, Greenberg, and Foa, 1992). As with much research in this area, there are numerous confounding factors in these studies; for example, as with many American studies conducted on rape, study volunteers were all paid a stipend and were all recruited from various emergency services (i.e., they had reported the sexual assault). In the above prospective studies, volunteers were paid for each assessment which increased if they completed all sessions. Even with this incentive, there were 31 non-completers in the first study (Rothbaum *et al.*, 1992). It may also be that the repeated assessments (weekly for 12 weeks) had a therapeutic effect, given that it results in repeated exposure to aspects of the traumatic event, which is a component of most cognitive-behavioural treatment approaches to PTSD. A further criticism might be directed towards whether or not the researchers in these two studies were correct in terming the earlier assessment findings as PTSD since DSM-III-R criteria specify symptoms should have been present for 1 month. However, the authors claimed to use an interview conforming to DSM criteria (Rothbaum *et al.*, 1992).

Little research has been conducted in the UK on rape-related PTSD. One study conducted in Belfast used DSM-III criteria to assess PTSD in 51 survivors of rape, seen on average 9 months post-rape. Of these, 70% were reported as having PTSD but a major confounding factor was that data collected formed part of a medico-legal assessment (referred to a psychiatrist by the police) towards Criminal Injury compensation claims (Bownes, O'Gorman, and Sayers, 1991b). Petrak and Campbell (1999) reported, in a sample of 19 women accessing a genitourinary medicine clinic who were on average 3 months post-rape, that 79% met the full criteria for PTSD.

Other factors that have been examined in relation to the development of PTSD post-sexual assault include anger, controllability of the event, and initial reactions to stress. In a group of 116 women who had experienced sexual and non-sexual criminal assaults, Riggs *et al.* (1992) reported that levels of anger were related to various aspects of the assault (e.g., use of weapon, her response to the attack). Elevated anger was positively related to the development of PTSD. In a related study, Kushner, Riggs, Foa, and Miller (1992) examined the perception of controllability felt during the assault, expected controllability over future assaults, and perceived controllability over aversive events generally in the development of PTSD. Only the latter aspect of controllability was associated with PTSD severity, and, interestingly, severity of the assault was not related to controllability measures. The impact of assault-related variables upon psychological response are considered below. Recent work has examined the influence of cognitive factors on the development and maintenance of PTSD after physical or sexual assault (Dunmore, Clark, and Ehlers, 1999). Factors associated with persistent PTSD included appraisal of aspects of the assault itself (e.g., mental defeat, mental confusion), appraisal of the sequelae of the assault (e.g., perceived negative responses of others), and high avoidance/safety seeking (Dunmore *et al.*, 1999). Initial severity of traumatic response is also associated with the development of PTSD (Adshead, 2000).

Research on PTSD following rape and sexual assault is at an early stage. While many of the symptoms of PTSD may aptly describe the psychological presentation in survivors, there is likely to be numerous variables associated with the development of (and recovery from) PTSD and other psychopathology post-rape; for example, recent work (e.g., Dunmore *et al.*, 1999) emphasizes the importance of cognitive appraisal of the assault situation in the development and maintenance of PTSD. Further work emphasizes the importance of screening for persistent shame reactions, in addition to fear reactions underpinning PTSD, with implications for psychological therapy (Adshead, 2000). Cognitive therapies for addressing shame and guilt may need to proceed before fear- and anxiety-focused therapies are used (see Chapter 7).

OTHER PSYCHOLOGICAL RESPONSES TO SEXUAL ASSAULT

Much research has focused on specific psychological and social responses post-sexual assault including anxiety and fear, depression, suicidal ideation and attempts, social adjustment, and sexual dysfunction. An overview will be presented here, while more detailed consideration of assessment and intervention for these responses will be covered throughout the chapters in this book.

Anxiety and fear predominate among psychological responses to rape; this may be intense fear of rape-associated situations and general diffused anxiety (Steketee and Foa, 1987). Kilpatrick, Resick, and Veronen (1981) studied the immediate response of 25 women post-rape, and 80–96% reported feeling scared, terrified, having racing thoughts, shaking, trembling, or palpitations. Intense fear persisted for 80% of the women 2–3 hours after the assault. Areas of rape-related fears identified include: (a) fears of stimuli or items that were directly associated with the attack (e.g., a man's penis, tough-looking people); (b) fears of rape consequences (e.g., going to court, pregnancy, sexually transmitted diseases); and (c) fears of future attack (e.g., being alone, being in a strange place, having people behind you: Kilpatrick *et al.*, 1981). Several authors have also commented on fear of HIV and AIDS as a primary concern for victims (Laszlo, Burgess, and Grant, 1991; Koss and Harvey, 1991) (see Chapter 9).

The course of anxiety and fear post-rape suggest these may be relatively long-term problems. Peterson, Olasov, and Foa (1987) suggest the anxiety induced by sexual assault reaches maximum levels in the third week, after which there are no further increases but significant decrements in fear may not begin for a long time. Thus, in a study comparing rape victims with non-victims, Veronen and Kilpatrick (1980) found the former had elevated scores on the Modified Fear Survey and phobic anxiety on the Symptom Check List (SCL-90) at 1 year post-rape. They reported that only 23% of those among the sample of 46 victims were asymptomatic on the Modified Fear Survey and 26% showed no abnormal phobic anxiety at 1 year post-rape (Veronen and Kilpatrick, 1983). Other studies report similar findings with small numbers of participants (e.g., Ellis, Atkeson, and Calhoun, 1981). A more extensive study, comparing 115 victims post-rape assessed at six time intervals over a 1-year period with 87 non-victims, reported that, although the victims' fearfulness declined from the first to the 2-month assessment, they were more fearful at all assessment periods than non-victims (Calhoun, Atkeson, and Resick, 1982).

In the UK, one study reports the use of standard measures of anxiety in a sample of 12 women reporting rape to the police, who were interviewed on three occasions over a 4-month period and compared with 12 women without a trauma history. Similar to the American studies, elevated scores on anxiety and phobic dimensions of the SCL-90 are reported compared with controls, but high scores decreased in the majority of cases by the end of the data collection (Mezey and Taylor, 1988). Most of the above studies focus on reporting symptoms but offer little in explanation as to causation of these other than the rape. Many do not specify details which may likely influence the course of anxiety or any other psychological response in survivors (e.g., whether or not individuals were reporting to medical and/or police services, awaiting court proceedings, relationship to assailant, prior history of victimization); for example, in Mezey and Taylor's (1988) study, 75% of rapes were committed by men not known to the survivors (and two cases involved multiple assailants). Two of the sample were technically 'attempted' rather than completed rapes although the authors stress these involved 'considerable violence' and three had histories of prior victimization (Mezey and Taylor, 1988). Some studies have attempted to separate out factors associated with psychological symptoms and outcome and these will be reviewed below, but many suffer from the methodological difficulty of small study samples and reporting unidimensional findings on what is clearly a complex, multi-factorial experience.

Research on the extent of depression in victims of sexual assault suggest that this reaction may resolve within months post-rape (Frank and Stewart, 1984) while other research suggests more chronic depressive reactions (Nadelson, Notman, Zackson, and Gornick, 1982; Ellis et al., 1981). Frank and Stewart (1984) used the Beck Depression Inventory (BDI) and a standardized interview to assess depression on a sample of 90 victims and reported 43% diagnosed as having major depression. These symptoms declined by 3 months post-assault. Other studies using non-victimized controls also found a similar pattern of depression being elevated in survivors soon after the rape but that this had diminished approximately 3 months later, and no differences were observed between the groups up to 1 year later (Atkeson, Calhoun, Resick, and Ellis, 1982; Kilpatrick, Veronen, and Resick, 1979). Findings from retrospective studies contrast the above results. Nadelson et al. (1982) found that 41% of women between 15 and 30 months post-rape continued to report episodes of depression related to the rape. Ellis et al. (1981) compared victims with matched non-victims 3 years after the rape and observed significantly more depression (as assessed by the BDI) in the former group.

Along with depression, suicidal ideation is prevalent among rape victims. Cross-sectional studies report suicidal ideation of between 33 and 50% in individuals with a history of sexual assault (Ellis et al., 1981; Koss, Dinero, Seibel, and Cox, 1988; Resick, Jordan, Girelli, Hutter, and Marhoefer-Dvorak, 1989). Kilpatrick et al. (1985) found that 19% had made a suicide attempt, and 44% reported suicidal ideation in a large-scale community (non-treatment seeking) survey of women who had been raped. There is a suggestion in the literature that young persons may be particularly at risk for suicidal behaviour following sexual assault (Burgess, 1995). As has been shown in other studies examining predictors of suicide, a previous history of suicidal behaviour is associated with the presence of suicidal ideation post-rape (Petrak and Campbell, 1999). Screening for a history of self-harming behaviour in the individual presenting post-sexual assault is important.

A number of studies have observed difficulties in social functioning and in the availability of social support post-rape (e.g., Frank, Turner, and Stewart, 1980; Calhoun, Atkeson, and Ellis, 1981; Baker, Skolnik, Davis, and Brickman, 1991). Nadelson et al. (1982) reported that more than half a sample of 41 women interviewed 15–30 months post-rape had a restricted social life and went out only in the company of friends. A prospective study by Calhoun et al. (1981), using the self-report Social Adjustment Survey, found that rape survivors differed from non-victims on economic, social, and leisure functioning at 2 months but improved thereafter. Work functioning, however, continued to be impaired 8 months later. In the same study, a combined index of marital, parental, and family functioning failed to differentiate victims from non-victims at any point post-assault. The investigators suggested that social network behaviour towards the survivors could have been altered by validation that stemmed from participation in the ongoing research (cited in Koss and Harvey, 1991). It could also be argued that participation in the ongoing research, involving contact with the investigators at least five times over a year, might have been socially supportive in itself. Other studies involving little contact with researchers demonstrate long-term negative effects of rape upon the family unit and in marital adjustment (e.g., Kilpatrick et al., 1987). Miller, Williams, and Bernstein (1982) reported 'serious relationship disturbance' in 57% of couples interviewed a mean of 2.4 years after the wife was raped. However, the latter study had no control sample, and individual psychopathology prior to the rape was also associated with relationship problems.

A more recent study compared rape victims and victims of other crimes on measures of positive and negative support from significant others. All ($n = 233$) were interviewed within 8 weeks of the crime, and findings suggest that, although there were no differences in positive supportive measures between the two groups, rape survivors were found to receive considerably more negative support from their significant others as compared with victims of other crimes. Negative support measures were designed by the researchers to include items such as: 'My significant other indicated that I should have fought back more' (Baker et al., 1991). This result suggests the social support in rape victims may to some extent be linked to perceived culpability. Frank et al. (1980) previously observed that victims of brutal assaults might receive more social support.

Aside from their impact on social support, social stereotypes of sexual assault may also lead to survivors developing negative internal representations about safety, power, trust, esteem, and intimacy (McCann, Sakheim, and Abrahamson, 1988). Decreased self-esteem is prevalent in women who have been raped compared with non-victims and may persist for years (Murphy et al., 1988). In addition, individuals may often experience significant levels of self-blame, shame, and self-disgust in the aftermath of sexual assault (Petrak, Doyle, Williams, Buchan, and Forster, 1997).

Problems in sexual functioning post-rape are common and may persist for many years (e.g. Burgess and Holmstrom, 1979). Becker, Skinner, Abel, and Cichon (1986) assessed 372 female sexual assault survivors (included rape, attempted rape, incest, and child abuse) and 99 controls and reported sexual dysfunction in 58.6% of the former group compared with 17.2% in the non-assaulted group. Seventy-one per cent of the survivors linked the onset of their problems to the assault. Various methodological difficulties are noted with this study; for example, significant differences emerged between the assault and control group on demographic characteristics (the control group were older and more highly educated), 60% of the survivor group had been assaulted more than once, and the timing of the development of sexual problems in relationship to the assaults are not noted other than that the survivor group varied between 2 months to 40 years post-assault. Nevertheless, this is the largest study addressing post-assault sexual functioning and suggests the extent of the problem. Sexual difficulties experienced post-sexual assault and their treatment will be considered in more detail in Chapter 8.

FACTORS ASSOCIATED WITH PSYCHOLOGICAL RESPONSE

Numerous studies have attempted to identify which variables may be associated with or predictive of psychological response following rape. The assumption underlying these studies is that individuals' post-traumatic responses are multiply determined and may be influenced by demographic, personality, social, historical, aspects of the rape situation, and environmental variables (Koss and Harvey, 1991). The evidence for and against various predictive variables is reviewed below.

Findings of the effect of demographic variables such as age, ethnicity, educational level, economic and marital status on psychological response post-sexual assault provide conflicting results, and their clinical relevance as reported is not clear. Kilpatrick, Veronen, and Best (1984) found no effect of age, ethnicity, education, and marital status, although economic status was inversely related to recovery (i.e., survivors of low socio-economic status experienced more psychological symptoms post-rape). Ruch and Leon (1983) found no effect associated with age but reported that non-Caucasians suffered greater trauma post-rape. Atkeson *et al.* (1982), however, reported that older sexual assault survivors presented with higher depression levels than younger survivors at 12 months following rape. In the same study, older women showed greater avoidance following the rape, more self-blaming attitudes, and had less social support. The lack of research on the relationship of demographic variables on psychological response post-sexual assault may reflect that, maybe, there is little reason to assume that a crime that cuts across all classes and cultures should differentially affect individuals. It may also reflect that the available research often focuses on the impact of sexual assault in a specific population (e.g., young people, older adults, different ethnic groups) and does not compare between them. However, in clinical practice, demographic variables such as culture and age may be very relevant to an individual response to sexual assault. The impact of gender and sexuality upon post-sexual assault, psychological functioning is considered in Chapter 3.

Social support emerges in a number of studies as an important factor in coping with both the short- and long-term aftermath of sexual assault (Atkeson *et al.*, 1982; Burgess and Holmstrom, 1979; Ruch and Chandler, 1983; Wyatt, Newcomb, and Notgrass, 1991). Related to social support studies, assessing the effect of having a stable relationship upon recovery provides contradictory results. Thus, Burgess and Holmstrom (1979) observed that rape survivors who had stable partners recovered more quickly while two studies report that married women had greater difficulties after the rape (McCahill, Meyer, and Fishman, 1979; Ruch and Chandler, 1983). Few studies, however, use social support measures, and in those that do the importance of looking at the type and quality of support (and of intimate relationships) is emphasized (Baker *et al.*, 1991). More recent research suggests that positive social support may also offset the development of PTSD post-sexual assault (Zoellner, Foa, and Brigidi, 1999).

Studies have also focused on specific aspects of the rape situation (e.g., stranger versus known assailant, use of weapons and violence, number of assailants, place of assault) in relation to the psychological aftermath. The degree of acquaintance of the assailant to the survivor is highlighted in a number of studies. Societal attitudes are more negative towards survivors of acquaintance rape and view stranger rape as the more serious assault (Tetreault and Barnett, 1987). Rapes by strangers are more likely to be reported to the police and more likely to be 'crimed' and achieve conviction (Lees and Gregory, 1993). It is also reported that the contextual nature of the rape may be different between stranger and acquaintance assaults, with the latter involving more attempts at interaction by the assailant after the rape (Bownes *et al.*, 1991a). Despite these contextual differences, the majority of research reports no significant differences in levels of psychological symptoms found between stranger and acquaintance rapes (Steketee and Foa, 1987; Koss *et al.*, 1988). However, women, who had some degree of acquaintance with their assailant, are reported as more likely to delay seeking treatment and are less likely to have revealed the rape to others compared with stranger rapes (Koss *et al.*, 1988). It remains unclear what long-term effects these findings have, although it seems likely that the rapist's relationship to the victim will affect the victim's perception of and the meaning attached to the incident in some way. Two large community surveys report that a history of sexual victimization may be related to overall greater utilization of medical systems and poorer health perceptions (Koss, Woodruff, and Koss, 1990; Golding, 1994). Therefore, it may be that women, who have some prior knowledge of their assailants (which account for the majority of rapes), are accessing services in different ways and not necessarily disclosing their sexual assault (Petrak, Skinner, and Claydon, 1995). The issue of whether there is a greater psychological benefit in reporting the sexual assault to the police as compared to not reporting it remains unclear. Some studies have suggested involvement with the criminal justice system increases levels of fear (Kilpatrick *et al.*, 1979), while others have suggested that those women who elected to proceed to prosecute their assailant reported higher self-esteem (Cluss, Boughton, Frank, Stewart, and West, 1983). While, clinically, it makes sense that attempting to take some kind of action towards increasing control over the event may be beneficial to the individual, the continued and not unfounded lack of faith in the criminal justice system to protect individuals remains high. It remains the task of the individual, and not the clinician, to decide whether or not to report their sexual assault to the police, proceed with examination, and legal proceedings. The understandable aversiveness of these proceedings is illustrated in Chapter 11. In most cases (excepting those workers attached to sexual assault centres with direct links to police), the clinician will encounter the majority of women and men who do not report coercive sexual experiences to the police (Petrak *et al.*, 1995).

Studies have used indices with regard to the degree of severity or brutality of the rape to examine the effect upon survivors' reactions. Life threat, physical injury, and completed rape contributed significantly to the development of PTSD (Kilpatrick *et al.*, 1989), and others report greater mood disturbance consequent on the more brutal the attack (McCahill *et al.*, 1979; Ellis *et al.*, 1981). Somewhat contradictory findings are reported by Cluss *et al.* (1983) who report that greater threat to the victim was associated with higher self-esteem. Others suggest it is the victim's perception of threat and not the characteristics of the event alone that predicts the extent of later fear reactions (Koss and Harvey, 1991).

Variables that are more consistently associated with psychological responses following rape include prior victimization, history of psychiatric treatment, and recent life events (Steketee and Foa, 1987). First, a prior history of sexual abuse is predictive of non-consenting sexual experiences as an adult in both women (Koss and Dinero, 1989; Gidycz, Hanson, and Layman, 1995) and men (Coxell, King, Mezey, and Gordon, 1999). Coxell *et al.* (1999), in a large sample of men attending general practice clinics in the UK, reported an increased likelihood of psychological symptomatology, high-risk alcohol consumption, and likelihood of self-harm in men with both child and adult non-consensual sexual experiences. Ruch, Amedeo, Leon, and Gartrell (1991), using interview data collected on 184 women attending a hospital sexual assault clinic, reported that individuals with a prior history of sexual assault had more severe trauma at 2-week follow-up than first assault victims. Prior assault victims were also more likely to have pre-existing mental health or substance abuse problems, and the combination of these difficulties appear to contribute to increased trauma level post-rape. Of note in this study, approximately 40% of the clinic attendees did not attend for follow-up (at which point the interview data was collected). This substantially reduced respondent numbers and suggests difficulties in obtaining follow-up when using a hospital clinic population where individuals are attending for reasons other than research purposes (i.e., respondents were not 'recruited' or paid a stipend). Ruch et al. (1991) do not provide longer term follow-up data, but, in an earlier study, Burgess and Holmstrom (1978) report that 47% of those previously victimized did not feel recovered versus 14% of single-incident assaults at 4–6 years post-rape. Ellis et al. (1982) reported that women with repeated histories of sexual assault were of lower socioeconomic status, more transient, and more dysfunctional in intrapersonal and interpersonal adjustment than women reporting a single incident. While this data cannot explain whether such differences were caused by the prior assault or led to multiple assaults, it does suggest increased vulnerability. Recent work suggests that one explanation for the increased likelihood of adult sexual assault, occurring in persons with previous sexual trauma, include difficulties recognizing the risk for potential danger. In particular, revictimized women may experience difficulty in accurately labelling and responding to danger which may cause them to remain in situations beyond the point at which they could escape (Meadows, Jaycox, Stafford, Hambree, and Foa, 1995). The impact of trauma symptoms upon risk of revictimization remains unclear. Some studies support differences between single- and multiple-incident survivors in dissociative symptoms, interpersonal problems, and psychological adjustment, and propose that dissociative symptoms may lessen revictimized women's awareness of environmental cues that a situation is potentially dangerous (Cloitre, Scarvalone, and Difede, 1997). Other studies found that variables related to psychological functioning failed to predict revictimization (Gidycz et al., 1995).

Prior psychiatric history or previous psychiatric consultation is reported to be associated with depressive symptoms (Atkeson et al., 1982), marital and sexual difficulties (Miller et al., 1982), and general recovery (Burgess and Holmstrom, 1979) post-rape. However, the design of some studies have excluded individuals with past or current psychiatric histories and, therefore, the relationship of this to, for example, post-traumatic stress symptoms remains unexplored (e.g., Rothbaum et al., 1992). Other studies have found a strong association between histories of drug and alcohol abuse and increased PTSD symptomatology (not using DSM-III criteria) following rape (Burgess and Holmstrom, 1979; Ruch and Leon, 1983).

A few studies have looked at the relationship between stressful life events and psychological response to rape. Ruch and Leon (1983) observed a curvilinear relationship between life changes occurring 1 year prior to the assault and the acute and long-term impact of the rape; those with a moderate degree of change fared best. Kilpatrick *et al.* (1984) reported that distress 3 months post-rape was greater in those who had suffered highly stressful events (e.g. bereavement) in the year prior to the rape. Contradictory results include Burgess and Holmstrom (1978) who report a lack of association between recent (within 6 months) life changes and recovery post-rape. However, such findings are difficult to interpret, as standard measures of life events were not used and their impact is undetermined.

SUMMARY

As can be seen, the psychological impact of sexual assault is wide-ranging and extends beyond the stress disorder diagnoses. Research on the prevalence of various psychological phenomena post-sexual assault generally suggests high rates of initial disturbance which, with the exception of fear and anxiety, dissipate over a period of about 4 months (Steketee and Foa, 1987). However, it is also likely that those individuals who come into clinical care will be those who, due to either vulnerability factors or other reasons, are experiencing more persistent emotional and behavioural disturbance. Little is known of those individuals who demonstrate particular resilience to trauma, but certainly it would seem that some individuals may reappraise negative life events (including sexual assault) as an opportunity for increasing personal cohesion and self-worth. Further research is needed on, for example, cognitive appraisal of traumatic events including sexual assault, which is likely to increase understanding of differential psychological response including resilience. The importance of including cultural factors (such as ethnicity and sexuality) which impact on cognitive appraisal will also be an important area for research. The importance of prior history upon psychological response to sexual assault is emphasized in the latter part of this chapter, and suggests the clinician may benefit from, at least, a good grounding in the understanding of assessment and treatment issues in child sexual abuse, substance misuse, and psychiatric problems. However, the greatest challenge to research in sexual assault will continue to be how to present findings in this difficult area that are sensitive to individual differences and do not compound an individual and societal view of 'victimization' as being the only response.

REFERENCES

Adshead, G. (2000) Psychological therapies for post-traumatic stress disorder. *British Journal of Psychiatry*, **177**, 144–148.

APA. (1987) *Diagnostic and statistical manual of mental disorders* (3rd edn, rev.). Washington, DC: American Psychiatric Association.

APA. (1994) *Diagnostic and statistical manual of mental disorders* (4th edn). Washington, DC: American Psychiatric Association

Atkeson, B., Calhoun, K., Resick, P., and Ellis, E. (1982) Victims of rape: Repeated assessment of depressive symptoms. *Journal of Consulting and Clinical Psychology*, **50**, 96–102.

Baker, T., Skolnik, L., Davis, R., and Brickman, E. (1991) The social support of survivors of rape: The differences between rape survivors and survivors of other violent crimes and between husbands, boyfriends, and women friends. In A. Burgess (ed.) *Rape and sexual assault III*. New York: Garland Publishing.

Becker, J., Skinner, L., Abel, G., and Cichon, J. (1986) Level of postassault sexual functioning in rape and incest victims. *Archives of Sexual Behavior*, **15**, 37–49.

Bownes, I., O'Gorman, E., and Sayers, A. (1991a) Rape—A comparison of stranger and acquaintance assaults. *Medical Science Law*, **31**, 102–109.

Bownes, I., O'Gorman, E., and Sayers, A. (1991b) Assault characteristics and posttraumatic stress disorder in rape victims. *Acta Psychiatrica Scandinavica*, **83**, 27–30.

Breslau, N. and Davis, G. (1987) Post-traumatic stress disorder: The stressor criterion. *Journal of Nervous and Mental Disease*, **175**, 255–264.

Breslau, N., Davis, G., Andreski, P., and Peterson, E. (1991) Traumatic events and posttraumatic stress disorder in an urban population of young adults. *Archives of General Psychiatry*, **48**, 216–222.

Burgess, A. (1995) Rape Trauma Syndrome. In P. Searles and R. Berger (eds) *Rape and society: Readings on the problem of sexual assault*. Boulder, CO: Westview Press.

Burgess, A. and Holmstrom, L. (1974) Rape Trauma Syndrome. *American Journal of Psychiatry*, **131**, 981–986.

Burgess, A. and Holmstrom, L. (1978) Recovery from rape and prior life stress. *Research in Nursing and Health*, **1**, 165–174.

Burgess, A. and Holmstrom, L. (1979) Adaptive strategies and recovery from rape. *American Journal of Psychiatry*, **136**, 1278–1282.

Calhoun, K., Atkeson, B., and Ellis, E. (1981) Social adjustment in victims of sexual assault. *Journal of Consulting and Clinical Psychology*, **49**, 705–712.

Calhoun, K., Atkeson, B., and Resick, P. (1982) A longitudinal examination of fear reactions in victims of rape. *Journal of Counseling Psychology*, **29**, 655–661.

Cloitre, M., Scarvalone, P., and Difede, J. (1997) Posttraumatic stress disorder: Self- and interpersonal dysfunction among sexually retraumatized women. *Journal of Traumatic Stress*, **10**, 437–452.

Cluss, P., Boughton, J., Frank, L., Stewart, B., and West, D. (1983) The rape victims: Psychological correlates of participation in the legal process. *Criminal Justice and Behavior*, **10**, 342–357.

Coxell, A., King, M., Mezey, G., and Gordon, D. (1999) Lifetime prevalence, characteristics, and associated problems of non-consensual sex in men: Cross sectional survey. *British Medical Journal*, **318**, 846–850.

Dunmore, E.C., Clark, D.M., and Ehlers, A. (1999) Cognitive factors involved in the onset and maintenance of post-traumatic stress disorder after physical or sexual assault. *Behaviour Research and Therapy*, **37**, 809–829.

Ellis, E., Atkeson, B., and Calhoun, K. (1981) An assessment of long-term reaction to rape. *Journal of Abnormal Psychology*, **90**, 263–266.

Ellis, E., Atkeson, B., and Calhoun, K. (1982) An examination of differences between multiple- and single-incident victims of sexual assault. *Journal of Abnormal Psychology*, **91**, 221–224.

Foa, E., Riggs, D., and Gershuny, B. (1995) Arousal, numbing, and intrusion: Symptom structure of PTSD following assault. *American Journal of Psychiatry*, **152**, 116–120.

Frank, E. and Stewart, B. (1984) Depressive symptoms in rape victims. *Journal of Affective Disorders*, **1**, 269–277.

Frank, E., Turner, S., and Stewart, B. (1980) Initial response to rape: The impact of factors within the rape situation. *Journal of Behavioral Assessment*, **2**, 39–53.

Gidycz, C. and Koss, M. (1990) A comparison of group and individual sexual assault victims. *Psychology of Women Quarterly*, **14**, 325–342.

Gidycz, C., Hanson, K., and Layman, M. (1995) A prospective analysis of the relationships among sexual assault experience: An extension of previous findings. *Psychology of Women Quarterly*, **19**, 5–29.

Golding, J. (1994) Sexual assault history and physical health in randomly selected Los Angeles women. *Health Psychology*, **13**, 130–138.

Holmes, M., Resnick, H., and Frampton, D. (1998) Follow-up of sexual assault victims. *American Journal of Obstetrics and Gynecology*, **179**, 336–342.

Kilpatrick, D. and Resnick, H. (1993) PTSD associated with exposure to criminal victimization in clinical and community populations. In J. Davidson and E. Foa (eds.) *PTSD in review: Recent research and future directions.* Washington, DC: American Psychiatric Press.

Kilpatrick, D., Best, C., Veronen, L., Ruff, M., Ruff, G., and Allison, J. (1985) Mental health correlates of criminal victimization: A random community survey. *Journal of Consulting and Clinical Psychology*, **53**, 866–873.

Kilpatrick, D., Resick, P., and Veronen, L. (1981) Effects of a rape experience: A longitudinal study. *Journal of Social Issues*, **37**, 105–121.

Kilpatrick, D., Saunders, B., Amick-McMullan, A., Best, C., Veronen, L., and Resnick, H. (1989) Victim and crime factors associated with the development of crime-related post-traumatic stress disorder. *Behavior Therapy*, **20**, 199–214.

Kilpatrick, D., Saunders, B., Veronen, L., Best, C., and Von, J. (1987) Criminal victimization: Lifetime prevalence, reporting to police, and psychological impact. *Crime and Delinquency*, **33**, 479–489.

Kilpatrick, D., Veronen, L., and Best, C. (1984) Factors predicting psychological distress among rape victims. In C. Figley (ed.) *Trauma and its wake.* New York: Brunner/Mazel.

Kilpatrick, D., Veronen, L., and Resick, P. (1979) The aftermath of rape: Recent empirical findings. *American Journal of Orthopsychiatry*, **49**, 658–659.

Koss, M. and Dinero, T. (1989) Discriminant analysis of risk factors for sexual victimization among a national sample of college women. *Journal of Consulting and Clinical Psychology*, **57**, 242–250.

Koss, M. and Harvey, M. (1991) *The rape victim: Clinical and community interventions*. Newbury Park, CA: Sage Publications.

Koss, M., Dinero, T., Seibel, C., and Cox, S. (1988) Stranger, acquaintance, and date rape: Is there a difference in the victim's experience? *Psychology of Women Quarterly*, **12**, 1–24.

Koss, M., Woodruff, W., and Koss, P. (1990) Relation of criminal victimization to health perceptions among women medical patients. *Journal of Consulting and Clinical Psychology*, **58**, 147–152.

Kushner, M., Riggs, D., Foa, E., and Miller, S. (1992) Perceived controllability and the development of posttraumatic stress disorder in crime victims. *Behavior Research Therapy*, **31**, 105–110.

Laszlo, A., Burgess, A. and Grant, C. (1991) HIV counseling issues and victims of sexual assault. In A. Burgess (ed.) *Rape and sexual assault III*. New York: Garland Publishing.

Lees, S. and Gregory, J. (1993) *Rape and sexual assault: A study of attrition*. London: Islington Council.

McCahill, T., Meyer, L., and Fishman, A. (1979) *The aftermath of rape*. Lexington, MA: Heath and Company.

McCann, I., Sakheim, D., and Abrahamson, D. (1988) Trauma and victimization: A model of psychological adaptation. *The Counselling Psychologist*, **6**, 531–594.

Meadows, E., Jaycox, L., Stafford, J., Hambree, E., and Foa, E. (1995) Recognition of risk in revictimized women. Poster session presented at the 29th Annual Meeting of the Association for the Advancement of Behavior Therapy, Washington, DC.

Mezey, G. and Taylor, P. (1988) Psychological reactions of women who have been raped. *British Journal of Psychiatry*, **152**, 330–339.

Miller, W., Williams, M., and Bernstein, M. (1982) The effects of rape on marital and sexual adjustment. *American Journal of Family Therapy*, **10**, 51–58.

Murphy, S., Amick-McMullan, S., Kilpatrick, D., Haskett, M. Veronen, L., Best, C., and Saunders, B. (1988) Rape victims' self-esteem: A longitudinal analysis. *Journal of Interpersonal Violence*, **3**, 355–370.

Nadelson, C., Notman, M., Zackson, H., and Gornick, J. (1982) A follow-up study of rape victims. *American Journal of Psychiatry*, **139**, 1266–1270.

Norris, F. and Kaniasty, K. (1994) Psychological distress following criminal victimization in the general population: Cross-sectional, longitudinal, and the prospective analyses. *Journal of Consulting and Clinical Psychology*, **62**, 111–123.

Peterson, D., Olasov, B., and Foa, E. (1987) Response patterns in sexual assault survivors. Paper presented at the Third World Congress on Victimology. Cited in Koss, M. and Harvey, M. (1991) *The rape victim: Clinical and community interventions*. Newbury Park, CA: Sage Publications.

Petrak, J. and Campbell, E. (1999) Post-traumatic stress disorder in female survivors of rape attending a genitourinary medicine clinic. *International Journal of STD and AIDS*, **10**, 531–535.

Petrak, J., Doyle, A., Williams, L., Buchan, L., and Forster, G. (1997) The psychological impact of sexual assault: A study of female attenders of a sexual health psychology service. *Sexual and Marital Therapy*, **12**, 339–345.

Petrak, J., Skinner, C., and Claydon, E. (1995) The prevalence of sexual assault in a genitourinary medicine clinic: Service implications. *Genitourinary Medicine*, **71**, 98–102.

Resick, P., Jordan, C., Girelli, S., Hutter, C., and Marhoefer-Dvorak, S. (1989) A comparative outcome study of behavioral group therapy for sexual assault victims. *Behavior Therapy*, **19**, 385–401.

Resnick, H., Kilpatrick, D., Dansky, B., Saunders, B., and Best, C. (1993) Prevalence of Civilian Trauma and Posttraumatic Stress Disorder in a representative national sample of women. *Journal of Consulting and Clinical Psychology*, **61**, 984–991.

Riggs, D., Dancu, C., Gershuny, B., Greenberg, D., and Foa, E. (1992) Anger and post traumatic stress disorder in female crime victims. *Journal of Traumatic Stress*, **5**, 613–625.

Rothbaum, B., Foa, E., Riggs, D., Murdock, T., and Walsh, W. (1992) A prospective examination of post-traumatic stress disorder in rape victims. *Journal of Traumatic Stress*, **5**, 455–475.

Ruch, L. and Chandler, K. (1983) Sexual assault trauma during the acute phase: An exploratory model and multivariate analysis. *Journal of Health and Social Behavior*, **24**, 184–185.

Ruch, L. and Leon, J. (1983) Sexual assault trauma and trauma change. *Women and Health*, **8**, 5–21.

Ruch, L., Amedeo, S., Leon, J., and Gartrell, J. (1991) Repeated sexual victimization and trauma change during the acute phase of the sexual assault trauma syndrome. *Women and Health*, **17**, 1–19.

Steketee, G., and Foa, E. (1987) Rape victims: Post-traumatic stress responses and their treatment: A review of the literature. *Journal of Anxiety Disorders*, **1**, 69–86.

Sutherland, S. and Scherl, D. (1970) Patterns of response among victims of rape. *American Journal of Orthopsychiatry*, **28**, 527–529.

Symonds, M. (1975) Victims of violence: Psychological effects and aftereffects. *American Journal of Psychoanalysis*, **36**, 27–34.

Tetreault, P. and Barnett, M. (1987) Reactions to stranger and acquaintance rape. *Psychology of Women Quarterly*, **11**, 353–358.

Veronen, L. and Kilpatrick, D. (1980) Self-reported fears of rape victims: A preliminary investigation. *Behavior Modification*, **4**, 383–396.

Veronen, L. and Kilpatrick, D. (1983) Stress management for rape victims. In D. Meichenbaum and M. Jaremko (eds) *Stress reduction and prevention*. New York: Plenum Press.

Wyatt, G., Newcomb, M., and Notgrass, C. (1991) Internal and external mediators of women's rape experiences. In A. Burgess (ed.) *Rape and sexual assault III*. New York: Garland Publishing.

Zoellner, L., Foa, B., and Brigidi, B.D. (1999) Interpersonal friction and PTSD in female victims of sexual and nonsexual assault. *Journal of Traumatic Stress*, **12**, 689–700.

Chapter 3

GENDER, SEXUAL ORIENTATION, AND SEXUAL ASSAULT

Adrian W. Coxell and Michael B. King

INTRODUCTION

This chapter compares and contrasts psychological and physical health in men and women who have experienced sexual assault. We briefly review the research on the effect of sexual assault on men and women with regard to various psychiatric disorders, health perception, limitations in physical function, and use of mental health and medical services. Next, we discuss social perceptions about sexual assault and how these may affect victims. Finally, we consider the relevance of gender and sexuality to treatment after sexual assault.

People can be sexually victimized in many different ways and at different times in their life. We use the term 'sexual assault' to describe these experiences except in cases where it is more correct to use another term (e.g., rape). We do not consider research solely concerned with sexual assault in children or adolescents in this chapter. Readers interested in research in this very important area should consider recent papers by Darves-Bornoz, Choquet, Ledoux, Gasquet, and Manfredi (1998) and Shrier, Pierce, Emans, and Durant (1998). In this chapter, we use the term 'victim' because we feel that Janoff-Bulman and Frieze (1983) are correct to argue that 'victim' and 'victimization' 'provide useful labels, for [they serve] to relieve victims of responsibility for their victimisation ... responsibility for the onset of the victimisation (i.e., the problem) differs from recovery from it (i.e., the solution)' (quoted in Otis and Skinner, 1996).

The Trauma of Sexual Assault. Edited by Jenny Petrak and Barbara Hedge.
© 2002 John Wiley & Sons Ltd.

HEALTH PROBLEMS ASSOCIATED WITH SEXUAL ASSAULT

In this section of the chapter, we consider psychological and physical health problems associated with sexual assault and the extent to which these associations are moderated by gender.

Psychological Health

There have been many studies into the association between sexual assault and psychological health (see Resnick, Acierno, and Kilpatrick (1997) for a review). The proportion of studies comparing male and female victims is quite small, however. In this section, we consider clinic based and epidemiological research.

Clinic Research

Clinic samples represent the clients that health professionals meet during their practice. However, these samples are unlikely to represent the 'average' sexual assault victim. Few victims seek help (DiVasto *et al.*, 1984) and those who do may be experiencing the most pathology or the greatest difficulty in adjustment.

Emergency Room Samples

Kaufman, DiVasto, Jackson, Voorhees, and Christy (1980) compared 14 male and 100 randomly selected female rape victims who presented at a hospital emergency room. Kaufman *et al.* observed that a higher proportion of men (12/14; 79%) seemed to display the 'controlled' style of acute emotional reaction described by Burgess and Holmstrom (1974), whereas the reactions of female victims were 'divided roughly equally' between the controlled and expressive style of acute reaction.

Frazier (1993) compared male (74) and female (1,380) rape victims who presented at a hospital-based rape crisis program. Nurses assessed victims using an instrument providing measures of anxiety, depression, and hostility. Male victims had significantly higher depression and hostility scores immediately post-rape, but differences were very small. Anxiety level was not significantly different between groups. These findings need to be interpreted with some caution, however. First, significantly more male victims had been raped by more than one person (31% of men, 19% of women: $\chi^2 = 4.2$, $p < 0.05$). Second, while nurses rated victims immediately post-rape, observed symptoms may not be rape sequelae.

Mental Health Clinic Sample

Hutchings and Dutton (1997) investigated gender differences in diagnoses and self-reported symptoms in clients of a community mental health centre (CMHC). Psychiatric diagnoses differed significantly between the men and women who had experienced sexual assault, but the authors argue that 'The reliability of the diagnosis process used by the CMHC clinicians is questionable ... The method of psychodiagnostic interview varied widely across clinicians, and reliability of chart diagnosis is notably weak'. CMHC clients also completed a self-report measure of psychological symptoms (SCL-90-R: Derogatis, 1983). Sexual assault victims had significantly higher scores on all scales. Overall, women had significantly higher scores on the anxiety, phobia, positive symptom distress index subscales, and the Global Symptom Index scale. No significant gender and abuse history interactions were found, and the authors argue that '... no support was found for the concept of differential gender effects of sexual assault or abuse'. These results are interesting, but need to be interpreted with caution, as very unequal numbers of men ($n = 9$) and women ($n = 60$) completed the SCL-90-R.

Epidemiological Research

Epidemiological research affords access to persons who have experienced sexual assault but have not presented for help. Furthermore, large samples permit multivariate statistical analyses that can be used to control for variables that might affect the relationship between sexual assault and symptomatology. We consider research using formal diagnostic criteria first and then consider research using self-report data of psychological difficulty.

Epidemiological Research Utilizing Formal Diagnostic Criteria

Sexual Assault and Mental Disorder in a Community Sample

Burnam et al. (1988) studied the effects of childhood and/or adulthood sexual assault on 432 men and women from an epidemiological survey of 3,132 adults in Los Angeles. Lay interviewers trained to use the National

Institute of Mental Health (NIMH) Diagnostic Interview Schedule (DIS: Robins, Helzer, Croughan, and Ratcliffe, 1981) identified disorders. Analyses using the variables 'gender', 'age', 'education', 'ethnic group', and 'age at first assault' were conducted to identify first onset of a number of psychiatric disorders. First onset of alcohol abuse/dependence after experiencing sexual assault was more common in men. Gender was not a significant predictor of any other psychiatric disorders (depression, drug use/dependence, phobia, panic or obsessive compulsive disorder). Burnam *et al.* conclude from their data that 'although women are at greater risk of becoming victims of sexual assault, the impact of sexual assault on mental health status does not differ considerably between the sexes'.

Epidemiological Research Utilizing Self-Report Data

Sexual Assault and Psychological Difficulty in a Community Sample

Siegel, Golding, Stein, Burnam, and Sorenson (1990) compared gender differences in reactions to sexual assault in the victims identified in the study by Burnam *et al.* (1988). Sexual assault victims were asked if their experiences of sexual assault had ever caused them to have certain feelings (e.g., 'feel angry') or engage in certain behaviours (e.g., 'drink more alcohol or use more drugs'). Women victims were significantly more likely to report 11 of the 15 reactions (being fearful; stopped doing things used to do; fearful of sex; less sexual interest; less sexual pleasure; feeling dishonoured or spoiled; feeling sad, blue, or depressed; feeling angry; feeling tense, nervous, or anxious; fear of being alone). Principal components analysis reduced the 15 items to a three-factor solution ('sexual distress', 'fear/anxiety', and 'depression'). Regression analyses using a number of demographic and assault-related predictors found that female gender was a significant predictor of scores on the 'fear/anxiety' factor only.

Sexual Assault and Psychosexual Disorders in a Community Sample

Negative sexual experiences are significantly associated with sexual difficulty in men and women (Laumann, Paik, and Rosen, 1999). Results from a large community sample (1,749 women and 1,410 men) in the USA show that:

1   Being sexually touched before puberty and being sexually forced by a man are significant predictors of arousal disorder (but not low desire or sexual pain) in women.

2 Being sexually touched before puberty is a predictor of premature ejaculation, erectile dysfunction, and low desire in men.
3 Ever having forced a woman to have sex is a significant predictor of erectile dysfunction in men.

Sexual Assault and Psychological Difficulty in a College/Community Sample

Zweig *et al.* (1997) researched the association between SA and measures of well being in 1,399 young people aged 19–22 years (872 women and 527 men). Statistical analysis comparing victims and non-victims of sexual assault controlling for gender and college/non-college student status did not find significant gender differences in those reporting sexual assault on measures of well-being (anger, coping, depressed mood, self-esteem, social anxiety, or social isolation). The authors then examined the data to establish whether differences in level of coercion (no coercion, coerced, violently coerced) were related to well-being in men and women. The relationship between level of coercion and well-being was moderated by gender on three measures (anger, depression, and social anxiety). Separate analyses for men and women found that:

• Violently coerced men were significantly more angry and depressed than men who had been coerced and men who had not experienced sexual coercion.
• Coerced women were significantly more: (1) depressed than those violently coerced and the non-coerced; (2) angry than the non-coerced group; and (3) socially anxious than the non-coerced and violently coerced group.

A final analysis found that violently coerced men had significantly higher depression scores than violently coerced women.

Sexual Assault and Psychological Difficulty in a Community Sample of Homosexuals

Otis and Skinner (1996) researched the association between depression and various forms of victimization experienced within the last 2 years in a sample of lesbians ($n = 500$) and gay men ($n = 567$: n calculated from percentages given in the text). Sexual assault by a male(s) was a significant predictor of depression for lesbians and gay men. Neither same-sex sexual assault for lesbians nor opposite-sex sexual assault for gays were significant predictors of depression (these events were rare, however).

Utilization of Mental Health Services in a Community Sample

Golding, Stein, Siegel, Burnam, and Sorenson (1988) investigated mental health service use (in the previous 6 months) in persons with and without a history of sexual assault. Use of mental health services was more common in persons with a history of sexual assault (18%) than those without (9%: $p < 0.01$). A multivariate analysis found that female gender was a significant predictor of mental health service utilization even after controlling for age, ethnicity, and 'need' and 'enabling' variables (see Golding *et al.*, 1988 for further details). The interaction between gender and sexual assault history was not significant and, thus, there was no evidence of significantly greater mental health service by female victims of sexual assault.

General Health

Self-Reported Health

Epidemiological studies utilizing diagnostic criteria identify persons who meet given diagnoses but are silent about the intensity of difficulty experienced by victims of sexual assault. Self-ratings of health can help provide this information. An analysis of seven population surveys (four adult surveys; three youth surveys: total $n = 10,001$) found that sexual assault was associated with poor subjective health (OR 1.6, 95% CI 1.36–1.95) regardless of gender or ethnic group (Golding, Cooper, and George, 1997).

Physical Functioning

Golding (1996) examined self-report data regarding physical functioning from 6,024 persons. Analyses controlling for a number of demographic factors found that sexual assault victims were more than:

- twice as likely to be confined to bed (in a given period) due to physical health problems; and
- one and a half times more likely to experience days when activities were limited due to physical problems.

No significant gender differences were found in sexual assault victims on these measures, however.

Utilization of Medical Services

Golding *et al.* (1988) investigated medical service use (in the previous 6 months) in persons with and without a history of sexual assault. Use of medical service was more common in persons with a history of sexual assault (60%) than those without (44%: $p < 0.01$). A multivariate analysis found that female gender was a significant predictor of medical service utilization even after controlling for age, ethnicity, and 'need' and 'enabling' variables (see Golding *et al.*, 1988 for further details). The interaction between gender and sexual assault history was not significant and, thus, there was no evidence of significantly greater medical service use by female victims of sexual assault.

REVICTIMIZATION

There is evidence that child sexual abuse is associated with an increased risk of sexual assault in adulthood. This association is found in both women (see Messman and Long, 1996 for a brief review) and men (Coxell, King, Mezey, and Gordon, 1999; Coxell, King, Mezey, and Kell, 2000). Sorenson *et al.* (1991) compared male and female victims of single and multiple SA on four demographic, fourteen mental disorder and thirteen measures of general functioning (see Sorenson, Siegel, Golding, and Stein, for details of variables). None of the comparisons was significant, this being true for comparisons conflating male and female victims of sexual assault, and for female sexual assault victims only. A multivariate analysis also revealed that gender was not a significant predictor of experiencing more than one sexual assault.

EFFECT OF SEXUAL ASSAULT AND SOCIAL MYTHS ON MASCULINITY, FEMININITY, AND SEXUAL IDENTITY

> we are part of our environment. One cannot separate ... experience of, or recovery from, sexual trauma from the sociocultural environment in which it is experienced (Lebowitz and Roth, 1994)

Sexual assault impacts on victims in ways not measured by formal diagnostic criteria, and it is important that it be understood within the context of societal beliefs about male and female sexuality, and about vulnerability to sexual assault; for example, Zweig, Barber, and Eccles (1997) point out that a number of researchers (Burkhart and Fromuth, 1991; Masters, Johnson, and Kolodny, 1986) have identified a 'sexual double standard' which 'encourages men to seek as much sexual activity as possible and encourages women to limit their sexual experience'. Zweig *et al.* further argue that 'These societal-level scripts manifest in different attitudes men and women have about sexual permissiveness, and the level of intimacy men and women require before sexual activity occurs'. A meta-analysis of research on gender differences in sexuality (including 177 studies) found that men are more permissive of casual and extramarital sex and report an earlier age of sexual intercourse and more sexual partners than do women (Oliver and Hyde, 1993). Women were found to report more anxiety or guilt about sex and were more likely to endorse the sexual double standard (i.e., 'Beliefs that female premarital sexual activity is less acceptable than male sexual activity': Oliver and Hyde, 1993).

Clearly, not every man or woman will have beliefs that conform to a society's sexual scripts. However, many will, and an understanding of how the impact of SA might be mediated by attitudes that are discrepant with events is likely to be useful. We also feel it important that clinicians are mindful of their own beliefs and how these might affect their response to the victim (we consider clinical matters later in this chapter).

We consider the effect of sexual assault on the victim's sense of masculinity or femininity and the effect of sexual assault on sexuality here. These are important areas for consideration in their own right, but they may also be mediators/moderators of various psychiatric disorders.

MALE SEXUAL ASSAULT VICTIMS

Sexual Assault of Men by Men

There are many myths about the sexual assault of men (Gonsiorek, Bera, and LeTourneau, 1994). We consider these myths and the impact they might have on male victims here.

Men Cannot Be Forced to Have Sex

This belief is based upon the idea that males are expected to defend themselves if threatened. Indeed, Stanko (1990) has argued that the perception of a 'real man' is:

> a strong, heterosexual male protector, capable of taking care of himself and, if necessary, guarding his and others' safety aggressively. He is the man who will stand up in a fight ... And, according to the mythology of the 'real man', he will do so fearlessly'.

Many people probably believe that they would exhibit strong physical resistance in response to sexual assault, but the data do not support this. A UK study of 119 cases of male sexual assault (non-consensual buggery with a male victim over 16 years of age) found that 'freezing' was a very common victim response to sexual assault (63% of heterosexuals, 59% of homosexuals, and 58% of bisexuals: Hodge and Canter, 1998). Mezey and King (1989) also found that most victims demonstrated 'helplessness and passive submission, engendered by an overwhelming sense of disbelief'. While such submission is often a source of shame to survivors (King, 1992), it has been argued to be a common self-preservation aid and a basic response to threatening situations (Storr, 1968).

Men Who Sexually Assault Other Men Must Be Gay

This myth is not supported by evidence which shows that sexual assault of men by strangers is significantly more likely to be perpetrated by heterosexual men and that 66% of all gang assaults are perpetrated by heterosexual men (Hodge and Canter, 1998).

Belief in this myth may be indicated in therapy if the victim exhibits a pathological fear or hatred of homosexuals. Myers (1989) found that 43% (6/14) of sexually assaulted men in his sample were 'quite homophobic' and had assumed that their assailant must be gay. These men exhibited prejudiced views about homosexual men (e.g., 'male homosexuals prey on young boys', 'all homosexuals are obsessed with sex and nothing else'). Furthermore, one of these men '... developed profound and un-relenting homophobia ...' and '... enjoyed "cruising the drag" in his hometown with his friends and taunting the "queers"'.

Erection and/or Ejaculation Imply that the Man Was Complicit in Some Way

Research on the male sexual response has led to the conclusion that '... the physiologic mechanism of any emotional response (anger, fright, pain, etc.) may be the mechanism of sexual response' (Kinsey, Pomeroy, and Martin, 1948; see Redmond, Koste, and Reiser, 1983 for a further discussion and case examples of men who have experienced ejaculation in anxiety provoking situations). Thus, erection and ejaculation can often be involuntary responses, and are not uncommon during sexual assault. A recent study found that 18% of victims ejaculated during sexual assault (King and Woollett, 1997). Such 'sexual' responses can lead to victim distress:

> I always thought that a guy couldn't get hard if he was scared, and when this guy took me off it really messed up my mind. I thought that maybe

something was wrong with me. I didn't know what it meant and it really bothered me (Groth and Burgess, 1980).

A Man Sexually Assaulted by Another Man Must Himself Be Gay or Have Been Acting like a Gay Man

Men sexually assaulted by men can fear that they must have been 'giving off gay signals' (King, 1992). Health professionals and family or friends can share this belief. Mezey and King (1989) report that a man who disclosed his sexual assault to a psychiatrist was '... politely disbelieved and told to come to terms with the homosexual side of himself ...', while another victim stated that 'My social life ended ... my friends accepted his counterclaim that I had attempted to seduce him and made false accusations when rebuffed. They treated me as if I had contracted leprosy' (King, 1992).

Masculinity

A sense of emasculation is not uncommon in men after experiencing sexual assault. Myers (1989) concluded that many men in his study 'equated tarnished masculinity with loss of power, control, identity ... confidence and independence'. Goyer and Eddleman (1984) also report very similar findings regarding the effect of sexual assault on male gender identity in their study. A quote from a prisoner in Lockwood's study of sexual assault in prison demonstrates the effect of violations of assumptions about men being able to defend themselves and the effect of rape on masculinity:

> I am thinking: What would a real man do in situations like this [rape] ... Well I was upset because first of all, most guys consider themselves a man, and you always say that in jail no one is ever going to do that to you. I was very upset about it for four or five months afterwards because I thought that I had lost my manhood (Lockwood, 1980 quoted in Stanko, 1990).

Sexuality

Confusion about sexual orientation is not uncommon following sexual assault by males, and occurs irrespective of orientation before assault (Myers, 1989; Mezey and King, 1989). Such confusion was reported by 64% (9/14) of men in Myers' (1989) sample and 27% (6/22) of men in Mezey and King's (1989) sample. Conflated data from a national epidemiological study (Coxell et al., 1999) and a study conducted in a genitourinary medicine clinic (Coxell et al., 2000) found a marginally significant trend for confusion about sexual orientation to be more common after sexual assault perpetrated by males (26%, 13/50) compared with females (11%, 4/35: $\chi^2 = 2.7$, 1 d.f., $p < 0.10$).

SEXUAL ASSAULT OF MEN BY WOMEN

A Woman Cannot Sexually Assault A Man

Female perpetrators are involved in a large proportion of sexual assaults on men (46% in the Coxell *et al.* (2000) sample). Female-perpetrated sexual assault raises a number of issues for men, since it is incongruent with many societal attitudes regarding masculinity and sexuality. Men may feel that they should be more able to defend themselves against female perpetrators. Furthermore, Zweig *et al.* (1997) argue that for men 'being a victim of sexual coercion is not compatible with the idea of always being willing to have sex'.

Sarrell and Masters (1982) studied a number of men sexually assaulted by women and concluded that 'the impact is potentially on all dimensions of sexuality—response, desire, sense of orientation and behaviour'. These authors also stated that men in their sample were concerned about their erection and/or ejaculation during the assault. These responses are not uncommon, however. Conflated data from a national epidemiological study (Coxell *et al.*, 1999) and from a study conducted in a genitourinary medicine clinic (Coxell *et al.*, 2000) found that high proportions of men report erection and/or ejaculation during sexual assault, and that this is more common where the perpetrator is female (78%, 36/46) than where the perpetrator is male (60%, 36/60: $\chi^2 = 3.99$, 1 d.f., $p < 0.05$, OR 2.4, 95% CI 1–5.7). It is not possible to tell from these data whether the man had been engaging in consensual sexual activity before the sexual assault experience, however.

FEMALE SEXUAL ASSAULT VICTIMS

First, we consider the impact of the sexual assault of women by men. Next, we consider the much underresearched area of the effect of female perpetrated sexual assault on women.

SEXUAL ASSAULT OF WOMEN BY MEN

The literature pertaining to the sexual assault of women is vastly greater than the research on men, and is impossible to fully consider here. We concentrate on 'macro' influences on the victim and their possible effect on successful recovery from sexual assault.

Blame Attached to the Victim

Many societies have 'rape-supportive cultures' which support and condone the rape of women (Brownmiller, 1975; Clarke and Lewis, 1977). Indeed, Stanko (1990) has argued that '... the very meaning of the word safety differs between the sexes. Women understand it to be both physical and sexual'. Furthermore, Stanko argues that much (if not most) of the responsibility for protecting women against sexual crime is seen to fall on women themselves:

> by the time they have reached adulthood, many women have developed an unconscious alarm system which monitors men's behaviour for possible danger ... When danger strikes, it is her behaviour that is scrutinised for its lure to physical and sexual aggressions.

Thus, it is argued that many people may believe that it is incumbent on women to behave in a manner that minimizes the possibility of being sexually assaulted in the first instance; for example, a recent survey found that nearly a quarter of 4th-year medical students 'strongly agreed' or 'agreed' that 'rape happens when women go out alone or are in unsafe places' (Williams, Forster, and Petrak, 1999). While courts may often question women about the level of resistance they offered to the perpetrator there is evidence that similar proportions of women (21/35, 60%: Galliano, Noble, Travis, and Peuchl, 1993) and men (approximately 60%: Hodge and Canter, 1998) report freezing or milder forms of being unable to resist.

Femininity and Sexuality

Siegel, Golding, Stein, Burnam, and Sorenson (1990) found that female gender was a significant predictor of 'sexual distress' (a combination of scores on the items: decreased sexual interest, decreased sexual pleasure, and fear of sex) after the 'physical threat' variable was removed from the regression analysis. As with men, some women experience orgasm during sexual assault and this can be a source of difficulty (Sarrell and Masters, 1982). We are not aware of research demonstrating how common this response is or the range and intensity of any difficulties with which it is associated.

Qualitative research has shown that rape has a powerful impact on women's sexuality and on their feelings about their worth as a woman.

Indeed, evidence from transcripts from female rape victims suggests that, for some women, 'The criteria for accruing value to female sexuality ... revolves around usage (meaning the number of men who have had sexual access to a woman). Specifically, high usage equals low worth' (Lebowitz and Roth, 1994). Rape increases 'usage' and this can result in the victim and others valuing the victim less highly than before the rape.

Lebowitz and Roth also found that a woman's value seemed tied to her sexuality. Thus, after being raped, one victim stated that '[my sexuality] was dirty, or there was something wrong with my sexuality and me ... [my sexuality] was bad and so I was bad'. Such feelings are not uncommon in female victims. Siegel *et al.* (1990) found that more than one-third of female sexual assault victims 'felt dishonoured or spoiled'. Significant others may also make unhelpful judgements about the value of the victim and the putative impact of the sexual assault:

> My mother ... said 'Now this has happened to you and you are going to have to have it the rest of your life' ... she didn't want to talk about it. I was soiled ... [and] now that I'm soiled I'm going to start living a loose life ... I really think she thinks I am whoring around. That I am a really no-good person ... that I really am unclean ... I don't believe any of it but it bothers me that she believes it. (Lebowitz and Roth, 1994).

Women may also feel that rape affects their attractiveness to current or future partners. In discussing one case, Lebowitz and Roth state that '... Lucy, after trying to talk her gun-wielding rapist out of raping her because 'my husband will never touch me again' apologized to her husband for getting raped. There is evidence that men respond differently to their female partners, contingent upon whether their partner is a victim of sexual or non-sexual assault. Female rape victims give higher ratings of unsupportive behaviours to their male romantic partners and male non-romantic partners than they do to female non-romantic and female significant others (Davis and Brickman, 1996).

The Impact of the Environment on Adjustment

Lebowitz and Roth (1994) argue that 'Living in an environment which is full of the symbols of objectification and degradation of women and laden with continuing threat of rape, may make it very difficult for a survivor to move towards resolution.' Thus, these authors also argue that women may be unable to get away from a number of potentially anxiety provoking stimuli such as the sight of sex shops or the experiencing of verbal or other sexual harassment. This situation is exemplified by the comments of rape victims in their research:

> When I'm in the movies or something, [and] you hear someone refer to a
> woman as a cunt it just sends me up a wall. I mean, that's not what we are.

Similarly, sexually aggressive language evoked fear and anger in a
woman who had heard a male friend state that he wanted to 'fuck' a
woman's 'brains out':

> And I tried real hard to dismiss that, you know to say 'Oh he's drinking.
> He's joking. And I can't dismiss that. I can't. Fucking someone's brains out
> is a violent thing. It's not, here I am with a person. At [its] best it's cutting
> someone up in pieces ... it's a violent thing.

We discuss possible treatment implications of the effect of cultural beliefs
and stereotypes later in this chapter.

SEXUAL ASSAULT OF WOMEN BY WOMEN

There has been little research on female-perpetrator/female-victim sexual
assault. However, it is known that both heterosexual women (Brand and
Kidd, 1986) and lesbians (Waldner-Haugrud and Vaden Gratch, 1997)
experience such assaults. This research has concentrated on the nature
and prevalence of these experiences, rather than on psychological and
behavioural sequelae. As such, little is known about the effects of such
assaults, and we consider this an important area for research.

We expect that victims of female-perpetrator/female-victim sexual assault
may be as likely to experience a similar range of psychiatric disorders as
those experienced by any other perpetrator/victim combination. Reports
from a very small sample ($n = 3$) of women who reported sexual
assault by another female while in prison found that all experienced
nervousness and distrust, one had bad dreams and flashbacks and yet
another reported depression (Struckman-Johnson, Struckman-Johnson,
Rucker, Bumby, and Donaldson, 1996). We make the obvious point here
that these victims may be especially likely to experience adjustment difficulties if they are fearful of potential sexual assault by men and also
distrustful and fearful of women.

Such assaults may raise similar concerns about sexuality and femininity as
male-perpetrator/male-victim sexual assault does for men. As with men,
we anticipate that this may occur regardless of sexual orientation before
experiencing sexual assault.

SEXUAL ASSAULT OF LESBIANS AND GAY MEN

We assume that gay men, lesbians, and bisexuals are as likely to experience the various forms of psychological sequelae and attributions about

themselves post-assault, discussed in previous sections of this chapter, as are heterosexual people. Further issues obtain, however. First, there is evidence that sexual assault is more common in homosexual people. Second, gay men and lesbians live in societies that are prejudiced against them, and this could affect their recovery from sexual assault.

Prevalence of Sexual Assault on Homosexuals

Prevalence research on a sample of students has found that homosexuals were more likely to have been a victim of sexual coercion than heterosexuals (37 vs 19%: Duncan, 1990). This finding held for both genders: the rate of sexual coercion was higher in gay men than in heterosexual men (12 vs 4%) and higher in lesbians than in heterosexual women (31 vs 18%: Duncan, 1990). Epidemiological work has also found that men who have male sexual partners are more likely to report sexual assault than are heterosexual men (Coxell et al., 1999).

Heterosexism and Homophobia

Homosexuals live in heterosexist societies in which 'heterosexism' '... denigrates, and stigmatizes any non-heterosexual form of behaviour, identity, relationship and community' (Herek, 1990). Gay men and lesbians who experience sexual assault may thus not only experience a traumatic event, but their subsequent adjustment may also be affected by experiencing homophobic reactions from others. We know of no systematic evidence relating to the effect of prejudicial comments or actions on recovery from sexual assault in gay men and lesbians, but anecdotal evidence suggests that prejudicial attitudes exist and that victims experience such attitudes strongly and negatively; for example, one victim (who had been raped by five men) described his treatment in the Emergency Room:

> A female resident came in ... asked what happened ... asked me if the [man] I was with was my lover. She barely looked at my cuts. She didn't examine me. She didn't do a rape kit. She didn't test me for any venereal diseases ... She gave me a cloth to wash off my hands ... She told me to be more careful next time and sent me home. I think her comment 'Be more careful next time,' was how she interpreted gay sex. She had this attitude of '... they all get rough. They're always doing something up the butt.' Even if she had meant 'be careful where you walk' or something like that ... it still would have been an instance of blaming the victim and a lack of sensitivity about male rape (Donnelly and Kenyon, 1996).

Gay Men and Lesbians as Victims of Bias (Prejudice) Crimes

Bias-motivated sexual assault is committed against lesbians and gay men (Otis and Skinner, 1996; Herek, Gillis and Cogan, 1999). Bias crimes (sexual and non-sexual) have more psychological impact on victims than do non-hate crimes. Herek *et al.* (1999) compared self-report data from lesbians and gay men and found that those who had experienced a bias crime within the last 5 years:

- had significantly higher scores on scales measuring depression, traumatic stress, and anger;
- were significantly more fearful of crime;
- felt significantly more vulnerable;
- were significantly more likely to attribute negative life events and setbacks to sexual prejudice;
- had significantly less belief in the benevolence of others; and
- had significantly lower self-mastery

than lesbians and gay men who had experienced no crimes, any crime 5 or more years previously, or any non-bias crime in the last 5 years.

It is unknown if victims of sexual hate crimes are more ambivalent about, or unhappy with, their sexual orientation than victims of non-sexual hate crimes. Intuitively, this might be the case since the behaviour in the crime would seem to be more related to a person's sexual identity; for example, Garnets, Herek, and Levy, (1990) have argued that 'gay men may experience their sexual assault as an attempt to degrade male sexuality, which may later give rise to fearful or aversive feelings associated with their normal sexual behaviour'. Garnets *et al.* argue a similar point for lesbian victims of sexual crime.

IMPLICATIONS OF GENDER AND SEXUALITY FOR THERAPEUTIC WORK WITH VICTIMS OF SEXUAL ASSAULT

for rape victims to receive desired services their cases may need to fit a rather constricted mold. When certain characteristics of the victim, the assault, and the community are in careful alignment, the likelihood of an outcome that is consistent with victims' needs is most probable. As these factors deviate from this narrow path, the number of services may drop off, the fit with victims' wishes may be compromised, and the advocacy needed to bring about beneficial outcomes may rise (Campbell, 1998).

Probably very few sexual assaults fit the 'constricted mould' which promotes an optimal response from helping agencies. In this section, we briefly consider the effect on victims of involvement with different helping agencies and how these can affect adjustment. Next, we consider important therapeutic issues relating to masculinity/femininity and sexuality as considered earlier in this chapter. Specialists in later chapters of this book present specific treatment issues. Readers interested in implications of sexual assault for clinical practice and public policy should consult the excellent paper by Kilpatrick, Resnick, Acierno (1997).

Responses of Helping Agencies

The terms 'second rape' and 'secondary victimisation' (Madigan and Gamble, 1991) have been used to describe the lack of, or inappropriate, services provided to victims of sexual assault. Such victimization is associated with increased levels of psychopathology; for example, post-traumatic stress symptoms were significantly elevated in a sample of women who were raped by a known person, received minimal help from legal and medical services, and experienced victim-blaming behaviour (Campbell, Sefl *et al.*, 1999). Crucially, there is evidence that secondary victimization is not something simply perceived by victims, it is also identified as problematic by rape advocates (Campbell, 1998).

The implications of research into secondary victimization are clear: all professionals must try to ensure that they minimize the impact of sexual assault on victims and be prepared to help victims who have experienced unhelpful interventions from different services. We state the obvious and empirically supported fact here that believing and not blaming the victim is crucial. No victim is responsible for sexual assault, whatever the circumstances: responsibility always lies with perpetrators.

Treatment Issues Related to Women

It is most unfortunate that many rape victims are raped by a known person and that this type of rape is often associated with secondary victimization and victim-blaming behaviour from services intended to provide help. This may in part be due to professionals' lack of knowledge about sexual assault; for example, a recent survey has found that only just over half (56%) of 'licensed mental health professionals' in one American state had received training on the sexual assault of women (Campbell, Raja, and Grining, 1999). Lack of training may result in incorrect judgements about victims; for example, nearly a quarter of 4-year medical students 'strongly agreed' or 'agreed' that 'A rape victim will be hysterical, shaky and distraught' (Williams *et al.*, 1999). In fact, a number of responses to rape have been observed in victims, including calmness and detachment (Burgess and Holmstrom, 1974).

Lebowitz and Roth (1994) have argued that therapy with women should also include helping a woman to '... critically examine the sociocultural context and the ways in which she has internalised its messages'. These authors argue that such an approach has both benefits and risks and readers interested in these issues should consider Lebowitz (1993). We cannot recommend or comment upon the possible efficacy of such an intervention since, to our knowledge, it remains untested. However, we certainly believe that professionals should be aware of damaging social constructions and have techniques/information to hand for dealing with them if raised by the client and deemed appropriate on a case-by-case basis; for example, the woman who blames herself (or is blamed by others) for not 'fighting back' can be reassured that 'freezing' or partial freezing is a very common human response in fear situations and may be equally common in men.

Treatment Issues Related to Men

Recent research has found that one-third of health professionals (psychologists, psychiatrists, nurses) in a teaching hospital never enquire about a history of child sexual abuse in male patients (Lab, Feigenbaum, and DeSilva, 2000). Furthermore, there is evidence that clinical psychologists are more likely to identify child sexual abuse as an aetiological factor of a patient's current presentation (presented in the form of a vignette) if they believe the patient to be female (Holmes and Offen, 1996). We are unaware of any research similar to that of Lab *et al.* (2000) or that of Holmes and Offen (1996) pertaining to sexual assault experienced by men in adulthood. It seems likely that many men who have experienced sexual assault in adulthood will not be considered to have, or be asked about, such a history. However, men should be asked about these experiences.

Where cases of sexual assault are identified, it is possible that victims are treated differently dependent upon their presentation. Kaufman *et al.* (1980) found that most of the male victims in their study demonstrated the 'controlled' style of acute emotional reaction described by Burgess and Holmstrom (1974). This is important since it has been suggested that medical personnel distinguish between 'good' and 'bad' victims (Madigan and Gamble, 1991). 'Good' victims show obvious signs of distress, are very receptive to help from others, and as such may receive more help. This may place men at a disadvantage, since many men would not consider it 'masculine' to demonstrate such behaviour in the presence of others, and may deliberately behave stoically to try to reassert their 'manhood'. We make the obvious point that all victims need to be treated sensitively and equally, irrespective of their presentation.

Helpful guidelines have been published for the management of male victims of sexual assault in genitourinary medicine clinics (Tomlinson and Harrison, 1998). With a few obvious changes, such guidelines are also likely to be useful in the management of female victims.

Treatment Issues Related to Gay Men and Lesbians

Many anecdotal reports from homosexual victims of sexual assault describe the heterosexist attitudes of some staff in the medical and legal professions. Training for professionals is certainly indicated since nearly 40% of social work schools (Mazur, 1978) and less than half of counsellor education programmes (Gray, Cummins, and Mason, 1989) offer courses in human sexuality generally. Training in lesbian and gay issues is even less common, with only 9% of American psychology departments offering clinical training on sexual orientation (Carlson, 1985). Lack of knowledge about gay and lesbian issues may have a number of clinical consequences; for example, research has found that mental health professionals have less accurate recall about homosexual clients, and make more errors in recall about issues discrepant with cultural stereotypes about lesbians and gays (Casas, Brady, and Pontoretto, 1983). Education for mental health professionals regarding gay and lesbian issues is thus indicated and should include: (1) knowledge concerning sexual orientation and lesbian/gay lifestyles; (2) the implications for gays/lesbians of living in a heterosexist and homophobic society; and (3) issues related to therapist/client interaction (Murphy, 1992).

Garnets et al. (1990) have written about a number of issues pertaining to sexual assault of lesbians and gay men. They make the important point that homosexuals who experience sexual assault may face the task of 'double disclosure' (i.e., disclosing both their sexuality and their sexual assault). Special consideration may need to be placed upon the confidentiality of a victim's sexual orientation as this could lead to discrimination if disclosed (Garnets et al., 1990).

Garnets et al. also consider research on the differential effects of sexual assault during different phases of the 'coming out' process; for example, these authors argue that victims in the early stages of 'coming out' are perhaps less likely to have supportive others and access to community resources for homosexuals. Furthermore, these victims may be less likely to have positive images of same-sex sexual contact with which to counter the effect of any same-sex sexual assault. It seems good clinical practice to enquire about how 'out' (i.e., the extent to which the person has disclosed their sexual orientation to others) and how comfortable the victim is with being 'out' when engaging in therapeutic work.

Sexual histories are an important part of any assessment of a victim of sexual assault. Professionals may assume that victims are heterosexual and ask inappropriate questions of persons who have a different sexuality to that assumed by the professional (Orzek, 1988). Such insensitivity is an obvious example of heterosexist practice and should be avoided. Professionals may also assume that a client is homosexual or bisexual and this may impact negatively on the client. In short, it is best that all questions are asked sensitively and that no assumptions are made.

Sexuality and Treatment

We have presented evidence that sexual assault can result in conflicted sexual orientation and that this can cause distress. However, it is also possible that after experiencing sexual assault a person could make an active decision to choose sexual partners of a different gender to that of the person who sexually assaulted them. If the client is happy with this decision, we do not consider it a treatment issue.

CONCLUSION

Research conducted so far suggests that observed psychiatric symptomatology, self-ratings of health, and use of mental health and medical services in persons who have experienced sexual assault does not differ greatly between men and women. Social constructions of masculinity, femininity, and sexuality combined with beliefs about the causes of crime and 'appropriate' victim behaviour during and after sexual assault may affect the victim's recovery and the helping response from legal, medical, and voluntary services. This is perhaps most likely to be true when the sexual assault does not fit the stereotypical or 'constricted mold' which provokes optimal responding from helping agencies. We feel that the impact of these social constructions should not be underestimated. Considering the possible range of victim/perpetrator combinations, it is likely that those intending to provide help to victims will need a wide range of knowledge and skills to provide help and support to victims. All those involved in assisting victims of sexual crime should be appropriately trained and aware of the potential negative impact of services intended to provide help.

REFERENCES

Brand, P.A. and Kidd, A.H. (1986) Frequency of physical aggression in heterosexual and homosexual dyads. *Psychological Reports*, **59**, 1307–1313.

Brownmiller, S. (1975) *Against our will: Men, women, and rape*. New York: Simon and Schuster.

Burgess, A.W. and Holmstrom, L.L. (1974) Rape trauma syndrome. *American Journal of Psychiatry*, **131**, 981–986.

Burkhart, B. and Fromuth, M.E. (1991) Individual psychological and social psychological understandings of sexual coercion. In E. Grauerholz, and Koralewski, M.A. (eds) *Sexual coercion: A sourcebook of its nature, causes and prevention* (pp. 75–89) Lexington, MA: Lexington.

Burnam, M.A., Stein, J.A., Golding, J.M., Siegel, J.M., Sorenson, S.B., Forsythe, A.B., and Telles, C.A. (1988) Sexual assault and mental disorders in a community population. *Journal of Consulting and Clinical Psychology*, **56**(6), 843–850.

Campbell, R. (1998) The community response to rape: Victims' experiences with the legal, medical and mental health systems. *American Journal of Community Psychology*, **26**, 355–379.

Campbell, R., Raja, S., and Grining, P.I. (1999) Training mental health professionals on violence against women. *Journal of Interpersonal Violence*, **14**(10), 1003–1013.

Campbell, R., Sefl, T., Barnes, H.E., Ahrens, C.E., Wasco, S.M., and Zaragoza-Diesfeld, Y. (1999) Community services for rape survivors: Enhancing psychological well-being or increasing trauma? *Journal of Consulting and Clinical Psychology*, **67**(6), 847–858.

Carlson, H. (1985) *Employment issues for researchers on lesbian and gay issues*. Paper presented at the 93rd Annual Convention of the American Psychological Association, Los Angeles, CA, August.

Casas, J.M., Brady, S., and Pontoretto, J.G. (1983) Sexual preference biases in counselling: An information processing approach. *Journal of Counselling Psychology*, **30**(2), 139–145.

Clarke, L. and Lewis, D.J. (1977) *Rape: The price of coercive sexuality*. Toronto: Women's Press.

Coxell, A.W., King, M.B., Mezey, G.C., and Gordon, D. (1999) Lifetime prevalence, characteristics, and associated problems of non-consensual sex in men: A cross sectional survey. *British Medical Journal*, **318**, 846–850.

Coxell, A.W., King, M.B., Mezey, G.C., and Kell, P. (2000) Sexual molestation of men: Interviews with 224 men attending a genitourinary medicine service. *International Journal of STD and AIDS*, **11**(9), 574–578.

Darves-Bornoz, J-M., Choquet, M., Ledoux, S., Gasquet, I., and Manfredi, R. (1998) Gender differences in symptoms of adolescents reporting sexual assault. *Social Psychiatry and Epidemiology*, **33**, 111–117.

Davis, R.C. and Brickman, E. (1996) Supportive and unsupportive aspects of the behaviour of others towards victims of sexual assault and nonsexual assault. *Journal of Interpersonal Violence*, **11**(2), 250–262.

Derogatis, L.R. (1983) *SCL-90-R Administration, scoring and procedures manual, II.* Towson, MD: Clinical Psychometric Research.

DiVasto, P.V., Kaufman, A., Rosner, L., Jackson, R., Christy, J., Pearson, S., and Burgett, T. (1984) The prevalence of sexually stressful events among females in the general population. *Archives of Sexual Behaviour*, **13**, 59–67.

Donnelly, D.A. and Kenyon, S. (1996) 'Honey, we don't do men': Gender stereotypes and the provision of services to sexually assaulted males. *Journal of Interpersonal Violence*, **11**(3), 441–448.

Duncan, D. (1990) Prevalence of sexual assault victimisation among heterosexual and gay/lesbian university students. *Psychological Reports*, **55**, 65–66.

Frazier, P.A. (1993) A comparative study of male and female rape victims seen at a hospital-based rape crisis program. *Journal of Interpersonal Violence*, **8**(1), 64–76.

Galliano, G., Noble, L.M., Travis, L.A., and Peuchl, C. (1993) Victim reactions during rape/sexual assault. *Journal of Interpersonal Violence*, **8**(1), 109–114.

Garnets, L., Herek, G.M., and Levy, B. (1990) Violence and victimisation of lesbians and gay men. *Journal of Interpersonal Violence*, **5**(3), 366–383.

Golding, J.M. (1996) Sexual assault history and limitations in physical functioning in two general population samples. *Research in Nursing and Health*, **19**, 33–44.

Golding, J.M., Cooper, M.L., and George, L.K. (1997) Sexual assault history and health perceptions: Seven general population surveys. *Health Psychology*, **16**(5), 417–425.

Golding, J.M., Stein, J.A., Siegel, J.M., Burnam, M.A., and Sorenson, S.B. (1988) Sexual assault history and use of health and medical services. *American Journal of Community Psychology*, **16**(5), 843–850.

Gonsiorek, J.C., Bera, W.H., and LeTourneau, D. (1994) *Male sexual abuse.* Thousand Oaks, CA: Sage Publications.

Goyer, P.F. and Eddleman, H.C. (1984) Same sex rape of non-incarcerated men. *American Journal of Psychiatry*, **141**, 576–579.

Gray, L.A., Cummins, E.J., and Mason, M.J. (1989) Human sexuality instruction in counsellor education curricula. *Counsellor Education and Supervision*, **28**, 305–317.

Groth, A.N. and Burgess, A.W. (1980) Male rape: Offenders and victims. *American Journal of Psychiatry*, **137**, 806–810.

Herek, G.M. (1990) The context of anti-gay violence: Notes on cultural and psychological heterosexism. *Journal of Interpersonal Violence*, **5**(3), 301–315.

Herek, G.M., Gillis, J.R., and Cogan, J.C. (1999) Psychological sequelae of hate-crime victimisation among lesbian, gay and bisexual adults. *Journal of Consulting and Clinical Psychology*, **67**(6), 945–951.

Hodge, S. and Canter, D. (1998) Victims and perpetrators of male sexual assault. *Journal of Interpersonal Violence*, **13**(2), 222–239.

Holmes, G.R. and Offen, L. (1996) Clinicians' hypotheses regarding clients' problems: Are they less likely to hypothesise sexual abuse in male compared to female clients? *Child Abuse and Neglect*, **20**, 493–501.

Hutchings, P.S. and Dutton, M.A. (1997) Symptom severity and diagnoses related to sexual assault history. *Journal of Anxiety Disorders*, **11**(6), 607–618.

Janoff-Bulman, R. and Frieze, I.H. (1983) Theoretical perspective for understanding reactions to victimisation. *Journal of Social Issues*, **39**(2), 1–17.

Kaufman, A., DiVasto, P., Jackson, R., Voorhees, D., and Christy, J. (1980) Male rape victims: Noninstitutionalised assault. *American Journal of Psychiatry*, **137**(2), 221–223.

Kilpatrick, D.G., Resnick, H.S., and Acierno, R. (1997) Health impact of interpersonal violence 3: Implications for clinical practice and public policy. *Behavioral Medicine*, **23**, 79–85.

King, M.B. (1992) *Male sexual assault in the community*. In G.C. Mezey and M.B. King (eds) *Male victims of sexual assault* (pp. 1–12) Oxford: Oxford University Press.

King, M.B. and Woollett, E. (1997) Sexually assaulted males: 115 men consulting a counselling service. *Archives of Sexual Behaviour*, **26**, 579–588.

Kinsey A.C., Pomeroy, W.B., and Martin, C.E. (1948) *Sexual behaviour in the human male*. Philadelphia: Saunders.

Lab, D., Feigenbaum, J.D., and DeSilva, P. (2000) Mental health professionals' attitudes towards male childhood sexual abuse. *Child Abuse and Neglect*, **24**(3), 391–409.

Laumann, E.O., Paik, A., and Rosen, R.C. (1999) Sexual dysfunction in the United States. *Journal of the American Medical Association*, **281**(6), 537–544.

Lebowitz, L. (1993) The convergence of feminism and trauma-focused therapy in the treatment of female sexual trauma survivors. *Journal of Training Practice Professional Psychology*, **7**, 81–99.

Lebowitz, L. and Roth, S. (1994) 'I felt like a slut': The cultural context and women's response to being raped. *Journal of Traumatic Stress*, **7**(3), 363–390.

Lockwood, D. (1980) *Prison sexual violence*. New York: Elsevia/Thomond Books.

Madigan, L. and Gamble, N. (1991) *The second rape: Society's continued betrayal of the victim*. New York: Lexington Books.

Masters, W.H., Johnson, V.E., and Kolodny, R.C. (1986) *Masters and Johnson on sex and human loving*. Boston: Little, Brown.

Mazur, C. (1978) A descriptive study of social work education in human sexuality: Curriculum design and instructor characteristics. Unpublished Masters Thesis, University of Hawaii, Honolulu.

Messman, T.L. and Long, P.J. (1996) Child sexual abuse and its relationship to revictimisation in adult women. *Clinical Psychology Review*, **16**(5), 397–420.

Mezey, G.C. and King, M.B. (1989) The effects of sexual assault on men: A survey of 22 victims. *Psychological Medicine*, **19**, 205–209.

Murphy, B.C. (1992) Educating mental health professionals about gay and lesbian issues. *Journal of Homosexuality*, 229–246.

Myers, M.F. (1989) Men sexually assaulted as adults and sexually abused as boys. *Archives of Sexual Behaviour*, **18**, 203–215.

Oliver, M.J. and Hyde, J.S. (1993) Gender differences in sexuality: A meta-analysis. *Psychological Bulletin*, **114**, 29–51.

Orzek, A.M. (1988) The lesbian victim of sexual assault: Special considerations for the mental health professional. *Women and Therapy*, **8**(1/2), 101–117.

Otis, M.G. and Skinner, W.F. (1996) The prevalence of victimisation and its effect on mental well-being among lesbian an gay people. *Journal of Homosexuality*, **30**(3), 93–117.

Redmond, D.E., Koste, T.R., and Reiser, M.F. (1983) Spontaneous ejaculation associated with anxiety: Psychophysiological considerations. *American Journal of Psychiatry*, **140**(9), 1163–1166.

Resnick, H.S., Acierno, R., and Kilpatrick, D.G. (1997) Health impact of interpersonal violence 2: Medical and mental health outcomes. *Behavioral Medicine*, **23**, 65–78.

Robins, L.N., Helzer, J.E., Croughan, J., and Ratcliffe, K. (1981) National Institute of Mental Health Diagnostic Interview Schedule: Its history, characteristics and validity. *Archives of General Psychiatry*, **38**, 381–389.

Sarrell, P.M. and Masters, W.H. (1982) Sexual molestation of men by women. *Archives of Sexual Behaviour*, **11**, 117–130.

Shrier, L.A., Pierce, J.D., Emans, S.J., and Durant, R.H. (1998) Gender differences in risk behaviours associated with forced or pressured sex. *Archives of Pediatric and Adolescent Medicine*, **152**, 57–63.

Siegel, J.M., Golding, J.M., Stein, J.A., Burnam, M.A., and Sorenson, S.B. (1990) Reactions to sexual assault. *Journal of Interpersonal Violence*, **5**(2), 229–246.

Sorenson, S.B., Siegel, J.M., Golding, J.M., and Stein, J.A. (1991) Repeated sexual victimisation. *Violence and Victims*, **6**(4), 299–308.

Stanko, E. (1990) *Everyday violence*. London: Pandora.

Storr, A. (1968) *Human aggression*. Harmondsworth, UK: Penguin.

Struckman-Johnson, C., Struckman-Johnson, D., Rucker, L., Bumby, K., and Donaldson, S. (1996) Sexual coercion reported by men and women in prison. *The Journal of Sex Research*, **33**(1), 67–76.

Tomlinson, D.R. and Harrison, J. (1998) The management of adult male victims of sexual assault in the GUM clinic: A practical guide. *International Journal of STD and AIDS*, **9**, 720–725.

Waldner-Haugrud, L.K. and Vaden Gratch, L. (1997) Sexual coercion in lesbian and gay relationships: Descriptives and gender differences. *Violence and Victims*, **12**(1), 87–98.

Williams, L, Forster, G., and Petrak, J. (1999) Rape attitudes among British medical students. *Medical Education*, **33**, 24–27.

Zweig, J.M., Barber, B.L., and Eccles, J.S. (1997) Sexual coercion and well-being in young adulthood. *Journal of Interpersonal Violence*, **12**(2), 291–308.

Chapter 4

A REVIEW OF TREATMENT AND OUTCOME OF POST-TRAUMA SEQUELAE IN SEXUAL ASSAULT SURVIVORS

Jennifer A. Bennice and Patricia A. Resick

The purpose of this chapter is to summarize the literature on psychosocial and pharmacological interventions for post-trauma reactions to sexual assault. The treatment models reviewed in this chapter will include crisis intervention, hypnotherapy, psychodynamic therapies, stress inoculation training, systematic desensitization, prolonged exposure, cognitive therapy, cognitive processing therapy, eye movement desensitization and reprocessing therapy, and pharmacotherapy. Although men are victims of sexual assault, the large majority of sexual assault victims are female. 'She' and 'her' will be used throughout the chapter for ease of language. Therapy procedures that have been developed and assessed for female sexual assault survivors should be considered for male clients as well.

This summary will take the form of an empirical review of various treatment models, evaluating each through a discussion of treatment outcome studies. We have included limited reference to studies involving survivors of various traumas because not all types of treatment have been evaluated with sexual assault victims, and there tends to be many similarities across traumas. This review will include the results of both controlled and uncontrolled group designs as well as relevant case studies. Well-controlled studies incorporate random assignment to treatment, comparison, or control groups; standardized treatment; objective measures of symptoms at pre- and post-treatment; and specific inclusion/exclusion criteria. While the results of uncontrolled studies offer few definitive conclusions,

The Trauma of Sexual Assault. Edited by Jenny Petrak and Barbara Hedge.
© 2002 John Wiley & Sons Ltd.

stronger evidence can be derived from the results of well-controlled studies. Therefore, our review will include a critical evaluation of treatment outcome results in light of each study's design. This discussion is intended to provide an empirically based rationale for the remaining chapters in which each treatment will be outlined in greater detail.

CRISIS INTERVENTION AND BRIEF TREATMENT APPROACHES

Crisis theory assumes that a trauma disrupts a person's homeostasis. A crisis state is defined as one in which a person is faced with a problem situation that cannot be modified or avoided by using standard means of coping. In response, the person enters a state of disequilibrium that lasts 6–8 weeks. During this period, the person experiences high levels of subjective distress and searches for new ways to handle the problem (Burgess and Holmstrom, 1976). If handled successfully, the person develops new and effective coping strategies and the distress diminishes. However, it is also possible that the person can develop maladaptive strategies to reduce distress (e.g., substance abuse, denial), which will result in chronic maladaptive coping and vulnerability to later problems.

Based on crisis theory, crisis counseling first emerged in the 1960s and 1970s. In general, crisis intervention is a supportive therapy aimed at the development of coping skills in the wake of a crisis situation. It focuses on the relative normalcy of victims' reactions to a crisis situation rather than characterological traits or psychopathology. The goal of crisis intervention is to prevent chronic post-trauma problems through the use of education, active listening and emotional support for the trauma survivor immediately following the traumatic event. Because crisis theory holds that the disequilibrium state following a crisis lasts 6–8 weeks, this approach assumes that distress subsides in the same brief period as well. Despite research countering this short recovery time period, crisis intervention is still used in the majority of rape crisis centers and victims assistance agencies.

Burgess and Holmstrom (1974a, 1974b) were the first to apply crisis theory to rape victims, and crisis counseling has since become the most common approach in rape crisis centers nationwide (Koss and Harvey, 1987). In general, there is not much research demonstrating the efficacy of crisis intervention for sexual assault victims. There have been no controlled studies, and existing uncontrolled studies, which have been conducted primarily with victims of other traumas (e.g., natural disaster), suggest that crisis intervention approaches aimed at preventing post-trauma symptomatology either do not work or can have deleterious effects for trauma survivors (e.g. Bisson, Jenkins, Alexander, and Bannister, 1997; Hytten and Hasle, 1989; Kenardy et al., 1996).

Moving beyond crisis intervention *per se*, some researchers have begun to examine the effectiveness of brief treatments within weeks after the trauma aimed at preventing or reducing post-trauma symptomatology; for example, Kilpatrick and Veronen (1983) examined a brief behavioral program aimed at reducing post-rape symptoms, but their findings are difficult to interpret due to methodological flaws. Foa, Hearst-Ikeda, and Perry (1995) and Foa, Rothbaum, and Molnar (1995) examined a brief prevention program for PTSD-positive female assault victims that included exposure, relaxation training, and cognitive restructuring. All techniques were found to be helpful in treating PTSD, and the brief prevention program participants showed significantly greater improvement in PTSD symptoms than the control group. Despite these encouraging results, they are limited by a small sample size.

Bryant and his colleagues (Bryant, Harvey, Dang, Sackville, and Basten, 1998; Bryant, Sackville, Dang, Moulds, and Guthrie, 1999) have conducted two studies of cognitive behavior therapy in order to determine if treatment within 2 weeks of the trauma could prevent the development of PTSD. In one study, a protocol including education, relaxation, exposure, and cognitive restructuring was compared with supportive therapy (Bryant et al., 1998). In the other study, prolonged exposure (PE), PE plus anxiety management, or supportive counseling were compared (Bryant et al., 1999). In both studies, the cognitive-behavioral treatments were superior to supportive therapy in preventing the development of PTSD. In the behavior therapy conditions, fewer than 25% had PTSD at 6 months post-trauma, while 67% of the supportive counseling group met the criteria for PTSD. While these studies did not include sexual assault survivors, the results could be considered promising for this population as well.

Overall, the use of crisis intervention techniques has not been empirically supported as a viable method for preventing post-trauma symptoms. Moreover, crisis intervention approaches do not account for the long-term reactions of sexual assault victims. The assumption of crisis theory is that distress subsides after 6–8 weeks, but this does not explain chronic PTSD and depressive symptomatology that is so frequently evident among sexual assault survivors (e.g., Ellis, Atkeson, and Calhoun, 1981; Kessler, Sonnega, Bromet, Hughes, and Nelson, 1995). Brief cognitive-behavioral treatment approaches that are initiated shortly after the trauma have demonstrated some promising results in the Foa, Hearst-Ikeda, and Perry (1995), Foa, Rothbaum, and Molner (1995), and Bryant et al. (1998, 1999) studies. It is possible that victims are better able to benefit from an intervention aimed at processing the trauma when they are no longer in an initial state of shock (e.g., 2 weeks post-rape). However, crisis intervention and brief treatment approaches such as supportive counseling are inherently unable to treat the long-term psychological sequelae presented by some trauma survivors.

HYPNOTHERAPY

Hypnotherapy was first used by Freud to treat traumatic stress. Freud believed that psychic conflict could be resolved by using hypnotherapy to produce the necessary catharsis in the client. More recently, Spiegel (1989) has suggested that hypnosis may be useful in treating PTSD for two reasons. First, dissociation, which is associated with hypnosis by nature, is a common coping mechanism for trauma survivors. Second, some traumatic events, which were originally encoded in a dissociative state, may be unavailable to conscious recollection. Spiegel has asserted that hypnosis may help to facilitate the recollection of such events.

To date, there have been several case studies that have found hypnosis to be useful in the treatment of PTSD (e.g., Leung, 1994; Spiegel, 1989; Spiegel, Hunt, and Dondershine, 1988). It is important to note, however, that only the Spiegel (1989) study examined the use of hypnosis with sexual assault victims. Nonetheless, the results of these uncontrolled studies are limited by methodological problems, including lack of specificity in targeted symptoms. Therefore, it is impossible to draw any definite conclusions about the efficacy of hypnotherapy based on this evidence alone.

Empirically based conclusions are further hampered by the scarcity of controlled studies of hypnotherapy and post-trauma symptomatology. Brom, Kleber, and Defares (1989) compared hypnosis, systematic desensitization, psychodynamic psychotherapy, and a wait-list control group in 112 PTSD-positive trauma victims (i.e., survivors of car accidents and various forms of violence). Results indicated that all three treatments were significantly more effective than the control, but there were no differences among the three treatments. Despite these encouraging results, additional controlled studies of the effectiveness of hypnotherapy in trauma populations are needed.

PSYCHODYNAMIC THERAPIES

Unlike its Freudian beginnings, modern psychodynamic thinking pays more attention to environmental stressors. Nonetheless, resolving intrapsychic conflict remains at the core of psychodynamic therapies. One of the most influential modern theories has been Horowitz's (1976) theory of trauma which emphasizes the concepts of denial, abreaction, catharsis, and stages of recovery. The goal of Horowitz's brief psychodynamic therapy is to resolve the intrapsychic conflict that has resulted from the traumatic experience. This approach stands in stark contrast to alternative therapies that aim to reduce specific symptoms.

Roth, Dye, and Lebowitz (1988) examined a group therapy that was based on Horowitz's model in female sexual assault victims. In the initial group session, members received a description of Horowitz's model and were encouraged to share their experiences as well as offer support to other group members. Of the original group membership, 13 sexual assault victims volunteered to be a part of a control group, and the remaining 13 women became a part of the group therapy. It is important to note that not only was assignment to the control condition non-random, but a high attrition rate from this group resulted as well. The goal of the group therapy for the clients was to work through the trauma by gradually re-experiencing the event at manageable levels. Results indicated improvements on measures of fear, intrusive symptoms, depression, and overall functioning for the treatment group. However, these improvements cannot be attributed solely to the group therapy because of the several methodological flaws that plagued this study, including non-random assignment, only partial control data, differences between treatment and control groups in the initial severity of symptoms, and the additional therapeutic component of individual therapy for the treatment group.

Since Horowitz's original conceptualization of trauma (1976), psychodynamic therapy has taken a more cognitive approach, focusing on the exploration of self as well as the conflict produced by the trauma. Although theoretically different, psychodynamic therapies contain elements that are similar to cognitive-behavioral interventions. However, psychodynamic therapists tend to place more emphasis on developmental issues, transference and countertransference reactions, and the therapeutic relationship.

Lindy (1996), Marmar, Weiss, and Pynoos (1995), and van der Kolk (1996) all emphasize the importance of the therapeutic relationship in the treatment of trauma survivors. They assert that a strong therapeutic alliance helps to create a safe holding environment in which the client can come to understand how the trauma has impacted her sense of self. In addition, such an environment can help to reduce the strong affective component related to the trauma as well as facilitate the integration of the trauma into current beliefs and future expectations. In sum, the mechanism of change in contemporary psychodynamic therapy is the transference of traumatic memories into the safe and non-judgmental therapeutic relationship where they can be processed fully.

Beyond the central importance of the therapeutic relationship, psychodynamic theorists have also made specific treatment recommendations for various subtypes of PTSD. Marmar *et al.* (1995) differentiated among simple/uncomplicated PTSD, complex PTSD, and PTSD with co-morbid Axis I disorders. Uncomplicated PTSD can be treated via brief therapy by establishing a strong therapeutic alliance, focusing on self-concepts, working through conflicts, linking the trauma to previous traumas, and attending to transference and countertransference issues. Similarly, PTSD with a co-morbid Axis I disorder is treated using the above approaches as well as treating the additional Axis I disorders simultaneously. One notable exception to this latter recommendation is in the case of co-morbid substance abuse/dependence, which must be treated prior to treating the PTSD. Complex PTSD, which is also referred to as PTSD personality disorder, requires a longer treatment process that potentially includes additional components such as interpersonal skills training, group or family therapy, medication, or hospitalization. Complex PTSD tends to be more likely in clients who suffered repeated abuse either in childhood or war. Herman (1992) and van der Kolk (1996) state that clients with complex PTSD often experience severe problems with affect regulation, dissociation, personal identity, and interpersonal and vocational functioning. Theorists suggest that once memories have been expressed fully and processed, dissociative boundaries are no longer needed.

Despite the attractiveness of such theories, little research exists beyond case studies in examining the effectiveness of psychodynamic therapies for trauma. Cryer and Beutler (1980) examined a brief dynamic group therapy in nine rape victims. Although they found significant reductions in fear and hostility, the absence of a control group and the small sample size limit these findings. Grigsby (1987) performed a single case study of a Vietnam veteran and found no improvement after 19 months of psychodynamic therapy. However, 10 additional sessions of behaviorally oriented imagery therapy resulted in a reduction of the client's self-reported PTSD symptoms.

In general, psychodynamic therapies have not been widely tested in controlled outcome studies. As cited previously, Brom *et al.* (1989) performed one of the few controlled studies of psychodynamic therapy in a trauma population. They randomly assigned 112 trauma survivors to psychodynamic therapy, hypnotherapy, systematic desensitization, or a wait-list control. Results indicated that all three treatment groups were more effective than the control group in decreasing PTSD symptoms, and there were no significant differences among the treatments.

Overall, the effectiveness of psychodynamic therapies in treating post-trauma reactions has not been empirically established. In order to draw more definite conclusions about treatment efficacy, additional methodologically rigorous studies are needed. In addition to the use of control groups, these studies need to utilize blind independent evaluators, standardized symptom measures, and samples of sexual assault victims.

STRESS INOCULATION TRAINING

Predating the concept of PTSD, early studies on sexual assault survivors focused solely on fear and anxiety reactions (Burgess and Holmstrom, 1974a, 1974b; Kilpatrick, Resick, and Veronen, 1981; Kilpatrick and Veronen, 1983). Stress inoculation training (SIT) was one of the first approaches used to treat trauma-related symptoms among sexual assault victims (e.g., Kilpatrick, Veronen, and Resick, 1982; Resick and Jordan, 1988; Veronen and Kilpatrick, 1983). Meichenbaum (1974) originally developed SIT as a cognitive-behavioral approach aimed at managing anxiety. Because sexual assault survivors tend to experience a great deal of anxiety when they are reminded of the trauma, it holds that SIT would be helpful to this population.

SIT is based on a two-factor learning theory model of fear and trauma-related symptoms. Since Mowrer's two-factor theory (1947), several authors have proposed that post-trauma reactions can be explained through classical and operant conditioning (e.g., Keane, Zimering, and Caddell, 1985; Kilpatrick, Veronen, and Resick, 1979; Kilpatrick et al., 1982). First, through classical conditioning, any stimulus associated with the traumatic event can become capable of eliciting a conditioned response similar to that associated with the original trauma (e.g., fear). In this framework, the trauma memory becomes the conditioned stimulus and fear becomes the conditioned response. Additional stimuli, which are indirectly associated with the trauma, create similar fear reactions through stimulus generalization and higher order conditioning. Second, operant conditioning accounts for the development of avoidance symptoms and maintenance of symptoms over time; that is, the trauma memory (i.e., conditioned stimulus) is avoided in order to escape or prevent fear and anxiety (i.e., conditioned response). In this manner, the avoidance of the trauma memory is negatively reinforced, which prevents the extinction of the stimulus-response link (i.e., traumatic memory–fear/anxiety link) and the maintenance of post-trauma symptoms.

The primary goal of SIT is to help clients understand and manage their trauma-related fear and anxiety reactions. SIT aims to manage anxiety via education and coping skills training. Within this approach, the initial treatment goal focuses on helping clients understand and manage trauma-related fear reactions. Accomplishment of this goal, in turn, helps to reduce the need for avoidance behavior of fear-producing stimuli. The fear and anxiety reactions are thus extinguished. Overall, SIT facilitates coping with intrusive recollections and reminders of the assault without having to resort to avoidance strategies.

SIT consists of three phases. First, the educational phase focuses on explaining post-trauma symptoms, including the development of fear. In addition, this phase helps to explain the relationship among fear cues, automatic fear reactions, intrusive thoughts, and avoidance behaviors. Second, the skill-building phase includes training in relaxation techniques, thought stopping, covert rehearsal, problem solving, and guided self-dialogue. Third, the application phase facilitates the use of these new skills to daily anxiety-provoking situations through the use of hierarchies in which fear cues are matched with coping skills and practised in their environment.

In terms of empirical support for the effectiveness of SIT, there are several single-case studies that have found this approach to be effective with sexual assault survivors (e.g., Kilpatrick and Amick, 1985; Pearson, Poquette, and Wasden, 1983). It is important to note that these studies included samples in which the participants were at least 3 months post-assault, and, thus, past the window of natural recovery. In addition to the supporting single-case studies, some uncontrolled multiple-case studies have examined the effectiveness of SIT as well; for example, Veronen and Kilpatrick (1983) examined SIT in 21 sexual assault victims and found this approach to be effective in reducing anxiety, fear, and a negative mood state.

There have been several controlled studies conducted on SIT that lend further empirical support. Resick, Jordan, Girelli, Hutter, and Marhoefer-Dvorak (1988) compared SIT, assertion training, supportive psychotherapy, and a wait-list control in a sample of rape victims. Results indicated that all three treatment groups improved equally on PTSD, depression, anxiety, rape-related and social fears, self-esteem and assertiveness.

Foa, Rothbaum, Riggs, and Murdock (1991) randomly assigned 45 rape victims to SIT, prolonged exposure (PE, see exposure-based therapies section of this chapter for a description), supportive counseling, or a wait-list control group. Findings showed significant improvement for the SIT and PE clients on measures of PTSD, depression, and anxiety. Although the SIT clients were most improved at post-treatment, there was a trend for the PE clients toward more improvement on PTSD at a 3-month follow-up. Foa *et al.* (1991) speculated that this latter finding might be due to the short-term nature of SIT as opposed to longer term effects of the cognitive and emotional processing of PE.

Foa *et al.* (1999) performed a large controlled study in which 96 female sexual assault victims with chronic PTSD were randomly assigned to PE, SIT, the combination of the two techniques, or a wait-list control group. In addition to the use of random assignment and a control condition, the strength of this study's design was also apparent in its use of blind, independent evaluators and the incorporation of 3-, 6-, and 12-month follow-up assessments. Results indicated that the combination of the two treatments did not improve upon the effectiveness of either treatment alone. Specifically, both treatments (either alone or in combination) were more effective in the treatment of PTSD and depression than the control group. These results were maintained through the follow-up assessments as well.

Overall, there seems to be substantial empirical support for the effectiveness of SIT in treating post-trauma symptoms. In addition to numerous case studies and uncontrolled studies, a few well-designed controlled studies have supported the effectiveness of SIT, particularly in reducing acute anxiety. It is also noteworthy that several of the studies that have examined SIT have utilized sexual assault samples rather than relying solely on veteran or mixed trauma populations.

SYSTEMATIC DESENSITIZATION

Systematic desensitization (SD) was a technique originally developed by Wolpe (1958) to treat phobias. This approach pairs relaxation techniques with short imaginal exposures to feared stimuli. These pairings begin with the least distressing scenario and proceed in a hierarchical manner. Client and therapist work together to generate a hierarchy of fear cues related to the trauma. The client is then trained in relaxation skills that she is taught to employ during the exposures. The client is exposed to increasingly distressing fearful images while in a relaxed state. SD utilizes brief exposures that are focused on one fear cue alone and repeated until mastery has been achieved.

Wolff (1977) was the first to use SD successfully with a female rape victim. Since then, this technique has been found to be effective in single-case and multiple-case uncontrolled studies of trauma victims (e.g., Bowen and Lambert, 1986; Frank and Stewart, 1983). However, these results are somewhat inconclusive due to methodological flaws, including inadequate single-case designs, unstandardized measures, and the absence of blind evaluators; for example, Frank and Stewart (1983) compared SD with cognitive therapy in a sample of 17 sexual assault survivors. SD resulted in significantly more improvement on self-report measures of depression, fear, anxiety, self-esteem, and social adjustment. However, these results are somewhat limited due to the absence of standardized measures.

Frank et al. (1988) further evaluated the effectiveness of SD by randomly assigning a large sample of sexual assault victims to SD or cognitive therapy. This study attempted to address some of the methodological problems of earlier studies. Results indicated that SD and cognitive therapy proved to be equally effective in reducing fear and anxiety. Moreover, several controlled studies have found SD to be effective in decreasing PTSD symptoms, particularly re-experiencing symptoms (e.g., Bowen and Lambert, 1986; Brom et al., 1989; Peniston, 1986). However, it is important to note that most of the existing controlled studies of SD have been performed on veteran or mixed trauma samples (e.g., car accidents, other crimes), which may limit the generalizability of such results to sexual assault survivors. It should also be noted that some of these findings are limited in that the studies comprised samples of recent trauma victims. Therefore, it is possible that the observed improvements are, in part, due to the natural reduction of symptoms common in the first few months following the trauma (Foa, Hearst-Ikeda, and Perry, 1995; Foa, Rothbaum, and Molner, 1995). Moreover, although research has supported the general effectiveness of SD, the active therapeutic component appears to be the exposure element of SD. This fact, coupled with the relative inefficiency of SD, suggests that more intense exposure-based therapies (e.g., flooding) may be more efficient and effective in the treatment of post-trauma sequelae.

EXPOSURE-BASED THERAPIES

The use of imaginal and *in vivo* exposure techniques emerged from conditioning theory in which sexual assault is viewed as a situation involving a threat of being killed or seriously injured as well as an experience of helplessness and loss of control. These experiences become unconditioned stimuli, which produce unconditioned responses of fear and anxiety. Consequently, any events, objects, or persons present during the assault may become conditioned stimuli capable of eliciting the conditioned responses of fear and anxiety. In response to these aversive conditioned responses, rape victims develop avoidance tactics. Foa and Kozak (1986) theorized that exposure corrects erroneous stimulus–stimulus and stimulus–response associations as well as mistaken evaluations.

This corrective process requires the activation of the fear memory structure. This cognitive structure contains elements related to the trauma, one's behavioral and affective response to the trauma, and the meaning attached to the trauma. The common post-trauma reactions of fear and PTSD symptomatology result in the incorporation of maladaptive components within an individual's fear memory structure. Therefore, treatment should focus on altering these maladaptive elements. In general, exposure techniques are designed to activate the traumatic memories in order to modify pathological aspects of these memories.

One of the first exposure-based therapies to be applied to the treatment of post-trauma symptoms was flooding, which was introduced in the 1980s as a treatment for PTSD. More recently, Foa's prolonged exposure (PE) treatment package has been developed to treat sexual assault survivors with chronic PTSD (Foa and Meadows, 1997; Foa, Steketee, and Rothbaum, 1989; Foa, Hearst-Ikeda, and Perry, 1995; Foa, Rothbaum and Molnar, 1995).

In order to facilitate the processing of the trauma, PE activates the client's fear structure through repeated exposures to feared stimuli. Imaginal exposures require the client to recall and relive the traumatic memories in the therapist's office by telling their account out loud, in present tense and first person. Although this reliving may be distressing initially for the client, it quickly becomes less distressing as exposures are repeated, and corrective information that is incompatible with the pathological elements of the fear structure is provided within a safe, therapeutic environment. This process allows trauma survivors to realize they do not need to fear safe situations that remind them of the trauma. In addition, imaginal exposures serve to disconfirm the mistaken belief that remembering the trauma is dangerous, thus reducing the need for avoidance behaviors. Finally, individuals learn that anxiety does not remain indefinitely in the presence of feared stimuli, but, instead, it decreases naturally without the necessity of avoidance or escape. Thus, experiencing anxiety and PTSD symptoms does not result in a loss of control (Foa and Jaycox, 1999). In addition to imaginal exposures to the entire rape memory, prolonged exposure also incorporates relaxation training and *in vivo* exposures to trauma-related cues. Thus, this approach requires the client to remember at least some details of the trauma as well as be aware of some cues that trigger the traumatic memory.

Of all treatments presently available for sexual assault, exposure-based techniques seem to have the most evidence supporting their efficacy and efficiency. Much of the early research in this area included flooding, which was one of the first exposure-based therapies introduced for the treatment of post-trauma symptoms. Since Haynes and Mooney (1975) first used flooding successfully with assault victims, several other case studies and non-controlled trials have demonstrated the effectiveness of flooding in the treatment of PTSD across trauma types (e.g., veterans, incest survivors) (Black and Keane, 1982; Fairbank, Gross, and Keane, 1983; Fairbank and Keane, 1982; Keane and Kaloupek, 1982; Richards, Lovell, and Marks, 1994; Rychtarick, Silverman, Van Landingham, and Prue, 1984; Thompson, Charlton, Kerry, and Lee, 1995).

In addition, a handful of controlled studies have also examined the effectiveness of exposure techniques in sexual assault samples; for example, Foa et al. (1991) conducted a well-designed study in which female sexual assault victims were randomly assigned to PE, SIT, supportive counseling, or a wait-list control. Results indicated that both the PE and SIT subjects improved on all three symptom clusters whereas supportive counseling and wait-list controls improved only on arousal symptoms. At 3 months post-treatment, a trend was noted in that the PE subjects showed fewer symptoms on all measures of psychopathology. At this time, 55% of the PE subjects no longer met criteria for PTSD vs 50 and 45% for the SIT and supportive counseling subjects, respectively.

As previously cited, Foa et al. (1999) conducted a well-controlled study of sexual assault victims in which PE, SIT, the combination of the two techniques, and a wait-list control were compared. Results indicated that both PE and SIT (either alone or in combination) were more effective in the treatment of PTSD and depression than the control group. These results were maintained through the follow-up periods. It is notable, however, that in the intent-to-treat sample, those treated with PE demonstrated the most improvement on measures of anxiety and global social adjustment at post-treatment. Moreover, in this sample, PE produced the largest effect sizes on measures of PTSD, depression, and anxiety at follow-up.

Resick, Nishith, Weaver, Astin, and Feuer (2000) compared PE with cognitive processing therapy (CPT; described below), and a waiting-list control group for the treatment of PTSD and depression for 171 women who had been raped. They found that both PE and CPT were equally and highly effective in reducing both PTSD and depressive symptoms compared with the waiting-list control group. Compared with pretreatment (in which 100% had PTSD and nearly 50% had major depressive disorder), at the 9-month follow-up after completing treatment, less than 20% of each group were diagnosed with PTSD and only 4% of the CPT and 15% of the PE group still met criteria for major depressive disorder.

Overall, many of the studies examining the effectiveness of exposure techniques have been based on veteran samples (e.g., Cooper and Clum, 1989; Keane, Fairbank, Caddell, and Zimering. 1989) and/or have included serious methodological flaws (e.g., lack of control groups or random assignment). However, it is important to note that recent studies (Foa *et al.*, 1991, 1999; Resick *et al.*, 2000) have addressed these problems by using well-designed control conditions, random assignment, and samples of sexual assault victims. Therefore, it can be concluded that prolonged exposure is an efficacious treatment for many of the post-trauma symptoms common among sexual assault survivors (e.g, PTSD, depression).

COGNITIVE THERAPY

Cognitive theories of post-trauma reactions have traditionally focused on the role of cognitions, beliefs, and expectations. According to Beck's theory (1967), individuals form stable cognitive structures that organize life experiences and include beliefs about the self, others, and the world. Although schemas are shaped by an individual's early life experiences, they can be activated later in life by similar conditions. When activated, the cognitions associated with these schemas impact an individual's mood and behavior. In addition, schemas organize new life experiences in ways that are consistent with existing thoughts and feelings. Those experiences that are already congruent serve to solidify a schema, and those that are discrepant are typically modified through the process of assimilation.

Based on Beck's theory, Veronen and Kilpatrick (1983) proposed that women hold beliefs about the circumstances under which rape occurs. By adhering to a 'just-world' hypothesis, individuals derive comfort from the belief that the universe is lawful and predictable. Therefore, after having experienced rape themselves, victims continually search for possible explanations in order to fit their experiences into existing schemas (Marhoefer-Dvorak, Resick, Hutter, and Girelli, 1988). Through the process of cognitive appraisal, rape victims attach meaning to their own traumas, and often distort their cognitions in such a way to assimilate their experiences into existing beliefs about themselves, others, and the world (Veronen and Kilpatrick, 1983).

In addition, an attribution model of self-blame for rape victims has been proposed in order to help explain the common post-trauma reactions of fear, depression, and self-esteem problems. Most notably, Janoff-Bulman (1979) differentiated two forms of self-blame attributions. First, sexual assault survivors who exhibit characterological self-blame attribute the rape to internal, stable personality traits. Second, behavioral self-blame is characterized by the victim attributing the rape to her own behavior. These cognitive distortions serve an important purpose for the trauma survivor in that they produce a false sense of control, which is important following an experience centered on a loss of control and helplessness; for example, by attributing the rape to her own behavior (i.e., behavioral self-blame) a victim comes to believe that future danger can be avoided by behaving in a specific manner.

Cognitive therapy helps trauma survivors learn how their thoughts, feelings, and behaviors are linked. Dysfunctional thoughts and common thinking errors are identified, and more rational responses are generated. Moreover, beliefs and attributions about the self, the trauma, and the world are reappraised.

There have been three primary studies that have examined the effectiveness of such cognitive approaches with trauma survivors. First, as cited previously, Frank *et al.* (1988) compared cognitive therapy with SD in a large sample of sexual assault victims and found equivalent effects in reducing anxiety and fear. The cognitive therapy used in this study incorporated the use of daily activities schedule, the identification of automatic negative thoughts and cognitive distortions, and the exploration of the subject's basic world assumptions.

Second, Marks, Lovell, Noshirvani, Livanou, and Thrasher (1998) randomly assigned 87 PTSD-positive trauma survivors to cognitive restructuring, exposure therapy, exposure plus cognitive restructuring, or relaxation training. For the purposes of this chapter, it is important to note that only 6% of the mixed trauma sample were sexual assault victims; the majority were survivors of physical assaults and car accidents. Results indicated that cognitive restructuring alone, exposure therapy alone, and the combined treatment were more effective than relaxation training, but there were no differences among the three treatments. Treatment gains were maintained at a 6-month follow-up as well.

Third, Tarrier *et al.* (1999) randomly assigned 72 trauma survivors (i.e., 52% crime victims, 34% accidents, 15% other traumas) to 16 sessions of either cognitive therapy (CT) or imaginal exposure (IE, based on Foa's PE). Results indicated significant improvements on PTSD scores at post-treatment although there were no significant differences found between the two treatments. These gains were maintained at a 6-month follow-up assessment. It should be noted, however, that there were significant differences between CT and IE with regard to treatment failures. The authors speculated that the worsening in PTSD severity scores for the IE group was perhaps due to inconsistent attendance, which resulted in sensitization (rather than desensitization) to trauma cues. Nonetheless, it is important to consider the heterogenous nature of this trauma sample when applying these results to sexual assault survivors. Given that sexual assault survivors often experience additional difficulties (e.g., trust, esteem, and intimacy) that accident or other crime victims may not experience, the generalizability of results based on such mixed trauma samples is called into question.

In sum, the results of these three studies indicate some promising treatment effects for the use of CT among trauma survivors. In fact, CT was found to be as effective as other cognitive-behavioral treatments (e.g., IE). In addition, these studies utilized random assignment, well-defined control or comparison groups, standardized measures, and an equivalent number of treatment sessions across therapy conditions. However, only one of these studies utilized a pure sample of sexual assault survivors. Therefore, such well-designed studies utilizing pure samples of sexual assault survivors are needed before more definitive conclusions can be made regarding the effectiveness of CT in the treatment of symptoms resulting from sexual assault.

COGNITIVE PROCESSING THERAPY

Cognitive processing therapy (CPT) combines both CT and exposure. CPT was originally developed for use with rape victims. It moves beyond the view that PTSD is associated only with fear. Instead, this therapy focuses on anger, humiliation, shame, guilt, and sadness as well. CPT is based on both cognitive and constructivist theories (Beck and Emery, 1985; McCann and Pearlman, 1990). The CT component of the therapy is adapted from other treatments for anxiety and depressive disorders. The thinking underlying this component is that beliefs about the trauma become distorted when the individual tries to maintain old beliefs about the self and the world. This process of distortion is referred to as assimilation. One of the primary goals of CPT is to correct such distortions and facilitate the appropriate accommodation of the traumatic event into more general schemas regarding oneself and the world. The process of accommodation requires changing existing schemata in order to include new, incompatible information. Although accommodation is necessary for successful integration of the trauma, over-accommodation (i.e. over-generalization) can lead to extreme distortions about the safety or trustability of others as well as overly harsh judgments about oneself (Resick and Schnicke, 1992, 1993). McCann and Pearlman (1990) identified domains that are most likely to be disrupted by trauma: safety, trust, control, esteem, and intimacy. CPT focuses on these domains as potential targets for modification.

In addition to CT, CPT contains an exposure component as well, which consists of describing the rape in writing and then reading it. Calhoun and Resick (1993) have proposed that only emotions resulting from danger, harm, or loss will habituate through exposure techniques; emotions resulting from distorted thinking will continue if left unattended. Therefore, this theory asserts that exposure as well as CT are essential components to therapy with sexual assault victims. The therapy begins with the trauma memory and focuses on the feelings, beliefs, and thoughts directly resulting from the trauma. Clients are taught to identify, challenge, and modify thoughts and beliefs that result in distress or maladaptive behavior.

The effectiveness of CPT was first examined by Resick and Schnicke (1992) who compared rape victims receiving CPT with a naturally occurring wait-list control group. Findings indicated CPT to be significantly more effective in reducing PTSD and depression as well as improving social adjustment. None of the CPT clients met diagnostic criteria for PTSD at follow-up. In addition, as cited earlier, Resick *et al.* (2000) conducted a controlled study of rape victims that compared CPT, PE, and a wait-list control group. Findings indicated that CPT and PE were highly effective in treating PTSD in contrast to the waiting-list control group, which did not improve at all. Similar treatment gains were found for depressive symptoms as well. No significant differences were found between the two treatments except that CPT appeared to be more effective in reducing guilt cognitions. These improvements were maintained through a 9-month follow-up.

Chard (2000) adapted CPT for treating symptoms (PTSD, depression, and disrupted self-esteem and cognitions) among adult survivors of child sexual abuse. In this modification, CPT has been expanded to 17 weeks with both group and individual treatment in the first 9 weeks and group treatment thereafter. Additional modules have been added to the original protocol to address developmental impact, communication training, and social support. In a controlled study comparing CPT with a waiting-list control, Chard found that those receiving active treatment showed significant and large improvements in symptoms compared with the non-treatment group, which did not change.

Overall, the empirical evidence thus far suggests that CPT is an effective treatment for post-trauma symptomatology. Although only three studies have been conducted, it is noteworthy that the recent studies are well-designed, controlled studies utilizing sexual assault samples. Given the strength of this initial empirical evidence, it is likely that future studies will further substantiate the efficacy of CPT with sexual assault survivors.

EYE MOVEMENT DESENSITIZATION AND REPROCESSING THERAPY

Eye movement desensitization and reprocessing therapy (EMDR) is a controversial therapy that was originally developed by Shapiro (1989b, 1995). Rather than evolving from theory or prior therapies, EMDR is based on Shapiro's personal observation that distressing thoughts were resolved when her eyes followed the movement of leaves in a park. Out of this observation, Shapiro proposed that lateral eye movements helped in the cognitive processing of a trauma. The resulting therapy combines both cognitive and exposure components as well as lateral eye movements.

EMDR could be conceptualized as a cognitive-behavioral treatment that facilitates the cognitive processing of a trauma as well as the cognitive restructuring of distorted trauma-related cognitions. During treatment, the client visualizes the traumatic memory, focuses on the accompanying cognitions and arousal, and visually tracks the therapist's finger. The client is instructed to generate a more adaptive thought and associate it with the visualized scene while moving her eyes. Subjective distress ratings are gathered after each set of eye movements, and the process is repeated until the client's distress ratings equal a zero or one.

Historically, EMDR has been criticized for its lack of theoretical foundation as well as a lack of supporting empirical data. In addition, those early studies that did seem to support the effectiveness of EMDR were tarnished by serious methodological flaws or used non-standardized treatments as comparison groups (e.g., Kleinknecht and Morgan, 1992; Lipke and Botkin, 1992; Shapiro, 1989a; Silver, Brooks, and Obenchain, 1995; Spector and Huthwaite, 1993; Wolpe and Abrams, 1991).

More recently, however, EMDR has been shown to be more effective than non-treatment or treatment-as-usual control groups in reducing symptoms of PTSD, depression and anxiety (e.g., Jensen, 1994; Rothbaum, 1997; Vaughan et al., 1994; Wilson, Becker, and Tinker, 1995; Wilson, Becker, and Tinker, 1997); for example, Rothbaum (1997) conducted a well-designed controlled study of EMDR by randomly assigning 21 female rape victims to either EMDR or a wait-list control group. In addition to random assignment and the use of a control group, this was one of the few studies to include standardized measures and blind evaluators as well, thus freeing itself from many of the methodological problems that plagued previous studies. It is important to note that this is the only controlled study that has examined the effectiveness of EMDR among sexual assault survivors. Results indicated that EMDR led to significantly more improvement on PTSD and depression symptoms than the control group, and these gains were maintained through a 3-month follow-up as well.

Overall, recent research has supported the effectiveness of EMDR in treating post-trauma symptoms. However, despite Shapiro's assertion that lateral eye movements are an essential therapeutic component of EMDR, this hypothesis has not been empirically supported; that is, dismantling studies utilizing veteran samples have produced somewhat equivocal results (e.g., Devilly, Spence, and Rapee, 1998; Pitman, Orr, Altman, and Longpre, 1996), suggesting that lateral eye movements may not be an essential therapeutic component of EMDR.

Instead, the efficacy of EMDR may be due to its facilitation of processing the traumatic memory, much like other forms of cognitive and/or exposure therapies. Therefore, the empirical support thus far for EMDR appears to be due to its IE and/or information processing components rather than its incorporation of lateral eye movements. In light of these conclusions, it is important to compare EMDR with other cognitive or exposure therapies. Devilly and Spence (1999) began this process by comparing EMDR and CBT in 23 trauma victims. Interestingly, CBT was found to be statistically and clinically more effective than EMDR in reducing PTSD symptoms at post-treatment. This finding became even more evident by the 3-month follow-up assessment. Nonetheless, further comparative studies of EMDR and other cognitive-behavioral therapies, particularly with sexual assault survivors, are needed before firm conclusions can be drawn regarding the necessity of lateral eye movements as a treatment component in EMDR.

PHARMACOTHERAPY

Biological abnormalities associated with PTSD have been detected among the serotonin, opioid, dopamine, thyroid, corticotropin-releasing factor (CRF), and glutamatergic systems (Bremner et al., 1997; Friedman, 1999; van der Kolk, 1987). In addition, disruption of the adrenergic and hypothalamic-pituitary-adrenocortical (HPA) mechanisms results in a decreased concentration of circulating cortisol, an increased glucocorticoid receptor sensitivity, and enhanced negative feedback in response to low doses of dexamethasone (Yehuda et al., 1990; Yehuda, Teicher, Levengood, Trestman, and Siever, 1994; Yehuda, Boisoneau, Lowy, and Giller, 1995; Yehuda, Teicher, Trestman, Levengood, and Siever, 1996). Finally, PTSD has also been associated with heightened noradrenergic neuronal reactivity and increased alpha-2 receptor sensitivity (Southwick et al., 1999). In short, PTSD seems to affect multiple physiological systems in a variety of differing ways.

In terms of pharmacotherapy, the far-reaching physiological effects of PTSD have resulted in nearly every drug class being tried as a potential medication treatment for PTSD symptoms. Historically, benzodiazepines (e.g., alprazolam and clonazepam) have been frequently prescribed, often in high doses, despite little existing empirical support for their use with trauma victims. One double-blind trial has been performed for alprazolam, and statistically significant differences were found between alprazolam and a placebo control in reducing anxiety symptoms. However, these differences were not deemed to be clinically significant (Foa and Rothbaum, 1998).

In addition to the limited empirical support for the use of benzodiazepines, there are potential accompanying risks that further argue against their use for PTSD. First, due to the notable risk for dependence, their use is contraindicated for patients with past or current alcohol or drug abuse/ dependence. Second, there is a risk of exacerbating symptoms in patients with co-morbid depression. In light of these risks, benzodiazepines may be best utilized as an adjunctive time-limited treatment for disrupted sleep or global anxiety.

Unfortunately, benzodiazepines are not the only drug class that has been used with trauma patients in an absence of strong empirical support. First, antiadrenergic agents (e.g., propranolol, clonidine, guanfacine) have been found to be somewhat effective when combined with tricyclic antidepressants, but these results are based entirely on naturalistic studies (e.g., Kinzie and Leung, 1989). Second, anticonvulsants have been found to be effective in several open trials and case studies. Carbamazepine has been found to be effective in improving re-experiencing and hyperarousal PTSD symptoms in two open trials (Lipper et al., 1986; Wolf, Alavi, and Mosnaim, 1988) and three case studies (Bennet and Curiel, 1988; Brodsky, Doerman, Palmar, Slade, and Munasifi, 1987; Stewart and Bartucci, 1986). In addition, valproate has been found to be effective in improving avoidance and hyperarousal PTSD symptoms in one open trial (Fesler, 1991) and two case studies (Brodsky, Doerman, Palmar, Slade, and Munasifi, 1990; Szymanski and Olympia, 1991). To date, however, the effectiveness of anticonvulsants has not been empirically tested in randomized clinical trials. Third, antipsychotics have been used in trauma survivors based on only a few published clinical anecdotes (e.g., Krashin and Oates, 1999). Overall, without additional support from controlled clinical trials, it is difficult to advocate further use of these drugs with trauma survivors.

In general, most studies of pharmacotherapy for PTSD have focused on antidepressant medications. Although the benefits of selective serotonin reuptake inhibitors (SSRIs) seem to be the most impressive thus far, the majority of controlled drug studies for PTSD have examined tricyclic antidepressants (e.g. imipramine, amitriptyline, desipramine) or monoamine oxidase inhibitors (MAOI: e.g., phenelzine).

Southwick, Yehuda, Giller, and Charney (1994) reviewed 15 studies that examined imipramine, amitriptyline, desipramine, and phenelzine and found all of them to be relatively effective for treating the re-experiencing symptoms of PTSD. Such effectiveness was not found for avoidance and hyperarousal symptoms. Although MAOIs appear to be more effective than tricyclic antidepressants, the clinician also needs to consider the potentially dangerous side effects and drug/food interactions resulting from MAOI use. In addition, compliance may be difficult for MAOIs due to the necessary dietary restrictions and abstinence from drug/ alcohol use.

While controlled clinical studies have begun to support the use of some tricyclic antidepressants and MAOIs, the most promising and most advocated choice for first line drug treatment in trauma survivors are SSRIs (e.g., Davidson and van der Kolk, 1996; Friedman and Southwick, 1995). There is some empirical support that SSRIs help to strengthen modulation of affect, impulse control, and sleep regulation. Friedman and Southwick (1995) assert that there are serotonin abnormalities in PTSD-positive individuals. In addition, serotonin plays a definite role in many common co-morbid conditions found in trauma survivors, including depression, suicidal ideation, substance abuse, impulsivity, and aggression.

Of the SSRIs, fluoxetine has been the most widely studied, partly because it has been available for the longest period of time. More recently, sertraline appears promising as well and tends to have fewer side effects than fluoxetine. In terms of research, two studies have found SSRIs (i.e., fluoxetine, sertraline, and fluvoxamine) to be effective in reducing post-trauma symptoms in veterans (Dow and Kline, 1997; Kline, Dow, Brown, and Matloff, 1994). In addition, Rothbaum, Ninan, and Thomas (1996) found sertraline to be effective, reducing PTSD scores by 53%, in an open trial with five female rape victims with chronic PTSD. Finally, Brady et al. (2000) conducted a well-designed randomized controlled study in which sertraline was compared with a placebo control in 187 PTSD-positive outpatients (i.e., 61.5% were survivors of either physical or sexual assault). Findings indicated that sertraline produced significantly greater improvements on PTSD avoidance and hyperarousal scores.

Overall, SSRIs appear to be the most promising medication thus far for treating PTSD because they seem as effective as phenelzine and more effective than the tricyclics. In addition, SSRIs produce fewer side effects and have fewer risks in terms of drug/food interactions. It is important to keep in mind, however, that medications are not a cure for post-trauma reactions. Instead, they simply enable an individual to function better, reducing anxiety and depressive symptoms and improving sleep. Therefore, trauma survivors can probably benefit most from medication by gaining temporary relief from symptoms, thus allowing them to focus their resources on processing the trauma. It is likely that most of the individual's symptoms would return after discontinuation of the medication if the trauma were not processed fully in therapy. Rothbaum *et al.* (1996) suggests that some PTSD-positive rape victims were better able to talk about and process their assault in therapy after being started on sertraline. In addition, the participants were able to successfully discontinue the medication once the trauma had been adequately processed.

In general, antidepressants should be considered only when PTSD symptoms seem to be taking a more chronic course. Some evidence exists that a minimum of 5–8 weeks of tricyclic or SSRI therapy is required for significant treatment effects. Some effects of phenelzine have been found to emerge after as little as 3–4 weeks of use. Moreover, some researchers have found gradual but persistent improvement with several months of antidepressant treatment (Bleich, Siegel, Garb, and Lerer, 1986; Kinzie and Leung, 1989). Finally, given that permanent structural changes have been associated with chronic PTSD, lifelong drug treatment may be necessary for some individuals (Foa and Rothbaum, 1998).

Perhaps the largest gap in pharmacotherapy research on PTSD is that there has yet to be a controlled study in which the majority of subjects were female PTSD-positive sexual assault survivors; for example, fewer than 20% of van der Kolk *et al.*'s (1994) sample had experienced a rape in adulthood. Instead, the majority of pharmacological studies have utilized male combat veteran samples from Veterans Administration Hospitals. Thus, more controlled research, examining the use of SSRIs in particular, needs to be performed on female sexual assault survivors before the extent of drug therapy's effectiveness with this population can be firmly concluded.

CONCLUDING REMARKS

Previous research has empirically established numerous post-trauma sequelae common to sexual assault survivors, including emotional, psychological, physiological, behavioral, and interpersonal consequences (e.g., Frank and Stewart, 1984; Kilpatrick *et al.*, 1981; Rothbaum, Foa, Riggs, Murdock, and Walsh, 1992). This chapter provided an empirical review of the existing psychosocial and pharmacological interventions for post-trauma reactions to sexual assault.

Therapy, particularly cognitive-behavioral therapy, seems to be the most promising treatment currently available for sexual assault survivors. There have been numerous research studies that have empirically supported the effectiveness of therapy in reducing the symptoms of PTSD, depression, general anxiety, and fear as well as improving social functioning. To date, no one treatment has been shown to be more effective overall than other forms of therapy. It is possible that this trend is an artifact of relatively small sample sizes, or perhaps it simply reflects the fact that these treatments are equally effective. However, an alternative explanation is that there may be substantial overlap in various therapies. Each of the proposed treatment packages are comprised of a number of individual components, some of which may be similar across therapies. Currently, it is not clear which of these therapeutic components are crucial for various post-trauma symptoms. Resick and Schnicke (1993) proposed that almost all of the current treatments utilized in comparison studies include, either formally or informally, corrective information, which may facilitate processing the sexual assault. Therefore, it will be important for future research to include dismantling studies of empirically validated treatments in order to better determine the active components and minimum number of sessions required to result in therapeutic success. In addition, long-term follow-up of therapy studies will be necessary in order to determine whether therapeutic gains made during treatment are permanent.

In addition to further evaluating various psychosocial therapies, it will be important for future research to continue to examine various pharmacological interventions. Although there is no one medication that has been empirically established as effective for treating the range of post-trauma symptomatology, SSRIs in particular appear to be the most promising in offering some relief. However, the clinician should keep in mind that the effectiveness of such medications is dependent upon client compliance, which may be hampered by possible side effects. Moreover, relapse in symptoms is highly probable upon discontinuation of medication. Therefore, pharmacological treatments may be best utilized as a supplementary form of treatment. Within this framework, medications could provide temporary relief from distressing symptoms so as to facilitate cognitive and emotional processing of the assault in the context of therapy.

Regardless, this review clearly illustrates the complexity of treating post-trauma sequelae among sexual assault survivors and the need for treatment packages comprised of a variety of empirically established therapeutic components. It is crucial for researchers and clinicians alike to keep in mind the range of symptoms that can result from sexual assault, and, consequently, work toward creating flexible treatment packages aimed at alleviating various symptom patterns.

REFERENCES

Beck, A.T. (1967) *Depression: Clinical, experimental and theoretical aspects*. New York: Harper and Row.

Beck, A.T. and Emery, G. (1985) *Anxiety disorders and phobias: A cognitive perspective*. New York: Basic Books.

Bennet, T.L. and Curiel, M.P. (1988) Complex partial seizures presenting as a psychiatric illness. *International Journal of Clinical Neuropsychology*, **10**, 41–44.

Bisson, J., Jenkins, P., Alexander, J., and Bannister, C. (1997) A randomized controlled trial of psychological debriefing for victims of acute burn trauma. *British Journal of Psychiatry*, **171**, 78–81.

Black, J.L. and Keane, T.M. (1982) Implosive therapy in the treatment of combat related fears in a World War II veteran. *Journal of Behavior Therapy and Experimental Psychiatry*, **13**, 163.

Bleich, A., Siegel, B., Garb, R., and Lerer, B. (1986) Post-traumatic stress disorder following combat exposure: Clinical features and psychopharmacological treatment. *British Journal of Psychiatry*, **149**, 365–369.

Bowen, G.R. and Lambert, J.A. (1986) Systematic desensitization therapy with post-traumatic stress disorder cases. In C.R. Figley (ed.) *Trauma and its wake* (Vol. II, pp. 280–291). New York: Brunner/Mazel.

Brady, K., Pearstein, T., Asnis, G., Baker, D., Rothbaum, B., Sikes, C.R., and Farfel, G.M. (2000) Efficacy and safety of sertraline treatment of posttraumatic stress disorder. *Journal of the American Medical Association*, **283**(14), 1837–1844.

Bremner, J.D., Licinio, J., Darnell, A., Krystal, J.H., Owens, M.J., Southwick, S.M., Nemeroff, C.B., and Charney, D.S. (1997) Elevated CSF corticotropin-releasing factor concentration in PTSD. *American Journal of Psychiatry*, **154**, 624–629.

Brodsky, L., Doerman, A.L., Palmar, L.S., Slade, G.F., and Munasifi, F.A. (1987) Post traumatic stress disorder: A tri-modal approach. *Psychiatric Journal of the University of Ottawa*, **12**(1), 41–46.

Brodsky, L., Doerman, A.L., Palmar, L.S., Slade, G.F., and Munasifi, F.A. (1990) Post-traumatic stress disorder: An eclectic approach. *International Journal of Psychosomatics*, **37**, 89–95.

Brom, D., Kleber, R.J., and Defares, P.B. (1989) Brief psychotherapy for post-traumatic stress disorders. *Journal of Consulting and Clinical Psychology*, **57**(5), 607–612.

Bryant, R.A., Harvey, A.G., Dang, S.T., Sackville, T., and Basten, C. (1998) Treatment of acute stress disorder: A comparison of cognitive-behavioral therapy and supportive counseling. *Journal of Consulting and Clinical Psychology*, **66**, 862–866.

Bryant, R.A., Sackville, T., Dang, S.T., Moulds, M., and Guthrie, R. (1999) Treating acute stress disorder: An evaluation of cognitive behavior therapy and supportive counseling techniques. *American Journal of Psychiatry*, **156**, 1780–1786.

Burgess, A. and Holmstrom, L. (1974a) The rape trauma syndrome. *American Journal of Psychiatry*, **131**, 981–986.

Burgess, A.W. and Holmstrom, L. (1974b) *Rape: Victims of crisis*. Bowie, MD: Robert J. Brady.

Burgess, A.W. and Holmstrom, L.L. (1976) Coping behavior of the rape victim. *American Journal of Psychiatry*, **133**, 413–418.

Calhoun, K.S. and Resick, P.A. (1993) Post-traumatic stress disorder. In D.H. Barlow (ed.) *Clinical handbook of psychological disorders* (pp. 48–98). New York: Guilford Press.

Chard, K.M. (2000) Cognitive processing therapy for sexual abuse: An outcome study. Unpublished manuscript, University of Kentucky.

Cooper, N.A. and Clum, G.A. (1989) Imaginal flooding as a supplementary treatment for PTSD in combat veterans: A controlled study. *Behavior Therapy*, **20**(3), 381–391.

Cryer, L. and Beutler, L. (1980) Group therapy: An alternative treatment approach for rape victims. *Journal of Sex and Marital Therapy*, **6**, 40–46.

Davidson, J. and van der Kolk, B. (1996) The psychopharmacological treatment of posttraumatic stress disorder. In B.A. van der Kolk, A.C. McFarlane and L. Weisaeth (eds) *Traumatic stress: The effects of overwhelming experience on mind, body, and society* (pp. 510–524). New York: Guilford Press.

Devilly, G.J. and Spence, S.H. (1999) The relative efficacy and treatment distress of EMDR and a cognitive-behavior trauma treatment protocol in the amelioration of posttraumatic stress disorder. *Journal of Anxiety Disorders*, **13**(1–2), 131–157.

Devilly, G.J., Spence, S.H., and Rapee, R.M. (1998) Statistical and reliable change with eye movement desensitization and reprocessing: Treating trauma within a veteran population. *Behavior Therapy*, **29**(3), 435–455.

Dow, B. and Kline, N. (1997) Antidepressant treatment of posttraumatic stress disorder and major depression in veterans. *Annals of Clinical Psychology*, **9**(1), 1–5.

Ellis, E., Atkeson, B., and Calhoun, K. (1981) An assessment of long-term reaction to rape. *Journal of Abnormal Psychology*, **90**, 263–266.

Fairbank, J.A. and Keane, T.M. (1982) Flooding for combat-related stress disorders: Assessment of anxiety reduction across traumatic memories. *Behavior Therapy*, **13**, 499–510.

Fairbank, J.A., Gross, R.T., and Keane, T.M. (1983) Treatment of posttraumatic stress disorder: Evaluating outcome with a behavioral code. *Behavior Modification*, **7**(4), 557–568.

Fesler, F.A. (1991) Valproate in combat-related post-traumatic stress disorder. *Journal of Clinical Psychiatry*, **52**(9), 361–364.

Foa, E.B. and Jaycox, L.H. (1999) Cognitive-behavioral theory and treatment of posttraumatic stress disorder. In D. Spiegel (ed.) *Efficacy and cost-effectiveness of psychotherapy* (pp. 23–61). Washington, DC: American Psychiatric Press.

Foa, E.B. and Kozak, M.J. (1986) Emotional processing of fear: Exposure to corrective information. *Psychological Bulletin*, **99**, 20–35.

Foa, E.B. and Meadows, E.A. (1997) Psychosocial treatments for post-traumatic stress disorder: A critical review. In J. Spence, J.M. Darley, and D.J. Foss (eds) *Annual review of psychology* (Vol. 48, pp. 449–480). Palo Alto, CA: Annual Reviews.

Foa, E.B. and Rothbaum, B.O. (1998) *Treating the trauma of rape: Cognitive-behavioral therapy for PTSD*. New York: Guilford Press.

Foa, E.B., Dancu, C.V., Hembree, E.A., Jaycox, L.H., Meadows, E.A., and Street, G.P. (1999) A comparison of exposure therapy, stress inoculation training, and their combination for reducing posttraumatic stress disorder in female assault victims. *Journal of Consulting and Clinical Psychology*, **67**(2), 194–200.

Foa, E.B., Hearst-Ikeda, D., and Perry, K.J. (1995) Evaluation of a brief cognitive behavioral program for the prevention of chronic PTSD in recent assault victims. *Journal of Consulting and Clinical Psychology*, **63**, 948–955.

Foa, E.B., Rothbaum, B.O., and Molnar, C. (1995) Cognitive-behavioral therapy of post-traumatic stress disorder. In M.J. Friedman, D.S. Charney, and A.Y. Deutch (eds) *Neurobiological and clinical consequences of stress: From normal adaptation to post-traumatic stress disorder* (pp. 483–494). New York: Lippincott-Raven.

Foa, E.B., Rothbaum, B.O., Riggs, D.S., and Murdock, T.B. (1991) Treatment of post-traumatic stress disorder in rape victims: A comparison between cognitive-behavioral procedures and counseling. *Journal of Counseling and Clinical Psychology*, **59**(5), 715–723.

Foa, E.B., Steketee, G., and Rothbaum, B.O. (1989) Behavioral/cognitive conceptualization of post-traumatic stress disorder. *Behavior Therapy*, **20**, 155–176.

Frank, E. and Stewart, B.D. (1983) Treating depression in victims of rape. *Clinical Psychologist*, **36**(4), 95–98.

Frank, E. and Stewart, B.D. (1984) Depressive symptoms in rape victims. *Journal of Affective Disorders*, **1**, 269–277.

Frank, E., Anderson, B., Stewart, B.D., Dancu, C., Hughes, C., and West, D. (1988) Efficacy of cognitive behavior therapy and systematic desensitization in the treatment of rape trauma. *Behavior Therapy*, **19**(3), 403–420.

Friedman, M.J. (1999) Pharmacotherapy for posttraumatic stress disorder. In M.J. Horowitz (ed.) *Essential papers on posttraumatic stress disorder. Essential papers in psychoanalysis* (pp. 473–483). New York: New York University Press.

Friedman, M.J. and Southwick, S.M. (1995) Towards pharmacotherapy for post-traumatic stress disorder. In M.J. Friedman, D.S. Charney, and A.Y. Deutch (eds) *Neurobiological and clinical consequences of stress: From normal adaptation to posttraumatic stress disorder* (pp. 465–481). Philadelphia: Lippincott-Raven.

Grigsby, J.P. (1987) The use of imagery in the treatment of posttraumatic stress disorder. *Journal of Nervous and Mental Disease*, **175**, 55–59.

Haynes, S.N. and Mooney, D.K. (1975) Nightmares: Etiological, theoretical, and behavioral treatment considerations. *Psychological Record*, **25**(2), 225–236.

Herman, J.L. (1992) *Trauma and recovery*. New York: Basic Books.

Horowitz, M.J. (1976) *Stress response syndromes*. New Jersey: Jason Aronson.

Hytten, K. and Hasle, A. (1989) Fire fighters: A study of stress and coping. *Acta Psychiatrica Scandinavica*, **80**, 50–55.

Janoff-Bulman, R. (1979) Characterological versus behavioral self-blame: Inquiries into depression and rape. *Journal of Personality and Social Psychology*, **37**, 1798–1809.

Jensen, J.A. (1994) An investigation of eye movement desensitization and reprocessing (EMDR) as a treatment for posttraumatic stress disorder (PTSD) symptoms of Vietnam combat veterans. *Behavior Therapy*, **25**(2), 311–325.

Keane, T.M. and Kaloupek, D.G. (1982) Imaginal flooding in the treatment of posttraumatic stress disorder. *Journal of Consulting and Clinical Psychology*, **50**(1), 138–140.

Keane, T.M., Fairbank, J.A., Caddell, J.M., and Zimering, R.T. (1989) Implosive (flooding) therapy reduces symptoms of PTSD in Vietnam combat veterans. *Behavior Therapy*, **20**(2), 245–260.

Keane, T.M., Zimering, R.T., and Caddell, J.M. (1985) A behavioral formulation of posttraumatic stress disorder in Vietnam veterans. *Behavioral Therapist*, **8**, 9–12.

Kenardy, J., Webster, R., Lewin, T., Carr, V., Hazell, P., and Carter, G. (1996) Stress debriefing and patterns of recovery following a natural disaster. *Journal of Traumatic Stress*, **9**, 37–49.

Kessler, R.C., Sonnega, A., Bromet, E., Hughes, M., and Nelson, C.B. (1995) Posttraumatic stress disorder in the national comorbidity survey. *Archives of General Psychiatry*, **52**, 1048–1060.

Kilpatrick, D.G. and Amick, A.E. (1985) Rape trauma. In M. Hersen and C. Last (eds.) *Behavior therapy casebook* (pp. 86–103). New York: Springer-Verlag.

Kilpatrick, D.G., and Veronen, L.J. (1983) Treatment for rape-related problems: Crisis intervention is not enough. In L. Cohen, W. Claiborn, and G. Specter (eds) *Crisis intervention* (2nd edn, pp. 165–185). New York: Human Sciences Press.

Kilpatrick, D.G., Resick, P., and Veronen, L. (1981) Effects of a rape experience: A longitudinal study. *Journal of Social Issues*, **37**, 105–122.

Kilpatrick, D.G., Veronen, L.J., and Resick, P.A. (1979) The aftermath of rape: Recent empirical findings. *American Journal of Orthopsychiatry*, **49**(4), 658–669.

Kilpatrick, D.G., Veronen, L.J., and Resick, P.A. (1982) Psychological sequelae to rape: Assessment and treatment strategies. In D.M. Dolays, R.L. Meredith, and A.R. Ciminero (eds.) *Behavioral medicine: Assessment and treatment strategies* (pp. 473–497). New York: Plenum Press.

Kinzie, J.D. and Leung, P. (1989) Clonidine in Cambodian patients with posttraumatic stress disorder. *Journal of Nervous and Mental Disease*, **177**, 546–550.

Kleinknecht, R. and Morgan, M.P. (1992) Treatment of posttraumatic stress disorder with eye movement desensitization. *Journal of Behavior Therapy and Experimental Psychiatry*, **23**(1), 43–49.

Kline, N.A., Dow, B.M., Brown, S.A., and Matloff, J.L. (1994) Sertraline efficacy in depressed combat veterans with posttraumatic stress disorder. *American Journal of Psychiatry*, **151**(4), 621.

Koss, M.P. and Harvey, M.R. (1987) *The rape victim: Clinical and community approaches to treatment*. Lexington, MA: Stephen Greene Press.

Krashin, D. and Oates, E.W. (1999) Risperidone as an adjunct therapy for posttraumatic stress disorder. *Military Medicine*, **164**(8), 605–606.

Leung, J. (1994) Treatment of post-traumatic stress disorder with hypnosis. *Australian Journal of Clinical and Experimental Hypnosis*, **22**(1), 87–96.

Lindy, J.D. (1996) Psychoanalytic psychotherapy of posttraumatic stress disorder: The nature of the relationship. In B.A. van der Kolk, A.C. McFarlane, and L. Weisaeth (eds) *Traumatic stress: The effects of overwhelming experience on mind, body, and society* (pp. 525–536). New York: Guilford Press.

Lipke, H. and Botkin, A. (1992) Brief case studies of eye movement desensitization and reprocessing with chronic posttraumatic stress disorder. *Psychotherapy*, **29**(4), 591–595.

Lipper, S., Davidson, J.R.T., Grady, T.A., Edingar, J.D., Hammett, E.B., Mahorney, S.L., and Cavenar, J.O. (1986) Preliminary study of carbamazepine in posttraumatic stress disorder. *Psychosomatics*, **27**, 849–854.

McCann, I.L. and Pearlman, L.A. (1990) *Psychological trauma and the adult survivor: Theory, therapy, and transformation*. New York: Brunner/Mazel.

Marhoefer-Dvorak, S., Resick, P.A., Hutter, C.K., and Girelli, S.A. (1988) Single vs. multiple incident rape victims: A comparison of psychological reactions to rape. *Journal of Interpersonal Violence*, **3**, 145–160.

Marks, I., Lovell, K., Noshirvani, H., Livanou, M., and Thrasher, S. (1998) Treatment of posttraumatic stress disorder by exposure and/or cognitive restructuring: A controlled study. *Archives of General Psychiatry*, **55**(4), 317–325.

Marmar, C.R., Weiss, D.S., and Pynoos, R.S. (1995) Dynamic psychotherapy for posttraumatic stress disorder. In M.J. Friedman, D.S. Charney, and A.Y. Deutch (eds) *Neurobiological and clinical consequences of stress: From normal adaptation to posttraumatic stress disorder* (pp. 495–506). Philadelphia: Lippincott-Raven.

Meichenbaum, D. (1974) *Cognitive behavior modification*. New Jersey: General Learning Press.

Mowrer, O.H. (1947) On the dual nature of learning: A reinterpretation of 'conditioning' and 'problem solving'. *Harvard Educational Review*, **17**, 102–148.

Pearson, M.A., Poquette, B.M., and Wasden, R.E. (1983) Stress inoculation and the treatment of post-rape trauma: A case report. *Behavior Therapist*, **6**, 58–59.

Peniston, E.G. (1986) EMG biofeedback-assisted desensitization treatment for Vietnam combat veterans post-traumatic stress disorder. *Clinical Biofeedback and Health: An International Journal*, **9**(1), 35–41.

Pitman, R.K., Orr, S.P., Altman, B., and Longpre, R.E. (1996) Emotional processing during eye-movement desensitization and reprocessing therapy of Vietnam veterans with chronic posttraumatic stress disorder. *Comprehensive Psychiatry*, **37**(6), 419–429.

Resick, P.A. and Jordan, C.G. (1988) Group stress inoculation training for victims of sexual assault: A therapists manual. In P.A. Keller and S.R. Heyman (eds) *Innovations in clinical practice: A source book* (pp. 99–111). Florida: Professional Resource Exchange.

Resick, P.A., Jordan, C.G., Girelli, S.A., Hutter, C.K., and Marhoefer-Dvorak, S. (1988) A comparative outcome study of behavioral group therapy for sexual assault victims. *Behavior Therapy*, **19**, 385–401.

Resick, P.A., Nishith, P., Weaver, T.L., Astin, M.C., and Feuer, C.A. (2000) A comparison of cognitive processing therapy, prolonged exposure, and a waiting condition for the treatment of posttraumatic stress disorder in female rape victims. Unpublished manuscript, University of Missouri-St Louis.

Resick, P.A. and Schnicke, M.K. (1992) Cognitive processing therapy for sexual assault victims. *Journal of Consulting and Clinical Psychology*, **60**, 748–756.

Resick, P.A. and Schnicke, M.K. (1993) *Cognitive processing therapy for rape victims: A treatment manual*. Newbury Park, CA: Sage Publications.

Richards, D.A., Lovell, K., and Marks, I.M. (1994) Post-traumatic stress disorder: Evaluation of a behavioral treatment program. *Journal of Traumatic Stress*, **7**(4), 669–680.

Roth, S., Dye, E., and Lebowitz, L. (1988) Group therapy for sexual assault victims. *Psychotherapy*, **25**(1), 82–93.

Rothbaum, B.O. (1997) A controlled study of eye movement desensitization and reprocessing in the treatment of posttraumatic stress disordered sexual assault victims. *Bulletin of the Menniger Clinic*, **61**(3), 317–334.

Rothbaum, B.O., Foa, E.B., Riggs, D.S., Murdock, T., and Walsh, W. (1992) A prospective examination of post-traumatic stress disorder in rape victims. *Journal of Traumatic Stress*, 5, 455–475.

Rothbaum, B.O., Ninan, P.T., and Thomas, L. (1996) Sertraline in the treatment of rape victims with posttraumatic stress disorder. *Journal of Traumatic Stress*, 9(4), 865–871.

Rychtarick, R.G., Silverman, W.K., Van Landingham, W.P., and Prue, D.M. (1984) Treatment of an incest victim with implosive therapy: A case study. *Behavior Therapy*, 15(4), 410–420.

Shapiro, F. (1989a) Efficacy of the Eye Movement Desensitization procedure in the treatment of traumatic memories. *Journal of Traumatic Stress*, 2(2), 199–223.

Shapiro, F. (1989b) Eye movement desensitization: A new treatment for posttraumatic stress disorder. *Journal of Behavior Therapy and Experimental Psychiatry*, 20(3), 211–217.

Shapiro, F. (1995) *Eye movement desensitization and reprocessing: Basic principles, protocols, and procedures*. New York: Guilford Press.

Silver, S.M., Brooks, A., and Obenchain, J. (1995) Treatment of Vietnam war veterans with PTSD: A comparison of eye movement desensitization and reprocessing, biofeedback, and relaxation training. *Journal of Traumatic Stress*, 8(2), 337–342.

Southwick, S.M., Bremner, J.D., Rasmusson, A., Morgan, C.A., Arnsten, A., and Charney, D.S. (1999) Role of norepinephrine in the pathophysiology and treatment of posttraumatic stress disorder. *Biological Psychiatry*, 46(9), 1192–1204.

Southwick, S.M., Yehuda, R., Giller, E.L., and Charney, D.S. (1994) Use of tricyclics and monoamine oxidase inhibitors in the treatment of PTSD: A quantitative review. In M.M Murburg (ed.) *Catecholamine function in post-traumatic stress disorder: Emerging concepts* (pp. 293–305). Washington, D.C.: American Psychiatric Press.

Spector, J. and Huthwaite, M. (1993) Eye movement desensitization to overcome post-traumatic stress disorder. *British Journal of Psychiatry*, 163, 106–108.

Spiegel, D. (1989) Hypnosis in the treatment of victims of sexual abuse. *Psychiatric Clinics of North America*, 12(2), 295–305.

Spiegel, D., Hunt, T., and Dondershine, H. (1988) Dissociation and hypnotizability in posttraumatic stress disorder. *American Journal of Psychiatry*, 145, 301–305.

Stewart, J.R. and Bartucci, R.J. (1986) Post-traumatic stress disorder and partial complex seizures. *American Journal of Psychiatry*, 143, 113–114.

Szymanski, H.V. and Olympia, J. (1991) Divalproex in posttraumatic stress disorder. *American Journal of Psychiatry*, 148(8), 1086–1087.

Tarrier, N., Pilgim, H., Sommerfield, C., Faragher, B., Reynold, M., Graham, E., and Barrowclough, C. (1999) A randomized trial of cognitive therapy and imaginal exposure in the treatment of chronic posttraumatic stress disorder. *Journal of Consulting and Clinical Psychology*, 67(1), 13–18.

Thompson, J.A., Charlton, P.F.C., Kerry, R., and Lee, D. (1995) An open trial of exposure therapy based on deconditioning for post-traumatic stress disorder. *British Journal of Clinical Psychology*, 34(3), 407–416.

van der Kolk, B.A. (1987) The drug treatment of post-traumatic stress disorder. *Journal of Affective Disorders*, 13(2), 203–213.

van der Kolk, B.A. (1996) The complexity of adaptation to trauma: Self-regulation, stimulus discrimination, and characterological development. In B.A. van der Kolk, A.C. McFarlane, and L. Weisaeth (eds), *Traumatic stress: The effects of overwhelming experience on mind, body, and society* (pp. 182–213). New York: Guilford Press.

van der Kolk, B.A., Dreyfuss, D., Michaels, M., Shera, D., Berkowitz, R., Fisler, R.E., Saxe, G.N., and Goldenberg, I. (1994) Fluoxetine in posttraumatic stress disorder. *Journal of Clinical Psychiatry*, **55**(12), 517–522.

Vaughan, K., Armstrong, M.S., Gold, R., O'Connor, N., Jenneke, W., and Tarrier, N. (1994) A trial of eye movement desensitization compared to image habituation training and applied muscle relaxation in post-traumatic stress disorder. *Journal of Behavior Therapy and Experimental Psychiatry*, **25**(4), 283–291.

Veronen, L.J. and Kilpatrick, D.G. (1983) Stress management for rape victims. In D. Meichenbaum and M.E. Jaremko (eds) *Stress reduction and prevention* (pp. 341–374). New York: Plenum Press.

Wilson, S.A., Becker, L.A., and Tinker, R. (1995) Eye movement desensitization and reprocessing (EMDR) treatment for psychologically traumatized individuals. *Journal of Consulting and Clinical Psychology*, **63**(6), 928–937.

Wilson, S.A., Becker, L.A., and Tinker, R.H. (1997) Fifteen-month follow-up of eye movement desensitization and reprocessing (EMDR) treatment for posttraumatic stress disorder and psychological trauma. *Journal of Consulting and Clinical Psychology*, **65**(6), 1047–1056.

Wolf, M.E., Alavi, A., and Mosnaim, A.D. (1988) Post-traumatic stress disorder in Vietnam veterans clinical and EEG findings; possible therapeutic effects of carbamazepine. *Biological Psychiatry*, **23**, 642–644.

Wolff, R. (1977) Systematic desensitization and negative practice to alter the after effects of a rape attempt. *Journal of Behavior Therapy and Experimental Psychiatry*, **8**, 423–425.

Wolpe, J. (1958) *Psychotherapy by reciprocal inhibition*. Stanford, CA: Stanford University Press.

Wolpe, J. and Abrams, J. (1991) Post-traumatic stress disorder overcome by eye movement desensitization: A case report. *Journal of Behavior Therapy and Experimental Psychiatry*, **22**(1), 39–43.

Yehuda, R., Boisoneau, D., Lowy, M.T., and Giller, E.L. (1995) Dose-response changes in plasma cortisol and lymphocyte glucocorticoid receptors following dexamethasone administration in combat veterans with and without posttraumatic stress disorder. *Archives of General Psychiatry*, **52**, 583–593.

Yehuda, R., Southwick, S.M., Nussbaum, G., Wahby, V., Giller, E.L., and Mason, J.W. (1990) Low urinary cortisol excretion in PTSD. *Journal of Nervous and Mental Diseases*, **178**, 366–369.

Yehuda, R., Teicher, M.H., Levengood, R.A., Trestman, R.L., and Siever, L.J. (1994) Circadian regulation of basal cortisol levels in posttraumatic stress disorder. *Annuals of New York Academy of Science*, **746**, 378–380.

Yehuda, R., Teicher, M.H., Trestman, R.L., Levengood, R.A., and Siever, L.J. (1996) Cortisol regulation in posttraumatic stress disorder and major depression: A chronobiological analysis. *Biological Psychiatry*, **40**, 79–88.

Chapter 5

PSYCHOLOGICAL ASSESSMENT OF SEXUAL ASSAULT

Anne-Marie Doyle and Susan Thornton

INTRODUCTION

A thorough assessment is the cornerstone of good psychological practice. It provides an initial case formulation of a client's difficulties and a rationale and guiding framework for psychological intervention. Assessment can be viewed as a process involving a number of tasks: the first is to establish rapport with the client and thereby gather relevant clinical information. The second is to identify and delineate the client's difficulties and, in the process, offer validation of the client's experiences. The third is to formulate a psychological understanding of the client's difficulties within a wider social framework, paying attention to issues such as gender and cultural background. The final task is to offer recommendations about clinical management including options for psychological therapy.

Assessment is based primarily upon clinical interview, through which information is gathered via client self-report and direct therapist observation. Referral information, pre-existing case history and scores on standardized psychological measures may all act to augment clinical interview material. Assessment generally takes between one and three sessions with the length varying according to the quality of information gathered, the complexity of the client's difficulties, and the skills of the assessor. The precise nature of an assessment will depend upon a range of factors including organizational context, training background of the assessor, available therapy resources, presenting difficulties, and client characteristics. A summary of the areas that will normally be covered during the assessment is given in Table 5.1.

The Trauma of Sexual Assault. Edited by Jenny Petrak and Barbara Hedge.
© 2002 John Wiley & Sons Ltd.

Table 5.1 Clinical assessment

- Description and history of presenting problems
- Observation of client's appearance, speech, behaviour, and affect
- Sexual assault and assailant information
- Physical health: injuries, sleeping and eating
- Pregnancy and termination issues
- Sexually transmitted infections including HIV
- Police and legal procedures
- Psychological responses to assault
- Relationship difficulties and sexual dysfunction
- Social support network and disclosure
- Family, educational, and occupational history
- Relationship and sexual history
- Significant life events history
- Previous trauma and abuse history
- Medical history
- Psychiatric history
- Risk assessment and management

The purpose of this chapter is to outline assessment procedures in the context of sexual assault. The chapter begins by addressing each of the areas listed in Table 5.1 (Section A) and is followed by a discussion of relevant psychiatric diagnoses (Section B), use of standardized psychological measures (Section C), and psychological formulation (Section D). The chapter concludes with a consideration of key assessment issues including organizational contexts, sociocultural values, and issues for the assessor (Section E). Case examples in this chapter are based on composite rather than individual cases in order to protect client confidentiality. The generic terms 'assessor' and 'therapist' are used interchangeably to refer to mental health professionals from a range of professional training backgrounds.

A CLINICAL ASSESSMENT

Provision of a Safe Physical and Emotional Space

Sexual assault can be viewed as essentially an act of extreme aggression against a person which is carried out sexually, rather than a sexual act carried out aggressively. The clients' experiences of sexual assault will vary; however, all will have been under the power and control of another person and suffered an unwanted sexual experience. Some may have been at the receiving end of overt expressions of hate and anger, and

Table 5.2   Starting the interview

- Room free from disturbance
- Introductions
- Confidentiality
- Professional boundaries
- Organizational boundaries
- Session boundaries
- Purpose of the meeting
- Referral information
- Demographic information and contact details

some may have suffered physical injury or been subjected to humiliating experiences in addition to the assault. Many will have been fearful for their lives, and some will have been assaulted in the context of 'male camaraderie'. Through their experience of assault, clients are likely to be in a vulnerable psychological position and will require respectful, sensitive management and a careful consideration of their needs. The assessor aims to provide a safe physical and emotional space to enable the client to disclose sensitive and distressing information. Since the central features of sexual assault are abuse of power, violation of personal boundaries, loss of control, and loss of a sense of safety, it is important that the therapist pays particular regard to issues of confidentiality, safety, trust, boundaries, and control.

Starting the Interview

In order to set the context of the interview, it is helpful to cover the following areas: introductions, boundaries of the session, boundaries of the organization, professional boundaries, confidentiality, referral information, purpose of the meeting, demographic and contact information. These areas are summarized in Table 5.2.

Establishing Rapport

Rapport is established through the assessor's ability to listen and communicate, as well as through the demonstration of empathy, concern, a non-judgemental attitude, and a commitment to helping the client. It is the initial work of the assessor, and later the therapist, to help the client begin to put into words experiences, thoughts, and feelings which previously may not have been expressed.

Good communication skills are a prerequisite for the assessor and act both to ameliorate a person's distress and facilitate disclosure of information, which is often experienced by the assaulted person as shameful. The valuing, supportive attitude of a health professional is central to a good assessment. The skill and experience of the assessor is clearly relevant in terms of ability to guide the interview, facilitate client communication, and formulate an understanding of the client's difficulties.

Containment and Validation

Validation of the client's experience is a crucial aspect of the assessment. It is through the assessor's acknowledgement of the client's experience that the process of containment and recovery begins. Many individuals who have been sexually assaulted struggle with the fear of being disbelieved or being held accountable for what happened to them and may face the actual experience of being disbelieved. Case Example 5.1 demonstrates this point.

Case Example 5.1

Ms H is a young, white, Scots woman who went out one evening with two friends to central London in August 1999. At a nightclub, the friends met two seemingly pleasant men who offered to buy them drinks. Unknown to them, one of the men added the drug flunitrazepam (a benzodiazepine used as a hypnotic, trade name Rohypnol) to Ms H's drink. Half an hour later, Ms H had no further recollection of the evening or events that followed. She later recalled that she had only drunk one alcoholic drink prior to meeting the two men. In a drug-induced state, probably appearing drunk to observers, she was unwittingly led out of the club and taken to one of the men's homes where she was anally and vaginally raped. She woke up the next day in the man's home feeling confused and physically unwell. She did not know where she was or how she had got there. As is not untypical for individuals assaulted whilst under the influence of Rohypnol, it was not until a week later that Ms H had a dawning realization that she had not been drunk that night. As her concern grew and events began to fall into place, she telephoned the police to report the incident. The first response of the police officer, the very first person she reported the crime to, was 'Well, what do you expect if you go down to the West End?' At this point, Ms H experienced a significant increase in distress, confusion, and self-blame.

The officer's response described in the above case is a clear example of an assaulted person being blamed for her misfortune while, at the same time, having her experience invalidated and trivialized. Two of the most-common defensive responses in therapists working with trauma survivors have been described by Fischman and Ross (1990) as either over-identification with the client or over-distancing and attempting to minimize the damage sustained. The police officer's response can be seen as an example of the second.

Presenting Problems

The timing of the assessment in relation to the occurrence of the assault is critical in assessing the response of the person and in formulating management. Some clients will present within the immediate aftermath of an assault and may be in a state of acute emotional shock. Others will be assessed several weeks or months afterwards, and some may be seen following the development of difficulties that relate to an assault that took place many years ago. For recent sexual assaults, the areas of physical health, sexual health, legal aspects, and acute stress reaction need to be addressed and managed first.

Following the introduction to the interview, the client can be asked to begin to describe his or her concerns. The aim is to obtain a good description of the individual problems, their pattern, and a history of when the problems began, together with any functional impairments brought about by the problems.

Observation of Appearance, Speech, Behaviour, and Affect

Observable features of the client including physical appearance, clothing, rate and tone of speech, behaviour, and emotional affect should be noted bearing in mind that individuals present in a variety of ways following an assault (Burgess and Holmstrom, 1974). This can include appearing calm and collected, emotionally flat and passive, tearful and distraught, aggressive and demanding, or even smiling and over-compliant. Each of these presentations can be indicative of a response to trauma and of emotional coping mechanisms in action. The overall pace of the interview needs to be judged according to the client's level of distress and general functioning. If the assault is very recent, it is likely that thinking processes and decision-making abilities will be impaired. If the assessment takes place within hours or days of an assault, the person may appear dazed or disoriented, and ability to concentrate and comprehend may be limited. An acute stress reaction typically occurs during or within minutes of the assault and disappears within 2 or 3 days, usually within a few hours.

There may be withdrawal in the form of a reduction or absence of voluntary movement or lack of responsiveness to external stimuli or both. Alternatively, the person may appear agitated and restless with autonomic signs of acute anxiety such as increased heart rate and sweating. According to ICD10 criteria for acute stress reaction (WHO, 1992), the clinical picture is mixed and usually changing with no one symptom predominating for long. Assessment at this stage can helpfully focus on normalizing the reaction and identifying specific needs for safety, comfort, support and possible referral to a physician for short-term tranquillizer or hypnotic medication. It may be useful to provide written information about common reactions to assault and what to expect over the following weeks as well as how to seek help if problems persist or become more severe.

Sexual Assault and Assailant Information

Some clients hold preconceived ideas that it is important to talk about their experiences as soon as possible. In such a case, the client can be encouraged to think about whether now is a good time to talk or whether it would be more helpful at a later stage in the context of an established therapeutic relationship. Many clients will want to talk about the assault but, for some, retelling their experience too soon or at an inappropriate time may have a retraumatizing effect (Symonds, 1980; Pitman *et al.*, 1991; Mayou, Ehlers, and Hobbs, 2000) and can increase feelings of vulnerability. This needs to be judged against the beneficial effects of acting as a witness to a client's experience of abuse and the opportunity for the assessor to more fully understand and thereby validate a client's experience.

A client may give specific details of an assault or make only vague passing references. It is not crucial to obtain all details of an assault at the assessment stage, and clinical sensitivity should be used to judge areas the client wishes to talk about and areas that remain overly distressing. Intrusive prompts to talk about the assault, particularly early on in the process of recovery, should be avoided. It is helpful to request a broad outline of the circumstances surrounding the incident, as well as summary details of the assault itself. In cases where the drug Rohypnol has been used, the person is unlikely to have a clear recollection of events.

The relationship of the assailant to the client should be ascertained. Contrary to popular belief, at least half the victims of assault know their assailant (Walmsley and White, 1979), and this can make it more difficult for clients to recognize fully that responsibility for the assault lies with the perpetrator. Information regarding the whereabouts of the assailant and the client's perception of his or her own safety should also be sought. Many clients, especially those who report to the police, fear further attack or reprisals from both the attacker and his or her family and friends. It is not uncommon for people to move to a new home or change job following an assault for these reasons.

Physical and Sexual Health

The nature and extent of any physical injuries should be documented as far as possible, and medical assessment and treatment arranged as required. Injuries to the face as well as to the body and genital region may occur, but the majority of sexual assaults involve no significant physical injury. The client should be asked also about basic physiological functioning including sleeping, eating, and maintenance of body weight.

Sexual assault naturally raises concerns about sexually transmitted infections including HIV and, for female clients, the possibility of pregnancy. Pregnancy testing and the option of referral to the GP or sexual health services to prevent or terminate pregnancy (e.g. use of intrauterine device or morning-after pill) should be considered, remembering that some women will decide to continue with a pregnancy following a sexual assault (see Case Example 5.2).

Case Example 5.2

Ms K is a 42-year-old, single, Irish, Catholic nurse living in Manchester who was raped in June 1998 while abroad on holiday in Italy. She did not report the rape to the police. When she returned home, she was shocked to discover that she was pregnant. She felt extremely distressed by the assault; however, after a great deal of heart-rending deliberation, she eventually decided to continue with the pregnancy. She chose this course of action for ethical and religious reasons and because she felt it might be her last and only chance to have a child.

A woman is likely to experience distress and emotional conflict whether she decides to continue with or terminate a pregnancy. Either decision is likely to give rise to a range of psychological issues that can be identified and addressed during the course of assessment and therapy.

A sexual health screen for sexually transmitted infections involves an external and internal genital examination with blood and tissue samples taken for investigations and diagnostic purposes. In the case of a forensic examination, a full sexual health screen is undertaken and prophylactic treatment administered as required.

HIV testing and post-exposure prophylaxis are provided in a number of settings including genitourinary medicine clinics. Testing for HIV infection is generally undertaken 3 months after possible exposure. The 3-month delay minimizes the risk of a false negative result since antibodies to the virus, on which the diagnostic test depends, are not present in an infected person until 6 to 12 weeks after exposure. In order to link an HIV infection to the time of assault, it is usual for an assaulted person to have blood taken and stored immediately afterwards. This can be tested if the subsequent test proves positive. In cases where the person has been assaulted by an individual known to be infected or in a high-risk category, prophylaxis in the form of anti-retroviral therapy can be prescribed. The client needs to attend an Accident & Emergency department or sexual health clinic immediately after the assault since treatment should begin as soon as possible after exposure (Lurie, Miller, Hecht, Lesney, and Lob, 1998).

Police and Legal Procedures

Whether the assault has been reported to the police and the current legal position should be established. Many clients will be motivated to report to the police because of a desire for justice and to protect others from the risk of future attack. Clients who decide not to report to the police may experience guilt. The police can work most effectively when an assault is reported as soon as possible after the event. Detailed police questions about the assault form the basis of the statement and a medical examination allows forensic evidence to be gathered, which acts to corroborate the statement.

Many survivors of sexual assault do not report to the police; however, the police request that crimes be reported even if clients do not wish legal procedures to go ahead. This allows them to gather statistical information about the nature and extent of rape and sexual assault as a local and national problem, and also provides a store of information about a particular assailant, which may be helpful in relation to other reported incidents.

The main role of the police is to investigate the attack, while it is the responsibility of the Crown Prosecution Service to prosecute the person charged with the attack. The legal process can be long and complicated and can act to maintain and exacerbate a client's distress. Often, cases do not go to court due to lack of evidence. If there is a court case, the client will need to appear as a witness and face questioning by the defence barrister. In many sexual assault cases, the charged person is found to be not guilty by the jury and the client can experience a significant increase in psychological distress at this time. Although clients often understand the mechanisms and limitations of the legal system, at the same time they can be left with a strong sense of injustice and feel that they have been disbelieved.

Clients who have reported the assault to the police should consider seeking criminal injuries compensation, which can be done by completing an application form. The purpose of the criminal injuries compensation scheme is to offer support in a tangible way to victims of crime, and all clients who have reported their case to the police are entitled to apply. An independent board assesses applications and the balance of evidence in each case is reviewed. There are eligibility criteria; for example, a claim needs to be submitted within 2 years of an assault and the case is tested against the concept of a 'good citizen' (i.e., the claimant ideally needs to have an unblemished criminal record and to have shown full co-operation with the police and prosecution services). Financial compensation is clearly helpful in relation to psychological recovery in that it represents a formal, societal recognition and validation of a client's experience. 10.

Psychological Responses to Assault

In the days, weeks, and months following an assault, there are a number of typical responses, and the most commonly reported behavioural, affective, physiological, and cognitive responses are described below. When the person is assessed within a few weeks of the assault, as with acute stress reactions, the most appropriate response is to normalize, explain, and contain the problems rather than to consider longer term therapy needs immediately. This is because there is evidence that, for many individuals, difficulties will resolve over a relatively short period. In a prospective study of 95 women who had been raped, almost all showed marked psychological disturbance in the following 2 weeks, but, by 2 months post-assault, only about half had persistent symptoms of post-traumatic stress disorder (PTSD: Rothbaum, Foa, Murdock, Riggs, and Walsh, 1992). Nevertheless, the situation should be monitored as sexual assault produces more severe and enduring reactions than other kinds of assault (Foa and Riggs, 1993). Although recommendations for specific therapy for post-traumatic stress, depression, or other disorders may not be the goal of assessment in the early stages following the assault, there are many indications for shorter term interventions; for example, developing strategies to overcome behavioural avoidance and to manage physiological arousal is likely to be helpful in preventing the establishment of phobic anxiety disorders.

Increased Physiological Arousal, Anxiety, and Behavioural Avoidance

Increased physiological arousal will frequently be present in the form of insomnia, exaggerated startle response, irritability, poor concentration, or hypervigilance (see Chapter 6). Partly as a consequence of this increased arousal, generalized anxiety, panic disorder, and conditioned anxiety responses often develop in conjunction with avoidance of assault-related stimuli. Behavioural avoidance of situations that remind the person of the assault is very common, and may be disabling in that it often prevents the individual from returning to a normal pattern of life. The client may not be able to go to work, may have to travel in unusual ways, or be unable to tolerate being alone. Assessment should aim to identify all the changes in a person's activity and the extent to which these constitute avoidance of distress as well as the extent to which their presence seriously compromises future relationships or employment. In this way, priorities for intervention can be established. Circumstances that make avoided activities more or less achievable can also be identified; for example, an individual may be able to go out in daylight if accompanied but not at night even if someone else is present.

Sometimes, a person tries to deal with the impact of an assault through a radical change in his or her life such as giving up a job or deciding to go to another country to start a new life. These forms of avoidance should also be assessed. Frequently, individuals express avoidance by a reluctance to attend any appointments in which they think they will be required to talk about their difficulties or about the assault (Veronen and Best, 1983). It is critically important that the assessment is conducted at the pace that the person can manage and that these problems are acknowledged in a sensitive way so that the opportunity to access intervention is not lost at the outset.

Assessment should aim to identify the physical, cognitive, behavioural, and environmental factors characterizing and maintaining the client's anxiety. In cognitive behavioural models of anxiety, a central principle is that behaviour is determined by a person's interpretations of the immediate situation and anxiety (often maintained by avoidance), so that clients should be asked for a detailed account of the times that they feel frightened. What physical sensations are reported? What are their thoughts about? What is their worst fear? How do they respond or cope? When and in what circumstances does the anxiety occur? How frequently? Does anything make it more or less likely? Is anything avoided because of the anxiety? In what circumstances can avoided situations be coped with? Did the person experience anxiety before the attack? These questions will help to determine which, if any, specific anxiety disorder is present.

Panic disorder involves the sudden onset of intense apprehension associated with a wide range of frightening physical sensations including breathlessness, chest pain, trembling, choking, dizziness, and sweating. Characteristically, the person interprets these physiological signs in a catastrophic way as indicating a serious physical or mental condition and often becomes hypervigilant about bodily sensations. Certain forms of avoidance of the perceived catastrophe are often seen such as walking near potential supports such as fences or walls in case of dizziness and fainting.

In *phobic anxiety*, excessive fear of objects and situations which are not objectively dangerous is principally maintained by behavioural avoidance which prevents the individual from learning that contact with the feared situation does not lead to the expected outcome.

In *generalized anxiety*, unlike the more discrete anxieties experienced in panic and phobic disorders, the problem is excessive and unrealistic worry about a wide range of life situations, rather than anxiety about specific situations or feared outcomes. Almost all anxiety states are characterized by increased arousal and, in generalized anxiety, the symptoms are less acute but more constant often involving continued muscle tension, fatigue, irritability, poor concentration, and feeling on edge as well as common autonomic signs. Typically, the person feels unable to control the worrying and feels that he or she has insufficient resources to cope with things in general.

Differentiating among anxiety disorders is important since they require somewhat different interventions; however, in practice, there may be some overlap, and some clients will experience one or more types of anxiety at different times following an assault. Clients may also resort to excessive use of alcohol or drugs to deal with arousal, insomnia, and anxiety (Frank, Turner, Steward, Jacob, and West, 1981; Burnam *et al.*, 1988).

Re-experiencing Phenomena

The assault may be re-experienced in a number of ways. This may include recurrent and intrusive recollections of the event such as images, thoughts, perceptions, or dreams. Flashbacks are distressing, vivid intrusions of memory that are associated with strong, negative affect. They can involve smell, sounds, or touch as well as visual images. Such intrusive memories may be partial or total and the person may move, act, and talk as if the assault is reccurring or may experience the feeling that the event is taking place again. Flashbacks may be brief but some can last for longer periods. Re-experiencing can be triggered by both internal (thoughts, physical sensations) and external cues which symbolize or resemble an aspect of the assault. External triggers for flashbacks and distress are client-specific and can include places (see Case Example 5.3), items of clothing, accents, colours, smells, and time of the day. Re-experiencing the assault in whatever form is likely to be associated with intense psychological distress and physiological reactivity. Avoidance of this distress may develop into a phobic disorder or into alcohol or drug dependence.

Case Example 5.3

Ms C was sexually assaulted by a work colleague while living and working in central Manchester. Following the assault, she felt unable to continue with her job and even to stay in the area. She moved to a rural district, which she recognized to be a response to the assault and a way of coping, but 1 year later was seen in a psychology service because of continued problems with intrusive flashbacks. These were usually triggered when she was sitting at her computer at work. She would feel as if she was back in her original workplace and be aware of the presence of her assailant. In particular, she would hear his voice. Her colleagues had noticed that while sitting at the computer she would suddenly appear frightened. At times, she would burst into tears. Ms C's subjective experience was that she had no control over when the flashbacks occurred nor over their content or length.

When assessing these symptoms, the therapist should remain aware that most people will not have experienced flashbacks before and may be worried that they could represent a serious mental health problem. Clients may not volunteer information about flashbacks as readily as they will about nightmares.

Dissociative Experiences: Numbing, Detachment, and Amnesia

Increased arousal, as expressed in fear, anxiety, irritability, and inability to concentrate, often alternates with various mechanisms to avoid feelings and thoughts usually described as dissociative experiences. Dissociative phenomena can be seen as involuntary attempts by the individual to protect her or himself from stimuli which are too painful or threatening. In recognizing these protective, functional coping mechanisms, it is important not to override them in the short term or in a time of ongoing stress by, for example, encouraging clients to give a detailed description of the assault during assessment.

The person may experience subjective emotional numbing or an absence of emotional response in situations where emotional responses are usual. The person may also experience a sense of detachment from other people and a reduction in awareness of his or her surroundings. Derealization and depersonalization may be experienced as well as amnesia for certain aspects of the assault. Depersonalization is a persistent and recurrent sense of unreality and strangeness about oneself, just as if the person is an outside observer of his/her thought processes or body although the person is aware that this is not actually the case. Derealization is a sense that the environment rather than the person is changed or unfamiliar. Dissociative amnesia is partial or complete loss of memory for the assault in the absence of any other cause such as head injury, extreme fatigue, the effects of medication or other drugs including alcohol. As with flashback symptoms, clients are sometimes reluctant to disclose unfamiliar experiences such as depersonalization because of fears about their meaning. It is usually helpful to be explicit and say that strange experiences are common soon after assault.

Case Example 5.4

Mr P was referred to the psychology service by his GP following a sexual assault. During the first clinical interview, he reported that he had been raped and then immediately fell silent, staring straight ahead with an impassive expression. This continued for 5 minutes until the therapist enquired how he was feeling. He made no reply and continued staring. The therapist's impression was that, had she not intervened, he would have remained in this dissociated state for at least the whole appointment time.

It is important to identify the presence of dissociative symptoms (see Case Example 5.4) since, while they can be seen as psychologically protective in the shorter term, it is proposed that in the longer term they may prevent the integration and resolution of the trauma (Koopman, Classen, Cardena, and Spiegel, 1995; Spiegel, 1996). There is also some evidence that their presence in the first 4 weeks following the assault predicts the development of PTSD (Harvey and Bryant, 1998).

Depression and Suicidal Feelings

Following an assault, people often feel a change or loss of identity as if they are in some way 'spoiled' or no longer the person they were. This may be exacerbated by a feeling of detachment from others, numbing of emotion, and social withdrawal. They may report the feeling that their future will not be as it is for others, or as it was before the assault, particularly if they meet the criteria for PTSD. These feelings may be associated with depression and hopelessness. As many as half of all those who have been assaulted have symptoms of a major depression soon after assault which may persist for longer periods in a smaller proportion (Frank and Stewart, 1984; Kilpatrick et al., 1987). Tearfulness, sadness, poor concentration, loss of interest and enjoyment in normal activities, relationships, and sexual activity are all commonly experienced after assault. The extent to which these difficulties represent a clinical depression must be carefully considered. In addition to the difficulties listed above, the following should be assessed: sleep disturbance (typically early waking), appetite change, weight loss, diurnal variation of mood, psychomotor retardation or agitation, feelings of guilt, worthlessness, and suicidal thoughts. These are all suggestive of a depressive disorder that requires intervention, possibly including medication, particularly if the symptoms have been present for 2 weeks or longer.

Shame, Guilt, and Self-Blame

Feelings of shame, guilt, and self-blame are common following a sexual assault. Individuals often report a feeling of shame for having been sexually assaulted as well as a sense of shame about their perceived responsibility for the assault. These feelings and beliefs may be functional, however, because they can reinforce a sense of individual control. Given that the client has experienced a complete loss of control and a physical, sexual assault, if there is a belief that he or she was responsible to an extent for what happened, then a sense of agency and retained control will remain. This may feel more comfortable and less frightening than a sense of the world and others being completely outside one's control.

There are specific gender and sexuality issues relevant to the issue of shame. The first is the widely held, implicit, social belief about responsibility in sexual encounters, which supports the idea that women, just by virtue of being female, are targets for a man's sexual interest, and, furthermore, that once a man is sexually aroused beyond a certain point, that he cannot be held responsible for his actions (Nicolson, 1993). Hence, if a woman, dresses in a sexually attractive manner or engages in any form of sexual activity with her assailant, she is somehow viewed as responsible for the attack. These ideas are deeply embedded in our culture, among both men and women, and may be another source of confusion and shame. The therapist needs to examine his or her attitudes carefully and reflect on how they may affect the conduct of the assessment interview.

Similarly, in a society in which men are expected to be able to defend themselves, the experience of being controlled and raped by another male is deeply shameful. This may be exacerbated if the assaulted man is a heterosexual who perceives that he has been assaulted by a homosexual man. Disgust or fear of sexual activity between men is prevalent among heterosexual men, and it is wrongly but widely assumed that assaults on males are perpetrated by gay men. Hence, for a heterosexual man, an assault may result in extreme psychological conflict and reluctance to report or disclose the assault. For gay men, while there may be less or no hostility to sexual acts between men in general, there is likely to be a sense of responsibility and self-blame and similarly less likelihood of reporting to the police (King, 1992).

There are also likely to be shameful feelings arising from the degree of resistance to the assault. Clients' perceptions of failure to resist sufficiently in the assault situation can make them vulnerable to depression. The overriding emotional experience for most during an assault is fear of death, and it is helpful for the client to be reminded that placatory behaviour or lack of resistance needs to be understood within the context of this.

Anger, Vengeance, and Desire for Justice

The emotion of anger is a common response to assault, and it may be necessary to help client articulate anger, vengeance, and justice fantasies and to differentiate these from real, intended plans of harm. It may be necessary in some cases to inform the client beforehand that disclosure of any plans or intention to harm the assailant will mean that client confidentiality may need to be broken and relevant information passed on to appropriate agencies (e.g., the police).

The client may be generally hostile towards particular groups of people following an assault (e.g., 'all men' or 'all strangers'). Anger may also be directed at people close to the client because he or she has difficulty in dealing with feelings of intimacy, which can stimulate reminders of vulnerability. In the case of reports of excessive irritability with children and difficulties managing them, perhaps in conjunction with depression or alcohol use, the possibility of risk to the children should be considered.

Relationship Difficulties and Sexual Dysfunction

Low mood, anxiety, anger, and poor self-image are just some of the factors that contribute to strained personal relationships following assault. It is not surprising that many clients lose interest in sexual activity or fear any sexual contact. Common sexual problems following assault include lack of sexual interest, sexual arousal difficulties, and lack of sexual pleasure. In addition, partners or others very close to the client may find it difficult to think about or acknowledge the assault because of their own distressing feelings. Psychological responses of partners can mirror those of the assaulted person (Holmstrom and Burgess, 1979). The presence, type, and severity of difficulties in close relationships and their history should be assessed. It may be appropriate to see the client's partner to gain another perspective of the difficulties.

Social Support Network and Disclosure

The extent and quality of a person's social network is related to overall adjustment both immediately and in the long term following assault (Burgess and Holmstrom, 1978). The social support available to the client should be determined, especially immediately after the assault and if the client is markedly depressed. Even if the client has a good social network, accessing support may be difficult because of social withdrawal, shame, or fear about other people's responses to disclosure. It is important, therefore, not only to identify important people, frequency of contact, geographical location, and the quality of the relationship the client has with them, but also to ask whether the client has told anyone about the assault and what the response was.

Background History

As in any assessment of potential psychological problems, all other relevant background information should be sought including family and developmental history, educational history, occupational history, sexual and relationship history, history of significant life events, medical history, trauma and abuse history, history of alcohol and drug dependence, and history of psychiatric problems. The most consistently reported factor associated with severe post-assault responses and slower recovery is a history of mental health and substance-abuse problems (Burgess and Holmstrom, 1979; Frank and Anderson, 1987). There is also evidence that previous experience of sexual assault, physical assault, sexual harassment, child sexual abuse, and parental and spouse violence are factors which may make recovery more difficult (Burgess and Holmstrom, 1978, 1979; Glenn and Resick, 1986). The number of life change events (Ruch, Chandler, and Harter, 1980) and the loss of a family member within the previous year (Kilpatrick, Veronen, and Best, 1985) have also been implicated in greater levels of distress. Predisposing vulnerability factors should be identified together with any other co-occurring problems that may influence the client's ability to cope and adjust.

Risk Assessment and Management

Suicidal ideation is common following assault (Atkeson, Calhoun, Resick, and Ellis, 1982), and elevated rates of deliberate self-harm have been reported among women with a history of sexual assault (Kilpatrick *et al.*, 1985). The risk of self-harm should be carefully assessed and appropriate steps for the safety of the client taken.

Enquiries should be made about the client's perception of current ways of coping and the client's use of functional and dysfunctional strategies in the short, medium, and long term considered. The use of recreational or prescribed drugs, in particular alcohol, should be established as well as self-care behaviour and possible risk-taking activities. Vulnerability factors and presenting difficulties in relation to coping strategies, personal resources, and levels of support should be assessed.

If the client initiates discussion about self-harm or suicidal thoughts, the subject should be followed up by asking about plans and previous experiences. If the client does not raise the subject, the therapist should enquire whether there have been any such thoughts or previous attempts. Examples of ways to ask about this fairly sensitive subject include: Have you recently thought that it's too difficult to carry on? Are you having any feelings that life is not worth living? Have you thought about ending it all? Have you sometimes felt that you might harm yourself in some way? It is generally recognized that suicide risk increases in the context of previous attempts, detailed plans, and explicit intention (Tuckman and Youngman, 1968; Pallis, Gibbons, and Pierce, 1984). An accurate history of previous self-harm incidents and suicide attempts is vital to risk assessment. The recency, severity, frequency, and pattern of any previous attempts should be elicited.

The client should be asked whether he or she has taken suicidal intent a stage further than that of planning. Thoughts of suicide without any plan or access to the means to do so carry a lower risk. The assessor must consider whether the client has access to means and how likely the plan is to succeed. Plans to avoid detection are of particular significance.

A statement from the client indicating an intention to kill or harm him or herself is the strongest indicator of risk and should not be dismissed. Equally, it is useful to bear in mind that an explicit denial of intention does not necessarily mean that there is no intent present.

In assessing the client's current mental state, the frequency and severity of suicidal ideation must be ascertained. If suicide is frequently considered and thoughts are persistent and intrusive, this indicates a higher risk even in the absence of planning. Restraints on action (e.g., religious beliefs, relationships, and family obligations) should be established. The general risk factors for suicide are being male, older, separated, divorced or widowed, having poor physical health, mental health diagnoses, and alcohol or drug dependence. Other risk factors include social isolation, history of exposure to traumatic events, unemployment, financial problems, and bereavement (Gelder, Gath, Mayou and Cowen, 1996). The assessor may also bear in mind that it can be therapeutic and containing for the client to have the time and space to talk about wishing to die, without meaning that there is direct suicidal intent.

Hospital care, possibly restriction under the Mental Health Act, should be considered when suicide risk is judged to be high. This can be organized via referral to a hospital or community duty psychiatric team who will undertake assessment and liaison work as appropriate. Alternatively, urgent referral to the local community mental health team and liaison with the general practitioner may be the best course of action. If the assessment is planned to continue for further appointments, these could be scheduled at short intervals or supplemented by telephone calls. The client should be encouraged to mobilize his or her social support, and it may be appropriate to arrange a programme of care and support with relatives and friends or day care attendance. The assessor should think about contingency plans if the client fails to attend an appointment and agree a contract with at-risk clients that they will not harm themselves. Access to various support agencies in times of emergency (e.g., 24-hour telephone helplines such as the Samaritans and hospital Accident & Emergency departments) should also be discussed.

B STRESS DISORDER DIAGNOSES

It is useful to be aware of two psychiatric diagnostic categories that have particular relevance in this area of work: these are acute stress disorder (ASD) and post-traumatic stress disorder (PTSD). The DSM-IV (American Psychiatric Association, 1994) diagnosis of ASD is used to classify trauma reactions occurring within 2 days of an assault and lasting for up to 4 weeks. The DSM-IV diagnosis of PTSD applies to trauma reactions that are present from 1 month after the assault. Longitudinal research suggests that about half of those experiencing sexual assault will experience problems consistent with a diagnosis of PTSD in the 3-month period following the assault (Rothbaum *et al.*, 1992). These problems can also last over longer periods of time: PTSD persisting for at least 1 year following the trauma is present in about 50% of cases (Davidson *et al.*, 1996).

Post-Traumatic Stress Disorder (DSM-IV)

Post-traumatic stress disorder is viewed as a delayed or protracted response to an acutely stressful event, which usually arises within 3 months of the event but can present many years later. The diagnosis is based on the fulfilment of six criteria shown in Table 5.3.

In order to meet the diagnostic criteria, at least one re-experiencing symptom, three avoidance symptoms, and two arousal symptoms must be present. Re-experiencing symptoms include distressing intrusive recollections, dreams, and dissociative flashback experiences. The other main classification system, ICD10 (WHO, 1992), confers a diagnosis of PTSD on a similar symptom pattern but differs from DSM-IV principally in not requiring avoidance, numbing, and autonomic arousal as essential for the diagnosis. In addition, a minimum duration of symptoms is not specified although the criteria indicate that latency ranges from a few weeks to a few months.

Table 5.3 Diagnostic criteria for post-traumatic stress disorder (DSM-IV) (reprinted with permission by APA, 1994)

A	Exposure to a traumatic event in which both the following were present: the person experienced, witnessed or was confronted by an event that involved actual or threatened death, serious injury or a threat to physical integrity; the person's response involved intense fear, helplessness or horror.
B	The event is persistently re-experienced.
C	Persistent avoidance of stimuli associated with the trauma.
D	Persistent symptoms of general arousal.
E	Duration of disturbance is more than one month.
F	Disturbance causes clinically significant distress or impairment in social, occupational or other important areas of functioning.

Table 5.4 Diagnostic criteria for acute stress disorder (DSM-IV) (reprinted with permission by APA, 1994)

A	Exposure to traumatic event.
B	Either while experiencing or after the event, the individual experiences three or more dissociative symptoms.
C	The traumatic event is persistently re-experienced (at least one symptom).
D	Marked avoidance of stimuli that arouse recollections of the trauma.
E	Marked symptoms of anxiety or increased arousal.
F	Disturbance causes clinically significant distress or impairment in social, occupational or other important areas of functioning or impairs ability to carry out necessary tasks such as obtaining assistance or telling family members about the experience.
G	Disturbance lasts for minimum of 2 days and a maximum of 4 weeks and occurs within 4 weeks of event.
H	Disturbance is not due to the direct physiological effects of a substance or a general medical disorder, is not better accounted for by a diagnosis of brief psychotic disorder and is not an exacerbation of a pre-existing axis Axis I or Axis II disorder.

Acute Stress Disorder (DSM-IV)

Acute stress disorder is conceptualized as an acute form of PTSD and shares many of the diagnostic criteria (i.e., re-experiencing, avoidance, and arousal symptoms), as shown in Table 5.4. The major difference is that a diagnosis of ASD requires that the person experience at least three dissociative symptoms during or after the event and that the symptoms occur within 4 weeks of the traumatic event. Because of the acute nature of the disorder, it is important to exclude the possibility of other explanations for the symptom picture such as substance use or pre-existing personality disorder. As mentioned earlier, the presence of dissociative symptoms may indicate a greater difficulty in processing the traumatic event and, if persistent, would suggest a particular therapeutic approach.

C STANDARDIZED PSYCHOLOGICAL MEASURES

It may be helpful to supplement interview material by the use of standardized measures. Generally, the choice of measure for particular problems will be guided by the following considerations: What is the purpose of using a measure? Is it to clarify symptom patterns or define the presenting disorder, quantify severity, assess change over time, or demonstrate to the client that the symptoms reported are expected in the situation? How acceptable to the client is the measure? How long is it? Are there any items which the client might find disturbing? Are there literacy problems?

There are a number of instruments available for the assessment of sexual assault related problems. Measures that are not sexual assault or trauma specific are also useful to assess other aspects of psychological distress. In most cases, the use of relatively lengthy assessment measures, such as those required in research, will not be appropriate. Instruments which have clinical relevance are described, but this is not a comprehensive list and clinicians will have their own preferences.

Rape Aftermath Symptom Test

There is only one well-documented rating scale specifically developed for sexual assault. This is the Rape Aftermath Symptom Test (Kilpatrick, 1988) which was developed from symptoms experienced by women in the 3-month period following rape. It is made up of 30 items from the Derogatis SCL-90-R (Derogatis, 1977) and 40 from the Veronen–Kilpatrick Modified Fear Survey (Veronen and Kilpatrick, 1980), which were found to best discriminate between rape and non-rape groups. Some examples of the items are:

- fear of persons behind you, being alone, darkness, sound of a doorbell;
- feeling that most people cannot be trusted;
- having to avoid certain things, places, or activities because they frighten you;
- being suddenly scared for no reason.

The measure distinguished between the assaulted and non-assaulted women at all time points in a 3-year follow-up and was sensitive to treatment effects in the Foa, Rothbaum, Riggs, and Murdock (1991) controlled trial of therapy approaches. This test is not easily available, however, and is included here for completeness because of its unique status.

Measures for PTSD

The Impact of Event Scale (Horowitz et al., 1979)

This widely used scale is a 15-item self-report measure which assesses two key aspects of PTSD: intrusion (8 items) and avoidance (7 items) which are scored separately. Respondents indicate the frequency with which they have experienced each item within the past week and the items are scored

0, 1, 3, and 5. The scale has high internal consistency and test–retest reliability, discriminates between different populations and changing symptom levels and its construct validity is supported by factor analysis (Zilberg, Weiss, and Horowitz, 1982; Schwarzwald, Solomon, Weisenberg, and Mikilincer, 1987). In relation to non-recent assault, it is known that scores can remain relatively high even after long periods of time. In a follow-up study of women who had been raped, after 2 years the mean intrusion score was 11.6 and that for avoidance was 16.0 (Kilpatrick and Veronen, 1984). Comparison data are available not only from the original report (Horowitz, Wilner, and Alvarez, 1979) but also from the many published studies of traumatized people using the scale, including those who have been sexually assaulted. The scale is particularly useful clinically because of its brevity, and, since typically either avoidance or intrusive phenomena predominate, it helps to guide intervention strategy.

There are a number of instruments, the primary purpose of which is to identify PTSD but which may also have utility in demonstrating clinical change before and after intervention. These include the Posttraumatic Stress Diagnostic Scale, The PENN Inventory and the Clinician Administered PTSD Scale (CAPS). The first two are self-report scales and differ in length and comprehensiveness while the third is clinician administered.

The Posttraumatic Stress Diagnostic Scale (Foa, 1995)

As the name indicates, this self-report scale is designed to aid in the diagnosis of PTSD and to quantify the severity of the symptoms. Its 49 items reflect closely the DSM-IV diagnostic criteria and are organized in four sections covering type of traumatic event, characteristics of specific event and time since occurrence, symptoms in past month and their duration, and areas of functioning affected by the symptoms. The scale has good psychometric properties and validity in terms of diagnostic agreement with the Structured Clinical Interview for DSM-III-R (Williams et al., 1992), and correlations of scores with other scales assessing symptoms associated with PTSD is high (Foa, 1995). Although it is not a substitute for a clinical assessment, this scale would be useful for the clinician who is less familiar with the presentation of PTSD.

The PENN Inventory for Posttraumatic Stress Disorder (Hammarberg, 1992)

The PENN Inventory is a scale consisting of 26 self-report items each made up of 4 statements in order of severity rated from 0 to 3. For example:

0 I rarely feel jumpy or uptight
1 I sometimes feel jumpy or uptight

2 I often feel jumpy or uptight
3 I feel jumpy and uptight all the time

The psychometric properties of the test were established in a series of studies among groups of combat veterans and survivors of an oil rig disaster. The inventory shows high internal consistency, test–retest reliability and validity in relation to PTSD diagnosis and measures of PTSD symptom dimensions (Hammarberg, 1992). The author suggests a score of 35 to give good specificity and sensitivity in distinguishing cases of PTSD from non-cases.

Clinician Administered PTSD Scale (CAPS) (Blake et al., 1997)

This is a semi-structured interview for arriving at a diagnosis of PTSD. Each of 17 symptoms relevant to diagnostic criteria for PTSD is given a frequency and intensity score in the range of 0–4 so that each symptom has a maximum score of 8. The scale has been shown to have adequate reliability and validity (Weathers and Litz, 1994).

The Scott Trauma Belief Inventory (Scott and Stradling, 1992)

This inventory consists of 20 dysfunctional trauma beliefs to be rated on a 5-point scale for how true each belief is of the person completing the scale. It is intended to help the clinician in assessing long-established, strongly held beliefs, which may hinder an individual's ability to overcome the consequences of a traumatic event. Sample items are:

- no one can be trusted;
- other people can never understand how I feel.

The scale awaits validation and no data are available regarding its psychometric properties. It can provide useful supplementary information when considering which therapeutic approach to recommend since an individual with strongly held dysfunctional beliefs may benefit from longer term therapy.

Measures for Anxiety, Depression, and General Psychological Distress

A wide range of measures is available for assessing the anxiety and depression that typically follow sexual assault. All the measures listed in this section have been widely used both in research studies and clinically, and have well-established reliability and validity properties. Specific measures of anxiety include the State-Trait Inventory (Spielberger, Gorsuch, and Lushene, 1970) which assesses transient, situational anxiety as well as longer term tendency to be anxious, and the Beck Anxiety Inventory (Beck, Epstein, Brown, and Steer, 1988) which has an emphasis on somatic symptoms. The Fear Survey Schedule (Wolpe and Lang, 1964) and the Fear Questionnaire (Marks and Matthews, 1979) are both instruments for assessing phobic anxiety. The latter is a brief scale which focuses on specific phobic avoidance.

The Beck Depression Inventory (Beck, Ward, Mendelson, Mock, and Erbaugh, 1961) is a well-established measure of depression and the Beck Hopelessness scale (Beck, Weissman, Lester, and Trexler, 1974) is useful in assessing suicidal risk since level of hopelessness has been shown to be associated with risk of suicide (Beck, Steer, Kovacs, and Garrison, 1985). The Hospital Anxiety and Depression Scale (Zigmund and Snaith, 1983) has the advantage of omitting somatic symptoms which may be useful when physical symptoms are present following the assault.

The General Hospital Questionnaire (Goldberg, 1972) is a measure of psychological distress which can be scored either to provide a dimensional measure of distress or to express the probability that a respondent might meet the criteria for a psychiatric illness. It has a number of different versions allowing for selection of a brief or longer measure, including the GHQ-28 which provides separate scores for somatic symptoms, anxiety and insomnia, social dysfunction and severe depression (Goldberg and Williams, 1988).

Because of the evidence that excessive alcohol use may follow sexual assault, it may be relevant to assess problem drinking. The CAGE questionnaire (Mayfield, McLeod, and Hall, 1974), which consists of only 4 items, is a useful measure as it does not cover alcohol consumption directly. Two or more positive responses indicate covert problem drinking. The Alcohol Use Disorders Identification Test (Babor, De la Fuente, Saunders, and Grant, 1989) is a 10-item measure which has been shown to identify not only harmful drinking but also heavy drinking which may develop into dependence (Saunders, Aasland, Babor, De la Fuente, and Grant, 1993).

D PSYCHOLOGICAL CASE FORMULATION

A case formulation is the assessor's hypothesis about the nature of the psychological mechanisms underlying the client's presenting problems (Persons, 1989). It organizes and links the problems in a meaningful way, gives an account of how they developed both in terms of immediate precipitants and predisposing factors, and describes how they are maintained. Formulations are based on both observation and inference about psychological processes involved in the expression and maintenance of client's difficulties. Importantly, a formulation will incorporate an understanding of issues of power, resources, economics, class, gender, sexuality, age, disability, religion, and cultural background in order that a sensitive and coherent understanding of a client's psychological difficulties is developed.

The main function of a formulation is to guide the treatment plan and make a successful outcome more probable. It also helps the therapist anticipate therapy-interfering events. In order to develop a hypothesis that can adequately explain the client's difficulties, it is always necessary to take account of the immediate antecedents and consequences of the presenting difficulties and, usually, also of experiences earlier in life which have contributed to characteristic beliefs and behaviour patterns. In terms of choice of intervention, a formulation may indicate the role of immediate factors maintaining the problems, for example, in simple phobic anxiety or the need to pay attention to longer term maintaining factors such as central beliefs about the self and the world, which might indicate the appropriateness of schema-focused or psychodynamic therapy (Beck *et al.*, 1990; Roth and Fonagy, 1996).

Psychiatric diagnoses such as major depression or PTSD provide a standardized way of classifying mental health difficulties and give a general indication of pharmacological treatment approaches that may prove helpful. Psychological formulation is an individualized understanding of a client's difficulties in the context of sociocultural factors, past and current relationships, and distal and proximal life events. It is useful in directing thinking about choices of psychological treatment and particular areas to target. Case Examples 5.5 and 5.6, Ms T and Ms N, demonstrate that the same psychiatric diagnoses can reflect very different difficulties and underlying psychological mechanisms, and therefore warrant different treatment approaches. In the two cases described, both clients meet the criteria for DSM-IV for PTSD after a sexual assault. Both have characteristic symptoms of arousal, re-experiencing, and avoidance of trauma-related stimuli.

Case Example 5.5

Ms T was sexually assaulted by a stranger while waiting on a train station platform. The attack took place in daylight and was extremely brutal. She attended the psychology service for assessment 10 months after the assault.

In addition to the PTSD symptoms, she had a number of somatic symptoms including blurred vision, weakness on the left side of her body, and irregular heartbeat, for which no pathological cause had been found. She was experiencing panic attacks which were usually preceded by catastrophic interpretation of her somatic symptoms and which had led her to avoid situations where she thought they would occur. Her history revealed that her father died 20 years previously, suddenly from a heart attack. In the period since the assault, her friend had been killed in a road accident. The underlying mechanism maintaining Ms T's problems was a group of beliefs that 'no one is secure: terrible things can happen and anyone can die at any moment'. These beliefs had been dormant for many years but were reactivated both by the assault and by her friend's death.

Ms T's formulation (Case Example 5.5) highlights the role of recent and distal life events in shaping a set of beliefs related to her perception of her own and others' vulnerability to harm. These beliefs acted to increase her attention to physical sensations experienced after the sexual assault which she interpreted as indicating a life-threatening condition, resulting in further somatic difficulties and panic attacks.

Case Example 5.6

Ms N worked as a teacher and had two young children. She was sexually assaulted by a friend of her husband's whom she had known for several years. She presented to the psychology service 8 months after the assault. Her problems were particularly focused on re-experiencing the assault in the form of nightmares and intrusive images and thoughts. When these occurred, she tried to blank them out by tensing her hands and concentrating on something else in her environment. She often thought about the circumstances of the assault, asking herself whether she had been responsible in some way for what happened, although she had not been able to talk about the assault itself. Exploration of her history, beliefs, and coping mechanisms revealed that her difficulties seemed to be maintained by repeated, unsuccessful attempts to regain control over events and, in particular, a belief that 'the best way to deal with distressing emotions is to suppress them'. Her coping strategies were based on a fundamental assumption that she would be overwhelmed if she did not remain in control. These beliefs had their origins in an unhappy early family life and a rigid upbringing. Her father had been a very angry, abusive man and had constantly shouted and bullied both his wife and the children.

Ms N's formulation (Case Example 5.6) indicates that she had learnt to cope with emotional difficulties by using primarily avoidant strategies.

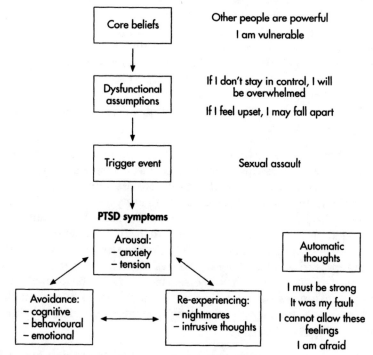

Figure 5.1 Cognitive formulation of Ms N's difficulties.

While, perhaps in the past, these had been functional and had allowed her to cope with difficult family situations during childhood, as an adult they served to suppress the expression of distress, which inadvertently acted to maintain anxieties and increase the feeling that she would, in her words, 'go mad' and 'have a complete mental breakdown'.

The formulations for these two people indicated that intervention needed to take account of the specific content of long-established beliefs which had become relevant in the context of the sexual assault since these could be seen to play a role in the maintenance and exacerbation of the post-traumatic difficulties. The formulation for Ms N is summarized in Figure 5.1.

E   KEY ASSESSMENT ISSUES

Organizational Contexts and Service Models

Psychological assessment services for people who have been sexually assaulted are offered by national health services (NHS), public sector services, and voluntary organizations. General practitioners act as the main referral gateway to a range of NHS adult mental health services which employ a variety of mental health professionals including, among others, clinical psychologists, counsellors, counselling psychologists, psychiatrists, psychoanalysts, and systemic therapists. NHS genitourinary medicine clinics offer direct client access to medical specialists in sexual health and typically offer referral on to specialized psychological and psychiatric services.

Public sector services include the police service and local authority social services. Social service care managers take lead responsibility for the co-ordination of complex social and health needs assessments, and the police, while not offering a direct assessment or therapy service, provide referral services and a police 'chaperone' to all sexual assault individuals until the end of legal procedures. The police refer all individuals who report crimes to the voluntary organization Victim Support. A number of other voluntary organizations offer support services and clients can mostly access these directly. Telephone helpline services include the Samaritans and Rape Crisis centres. 'Respond' is a voluntary organization that offers assessment and therapy to people with learning difficulties who have been sexually assaulted.

A variety of service models are employed within the mental health field. In a typical service model the mental health professional who undertakes the assessment also provides the therapy. Other service models are based upon separate procedures of assessment and therapy and are undertaken by two different health professionals.

Psychology Theory

Since assessment is underpinned by psychology theory and is intrinsically linked to the process of therapy, it is significantly influenced by the theoretical orientation of the assessor so that varying styles of assessment will be offered according to the therapist's training background. There are a number of psychological theories and therapies that have application within the field of sexual assault (see Chapter 4). While the number of studies on the outcome of therapeutic interventions for the psychological sequelae of sexual assault are limited, those that do exist support the effectiveness of a cognitive-behavioural approach (Solomon, Gerrity, and Muff, 1992; Van Etten and Taylor, 1998; see also Chapter 4). Cognitive-behavioural therapy is guided by principles of therapist–client collaboration, client education, hypothesis-testing, experimentation, client work between sessions, active change, and development of client self-help skills. During the assessment period, the client may be asked to keep a diary of relevant observations (e.g., a record of thoughts and emotions). By the end of a cognitive-behavioural assessment, the therapist in conjunction with the client would aim to have achieved an initial formulation of presenting difficulties, identified precipitants of distress and factors likely to be maintaining the difficulties, designed a plan for therapy, and presented introductory educational material to the client about the cognitive-behavioural model. The assessment guidelines in this chapter have been broadly based upon a cognitive-behavioural framework.

Values and Sociocultural Issues

Attention to the client's cultural and social position is clearly relevant in terms of beginning to understand that person's experience and the meaning the sexual assault has come to have. Therapists can usefully remain aware of their own cultural and social position and of their personal values and beliefs during assessment. While no single therapist can have detailed knowledge of all cultural and social backgrounds, the key to assessment is a demonstrated sensitivity to areas of difference and a willingness to ask the client about his or her experience in order to further the therapist's understanding. It is the endeavour to understand the client that is likely to be experienced as helpful rather than knowledge *per se*.

In terms of reporting an assault to the police, it is important to remember that certain groups of women and men may be more wary than others about involving the police or other public organizations because of prevailing negative attitudes and biased procedures within such institutions. In cases of sexual assault within long-term relationships, particularly in cases of stigmatized, disenfranchised social groups and in the context of some religious cultures, individuals may feel under considerable pressure to remain within the relationship.

Case Example 5.7

Ms S is a young, married, Bangladeshi, Muslim woman who was indirectly affected by a sexual assault when she discovered that her husband had sexually assaulted one of her younger sisters. She experienced tremendous psychological conflict and great torment because, while she wanted to leave her husband, she also strongly feared many of the consequences. She was concerned about the stigma of divorce, worried about the impact of a family break-up upon her three young children, and fearful about managing as a single parent. She feared her parents' reaction who, although they knew about the assault, had nevertheless threatened to cut all social ties with her if she left her husband. She was also concerned about the impact on her two younger sisters who were awaiting marriage arrangements. She felt that if the wider Bangladeshi community were to become aware of either a divorce in the family or the sexual assault itself, then her sisters' marriage opportunities would be significantly reduced.

Cultural and religious concepts such as 'virginity' and 'monogamy' may be relevant to a psychological understanding of a client's guilt, shame and distress. Ms S, described in Case Example 5.7, was concerned about the possibility of her sister being rejected by a potential partner on account of her sister having been 'touched' by another man, even though the contact was by force.

For clients whose first language is not shared by the therapist, or for those with hearing or speech impairments, communication can be facilitated through access to interpreting and signing services. It is increasingly recognized that people with learning difficulties are particularly vulnerable to sexual assault (Turk and Brown, 1993) by strangers, friends, partners, family members, paid carers, and other people with learning difficulties. Specialist health and social services for people with learning difficulties may need to be involved during assessment procedures, particularly when the client is known to a service and is likely to benefit both from specialist skills and from the support of someone well known to him or her.

A number of issues relate specifically to sexual orientation. For a lesbian to disclose that she has been sexually assaulted by a female partner may prove difficult in the light of stereotypical ideas about male violence and more general fears about disapproval of her sexuality. Heterosexual men may be reluctant to disclose an assault by another man, whether the assault was by a straight or gay man, because of perceived implications about their own sexuality. Gay men who have been sexually assaulted in places where casual sexual encounters occur may fear being blamed (see Case Example 5.8).

Case Example 5.8

Mr P is a Spanish gay man who was sexually assaulted by two men in the toilets of a central London gay nightclub. The club was popular and well known for (consenting) casual sexual encounters. After the assault, Mr P reported that he felt very much to blame for what had happened, particularly as he had heard afterwards from other gay men that 'this kind of thing' took place in the club 'all the time'. This information both exacerbated his sense of self-blame and led him to feel naive that he had not considered it a possibility before.

Although sexual assaults by men on other men, and by women on other women and men, are acknowledged and recognized to be underreported, it remains true that the vast majority of current sexual assault work is with female clients who have been sexually assaulted by male assailants.

Clinical practice indicates that, generally, female clients are assessed by female therapists. Two important factors to consider are the client's preference and whether the therapist feels comfortable undertaking sexual assault work. It is recommended that gender, alongside wider sociocultural issues, remains on the agenda both during client assessment meetings and within supervision forums.

Issues for the Assessor

A vital aspect of assessment work is the therapist's management of his or her own psychological response to the client and the presented clinical material. Listening to an account of a distressing event can evoke strong emotions in the therapist both within the session and for an extended period. The term 'vicarious traumatization' is used to refer to indirect effects upon those who witness an account of a trauma. Trauma can impact upon partners, friends, and family of the assaulted person, as well as upon the therapist. The effects on the therapist can be managed with the help of a range of support systems, which may include clinical supervision, access to informal peer support, access to relevant literature, use of personal self-care strategies, and use of personal therapy. The availability of a forum for regular clinical supervision is recommended for therapists undertaking assessment and therapy with assaulted clients.

While acknowledging the negative emotional impact of trauma upon the therapist, it is important to consider another aspect of this work. It is generally recognized that there exists a social fascination with subjects concerned with sex, violence, death, and horror. This interest is seen, for example, at the site of a road traffic accident when pedestrians and motorists gather around the scene. Similarly, popular news programmes and newspapers regularly offer detailed accounts of trauma, abuse, and murder cases, and the popularity of horror films is clear. If therapists acknowledge this wider societal fascination with trauma, then they become better positioned to recognize similar dynamics within themselves and the risks of intrusive and inappropriate client questioning are reduced.

SUMMARY

This chapter has addressed issues regarding the psychological assessment of sexual assault. The process of assessment involves identifying and differentiating responses to sexual assault, distinguishing between those that are normal in the circumstances and likely to be resolved and those that require intervention, agreeing a formulation and intervention plan with the client and finally identifying priorities for intervention, including areas that need to be dealt with as an emergency. In order to do this, it is helpful if the assessor is familiar with what to expect, knows how to recognize patterns of response, and has knowledge of diagnostic criteria for relevant psychiatric diagnoses. Since there are wide individual variations in response to sexual assault and since clients often present a mixed picture of psychological difficulties with several disorders co-existing, assessment needs to be thorough yet remain individually tailored and sensitive to presenting needs.

ACKNOWLEDGEMENTS

The work of this chapter is based upon research and clinical work with female and male clients who have suffered sexual assault. Acknowledgement is given to the role that clients have played in the development of psychological expertise in this area. It is through clients' willingness to seek support, face their difficulties, and talk openly about their experiences with health professionals that the development of mental health practice has been facilitated.

REFERENCES

APA. (1994) *Diagnostic and Statistical Manual of Mental Disorders* (4th edn). Washington, DC: American Psychiatric Association.

Atkeson, B.M., Calhoun, K.S., Resick, P.A., and Ellis, E.M. (1982) Victims of rape: Repeated assessment of depressive symptoms. *Journal of Clinical and Consulting Psychology*, **50**, 96–102.

Babor, T.F., De la Fuente, J.R., Saunders, J., and Grant, M. (1989) *AUDIT—the alcohol use identification test: Guidelines for use in primary health care*. Geneva: World Health Organization.

Beck, A.T., Epstein, W., Brown, G., and Steer, R.A. (1988) An inventory for measuring clinical anxiety: Psychometric properties. *Journal of Clinical and Consulting Psychology*, **56**, 893–897.

Beck , A.T., Freeman, A., Pretzer, J., Davis, D.D., Fleming, B., Ottaviani, R., Beck, J.,

Simon, K., Padesky, C., Meyer, J., and Trexler, L. (1990) *Cognitive therapy of personality disorders*. New York: Guilford Press.

Beck, A.T., Steer, R.A., Kovacs, M., and Garrison, B. (1985) Hopelessness and eventual suicide: A 10-year prospective study of patients hospitalised with suicidal ideation. *American Journal of Psychiatry*, 145, 559–563.

Beck, A.T., Ward, C.H., Mendelson, M., Mock, J.E., and Erbaugh, J.K. (1961) An inventory for measuring depression. *Archives of General Psychiatry*, 4, 561–571.

Beck, A.T., Weissman, A., Lester, D., and Trexler, L. (1974) The measurement of pessimism: The Hopelessness Scale. *Journal of Clinical and Consulting Psychology*, 42, 861–865.

Blake, D., Weathers, F., Nagy, L., Kaloupek, D., Klauminzer, G., Charney, D., and Keane, T. (1997) *Clinician-administered PTSD Scale (CAPS)*. Boston: National Centre for Post-traumatic Stress Disorder, Behavioural Science Division-Boston, VA.

Burgess, A.W. and Holmstrom, L.L. (1974) Rape trauma syndrome. *American Journal of Psychiatry*, 131, 981–986.

Burgess, A.W. and Holmstrom, L.L. (1978) Recovery from rape and prior life stress. *Research in Nursing and Health*, 1, 165–174.

Burgess, A.W. and Holmstrom, L.L. (1979) *Rape: Crisis and recovery*. Bowie, MD: Robert J. Brady.

Burnam, M.A., Stein, J.A., Golding, J.M., Siegel, J.M., Sorenson, S.B., Forsyth, A.B., and Telles, C.A. (1988) Sexual assault and mental disorders in a community poulation. *Journal of Consulting and Clinical Psychology*, 56, 843–850.

Davidson, J., Foa, E.B., Blank, A.S., Brett, E.A., Fairbank, J., Green, B. L., Herman, J. L., Keane, T.M., Kilpatrick, D.L., March, J.S., McNally, R.J., Pitman, R.K., Resnick, H.S., and Rothbaum, B.O. (1996) Post-traumatic stress disorder. In T.A. Widiger, A.J. Francis, H.A. Pincus, R. Ross, M.B. First, and W.W. Davis (eds) *DSM-IV Sourcebook* (Vol. 2, pp. 507–605). Washington, DC: American Psychiatric Association.

Derogatis, L.R. (1977) *SCL-90-R: Administration, scoring and procedures manual I.* Baltimore: Clinical Psychometrics Research.

Fischman, Y. and Ross, J. (1990) Group treatment of exiled survivors of trauma. *American Journal of Orthopsychiatry*, 60, 135–142.

Foa, E.B. (1995) *Posttraumatic Stress Diagnostic Scale*. Minneapolis, MN: National Computer Systems.

Foa, E.B. and Riggs, D.S. (1993) Post-traumatic stress in rape victims. In J. Oldham, M.B. Riba, and A. Tasman (eds) *American Psychiatric Press Review of Psychiatry* (Vol. 12). Washington, DC: American Psychiatric Press.

Foa, E.B., Rothbaum, B.O., Riggs, D.S., and Murdock, T.B. (1991) Treatment of post-traumatic stress disorder in rape victims: A comparison of cognitive-behavioural procedures and counseling. *Journal of Consulting and Clinical Psychology*, 59, 715–723.

Frank, E. and Anderson, B.P. (1987) Psychiatric disorders in rape victims: Past history and current symptomatology. *Comprehensive Psychiatry*, 28, 77–82.

Frank, E. and Stewart, B.D. (1984) Depressive symptoms in rape victims: A revisit. *Journal of Affective Disorders*, 7, 77–85.

Frank, E., Turner, S.M., Stewart, B.D., Jacob, M., and West, D. (1981) Past psychiatric symptoms and the response to sexual assault. *Comprehensive Psychiatry*, **22**, 479–487.

Gelder, M., Gath, D., Mayou, R., and Cowen, P. (1996) *Oxford Textbook of Psychiatry* (3rd edn). Oxford: Oxford University Press.

Glenn, F. and Resick, P.A. (1986) Incest and domestic violence as factors predicting adjustment to victimisation. Paper presented at the Association for Advancement of Behaviour Therapy, Chicago, IL, November 1986.

Goldberg, D.P. (1972) *The detection of psychiatric illness by questionnaire*. London: Oxford University Press.

Goldberg, D.P. and Williams, P. (1988) *A user's guide to the General Health Questionnaire*. Windsor: NFER-Nelson.

Hammarberg, M. (1992) PENN inventory for post-traumatic stress disorder: Psychometric properties. *Psychological Assessment: A Journal of Consulting and Clinical Psychology*, **4**, 67–76.

Harvey, A. and Bryant, R.A. (1998) The relationship between acute stress disorder and posttraumatic stress disorder: A prospective evaluation of motor vehicle accident survivors. *Journal of Consulting and Clinical Psychology*, **66**, 507–512.

Holmstrom, L.L and Burgess, A.W. (1979) Rape: The husband's and boyfriend's initial reactions. *The Family Co-ordinator*, **28**, 321–330.

Horowitz, M., Wilner, N., and Alvarez, W. (1979) Impact of Event Scale: A measure of subjective stress. *Psychological Medicine*, **41**, 209–218.

Kilpatrick, D.G. (1988) Rape aftermath symptom test. In M. Hersen and A.S. Bellack (eds) *Dictionary of behavioural assessment techniques*. Oxford: Pergamon Press.

Kilpatrick, D.G. and Veronen, L.J. (1984) *Treatment of fear and anxiety in victims of rape* (Final Report, Grant No. ROI MH 29062). Rockville, MD: National Institute of Mental Health.

Kilpatrick, D.G., Veronen, L.J., and Best, C.L. (1985) Factors predicting psychological distress among rape victims. In C.R. Figley (ed.). *Trauma and its wake*. New York: Brunner/Mazel.

Kilpatrick, D.G., Veronen, L.J., Saunders, B.E., Best, C.L., Amick-McMullen, A.E., and Paduhovich, J. (1987) *The psychological impact of crime: A study of randomly surveyed crime victims* (Final Report, Grant No. 84-IJ-CX-0039). Washington, DC: National Institute of Justice.

King, M.B. (1992) Male sexual assault in the community. In G.C. Mezey and M.B. King (eds) *Male victims of sexual assault*. London: Oxford Medical Publications.

Koopman, C., Classen, C., Cardena, E., and Spiegel, D. (1995) When disaster strikes, acute stress disorder may follow. *Journal of Traumatic Stress*, **8**, 29–46.

Lurie, P., Miller. S., Hecht, F., Lesney, C., and Lob, M. (1998) Post exposure prophylaxis after non-occupational HIV exposure: Clinical, ethical and policy considerations. *Journal of the American Medical Association*, **280**, 1769–1773.

Marks, I.M. and Matthews, A. (1979) A brief standard rating scale for phobic patients. *Behaviour Research and Therapy*, **17**, 263–267.

Mayfield, D., McLeod, G., and Hall, P. (1974) The CAGE questionnaire: Validation of a new alcoholism screening instrument. *American Journal of Psychiatry*, **131**, 1121–1123.

Mayou, R.A., Ehlers, A., and Hobbs, M. (2000) Psychological debriefing for road traffic accident victims. Three year follow up of a randomised controlled trial. *British Journal of Psychiatry*, **176**, 589–593.

Nicolson, P. (1993) Public values and private beliefs. In J.M. Ussher and C.D. Baker (eds) *Psychological perspectives on sexual problems: New directions in theory and practice*. London: Routledge.

Pallis, D.J., Gibbons, J.S., and Pierce, D.W. (1984) Estimating suicide risk among attempted suicides: II, Efficiency of predictive scales after the attempt. *British Journal of Psychiatry*, **144**, 139–148.

Persons, J. (1989) *Cognitive therapy in practice: A case formulation approach*. New York: W.W. Norton.

Pitman, R.K., Altman, B., Greenwald, E., Longpre, R.E, Macklin, M.L., Poire, R.E., and Steketee, G.S. (1991) Psychiatric complications during flooding therapy for post-traumatic stress disorder. *Journal of Clinical Psychiatry*, **52**, 17–20.

Roth, A. and Fonagy, P. (1996) *What works for whom? A critical review of psychotherapy research*. New York: Guilford Press.

Rothbaum, B.O., Foa, E.B., Murdock, T., Riggs, D., and Walsh, W. (1992) A prospective examination of post-traumatic stress disorder in rape victims. *Journal of Traumatic Stress*, **5**, 455–475.

Ruch, L.O., Chandler, S.M., and Harter, R.A. (1980) Life change and rape impact. *Journal of Health and Social Behaviour*, **21**, 248–260.

Saunders, J.B., Aasland, O.G., Babor, T.F., De la Fuente, J.R., and Grant, M. (1993) Development of the alcohol use identification test (AUDIT): WHO collaborative project on early detection of persons with harmful alcohol consumption. *Addiction*, **88**, 791–803.

Schwarzwald, J., Solomon, Z., Weisenberg, M., and Mikilincer, M. (1987) Validation of Impact of Event Scale for psychological sequelae of combat. *Journal of Consulting and Clinical Psychology*, **55**, 251–256.

Scott, M.J. and Stradling, S.C. (1992) *Counselling for post-traumatic stress disorder*. London: Sage Publications.

Solomon, S.D., Gerrity, E.T., and Muff, A.M. (1992) Efficacy of treatments for post-traumatic stress disorder: An empirical review. *Journal of the American Medical Association*, **263**, 633–638.

Spiegel, D. (1996) Dissociative disorders. In R.E. Hales and S.C. Yudofsky (eds) *Synopsis of psychiatry*. Washington, DC: American Psychiatric Press.

Spielberger, C.D., Gorsuch, R.L., and Lushene, R.E. (1970) Manual for the *State-Trait Anxiety Inventory (self-evaluation questionnaire)*. Palo Alto, CA: Consulting Psychologists Press.

Symonds, M. (1980) The 'second injury' to victims. *Evaluate and Change*, Special issue, 36–38.

Tuckman, J. and Youngman, W.F. (1968) A scale for assessing suicide risk of attempted suicides. *Journal of Clinical Psychology*, **24**, 17–19.

Turk, V. and Brown, H. (1993) The sexual abuse of adults with learning difficulties; results of a two year incidence survey. *Mental Handicap Research*, **6**, 193–216.

Van Etten, M.L. and Taylor, S. (1998) Efficacy of treatments for post-traumatic stress disorder. *Clinical Psychology and Psychotherapy*, **5**, 126–144.

Veronen, L.J. and Best, C. (1983) Assessment and treatment of fear and anxiety in rape victims. *The Clinical Psychologist*, **6**, 99–101.

Veronen, L.J. and Kilpatrick, D.G. (1980) Self-reported fear of rape victims: A preliminary investigation. *Behaviour Modification*, **4**, 383–396.

Walmsley, R. and White, K. (1979) *Sexual offences, consent and sentencing* (Home Office Research Study No. 54). London: Her Majesty's Stationery Office.

Weathers, F.W. and Litz, B.T. (1994) Psychometric properties of the Clinician-Administered PTSD Scale CAPS-I. *PTSD Research Quarterly*, **5**, 2–6.

WHO. (1992) *ICD10: Classification of mental and behavioural disorders*. Geneva: World Health Organization.

Williams, J.B.W., Gibbon, M., First, M.B., Spitzer, R.L., Davies, M., Borus, J., Howes, M.J., Kane, J., Pope, H.G., Rounsaville, B., and Wittchen, H.U. (1992) The Structured Clinical Interview for DSM-III-R (SCID). *Archives of General Psychiatry*, **49**, 630–636.

Wolpe, J. and Lang, P.J. (1964) A fear survey schedule for use in behaviour therapy. *Behaviour Research and Therapy*, **2**, 27–30.

Zigmund, A.S and Snaith, R.P. (1983) The Hospital Anxiety and Depression Scale. *Acta Psychiatrica Scandinavica*, **67**, 361–370.

Zilberg, N.J., Weiss, D.S., and Horowitz, M.J. (1982) Impact of Event Scale: A cross validation study and some empirical evidence supporting a concept model of stress response syndromes. *Journal of Consulting and Clinical Psychology*, **50**, 407–414.

Chapter 6

TREATMENT FOR ACUTE STRESS AND PTSD FOLLOWING RAPE

Amy E. Naugle, Heidi S. Resnick, Matt J. Gray, and Ron Acierno

INTRODUCTION

The primary goal of this chapter is to provide the reader with an overview of cognitive-behavioral strategies for treating acute stress reactions and PTSD. Intervening as early as possible post-assault may be effective in reducing longer term, chronic symptomatology; however, this needs to be demonstrated empirically. In order to place cognitive-behavioral treatment strategies outlined in the chapter within a coherent framework, we first offer a behavioral conceptualization for understanding the development of PTSD symptoms among rape victims. In the section that follows, we describe several cognitive-behavioral treatment techniques, many of which have been shown to be effective in reducing symptoms of anxiety characteristic of PTSD. Intervention strategies presented in the chapter are primarily a summary of extant cognitive-behavioral treatments for PTSD that are described in greater detail in other sources. We also describe a video-based program that has been implemented into a hospital emergency department setting and has preliminarily produced some encouraging results. Finally, we offer a section on additional factors that should be considered when planning and executing treatment with rape victims.

The Trauma of Sexual Assault. Edited by Jenny Petrak and Barbara Hedge.
© 2002 John Wiley & Sons Ltd.

A CONCEPTUAL FRAMEWORK FOR UNDERSTANDING PTSD

Existing cognitive-behavioral treatments available for rape victims evolved directly out of a behavioral tradition. We believe that it is imperative for clinicians to be well grounded in the classical conditioning and operant learning principles from which the treatments are derived. Approaching treatment from a coherent theoretical perspective allows the clinician to apply treatment strategies with more flexibility, and to effectively tailor the treatment plan to the individual. Moreover, the clinician can more effectively explain the treatment rationale to the client in a clear and convincing way.

CLASSICAL CONDITIONING

A classical conditioning model can explain the etiology of many posttrauma reactions, particularly anxiety or physiological arousal symptoms (Keane, Zimering, and Caddell, 1985; Kilpatrick, Veronen, and Resick, 1982; Foa, Steketee, and Rothbaum, 1989). Central to this model is the notion that stimuli that are associated with the sexual assault come to elicit a conditioned response that is similar to the unconditioned response experienced at the actual time of the trauma. At a concrete level, the experience of rape can be viewed as a classical conditioning situation in which aspects of the rape, such as actual or threat of injury, operate as unconditioned stimuli. During the rape, an unconditioned response is elicited, such as pain or intense feelings of fear and anxiety. At the time of the assault, there are certain previously neutral situations or elements of the rape situation that are paired with the sexual assault experience and become conditioned stimuli for the conditioned response of fear and avoidance; for example, specific physical characteristics of the perpetrator (e.g., a beard) or certain smells (e.g., alcohol on the perpetrator's breath) may become conditioned to elicit conditioned fear responses similar to the original unconditioned response. Through the process of stimulus generalization and second-order conditioning, stimuli associated with the original feared stimuli and the conditioned stimuli can also evoke a fear or anxiety reaction; that is, a victim may become anxious when interacting with any man with a beard, or may experience physiological arousal when her boyfriend is drinking alcohol even though this scenario had never bothered her in the past.

OPERANT CONDITIONING

Operant learning theory explains behavior by examining the environmental conditions under which the behavior occurs. Kilpatrick *et al.* (1982) also applied an operant analysis specifically to their understanding of symptomatology among rape victims. As the environmental conditions change, so does behavior. By environmental conditions, we mean both the antecedents and consequences of behavior. Antecedents are the environmental stimuli that precede behavior. Consequences (generally thought of as either reinforcing or punishing) are those stimuli that follow behavior and have a direct influence on the probability of its occurrence. 'Positive reinforcement' is used to describe the delivery of environmental stimuli that strengthen behavior and increase the likelihood of it occurring in the future. 'Negative reinforcement' also strengthens behavior but through the removal of an aversive stimulus. Escape and avoidance behaviors are examples of the principle of negative reinforcement. In order to escape intrusive thoughts about her sexual assault, a rape victim may have a beer or two or may avoid going to work. In this example, drinking alcohol or staying away from work are negatively reinforced in that these behaviors allow an individual to avoid the negative consequences (i.e., physiological arousal and intrusive thoughts). A careful analysis of the environmental conditions that maintain specific escape and avoidance behaviors is essential (Naugle and Follette, 1999) in order to tailor exposure-based strategies to the individual client.

Many of the treatment strategies we will discuss follow directly from these behavioral underpinnings; for example, exposure-based interventions involve having the client confront feared conditioned stimuli in the absence of the original unconditioned stimuli until the conditioned fear response dissipates (known as the process of extinction). This can be accomplished through a number of different techniques, including systematic desensitization, *in vivo* exposure, and imaginal exposure.

COGNITIVE PRINCIPLES

In contrast to learning and conditioning theories, cognitive theories of psychopathology assert that distressing emotional reactions result from one's interpretations of events that evoke psychological distress (e.g., Resick and Schnicke, 1993); for example, rape victims often engage in self-blaming statements following a sexual assault. A victim may tell herself such things as 'I shouldn't have flirted with him like that' or 'I shouldn't have been walking at night by myself.' Such self-blaming thoughts can evoke feelings of guilt. In addition, after a sexual assault, a rape victim may perceive that she or he has no control over interpersonal situations. Such perceptions may lead to feelings of fear which interfere with the victim's ability to engage in relationships effectively.

Cognitive restructuring focuses on targeting dysfunctional patterns of thinking that lead to exaggerated emotional responses. As clients become aware of these problematic ways of perceiving themselves and their environment, the dysfunctional thoughts are corrected and replaced with more effective ways of thinking. Cognitive restructuring is a component of many treatment packages for PTSD, including Stress Inoculation Training (SIT: Kilpatrick *et al.*, 1982) and Cognitive Processing Therapy (Resick and Schnicke, 1993).

Additional models for understanding the development of PTSD symptoms have been proposed. Most of these models are adaptations, explications, or combinations of the basic behavioral and cognitive principles outlined above. Detailed descriptions of these additional theoretical models are beyond the scope of this chapter. However, relevant aspects of the theories will be discussed in reference to specific treatment modalities when warranted.

COGNITIVE-BEHAVIORAL STRATEGIES FOR TREATING RAPE VICTIMS

Orienting the Client to Treatment

Prior to implementing any specific cognitive-behavioral techniques, the first session following assessment should be used to provide feedback to the client and to develop a treatment plan. In our work with sexual assault victims, we provide education regarding common responses to sexual assault, explain the theoretical foundations of stress reactions, and provide a framework for the cognitive-behavioral interventions to be used over the course of treatment (see Example 6.1).

Example 6.1

Sexual assault is a traumatic event that is often emotionally shocking. While each person may respond to trauma in her or his own unique way, many of the problems you have described to me are common or typical reactions that victims experience following a sexual assault. We call these responses post-traumatic stress reactions.

The most common reaction to sexual assault is fear. At the time of the sexual assault itself, many victims experience intense fear—fear of being physically injured and even fear of being killed. For many victims, the fear response occurs again, after the rape, when one is confronted with sights, sounds, smells, thoughts, places, situations, people, etc. that remind her or him of the sexual assault. Many victims repeatedly think about the sexual assault when they don't want to or have dreams about it. Sometimes, the thoughts and memories seem real, as if the sexual assault is occurring again. We call this a flashback.

Following a sexual assault, many victims also experience a number of problems that are the result of heightened physical arousal. These include sleep problems, having trouble concentrating, feeling restless and irritable, and being more jumpy or on edge than usual. This physical arousal can also be extremely distressing. One of the goals of treatment is to teach you ways of decreasing your level of physical arousal so that you are able to deal more effectively with the demands of daily living.

Finally, I want to mention a third set of reactions often described by people who have experienced a traumatic event. In an attempt to control the physical and mental aspects of fear, many victims go to great lengths to avoid persons, places, things, and situations that remind them of the assault. Some victims become so fearful they greatly restrict their activities and are even unable to leave their homes or be left alone. While avoiding these reminders may alleviate discomfort in the short term, it can interfere with daily functioning, as well as get in the way of resolving the sexual assault and dealing effectively with the experience. The treatment approach we use will address each of these problems. I will explain specific strategies in much more detail as we go along. Overall, the goal is for us to work together as a team to reduce the symptoms you are experiencing as efficiently as possible.

(modified from Kilpatrick et al., 1982)

The treatment rationale presented in Example 6.1 is an abbreviated version of what is covered in the initial session following assessment. During this session, it is important to use examples of the individual client's presenting problems and unique situation to illustrate the information outlined above. Basically, the goal of the initial session is to provide clients with information regarding acute stress reactions and PTSD, to normalize their experience, and to begin developing a rationale for the specific intervention strategies that will be utilized.

Strategies for Managing Physiological Arousal and Anxiety

We have found that teaching clients anxiety-management strategies is a useful first step in treatment. Indeed, many of our clients report that these strategies provide them with some immediate relief from their distress. The skills are relatively easy to learn and implement. The primary goal of anxiety-management exercises is to decrease the physiological arousal many rape victims experience following a sexual assault to less distressing levels. We are careful to explain to clients that the goal of these anxiety-management strategies is to help them *manage* the anxiety, not eliminate it. Anxiety is an unavoidable aspect of life. We are interested in providing clients with tools that allow them to manage the anxiety and function more effectively.

Anxiety-management skills are taught and rehearsed during therapy sessions. Clients are also instructed to practice the strategies on a daily basis in order to maximize effectiveness. We have found it useful to provide clients with a daily practice card for them to record rehearsal of exercises, as well as to monitor their level of subjective distress on a daily basis. An example of a practice card is provided in Figure 6.1.

Progressive Muscle Relaxation Skills

Several different approaches to muscle-relaxation training are offered in the literature on the treatment of anxiety. The relaxation skills described in this chapter are based on the Jacobsonian tension-relaxation contrast method (Jacobson, 1938). During the first session, clients are taught to relax all major muscle groups. Therapists should be prepared to demonstrate procedures for each muscle group for the client. In addition, an audiotape of the session should be made so that the client can practice the skills between sessions. It should be emphasized that learning relaxation skills, like learning any new skill, requires a great deal of practice. Clients should be encouraged to incorporate specific relaxation skills into a variety of their daily activities.

Foa and Rothbaum (1998) provide a detailed explanation of the relaxation procedure that they incorporate into their work with sexual assault victims. Clients are instructed to focus on each muscle group as the procedure progresses. The tension phase should last approximately 10 sec, followed by a 30-sec relaxation phase for each muscle group. During the relaxation phase, the clinician may want to make statements to encourage clients to relax such as 'Allow your muscles to completely relax' or 'Notice how different your muscles feel when they are relaxed'. Table 6.1 offers a list of the muscle groups on which the client is asked to focus.

ANXIETY MANAGEMENT SKILLS PRACTICE RECORD

	Type of skill used RT = Relaxation DB = Deep breathing GT = Guided imagery	Anxiety before practice (0–10)	Anxiety after practice (0–10)
Monday a.m.			
Monday p.m.			
Tuesday a.m.			
Tuesday p.m.			
Wednesday a.m.			
Wednesday p.m.			
Thursday a.m.			
Thursday p.m.			
Friday a.m.			
Friday p.m.			
Saturday a.m.			
Saturday p.m.			
Sunday a.m.			
Sunday p.m.			

Figure 6.1 Anxiety management skills weekly homework card.

Breathing Control Skills

Sexually assaulted individuals often experience symptoms of panic, including hyperventilation (Falsetti and Resnick, 1997). Strategies that emphasize slow, diaphragmatic breathing can be extremely beneficial to these individuals. The breathing retraining techniques developed by Barlow and Craske (1989) are particularly helpful in teaching sexual assault victims to change their breathing patterns. A primary goal of deep-breathing exercises is to teach clients how to slow down their breathing. The exercises first require that clients take in normal, smooth breaths through the nose and exhale slowly and smoothly through the mouth. At the same time, clients are encouraged to focus on their breathing. Through

Table 6.1   Muscle groups for relaxation training

Muscle group	Tension phase (hold for 10-sec)	Relaxation phase (hold for 30-sec)
Arms and hands		
Fists	Clench fists	Relax fists
Wrists	Bend wrists backward	Let hands relax
Biceps	Flex biceps	Relax biceps
Neck and shoulders		
Shoulders	Raise shoulders to ears	Drop shoulders
	Push shoulders back into chair	Relax shoulders and chest
Neck	Tilt head to left/right shoulder	Raise head
	Tuck chin toward chest	Raise head
Face and jaw		
Jaw	Clench jaw	Relax jaw
	Open mouth wide	Close mouth and relax
Face	Close eyes tightly	Relax eyes (but keep closed)
	Wrinkle forehead	Relax forehead
Stomach	Tighten stomach	Relax stomach
Buttocks	Tighten buttocks	Relax buttocks
Back	Arch back	Relax back
Legs and feet	Stretch out left/right leg and bend toes back	Relax legs and toes
	Stretch out left/right leg and point toes forward	Relax legs and toes
	Curl up toes inside shoe	Relax toes

this focus, clients can learn to slow down their breathing to a rate of about 10 breaths per minute. Again, clients are asked to practice this exercise between sessions.

Guided Imagery

Guided imagery is another technique that clients may find useful in managing anxiety and facilitating relaxation. Visualization exercises generally involve having the client imagine herself or himself in a pleasant, peaceful setting. The clinician then guides the client through this positive scene, while, simultaneously, having them focus on becoming increasingly relaxed. The visualization exercises use language that concentrates on the senses and reference to vivid details. Such guided imagery allows clients to become relaxed, instead of focusing on their anxious thoughts and feelings. Many of the muscle relaxation and breathing techniques described above can be incorporated into the guided imagery exercises.

Strategies for Managing Problematic Cognitions

Some evidence suggests that the ways sexual assault victims think about and appraise their assault experience are directly related to post-trauma symptomatology; for example, one conceptualization, information processing theory (Resick and Schnicke, 1993), outlines how sexual assault impacts how one thinks about and perceives the world. The concept of *schema* is used to describe how individuals encode, organize, and recall information. Schemata are believed to interact with and influence attention, interpretations, and retrieval of incoming information. When a person is sexually assaulted, this experience is often inconsistent with one's existing beliefs or schemata. Therefore, in order to make sense of the experience, sexual assault victims adapt in one of two ways. They alter or distort the experience into their existing beliefs (assimilation; e.g., blame themselves) or they shift their beliefs to incorporate the new experience (accommodation). Often, rape victims make extreme accommodations in their belief systems, which can significantly interfere with functioning. Victimization experiences are thought to affect five major areas or themes: safety, trust, power, esteem, and intimacy (McCann, Sakheim, and Abrahamson, 1988; Resick and Schnicke, 1993). The primary goal of cognitive techniques is to address these, as well as other, maladaptive patterns of thinking about and perceiving oneself and one's environment.

Cognitive Restructuring

Cognitive restructuring is designed to reduce psychological distress by teaching clients to identify and change dysfunctional thoughts and beliefs (Beck, Rush, Shaw, and Emery, 1979; Foa and Rothbaum, 1998). By teaching clients more realistic ways of thinking about themselves and the world, the goal is to enhance coping skills for dealing with the world in general and trauma-related situations in particular. Negative or dysfunctional thoughts following a sexual assault can become automatic for the client; that is, they may be perceived to 'come out of nowhere'. Treatment assists clients in identifying these automatic thoughts and understanding how they are associated with negative feelings. The goal is then to work with the client to differentiate between realistic and unrealistic ways of thinking about and perceiving the world. Cognitive restructuring involves generating and challenging hypotheses through questioning and drawing attention to inconsistencies between clients' thoughts and the available evidence.

During treatment, the therapist's job is to watch for examples of dysfunctional thinking. When dysfunctional thoughts or beliefs are identified, the task is to assist clients in challenging the problematic statements. Clients are encouraged to challenge maladaptive cognitions by asking themselves questions about the thought or belief. It is helpful to present an outline of these questions for clients to refer to between sessions. Again, clients benefit by incorporating cognitive restructuring techniques between therapy sessions. Homework exercises that require clients to monitor irrational thought patterns and challenge irrational beliefs provide useful information to address in subsequent treatment sessions (see Figure 6.2).

Guided Self-Dialogue

This coping skill involves teaching clients to attend to what they are saying to themselves and to replace irrational, negative self-talk with more reasonable, effective self-dialogue. Guided self-dialogue skills have been adapted for rape victims from Meichenbaum's (1985) stress inoculation training examples (Kilpatrick *et al.*, 1982; Veronen and Kilpatrick, 1983). The coping skill requires clients to generate specific self-statements and questions across four categories: (1) preparing for a stressful situation; (2) confronting and managing a stressful situation; (3) coping with overwhelming feelings; (4) reinforcing or encouraging self-statements. The statements are designed to address target fears unique to the individual client. Writing the self-statements on note cards allows clients to take them home and practice outside of treatment. Clients are encouraged to utilize these coping skills for managing everyday stressors or difficulties.

Strategies for Managing Ineffective Behavior

Role Play

Role playing is a broadly applicable technique for correcting ineffectual behaviors and practicing more adaptive behaviors. With respect to trauma-related behavioral deficits, the most common ineffective behavior is avoidance of anxiety-provoking situations, settings, and individuals. As stated previously, avoidance of trauma-related cues is remarkably prevalent because it yields a short-lived reduction in anxiety. Unfortunately,

MY THOUGHT RECORD

Thought or belief:

Situation in which thought/belief arose:

Strength of belief (1 to 10):

1	2		3	4	5		6	7	8		9	10

Not at all strong   Somewhat strong   Moderately strong   Extremely strong

What I am feeling:

Questions to ask yourself:

On a scale from 1 to 100, how realistic is the belief?

What are the facts?

    Facts that support the belief:

    Facts that counter the belief:

How is the information relevant?

What words indicate I am thinking in extremes?

Am I basing my actions on feelings or facts?

What aspects of the situation am I disregarding?

I could say this to myself instead:

And then I would feel:

Figure 6.2 Sample record for challenging thoughts and beliefs.

such avoidance serves to maintain disorders such as ASD and PTSD in the long run. The utility of role playing is that it provides an opportunity to rehearse potentially anxiety-provoking encounters with individuals, situations, or settings that are reminiscent of the original traumatic event, in an objectively safe environment. This form of behavioral rehearsal serves to reduce anxiety and to enhance the likelihood of successfully confronting previously avoided stimuli.

Foa and Rothbaum (1998) provide guidelines for appropriate use of role play in therapy. As a general rule, the therapist should model the appropriate behavior first. After the client rehearses the behavior in question (e.g., declining a sexual advance), it is important that the therapist reinforce positive aspects of the role play and praise him or her for engaging in appropriate behaviors in addition to citing areas in need of improvement. These authors also note that it is prudent to begin with more innocuous or benign scenarios before proceeding to more fear-eliciting scenarios such as situations related to the traumatic event. This allows for successful experiences using role play techniques, which may facilitate the use of role playing for more difficult scenarios.

Goldfried and Davison (1994) note that some clients are initially resistant to the idea of role playing, believing it to be too contrived or awkward. As they correctly point out, it is necessary to communicate to such clients that any new behavior initially seems awkward. The advantage of rehearsing the behavior (e.g., assertiveness) with the therapist is that initial, awkward attempts occur in a setting in which mistakes are inconsequential. With practice, the new behavior becomes more natural and the client can engage in that behavior more adeptly in real life situations.

Covert Modeling

A variant of role playing is covert modeling. In essence, this technique represents imaginal role playing; that is, instead of actually acting out a scenario with a therapist, the client visualizes himself or herself successfully confronting a fear-provoking situation (Calhoun and Resick, 1993). This technique may be used as an adjunct to role play. A client may rehearse a scenario in session with the therapist, and may then employ covert modeling between sessions to enhance performance.

Although covert modeling can be a valuable therapeutic technique, some words of caution are warranted. Specifically, it is essential that the therapist determine whether the client is, in fact, visualizing behavior that is adaptive and effective. If the client does not know what constitutes appropriate or effective behavior in a given situation, covert modeling will be fruitless. It is worthwhile to have the client vividly describe, in session, the scenario and his or her behavior (Foa and Rothbaum, 1998). In this manner, the therapist can determine whether skills training or behavioral rehearsal is warranted. Finally, because avoidance of anxiety-provoking, trauma-related cues is a hallmark of PTSD and ASD, the therapist must recognize that covert rehearsals of anxiety-provoking situations may be tempting for clients to avoid. Accordingly, the therapist should discuss this possibility with clients, and should provide a compelling explanation of the merits of this technique in treating ASD or PTSD.

EXPOSURE-BASED INTERVENTIONS

Exposure-based treatments for ASD and PTSD follow logically from etiological models that are informed by learning theory. To review, a traumatic event such as a sexual assault results in an unconditioned response of intense fear, helplessness, or horror. Previously neutral stimuli that are present at the time of the traumatic event (e.g., the smell of alcohol) are paired with these feelings of intense fear or anxiety, such that they are subsequently capable of eliciting similar feelings of fear or anxiety long after the actual traumatic event. Repeated exposure to these stimuli in the absence of actual threat or harm will eventually result in a reduction of anxiety, as conditioned fear to these stimuli gradually extinguishes. Unfortunately, because trauma victims often go to great lengths to avoid cues or reminders of their traumas, such extinction or fear habituation does not occur, resulting in chronic psychopathology. The purpose of exposure-based therapies, then, is to allow the trauma victim to encounter anxiety-eliciting trauma cues for a longer duration such that fear associated with these cues may extinguish.

Individuals suffering from ASD and PTSD experience fear when faced not only by external trauma cues, but also by the memory of the traumatic event (Rothbaum and Foa, 1992). Because of this, such individuals typically avoid thinking about or recalling the traumatic event. Accordingly, exposure-based techniques involve confronting external stimuli and situations reminiscent of the traumatic event (i.e., *in vivo* exposure), as well as memories of the trauma (i.e., imaginal exposure). *In vivo* exposure involves purposely confronting typically avoided situations or trauma cues. For victims of rape and sexual assault, this may include reading newspaper articles or watching television programs related to sexual assault or engaging in intimate behaviors with significant others (Foa and Rothbaum, 1998). As with role playing techniques, it may be prudent to begin with relatively less distressing stimuli or activities. Only situations that are objectively safe should be used for the purposes of *in vivo* exposure. When exposed to fear-eliciting stimuli, clients must continue exposure until significant anxiety reduction (i.e., habituation) has occurred. To terminate an exposure session while the client is still significantly distressed is counter-therapeutic in that it reinforces pathological avoidance and may increase anxiety related to the trauma cue in question. When using *in vivo* exposure, clients rate their anxiety from 1–100 when initially exposed to the trauma cue. It is generally recommended that the exposure session continue until the client's anxiety has fallen to no more than 50% of the initial rating (Foa and Rothbaum, 1998). These sessions should be repeated frequently until initial exposure to the feared stimulus does not produce substantive fear or anxiety.

Imaginal exposure requires that the client vividly imagine the traumatic event to allow the severe anxiety surrounding the traumatic memory to dissipate. The purpose of imaginal exposure is not to render the traumatic memory neutral. Even after successful therapy, the memory will invariably continue to be unpleasant. Following successful exposure therapy, however, the traumatic memory does not result in severe or incapacitating fear and anxiety.

During the initial, imaginal exposure session, the level of detail that the client provides is not important. It is more important that the client experience a successful exposure session as evidenced by a reduction in anxiety when thinking about the traumatic event. During subsequent exposure sessions, the client should be encouraged to describe the event in as much detail as possible—including thoughts or fears he or she may have been experiencing at the time, physiological reactions (e.g., accelerated heartbeat), and so forth. As with *in vivo* exposure, the client is asked to repeat the scenario until there is a significant reduction in anxiety relative to initial ratings. This typically takes 45–60 min (Rothbaum, Foa, Riggs, Murdock, and Walsh, 1992). However, it bears repeating that anxiety reduction, as opposed to elapsed time, dictates the length of an exposure session.

Although the number of sessions required for successful exposure therapy varies by client, the treatment developed by Foa and Rothbaum (1998) consists of nine 90-min sessions, the first two of which are devoted to information gathering and providing a rationale for exposure therapy to clients. Because of the lengths that trauma victims will go to in order to avoid thinking about or being exposed to reminders of their traumatic events, the importance of providing a compelling rationale for exposure therapy cannot be emphasized enough. More detailed descriptions of exposure-based therapies for treating ASD and PTSD are available (e.g., Foa and Rothbaum, 1998); however, these procedures should not be attempted in the absence of intensive training and supervision by clinicians well versed in exposure-based techniques.

Falsetti and Resnick (2000) also have obtained preliminary support for the efficacy of an intervention that includes interoceptive exposure strategies as well as strategies to provide exposure to cognitions and memories of assault and behaviors that have been avoided following assault or other crime. Some components of the treatment addressing cognitions and trauma-related memory exposure were adapted from Resick and Schnicke (1993), including the strategy of writing about the traumatic event. This treatment was designed for those exposed to traumatic events who have developed PTSD and co-morbid panic attacks. The interoceptive exposure phase of treatment was adapted from Barlow and Craske's (1989) treatment for panic disorder and involves having clients practice a set of exercises, such as hyperventilation, that will evoke physical sensations similar to those they experience during a panic attack or when exposed to trauma-related cues. Once clients have mastered interoceptive exposure to relevant physiological cues, they proceed to cognitive and behavioral exposure elements of treatment (Falsetti and Resnick, 2000).

Despite the fact that exposure-based therapy techniques have repeatedly been shown to effectively treat symptoms of PTSD and ASD, and have also been shown to result in greater treatment gains than other commonly used interventions for these disorders, these techniques tend to be under-utilized by practitioners (Foy et al., 1996). Frequently cited reasons for not using exposure-based techniques, such as concerns that clients will be inordinately distressed or may have crisis reactions such as suicidal ideation, appear to be based more on myth than fact. Empirical evaluations of these reactions have not substantiated such concerns (Foy et al., 1996).

ACCEPTANCE-BASED INTERVENTIONS

Among behaviorally oriented clinicians, a great deal of attention has recently been given to acceptance-based approaches for treating problems of emotional or experiential avoidance (Hayes, Strosahl, and Wilson, 1999). Experiential avoidance can be understood as an unwillingness to experience unpleasant psychological events, including thoughts, memories, feelings, and physiological states. Certainly, this concept characterizes the experiences that lead sexual assault victims to seek treatment.

An acceptance-based approach to working with rape victims is offered as a contrasting alternative to the 'control' strategies described above. Acceptance involves abandoning the agenda of change that is characteristic of the aforementioned techniques. It requires the client (and the therapist) to be open to one's emotional and cognitive experiences.

Hayes *et al.* (1999) have developed a treatment called Acceptance and Commitment Therapy (ACT) that is based on principles of experiential avoidance and acceptance strategies. ACT is a collection of exercises, metaphors, and other techniques, many borrowed from non-behavioral traditions, which are implemented from a coherent theory or philosophy of the human condition. In this treatment approach, psychological distress *per se* is not viewed as the primary problem. Rather, it is the individual's avoidance of emotions and other private events that are addressed in treatment (Follette, 1992; Hayes, 1987; Hayes *et al.*, 1999; Walser and Hayes, 1999). The techniques are used to promote acceptance of 'normal' psychological processes, in contrast to viewing the psychological processes (e.g., thoughts, feelings, memories) as pathological. Versions of the treatment approach have been applied to clients with a history of trauma (Follette, 1992). The therapy centers on facilitating clients' acceptance of their histories, emotions, and thoughts while continuing to engage in behavioral change.

Treatment Termination

Ending treatment with sexual assault victims can raise some unique and important considerations. Prior to terminating treatment, it is important to assess clients' perceptions of their progress and evaluate the need for additional sessions. It is appropriate to conduct additional sessions if the client may profit from them. One strategy is to conduct 'booster' sessions across a longer period of time. By spacing out additional sessions, clients are given an opportunity to practise specific skills, evaluate their effectiveness, and identify ongoing problem areas.

In general, termination sessions should focus on highlighting the client's progress in treatment and reviewing the specific techniques covered in treatment (Foa and Rothbaum, 1998). Identifying skills that require particular reinforcement can assist the therapist in deciding how to allocate time to reviewing these specific skills. Termination sessions can also provide an opportunity to solicit feedback from clients about the relative usefulness of the treatment components. Helping clients anticipate future stressors or difficulties, as well as generating strategies for managing them, can be a fruitful strategy for promoting success. Arrangements for follow-up should also be discussed with clients prior to ending treatment. Clients should be encouraged to contact the therapist and utilize additional sessions in the event further services are warranted.

EARLY INTERVENTION

Effectiveness of Early Interventions with Victims of Rape

While early intervention programs are generally presumed to be effective, research evaluating the efficacy of early intervention programs for sexual assault victims actually has yielded mixed results; for example, a brief behavioral intervention program implemented at 3 weeks post-rape did not reveal differences between women receiving the treatment and a no-treatment comparison group at the 3-month follow-up (Kilpatrick and Veronen, 1984). Similarly, Foa and colleagues (1995) compared a brief prevention program with a matched control group with victims of rape or physical assault who were less than 1 month post-assault. While lower rates of PTSD were found among the treatment group versus the comparison group at 2 months post-assault, the groups did not differ in terms of PTSD diagnosis at the assessment almost 6 months post-assault (Foa, Hearst-Ikeda, and Perry, 1995). These studies indicate that the strategies described earlier, that address coping in physiological, cognitive, and behavioral channels and that include exposure to realistically non-dangerous cues, can be implemented with acute assault survivors. More research needs to be conducted to further evaluate the efficacy of such early intervention strategies, controlling for intensity of initial post-assault distress or ASD diagnosis. This strategy was used by Bryant, Harvey, Baston, Dang, and Sackville (1998) who found that a five-session CBT treatment implemented within 2 weeks post-trauma was effective in reducing subsequent rates of PTSD among automobile accident victims, all of whom met criteria for ASD.

Video-based Intervention in Emergency Department Setting

Resnick, Acierno, Holmes, Kilpatrick, and Jager (1999) are currently conducting a study evaluating an early intervention program for sexual assault victims within an emergency department medical setting. The program is multidisciplinary and is integrated within a setting that provides forensic medical care to sexual assault victims within 72 hours post-rape. The program is co-ordinated with services provided by the local rape crisis center and Sexual Assault Nurse and Physician Examiner team. Due to the many rape-related cues that are present during a forensic medical exam, the exam procedures may exacerbate distress. Therefore, one component of the video-based intervention is designed to reduce anxiety in the medical setting that may have a mediating impact on the development of longer term mental health problems. The brief cognitive-behavioral intervention offered prior to the medical examination is delivered in a video format. Therefore, the content of the intervention is highly standardized and implemented relatively easily. The video is approximately 20 min in length and includes psychoeducation, modeling, and other cognitive-behavioral strategies, including instructions in exposure techniques to realistic, safe, rape-related cues.

To demonstrate the efficacy of this brief intervention program, eligible rape victims who present at the emergency medical setting within 72 hours post-assault are randomly assigned to either the video-intervention or to standard medical treatment and rape crisis advocacy support as usual. A subjective measure of anxiety is administered both pre- and post-emergency medical exam. In addition, an extensive assessment of psychological symptoms, victimization history, substance use, and other mental health factors is conducted at 6 weeks and again at 6 months post-rape.

Preliminary data indicated that psychological distress at the time of the medical exam was strongly related to the presence of PTSD symptoms and other symptomatology at the 6-week follow-up. In addition, the data suggested that, after controlling for pre-exam distress, women in the video condition were less distressed following the medical examination than women in the control condition (Resnick et al., 1999). These preliminary data indicate that an intervention that is delivered as early as possible post-rape (within 72 hours) may be effective in reducing longer term negative mental health outcomes. This study also employed the strategy of controlling for initial distress within hours post-rape when evaluating the effect of this early intervention.

ADDITIONAL CONSIDERATIONS WHEN TREATING RAPE VICTIMS

PTSD and Substance Abuse

The relationship between substance abuse and PTSD among sexual assault victims has been well documented (Kessler, Sonnega, Bromet, Hughes, and Nelson, 1995; Kilpatrick, Acierno, Resnick, Saunders, and Best, 1997). Not only is a diagnosis of PTSD associated with increased risk for substance abuse, but individuals with substance abuse problems are also at increased risk for sexual victimization (Kilpatrick et al., 1997; Polusny and Follette, 1995). Given this strong relationship between PTSD and substance abuse, it is essential that clinicians assess for substance use and appropriately intervene when working with individuals who have been sexually assaulted. Sexual assault victims may use alcohol or other drugs as a way to cope with overwhelming psychological distress. When substance use is used as a strategy to avoid negative affect associated with reminders of the sexual assault, such behavior interferes with the goals of a cognitive-behavioral approach to treatment. Therefore, treatment effectiveness is maximized when clients maintain a period of abstinence for a stable period of time prior to doing trauma-specific therapy. In cases where substance abuse has been a long-standing problem, a referral for intensive, specialized substance abuse treatment may be required. The important issue is that substance abuse issues are addressed when providing treatment for PTSD and other trauma-related problems (Ruzek, Polusny, and Abueg, 1998).

RISK FOR REVICTIMIZATION

Women with a prior history of sexual victimization are at significantly greater risk for being revictimized than women without such a history. In one study investigating risk factors for sexual assault, Koss and Dinero (1989) found that 66% of the women who reported rape or attempted rape also had a prior history of sexual victimization. In the Koss and Dinero study, only the variables indicating past traumatic experiences improved predictions over base rates for identifying rape victims. Greene and Navarro (1998) reported similar findings. In a prospective study investigating protective and risk factors for sexual assault, prior victimization was the strongest predictor of future incidents of sexual victimization.

Revictimization is also associated with a number of psychological consequences. Revictimized women had higher levels of trauma-related symptoms than women who reported only one type of victimization experience (Gold, Milan, Mayall, and Johnson, 1994). Moreover, Follette, Polusny, Bechtle, and Naugle (1996) offer evidence for the cumulative impact of multiple victimization experiences. Women who had experienced multiple types of victimization experiences reported increasing levels of post-trauma symptoms. Additionally, according to Cloitre, Scarvalone, and Difede (1997), revictimized subjects are more likely to attempt suicide and experience problems in areas such as intimacy and trust than either women who had never been sexually victimized or sexually assaulted women without a prior victimization history.

These data support the strong need for treatment components that specifically address risk factors for revictimization and introduce skills to minimize risk. It has been hypothesized that one factor that places individuals at risk for revictimization is an inability to recognize and respond to environmental cues that suggest risk or danger (Naugle, 1999; Wilson, Calhoun, and Bernat, 1999). Sexual assault victims may benefit from education regarding high-risk situations, as well as from building skills for confronting risky situations when they occur. Cloitre (1998) has proposed one treatment model for revictimized women that combines prolonged exposure techniques with additional affect regulation and interpersonal skills. Such skills training focuses on enhancing emotional awareness, including teaching clients to identify and label feelings and providing skills to assist them in modulating negative emotions and tolerating distress associated with situations that call for protective behavior. In addition, the skills training focuses on strengthening interpersonal skills, including assertive behavior and conflict-resolution skills.

CONCLUSION

The high rates of trauma-related symptomatology among rape victims suggest the need for effective treatment strategies to reduce psychological distress and to promote successful functioning. The cognitive-behavioral strategies outlined in this chapter have been demonstrated to be successful at strengthening the coping skills of rape victims and subsequently alleviating PTSD and acute stress symptoms. Many of the treatment components we have described have been incorporated in comprehensive treatment packages for rape victims. In cases where these strategies are not included in the treatment package, it has been our experience that the addition of these coping skills enhances the effectiveness of other treatment strategies. Therefore, the cognitive-behavioral interventions described above offer a number of advantages to the clinician and to the clients they serve.

REFERENCES

Barlow, D.H. and Craske, M.G. (1989) *Master of your anxiety and panic*. Albany, NY: Graywind.

Beck, A.T., Rush, A.J., Shaw, B.F., and Emery, G. (1979) *Cognitive therapy of depression*. New York: Guilford Press.

Bryant, R.A., Harvey, A.G., Basten, C., Dang, S.T., and Sackville, T. (1998) Treatment of acute stress disorder: A comparison of cognitive-behavioral therapy and supportive counseling. *Journal of Consulting and Clinical Psychology*, 66, 862–866.

Calhoun, K.S. and Resick, P.A. (1993) Post-traumatic stress disorder. In D. Barlow (ed.) *Clinical handbook of psychological disorders* (2nd edn) New York: Guilford Press.

Cloitre, M. (1998) Sexual revictimization: Risk factors and prevention. In V.M. Follette, J.I. Ruzek, and F.R. Abueg (eds) *Cognitive-behavioral therapies for trauma* (pp. 278–304). New York: Guilford Press.

Cloitre, M., Scarvalone, P., and Difede, J. (1997) Post-traumatic stress disorder, self, and interpersonal dysfunction among sexually revictimized women. *Journal of Traumatic Stress*, **10**, 435–450.

Falsetti, S.A. and Resnick, H.S. (1997) Frequency and severity of panic attack symptoms in a treatment seeking sample of trauma victims. *Journal of Traumatic Stress*, **10**, 683–689.

Falsetti, S.A. and Resnick, H.S. (2000) Treatment of PTSD using cognitive and cognitive behavioral therapies. *Journal of Cognitive Psychotherapy: An International Quarterly*, **14**, 97–122.

Foa, E.B. and Rothbaum, B.O. (1998) *Treating the trauma of rape: Cognitive-behavioral therapy for PTSD*. New York: Guilford Press.

Foa, E.B., Hearst-Ikeda, D., and Perry, K.J. (1995) Evaluation of a brief cognitive-behavioral program for the prevention of PTSD in recent sexual assault victims. *Journal of Consulting and Clinical Psychology*, **63**, 948–955.

Foa, E.B., Steketee, G., and Rothbaum, B.O. (1989) Behavioral/cognitive conceptualization of post-traumatic stress disorder. *Behavior Therapy*, **20**, 155–176.

Follette, V. M. (1992) Survivors of child sexual abuse: Treatment using a contextual analysis. In S.C. Hayes, N.S. Jacobson, V.M. Follette, and M.J. Dougher (eds) *Acceptance and change: Content and context in psychotherapy* (pp. 255–268). Reno, NV: Context Press.

Follette, V.M., Polusny, M.A., Bechtle, A.E., and Naugle, A.E. (1996) Cumulative trauma: The impact of child sexual abuse, adult sexual assault, and spouse abuse. *Journal of Traumatic Stress*, **9**, 25–35.

Foy, D.W., Kagan, B., McDermott, C., Leskin, G., Sipprelle, R., and Paz, G. (1996) Practical parameters in the use of flooding for treating chronic PTSD. *Clinical Psychology and Psychotherapy*, **3**, 169–175.

Gold, S.R., Milan, L.D., Mayall, A., and Johnson, A.E. (1994) A cross-validation study of the Trauma Symptom Checklist: The role of mediating variables. *Journal of Interpersonal Violence*, **9**, 12–26.

Goldfried, M.R. and Davison, G.C. (1994) *Clinical Behavior Therapy*. New York: John Wiley and Sons.

Greene, D.M. and Navarro, R.L. (1998) Situation-specific assertiveness in the epidemiology of sexual victimization among university women. *Psychology of Women Quarterly*, **22**, 589–604.

Hayes, S.C. (1987) A contextual approach to therapeutic change. In N.S. Jacobson (ed.) *Psychotherapists in clinical practice: Cognitive and behavioral perspectives* (pp. 327–387). New York: Guilford Press.

Hayes, S.C., Strosahl, K.D., and Wilson, K.G. (1999) *Acceptance and commitment therapy: An experiential approach to behavior change*. New York: Guilford Press.

Jacobson, E. (1938) *Progressive relaxation*. Chicago: University of Chicago Press.

Keane, T.M., Zimering, R.T., and Caddell, J.M. (1985). A behavioral formulation of posttraumatic stress disorder. *The Behavior Therapist*, **8**, 9–12.

Kessler, R.C., Sonnega, A., Bromet, E., Hughes, M., and Nelson, C.B. (1995) Posttraumatic stress disorder in the National Comorbidity Survey. *Archives of General Psychiatry*, **52**, 1048–1060.

Kilpatrick, D.G. and Veronen, L.J. (1984) Treatment for rape-related problems: Crisis intervention is not enough. In L. Cohen, W. Claiborn, and G. Specter (eds) *Crisis intervention (2nd edn): Community-clinical psychology series*. New York: Human Services Press.

Kilpatrick., D.G, Acierno, R., Resnick, H.S., Saunders, B.E., and Best, C.L. (1997) A 2-year longitudinal analysis of the relationships between violent assault and substance use in women. *Journal of Consulting and Clinical Psychology*, **65**, 834–847.

Kilpatrick, D.G., Veronen, L.J., and Resick, P.A. (1982) Psychological sequelae to rape: Assessment and treatment strategies. In D.M. Doleys, R.L. Meredith, and A.R. Ciminero (eds) *Behavioral medicine and treatment strategies* (pp. 473–497). New York: Plenum Press.

Koss, M.P. and Dinero, T. E. (1989) Discriminant analysis of risk factors for sexual victimization among a national sample of college women. *Journal of Consulting and Clinical Psychology*, **57**, 242–250.

McCann, I.L., Sakheim, D.K., and Abrahamson, D.J. (1988) Trauma and victimization: A model of psychological adaptation. *The Counseling Psychologist*, **16**, 531–594.

Meichenbaum, D.H. (1985) *Stress inoculation training*. New York: Pergamon Press.

Naugle, A.E. (1999) Identifying behavioral risk factors for repeated victimization using video-taped stimulus materials. Unpublished doctoral dissertation, University of Nevada, Reno.

Naugle, A.E. and Follette, W.C. (1999) A functional analysis of trauma symptoms. In V.M. Follette, J.I. Ruzek, and F.R. Abueg (eds) *Cognitive-behavioral therapies for trauma* (pp. 48–73). New York: Guilford Press.

Polusny, M.A. and Follette, V. M. (1995) Long-term correlates of child sexual abuse: Theory and review of the empirical literature. *Applied and Preventive Psychology*, **4**, 143–166.

Resick, P.A. and Schnicke, M.K. (1993) *Cognitive processing therapy for rape victims: A treatment manual*. Newbury Park, CA: Sage Publications.

Resnick, H., Acierno, R., Holmes, M., Kilpatrick, D.G., and Jager, N. (1999) Prevention of post rape symptomatology: Preliminary findings of a controlled acute rape treatment study. *Journal of Anxiety Disorders*, **13**, 359–370.

Rothbaum, B.O. and Foa, E.B. (1992) Exposure therapy for rape victims with Post-Traumatic Stress Disorder. *The Behavior Therapist*, 219–222.

Rothbaum, B.O., Foa, E.B., Riggs, D., Murdock, T., and Walsh, W. (1992) A prospective examination of post-traumatic stress disorder in rape victims. *Journal of Traumatic Stress*, **5**, 455–475.

Ruzek, J.I., Polusny, M.A., and Abueg, F.R. (1998) Assessment and treatment of concurrent posttraumatic stress disorder and substance abuse. In V.M. Follette, J.I. Ruzek, and F.R. Abueg (eds) *Cognitive-behavioral therapies for trauma* (pp. 226–255). New York: Guilford Press.

Veronen, L.J. and Kilpatrick, D.G. (1983) Stress management for rape victims. In D. Meichenbaum and M.E. Jaremko (eds) *Stress reduction and prevention* (pp. 341–374). New York: Plenum Press.

Walser, R.D. and Hayes, S.C. (1999) Acceptance and trauma survivors: Applied issues and problems. In V.M. Follette, J.I. Ruzek, and F.R. Abueg (eds) *Cognitive-behavioral therapies for trauma* (pp. 256–277). New York: Guilford Press.

Wilson, A.E., Calhoun, K.S., and Bernat, J.A. (1999) Risk recognition and trauma-related symptoms among sexually revictimized women. *Journal of Consulting and Clinical Psychology*, **67**, 705–710.

Chapter 7

COGNITIVE-BEHAVIOURAL THERAPY FOR MOOD AND BEHAVIOURAL PROBLEMS

Helen Kennerley

As you will see, cognitive-behavioural therapy (CBT) is effective with a range of psychological problems and is, thus, a very reasonable therapy option for many survivors of sexual trauma. However, when working with this client group, the therapist is often applying the principles and practice of CBT in the face of chronic difficulties, interpersonal stresses, and the therapist's own strong reactions to a client's history and/or behaviour. So, the therapist needs to think not only about the clinical utility of CBT, but how best to implement treatment so that it is sensitive to both client and therapist needs and issues.

Of course, not all victims of sexual assault will develop significant problems. However, many do seek professional help and therapists working with such clients will be well aware that they can present with widely varying difficulties including, anxiety disorders, impulsive behaviours, depression, and personality disorders.

With this in mind, this chapter will first review CBT and its clinical applications, then consider what mood and behaviour problems face survivors of sexual assault and how CBT can be adapted to meet their needs. Finally, I will touch on the field of schema-focused cognitive therapy, indicating how, and when, it might be a helpful development in therapy. Of course, within a single chapter, one can only scratch the surface of the field of CBT and hope to whet the appetite for further reading.

The Trauma of Sexual Assault. Edited by Jenny Petrak and Barbara Hedge.
© 2002 John Wiley & Sons Ltd.

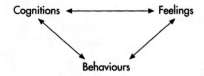

Figure 7.1   The interaction of cognitions, feelings, and behaviours.

COGNITIVE-BEHAVIOURAL THERAPY (CBT) AND ITS CLINICAL APPLICATIONS

CBT was developed by A.T. Beck throughout the 1960s and 1970s, and is one of several cognitive therapies that emerged to fill a niche left by the behavioural and the psychodynamic therapies. Any cognitive therapy recognizes the reciprocal role of cognitions (mental representations in the form of thoughts or images) and affect: the way we think colours the way we feel, which affects the way we think. Of course, our cognitions and feelings also influence our behaviour and vice versa (see Figure 7.1).

If our cognitions or interpretations are accurate, we feel (and react) appropriately; if our interpretations are skewed or distorted, we feel (and behave) in ways that do not reflect reality and which can cause difficulties; for example, if a woman is waiting for a friend who does not turn up, she might think: 'She doesn't care about me. No one really bothers about my feelings.' She might then feel miserable and hopeless and decide to leave the cafe without giving her friend a chance to explain: thus jeopardizing her friendship and deepening her sense of misery. If, on the other hand, she thinks: 'Something awful has happened: an accident!', she will feel anxious and show agitation. The more agitated she gets, the more catastrophic her thinking. However, if it crosses her mind that the friend might be held up in traffic or has lost her way, the woman is likely to remain calm and avoid getting caught up in unhelpful cycles of misery or anxiety.

Cognitive therapy focuses on reappraising those interpretations that give rise to mood and/or behavioural difficulties. Beckian cognitive therapy both emphasizes the understanding and examination of the cognitive element of the problem and utilizes the powerful role of behaviour in maintaining and changing the way that we think and feel: hence the term *cognitive-behavioural* therapy.

The basic psychological model which guides CBT is shown in Figure 7.2. In his early description of the emotional problems, Beck (1976) recognized that biology and external environment impact on our well-being, and he accepted that readily accessible cognitions and observable behaviours were underpinned by fundamental belief systems or schemata which

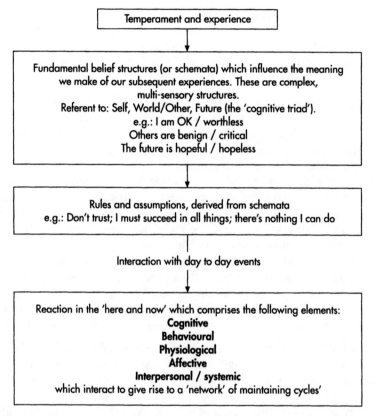

Figure 7.2 The psychological model underpinning CBT.

were shaped by both personal experience and temperament. However, 'classic' CBT was evolved to maximize the fact that much radical change (impacting on deeper structures) can be effected through active work at the level of current cognitions and behaviours: work in the 'here and now'.

CBT first helps the client identify the cognitions which drive problem behaviours and/or emotional states, and then guides that person in re-evaluating the relevant cognitions. Insights that are evolved in this way are then 'tested', in that the client is encouraged to check out the veracity of the new perspective or belief. This 'testing' typically, though not necessarily, involves behavioural work; for example, a man who feared dogs might develop the insight that his fears derive from a traumatic childhood experience with a fierce Labrador and that the majority of dogs are, in fact, benign. He would then be encouraged to consider ways in which he could assess the validity of this new conclusion. He has several options:

for instance, he might canvass friends to collect their views on the danger-ousness of dogs, he might study books on pets and discover more about the nature of dogs that way, he might begin to approach small, placid dogs and note what happens, or he might find the courage to face a large dog in order to test his new view.

Clearly, it is necessary to identify the cognitions crucial to a client's difficulties, and there are two standard methods in CBT: 'Socratic question-ing' and 'Daily thought records'. In sessions, insights are developed using 'Socratic questioning' or 'Guided discovery', a form of systematic, but em-pathic, exploratory questioning, initiated by the therapist with a view to 'training' the client in the skill of analysing problem reactions and synthe-sizing new responses. Socratic questioning is not leading or suggestive but, rather, aims to help the client uncover knowledge that they have overlooked. Between sessions, the client is encouraged to self-monitor key cognitions, moods and behaviours in the form of daily thought records, which actually tap into more than just thoughts. Clients are urged to keep organized notes of thoughts, images, emotions, behaviours which can shed light on their current problems. They are helped in iden-tifying unhelpful patterns of behaviour and the assumptions and deeper meanings which underlie the more readily accessible cognitions.

By now, it is probably evident that the aim of CBT is to help the client learn methods of self-management. So, in addition to the techniques they learn to better understanding problems, they are also guided in methods of appraising automatic thoughts and images, identifying cognitive dis-tortions and substituting statements (or images) that carry greater validity and which do not promote the problem affect and/or behaviours. As mentioned earlier, clients are also encouraged to use structured data collection and behavioural tests to evaluate all new perspectives. In summary, there is an emphasis on clients 'discovering' insights and solu-tions for themselves and on insights being tested.

Although clearly structured, CBT has always been more than a protocol-driven therapy that can be applied to particular psychological problems: Beck et al. (1979) emphasizes the importance of developing and using the therapeutic relationship (ibid.: 27) and tailoring the therapy to meet the needs of the individual (ibid.: 45). He also warns the therapist against being overly didactic or interpretative and, instead, encourages genuine 'collaborative empiricism' (ibid.: 6). This last point was summarized by Padesky (1993) when she urged therapists towards 'guiding discovery' rather than 'changing minds'.

With regard to the usefulness of CBT, it has been widely evaluated in clinical trials and is clearly an effective treatment approach for a range of DSM-IV (APA, 1994) axis I disorders, including: depression and anxiety disorders (Chambless and Gillis, 1993; Hollon, Shelton, and Davis, 1993), particularly panic disorder (Clark *et al.*, 1994), flashback management in PTSD (Marks, Lovell, Noshirvani, Livanou, and Thrasher, 1998), and eating disorders (Fairburn, 1981). There are also established treatment approaches for substance misuse (Beck, Wright, Newman, and Liese, 1993) and relationship problems (Safran and Segal, 1990), for example. In addition, there are indications that CBT is helpful in both managing axis I disorders suffered by those with concurrent axis II problems (for a review see Dreessen and Arntz, 1998) and in modifying the axis II presentation itself (Shea, 1993). However, given the paucity of clinical trials of CBT with axis II difficulties, conclusions should be viewed with some caution.

Although CBT is a widely used and useful psychological therapy, it should be remembered that it is not a panacea and the approach will not benefit everyone. It is crucial, at assessment, that the therapist be sensitive to the needs and characteristics of the client as there are bound to be those who will benefit more from another approach such as, counselling, drug treatment, social intervention, and so on.

In deciding whether or not CBT will be relevant to those who have survived sexual assault, we need to consider just what mood and behavioural problems face survivors; in particular, what cognitive-related difficulties might underpin their problems.

SURVIVORS OF SEXUAL ASSAULT: WHAT PROBLEMS DO THEY FACE?

Broadly speaking, there are three groups of survivors: those who experience childhood sexual assault (repeated or single) without further trauma; those who experience both childhood and adulthood sexual assault; those who experience a single sexual assault as an adult in the absence of significant previous trauma (physical, sexual, or emotional). The acute stress and PTSD commonly experienced by adult survivors is addressed in Chapter 6 by Amy Naugle, Heidi Resrick, Matt Gray and Ron Acierno, but there are other, widely recognized sequelae of assault which survivors of sexual trauma have to deal with.

Survivors of Childhood Sexual Assault

The long-term consequences of childhood sexual assault (CSA) vary because the outcome is very much influenced by the child's perception of the abuse, the family, or system dynamics and its reaction when abuse was disclosed. However, for some time, it has been accepted that there is a common set of sequelae: the terms 'CSA accommodation syndrome' (Summit, 1983) and 'Post-sexual abuse trauma' (Briere, 1984) have been used to describe problems which, typically, manifest post-abuse. These include conduct disorders, depression, anger management problems, dissociation, somatization and anxiety disorders, substance misuse, promiscuity, suicidal ideas, sexual dysfunction, and victimization of others.

Extensive exploration in the 1980s and 1990s indicates that there is, indeed, an association between childhood sexual assault and a wide range of problems in adulthood; for example: depression (Cheasty, Clare, and Colins, 1998), suicidal behaviours (Briere and Zaidi, 1989), PTSD (Rodriguez, Ryan, van der Kemp, and Foy, 1997), eating disorders (Everill and Waller, 1995), interpersonal difficulties (Herman and Hirschman, 1981), self-harm (Briere and Zaidi, 1989, Romans, Martin, Anderson, Herbison, and Mullen, 1995). In addition to mood and behavioural problems, physical associations have been found to exist between childhood abuse and somatization and hypochondriasis (Salmon and Caulderbank, 1995), genitourinary problems (Leserman et al., 1997), dyspareunia (Jehu, 1989a), and body shame (Andrews, 1995).

Over time, it has become clear that childhood sexual assault is not so much linked with specific axis I problems, but that the experience increases an individual's risk of developing psychological problems in general (Mullen, Martin, Anderson, Romans, and Herbison, 1993) and that the degree of adult psychopathology increases as the 'severity' of the abusive experience increases (Pribor and Dinwiddie, 1992; Mullen et al., 1993). 'Severity' tends to be determined by the age of onset of the abuse, the degree of sexuality, the amount of force or violence used, the number of perpetrators involved, and the frequency of abuse. Thus, the therapist working with survivors of sexual assault must be prepared to face a range of presenting problems and the generic model described in Figure 7.2 is particularly adaptable in the understanding of a wide range of difficulties.

Any cognitive therapist, Beckian or otherwise, will be especially concerned with the cognitive correlates of childhood sexual assault, their impact on the well-being of the client and their impact on the therapeutic process. For ease, cognitive correlates can be considered as those of process and content, and of memory (including flashbacks), each of which can powerfully influence mood and behaviour.

Cognitive Process and Content

Cognitive processing in survivors may show patterns or biases; for example: dissociation (Jehu, 1989b; Waller, Quinton, and Watson, 1995; Vanderlinden, 1993) and attentional bias for abuse (Waller and Smith, 1994). With regard to *cognitive content or beliefs*, there is clearly a trend towards the negative. The self-image of survivors of abuse is poor (Herman and Hirschman, 1981), with survivors holding negative personal constructs (Clarke and Llewelyn, 1994). Jehu (1988) identified abused women's views of themselves as unusual, bad, worthless and blameworthy, while their concept of others was as untrustworthy and rejecting, and their notion of the future was hopeless. Kennerley (1995) carried out a simple factor analysis of the beliefs and assumptions of childhood sexual assault survivors and discovered five 'clusters' of personal beliefs which reflected badness, helplessness, uncleanness, being a misfit, and being 'nothing'—a person with no personal identity or purpose.

This might well present particular challenges for the therapist; for example, therapy sessions can be disrupted by clients dissociating, the therapeutic alliance can be undermined by the client's acute sensitivity to the therapist's enquiry about their difficulties and history or by their negative self-appraisal, and high levels of shame might inhibit disclosure and collaboration.

Memory in Survivors of Sexual Assault

It is accepted that *traumatic memories* are a sequel of trauma, but there has been much concern about the possibility of false memories for trauma: confabulated recollections of abuse which are believed, by the survivor, to be true. To some extent, this problem is insoluble, however, we do have some understanding of the nature of memory that can guide therapists in their work. The most thorough review of this phenomenon was carried out by a working party of the British Psychological Society, in 1995, which derived several conclusions. First, that memory is largely accurate, but can be distorted or elaborated; second, memories can be in error, but this is more likely to reflect incorrect rather than false memory; third, sustained pressure or repetition can create false memories in some; fourth, memory loss from trauma is reported and recall can occur within or independent of psychotherapy.

Clearly, this can raise many issues for both therapist and client. There can be times when the therapist doubts the client and when clients doubt themselves, therapists can fear promoting false memories through inappropriate questioning or overinterpretation, trust within the relationship can be compromised, to name but a few. There will be instances when verification of events is necessary (e.g., for legal purposes), but there will also be occasions when the therapist is able to focus on the meaning of events rather than the events themselves and, thus, accurate recall is not so vital.

With regard to good practice, the cognitive therapist needs to remain open-minded about the veracity of a client's account which might be accurate, unwittingly distorted, or knowingly misrepresented: good supervision is often vital in helping the therapist retain an objectivity. Also, the therapist must be conscientious in not asking leading questions, resisting overt interpretation and perseveration on past events in order to avoid encouraging confabulation.

Flashbacks of the trauma are memories which the individual might experience as both intrusive and uncontrollable. For some, flashbacks are simply a 'sense' of a previous trauma, while others experience full sensory recall as if the event is being relived. The recollection can be intense, comprising visual, auditory, olfactory and/or tactile memories and, although the incident may be some time in the past, the experience for the client in flashback can be very immediate.

The memory is often triggered by sounds, the feel of a fabric, smells, certain words, being touched in a certain way, etc. The triggers can be internal, such as the physical sensations of anxiety, or external, such as the smell of a certain aftershave. Flashbacks can be alarming and misinterpreted by the individual as indicating madness, for example. The distress that they cause can then lead to compensatory behaviours to disrupt the flashback, such as self-mutilation or substance misuse.

As flashbacks can occur in sessions or their onset can be triggered by therapy, therapists should be prepared to help clients understand what is happening, its natural course, and some basic techniques for taking control of the intrusions such as refocussing techniques and applied relaxation which serve to soothe and distract the client who has not had the opportunity to develop ways of restructuring and reconceptualizing the trauma.

Survivors of Adult Experience of Sexual Assault

Although the experience of sexual assault in adulthood will be traumatic, persistent difficulties following sexual assault are not inevitable and shouldn't be assumed. Albeit in a small (controlled) study of 12 rape victims, Mezey and Taylor (1988) recognized that a 'considerable psychopathology' was elicited soon after the event, but found that, 4 months later, these feelings had improved in the majority of victims. Having said that, anyone working in the clinical field well knows that many survivors do experience enduring problems for which psychotherapy can offer relief.

Some adult survivors of sexual assault will not have an earlier history of abuse, while others will have suffered as children as well. It is of note that revictimization among abuse survivors is not uncommon (Herman and Hirschman, 1981). Clearly, those who suffer both adult assault and childhood abuse will be vulnerable to the difficulties described above, the later assault acting as trigger for the development of psychological problems or exacerbating existing difficulties. This reminds us that, when assessing the adult survivor of assault, it is important to attend to as full a personal history as possible, particularly as it is well established that pre-assault psychological adjustment is an important factor in determining a person's prognosis (Burgess and Holmstrom, 1974; Miller *et al.*, 1978).

A commonly reported post-rape reaction is PTSD. Resnick, Kilpatrick, Dansley, Saunders, and Best (1993) studied a cohort of female rape victims and found a lifetime prevalence of PTSD in just under one-third and a point prevalence of 12.4%. The psychological symptoms of PTSD are characterized by a sense of re-experiencing the trauma (usually in the form of nightmares or flashbacks), emotional numbing and/or avoidance, and increased arousal—often distingushed by a marked startle response, irritability, and difficulty sleeping (see DSM-IV: APA, 1994). In addition to the problems presented by this post-traumatic syndrome itself, PTSD (whatever the precipitating trauma) enhances the risk of the development of other psychological problems such as depression and alcohol misuse (Breslau, Davis, Peterson, and Schultz, 1997), so it is important that it be recognized and addressed. The management of PTSD and acute stress, following sexual assault, is dealt with in Chapter 6.

Not all survivors of sexual trauma who experience problems will fulfil criteria for PTSD, yet they will be suffering from post-traumatic responses or reactions which impair mood and behaviours: responses such as shame and depression (Andrews, 1995); guilt, anxiety, phobic disturbance, and a deep sense of stigmatization (Mezey and Taylor, 1988). These, in turn, can fuel relationship difficulties. Clearly, cognitions will play a part in the onset and maintenance of such problems and the established cognitive therapies for such difficulties will be relevant to those traumatized by assault, while the understanding that we have of the relationship between cognitions and PTSD can further refine treatments offered to our clients. Thus, there is much scope for the cognitive therapist.

Cognitive Processing and Content

Since the 1980s, research in the field of post-traumatic responses has high-lighted the role of cognitive factors in their development and persistence. From such research, it is evident that cognitive factors contribute to the course of the post-traumatic reaction, perhaps as much as the severity of the trauma itself (Janoff-Bulman, 1985; Ehlers and Stiel, 1995; Dunmore, Clark, and Ehlers, 1997). For the cognitive therapist, a better under-standing of the cognitive processes which precipitate and perpetuate psychological problems presents an opportunity for specific targeting of symptoms.

In a recent study, Dunmore, Clark, and Ehlers (1999) investigated the cognitive factors involved in the onset and maintenance of PTSD. They established that cognitive factors associated only with the *onset* of PTSD were: dissociation during the assault, failure to perceive positive re-sponses from others, and subsequent rumination on how things could have been different. Cognitive factors associated with both the *onset and maintenance* of PTSD were: negative appraisal of the assault itself, negative appraisal of the sequelae of the assault, dysfunctional coping strategies and the victim's global belief system (i.e. their view of self, others, and the future) being negatively influenced by the assault.

As is evident from the Dunmore study, rumination on traumatic events contributes to the chronicity of post-traumatic difficulties and the re-experiencing of the event, in the form of nightmares and flashbacks, has been considered the hallmark of PTSD (e.g., Foa and Rothbaum, 1992). As such cognitive phenomena are not limited to those who fulfil criteria for PTSD, therapists working with survivors need to be familiar with the forms that flashbacks take and aware of interventions that can offer respite to the client. Cognitive restructuring (Marks *et al.*, 1998) and ex-posure (Foa, Rothbaum, Riggs, and Murdoch, 1991) have been shown to be effective in trials. However, there are those who do not readily habit-uate to the traumatic content of their flashbacks and, in these instances, judicious use of distraction and 'grounding techniques' might give some relief to sufferers (Kennerley, 1996).

Therapists' Considerations

By now, it will be clear that any therapist offering help to a person who has suffered sexual trauma will need to consider a variety of issues which could impact on that therapy: questions about the veracity of accounts, establishing the precise and personal meaning of the assault, relationship difficulties within the therapy session, not to mention the vicarious trauma or restimulation of trauma that the therapist might experience.

Establishing the Meaning of the Assault

Although clients might be referred for therapy because of an experience of sexual trauma, CBT tends to focus on the 'meaning' of that trauma rather than the events themselves. The meaning of an assault, or series of assaults, can be very different for different persons and one cannot assume that objective 'severity' determines the degree of impairment or that a client will 'fit' the stereotype of a survivor of trauma; for example, consider the cases of 'Simon' and 'Suzie'.

Simon was sexually assaulted by a teacher when he was 8 years old. The assault involved penetration, was repeated, and the abuser used threats to secure Simon's silence. The boy, however, told his parents who swiftly took action against the teacher, protected Simon from the legal aspects of bringing the perpetrator to justice and took him on a family holiday—where he was under no pressure to talk about the incident, yet it was never a taboo subject. As an adult, Simon was not aware of experiencing enduring difficulties because of the rape, but he did recall a time of trauma in his life mixed with a sense of security in knowing that his family cared for and supported him.

Suzie was an inpatient with chronic social anxieties and a depression which had driven her to attempt suicide. From early puberty, her stepfather had made sexual remarks to her, although he had never touched her in a sexual way. He had also insisted that there was no lock on her bedroom or bathroom door and then he had regularly walked in to watch her dress, bathe, or go to the lavatory. Suzie had turned to her mother who dismissed Suzie's story as malicious fantasy. As a young adult, she felt vulnerable, unloved, and terrified of intimacy.

Simon's experience was horrific, and yet does not seem to have left him with psychological problems in adulthood. In Suzie's case, however, despite, in Suzie's own words, 'He never laid a finger on me', her experience appears to have handicapped her profoundly. Without a proper understanding of the personal meaning that the experience held for each child, we could not fully understand the implications of the abuse resulting in failure to target the most relevant cognitions in therapy.

Relationship Difficulties and Therapists' Own Reactions

A further issue for therapists working with this client group are the possible difficulties arising within the therapeutic relationship. Collaboration, so necessary for cognitive therapy, can be impeded by a client's difficulties in developing trust, perhaps because of the fear, self-blame, shame, and anger that can arise from being sexually assaulted. Relationship difficulties can also arise because of the therapist's own reactions; for example, doubts about the veracity of a client's account, fears, or revulsion triggered by the therapist, restimulation of a therapist's own trauma, and so on. Within the world of cognitive therapy, problems within the working alliance and therapist-related issues have been explored. Of particular relevance is Safran and Segal's work on interpersonal processes in cognitive therapy (1990) and Padesky's observations (1996) concerning the importance of therapy supervision. Perhaps most disturbing is Jehu's (1994) investigation of therapist abuse of clients which, although unpalatable, we cannot ignore.

ADAPTING CBT TO MEET THE NEEDS OF SURVIVORS OF SEXUAL ASSAULT

What Can the Cognitive Therapist Offer?

The task facing any cognitive therapist is to provide good-quality treatment, sensitive to the client's particular needs; given what we understand of the inner world of the victim of assault, therapists can begin to tailor therapy accordingly from the outset. As we have seen, it is not unusual for the victim of assault to suffer interpersonal difficulties and, along with many other psychological therapies, CBT emphasizes the importance of fostering a supporting and empathic therapeutic relationship (Beck *et al.*, 1979). Concern for, and appraisal of, the quality of the relationship should be prominent from the first meeting.

CBT follows clear stages, beginning with the development of a conceptualization of the problem, which is always shared with the client. The therapist is then able to discuss the option of CBT and its relevance. Where it is appropriate, the conceptualization guides an intervention which aims to be overt, collaborative, focused, and active.

Making Sense of Current Difficulties: Conceptualizing the Problem(s)

This part of the therapeutic work answers questions that are crucial to both therapist and client: the 'Why me?', 'Why now?', and 'Why aren't things getting better?' questions. Beck (1995) emphasizes the importance of first developing a very personalized, idiosyncratic conceptualization based on the generic heuristic (shown in Figure 7.2), which is tailored to the client's experience and then 'fine-tuned' using our current understanding of specific difficulties; for example, those survivors of assault who experience panic are likely to benefit from a conceptualization that is augmented by our understanding of the cognitive model of panic (Clark, Salkovskis, and Chalkley, 1985). Subsequently, therapy can be enhanced by the interventions suggested by Clark's panic model. Beck (1995) reminds us that the conceptualization should emphasize the person rather than the model.

In the example on p. 170, 'Sophie's' difficulties were initially understood with reference to the generic model. Once it became clear that bulimia nervosa played a part in her problem, an established cognitive model of bulimia nervosa (Fairburn, 1981) could be used to formulate hypotheses regarding her condition, which could then be explored using Socratic methods.

In CBT, therapists overtly discuss the development and purpose of the conceptualization, the result reflects a joint effort which makes sense to both the therapist and the client. This also presents an opportunity for the therapist to begin to educate the client about CBT and to set up a collaborative endeavour. In addition, discussion helps to minimize misunderstandings regarding the client's past or present experiences.

Deciding If a Person Can Benefit from CBT

The model which guides cognitive therapy provides such a general heuristic for understanding human learning, behaviour, emotion, and information processing that it is impossible to encounter the client that does not 'fit' the model. Even so, not every patient can benefit from CBT. Safran and Segal (1990) have identified certain client characteristics as being necessary if CBT is to be accessible to the client. These include an ability to access relevant cognitions; an awareness of, and ability to differentiate, emotional states; acceptance of the cognitive rationale for treatment; acceptance of personal responsibility for change; and the ability to form a real 'working alliance' with the therapist.

Not all potential clients show these characteristics, and they may be better suited to other forms of psychotherapy such as analytic, systemic, social, or pharmacological approaches. It is a task of the assessing therapist to best match client and therapy; for example, in my experience, a proportion of clients are referred prematurely when their need is for disclosure

Example: Sophie

Sophie is a 26 year-old accountant, referred because she has a 10-year history of intermittent bulimia nervosa preceded by a 2-year episode of anorexia nervosa. Despite her current difficulties, she has a successful academic background, is now employed in a high-status and lucrative job and she has a stable, 5-year relationship.

Temperament and experience
Ambitious family which stressed achievement. Tendency to be competitive. Many experiences of aiming high and being successful

▼

Fundamental beliefs: relating to schemata
I can achieve/be in control
Others expect me to achieve and reward this
The future [my life] is controllable

▼

Rules and assumptions
I must achieve and be in control. In order to be valued, I must be the best
Others value me because I am successful: they will not value me if I am not

▼

Critical incident
Sexual molestation by uncle when 14 years old

▼

Reaction in the 'here and now': this reflects Sophie's current problem

Cognitive: 'I have to regain control of my life. I have to regain control over my body which now repels me. Others must not know of this.' Dichotomous thinking style is dominant

Behavioural: Restricted eating (anorexia nervosa) in order to exert control. Later replaced by bulimia nervosa when self-starvation can no longer be sustained

Physiological: Cycle of starvation, triggering craving and hunger which triggers binge-eating

Affective: Shame, particularly 'body shame'. Panic when perceives loss of control (hence excessive attempts to regain control in the form of self-starvation)

Interpersonal/systemic: Withdrawal from those close to her (thus no confidants) and excessive energies directed towards her work achievement and validation rather than for structured, focused therapy. In such cases, counselling would seem more appropriate.

Sophie was amenable to CBT. She was 'psychologically minded' in so far as she took on board the shared conceptualization, and she could see the powerful part that maintaining cycles played in the persistence of her bulimia. She seemed to derive some relief from having an explanation for her eating disorder that didn't simply focus on 'failure', as did her own explanation. She was also a woman who was ready to risk making changes: she was motivated to collaborate with the therapist to change the behaviours and question the cognitions that she had relied upon for most of her life.

Organizing Cognitive Therapy Sessions

The framework for a cognitive therapy session is clearly delineated, but flexible. Generally, work begins with agenda setting, the agenda being mutually agreeable to client and therapist. This active involvement is a first step towards the client's learning to define and prioritize aspects of their difficulties—which is a necessary step in problem solving. The shared task also fosters collaboration and makes explicit the content and purpose of the session. Cognitive therapy is a very 'active' therapy, and the next task is to review any between-session assignments which the client had planned in the previous session. Whether the task has gone well or badly, the client is encouraged to identify what they have learnt from the experience and how they might take this forward: thus introducing relapse management. In my view, in the case of chronic problems, relapse management is the most crucial aspect of the therapy.

Next, the topics or issues raised during agenda setting are taken up and, whenever possible, between-session assignments are generated from this work. Alternatively, assignments might be negotiated towards the end of a session in the light of discoveries made during therapy. Finally, the therapist collects feedback from the client concerning the client's views of the session; for example, what main message the client will take away from the meeting, or how sessions might be improved or made more comfortable. Simple changes such as repositioning chairs or using the client's preferred forename can create a sense of safety that can enhance sessions.

The starting point for therapy should be in the 'here and now' (i.e., using the principles and methods of 'classic' CBT) even though a conceptualization might be schema-based, as was Sophie's. Although some problems might ultimately justify extending into schema-focused work (see 'Further developments in cognitive therapy' on p. 175), this should be done with caution as we do not have the same wealth of empirical support for schema-focused work as we do for 'classic' interventions.

Using the Conceptualization to Guide the Intervention

Therapy, itself, tends to begin with the identification of key maintaining cycles illustrated by the conceptualization. In Sophie's case, there was a clear behavioural/physiological maintaining cycle interacting with her cognitions and affect. Bearing in mind that those cognitive models which have been developed to describe specific psychiatric problems and their management can guide therapy plans, reference was made to the treatment guidelines suggested by the cognitive model and treatment of bulimia nervosa (Fairburn, 1981). This involved Sophie monitoring her eating pattern, her cravings, and her thoughts concerning her eating habits. She was able to use these data to further understand the interaction of cognitions, feelings and behaviours (Figure 7.3).

In the first instance, this gave her insights into predictable patterns. Once she was aware of this, she could begin to plan to sabotage the vicious cycle. Sophie decided to try to break the patterns by reorganizing her eating regime so that she avoided self-starvation while avoiding foods which triggered binge-eating. Later in therapy, she was able to relax her control and incorporate a wide variety of foods into her diet.

By collecting her automatic thoughts, she was able to gain a greater appreciation of the role played by cognitions. The first skill she developed was identifying systematic biases in her thinking—the cognitive distortions that pervade all our thinking at one time or another. For her, a dichotomous thinking style was predominant (which was evident, for example, in her view of control being 'all or nothing'); this was addressed

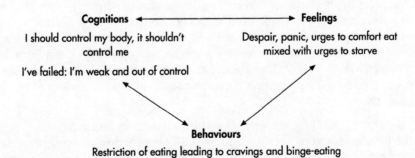

Figure 7.3 The interaction of Sophie's cognitions, feelings, and behaviours.

and she began to recognize that many concepts are best represented by a spectrum rather than a dichotomy, which gave her much more flexibility. Second, she learnt how her cognitions related to her problem feelings and behaviours and she isolated the underlying assumptions which contributed to their maintenance. Underlying assumptions present us with testable 'if ... then' type statements and rules. In Sophie's case, they included: *'I must achieve and be in control', 'In order to be valued I must be the best'*, and *'Others value me because I am successful: they will not value me if I am not'*. Sophie was able to put this to the test by gradually lowering her standards and observing how others reacted. Quickly she learnt that her friends and colleagues retained a respect and liking for her which was independent of her performance on a particular task. Through self-monitoring, she was also able to identify those cognitions which gave her license to binge or to starve such as: *'This will be the last binge'* or *'Starving is the only way of coping'*. She learnt to recognize and challenge these 'permission-giving' statements and further disrupted the maintaining cycles of bulimia.

Through learning how to monitor and analyse cognitions, Sophie also grew very aware of the fundamental belief systems which underpinned her problem assumptions, and she observed the way in which they shifted and modified in the light of her new experiences. Even her 'felt sense', her visceral perception, of being overweight and ugly changed as she began to value herself more and to appreciate that she had qualities which made her likeable. Thus, in Sophie's case, it was unnecessary to consider a mode of working which addressed the fundamental belief systems directly— they took care of themselves.

In some instances, however, the deeper belief systems seem to be persistent even in the face of consistent conflicting experiences and they then seem to serve to maintain problem cognitions, feelings, and behaviours despite the client's best endeavours. In such cases, schema-focused cognitive therapy could be considered as a possible treatment option (see 'Further developments in cognitive therapy' on p. 175).

What Do Clients Tell Us that They Need from Therapy?

In Oxford, we have been running a cognitive therapy programme for survivors of childhood abuse for over 10 years (Kennerley, Whitehead, Butler, and Norris, 1998). In that time, those who have been through the programme have given us feedback and made suggestions for improving our therapy. Three suggestions have been clear and consistent:

1 Clients told us that they need an overt structure to their therapy, they needed to know what was in store so that they could prepare themselves; for this reason, we developed a well-defined 18-session programme, which ran for 6 months. This was the preferred time span for the majority.

2 They asked for initial sessions to focus on developing day-to-day survival skills; namely, the basics of mood, stress, and relapse management. Clients chose to delay the 'formal' introduction to the model and methods of cognitive therapy until they felt that they had some essential coping skills and stability. As some, if not many, of our clients lived in a dangerous environment (an abusive family, a volatile relationship, or their own self-destructive inner world), the emphasis of coping strategies and methods of self-protection was clearly essential.

3 Perhaps most importantly, they told us that they needed careful preparation for the personal and systemic stresses of changing key beliefs; for example, some struggled with the implications of developing a sense of self-worth, shifting blame, or learning to trust. On the face of it, each of these shifts would seem to offer relief; however, changes occur within a system which has supported the old perspective and which might be resistant to change. Below are four instances of distress or harm coming to clients who modified a specific belief , or belief system, prematurely.

In therapy, Annie developed a sense of self-worth and began to assert herself within an abusive relationship. She was brutally assaulted by her partner.

In group therapy, Billy suddenly realized that he was not to blame for the sexual abuse he had experienced as a child and he became more depressed. He was now faced with a new reality: that his father was a paedophile, his mother a willing bystander and he lost hope that he would ever achieve a 'normal' relationship with his parents. Furthermore, he did not know how to handle the feelings of anger that welled up in him and terrified him.

Chrissie had mistrusted men all her life but had shifted this belief in therapy and, in middle age, had begun to date. She was faced with the grief of the lost years and the children that she would not now have; she was faced with acute embarrassment stemming from her social and sexual naivety and she was filled with the misery of self-reproach.

David first described his most core feeling being that of 'victim'. This was eroded in therapy but, far from giving him relief, this exposed a deeper and more painful sense of being 'nothing' and his mood deteriorated.

Again, this emphasizes the need for therapists to pre-empt such complications, which, in turn, reminds us of the importance of supervision. Clearly, one cannot guard against all adverse reactions to progress in therapy, but, as therapists, we can strive to keep in mind the 'bigger picture', to plan sensitively, and, thus, minimize the client's pain.

FURTHER DEVELOPMENTS IN COGNITIVE THERAPY: SCHEMA-FOCUSED COGNITIVE THERAPY (SFCT)

A schema is generally defined as a mental structure that: 'consists of a stored domain of knowledge which interacts with the processing of new information' (Williams, Watts, Macleod, and Mathews, 1997). It is a dynamic mental 'filter', shaped by our previous experiences, which colours subsequent interpretations. CBT has always recognized that such structures underpin emotional and behavioural experience, but 'classic' CBT, though effective with a range of psychological problems, has de-emphasized the role of schemata and often fails to generate sufficient understanding of complex, chronic, and characterological problems. Fortunately, by the late 1980s, the aetiological factors in the development of persistent dysfunctional beliefs and schemata were made more explicit by cognitive therapists, and their role in the maintenance of problems was refined (Beck *et al.*, 1990; Young, 1994). This enabled us to better understand the persistence and complexity of certain psychological problems.

Recently, several theoretical models have been advanced to better describe the schema (e.g., Layden, Newman, Freeman, and Byers-Norse, 1993; Beck, 1996; Teasdale, 1996; Power, 1997), and they have several common features. First, schemata are seen as multimodal structures—a schema is rich in meaning and represents much more than a single belief. It is proposed that they comprise 'meaning', held in physical, emotional, verbal, visual, acoustic, kinetic, olfactory, tactile, and kinaesthetic forms. These aspects of meaning interact to convey the powerful 'sense' that is carried by the schema; for example:

William's early abuse had left him with a schema which was best represented by a simple label: 'I am worthless'. It was this that made sense of his low self-esteem, his difficulty in relationships, and his compensatory perfectionism. When a colleague said, 'That's not a bad job', his interpretation (coloured by his belief system) was, 'He thinks that my work isn't good enough.' This activated the schema which triggered a powerful 'felt sense' of vulnerability and self-revulsion with a physiological reaction of nausea and a flood of adrenaline. He also had an uneasy sense of *déjà vu* and a negative projection into the future, accompanied by a fleeting image of being rejected—a memory of a past experience. This promoted a drive to protect himself by running away. Within an instant, William had an experience which was physical, visual, affective, and motivational; however, he was only aware that he had felt something very awful that he could not easily put into words but which was best represented by the component core belief: 'I am worthless'.

An activated schema is complex and ephemeral and, thus, often resilient to the methods of 'classic' cognitive therapy. Schema-focused cognitive therapy aims to address the schemata directly and is an extension or elaboration of CBT: it is not distinct from CBT. Schemata can often be identified using guided discovery, as in 'classic' CBT, although the use of phrases like 'How does that feel?' and 'What's happening in your body?' might commonly supplement 'What images or thoughts run through your mind?' The process of 'unpacking' the meaning can take considerably longer and might be helped by questionnaires devised to aid schema identification (e.g., Young and Brown, 1994).

Schema-focused strategies in cognitive therapy often require simple modification of standard techniques. Commonly used schema-change approaches which illustrate this include scaling, positive data logs, historical review, and visual restructuring. Pretzer's scaling (or continuum) technique is an elaboration of the exploration and balancing of dichotomous thinking style which is commonly used in 'classic' work (see Beck *et al.*, 1990), while Padesky's positive data logs (Padesky, 1994) require focused, systematic collection of evidence supporting the development of an adaptive core belief and, as such, the technique has its roots in typical data collection exercises of 'classic' CBT. Young's historical reviews (Young, 1994) represent an elaboration of the familiar 'daily thought records', but the identification and challenging of key cognitions becomes a retrospective exercise to evaluate schema-relevant experiences and beliefs. Also, much of Layden's visual restructuring (Layden *et al.*, 1993), which aims to transform the meanings held by memories and images, has built on the imagery exercises which have been a component of CBT since the 1970s. The use of schema-focused techniques, which emphasize experiential approaches to reviewing childhood memories associated with dysfunctional belief systems, is, increasingly, recommended as a necessary part of the standard treatment of complex cases (Layden *et al.*, 1993; McGinn and Young, 1996). Recently, Arntz and Weertmann (1999) have conducted an experimental study which does suggest that these methods are more powerful than non-experiential methods in inducing schema change.

In addition to this, Safran and Segal (1990) have established a further branch of cognitive therapy which targets interpersonal schemata and which uses the interpersonal domain as a medium for change. This approach is very relevant for those clients with interpersonal difficulties, such as are experienced by clients with personality disorders, for example.

Two very useful sources of descriptions of schema-change strategies are Beck et al. (1990) and Padesky (1994). However, it must be stressed that SFCT should be used only if the formulation and the course of therapy justify it.

Finally, we all have mental representations of our body size, state, and position (i.e. 'body schemata': Berlucchi and Aglioti, 1997). These internal representations of body state can be distorted, and it has been recognized for some time that abnormality of body image frequently plays a part in the maintenance of dysmorphophobia and eating disorders—and this remains one of the diagnostic criteria for both anorexia nervosa and bulimia nervosa (APA, 1994). Survivors of sexual assault often struggle with a sense of body shame and loathing that can be experienced physically, rather than cognitively, and, recently, there have been developments in helping clients combat unhelpful 'felt-sense' (Kennerley, 1996; Mills and Williams, 1997; Rosen, 1997) using 'visceral' guided discovery and challenging.

In principle, schema-change strategies can target meanings that are held in verbal, visual, and viscerally accessible modalities, each of which interacts with affect and motivation.

Can SFCT Contribute to our Work with Survivors of Sexual Assault?

Given that some survivors of assault do present with chronic and/or complex problems, such as long-term dysphoria or multi-impulsive behaviours, and given that some survivors develop characterological and interpersonal problems, SFCT would seem to have a place in the management of such presentations if 'classic' CBT methods are clearly insufficient to help the client. Nonetheless, the efficacy of schema-focused work is not yet well established and should be introduced with caution, with rigorous preparation of the client and with the support of good supervision.

CONCLUSIONS

By now, it will be evident that Beckian cognitive therapy can address many of the mood and behaviour problems which develop in those who have experienced sexual assault. The psychological model which guides CBT and SFCT can render complex difficulties understandable and can guide appropriate intervention, while the approach taken by cognitive therapists should foster confidence and independent skills in the client. When offered appropriately, this form of cognitive therapy provides a valuable addition to the range of psychotherapies which can help survivors of sexual trauma.

REFERENCES

Andrews, B. (1995) Bodily shame as a mediator between abusive experiences and depression. *Journal of Abnormal Psychology*, **104**(2), 277–285.

APA. (1994) *Diagnostic and statistical manual of mental disorders* (4th edn, DSM-IV). Washington, DC: American Psychiatric Association.

Arntz, A. and Weertmann, A. (1999) Treatment of childhood memories: Theory and practice. *Behavioural Research and Therapy*, **37**, 715–740.

Beck, A.T. (1976) Cognitive therapy and the emotional disorders. New York: International Universities Press.

Beck, A.T., Freeman, A., and Associates (1990) *Cognitive therapy of personality disorders*. New York: Guilford Press.

Beck, A.T. (1995) Presentation in The Department of Psychiatry, University of Oxford.

Beck, A.T. (1996) Beyond belief: A theory of modes, personality and psychopathology. In: P.M. Salkovskis (ed.) *Frontiers of cognitive therapy* (pp. 1–25). New York: Guilford Press.

Beck, A.T., Rush, A.J., Shaw, B.F., and Emery, G. (1979) *Cognitive therapy of depression*. New York, Guilford Press.

Beck, A.T., Wright, F.D., Newman, C.F., and Liese, B.S. (1993) *Cognitive therapy of substance abuse*. New York: Guilford Press.

Berlucchi, G. and Aglioti, S. (1997) The body in the brain: Neural bases of corporeal awareness. *Trends in Neuroscience*, **20**, 560–564.

Breslau, N., Davis, G.C., Peterson, E.L., and Schultz, L. (1997) Psychiatric sequelae of post-traumatic stress disorder in women. *Archives of General Psychiatry*, **54**, 81–87.

Briere, J. (1984) The effects of childhood sexual abuse on later psychological functioning: Defining a post sexual abuse syndrome. Paper presented at the 3rd National Conference of Sexual Victimization of Children, Washington, DC.

Briere, J. and Zaidi, L.Y. (1989) Sexual abuse histories and sequelae in female psychiatric emergency room patents. *American Journal of Psychiatry*, **146**, 1602–1606.

British Psychological Society. (1995) *Recovered memories: The report of the working party of the BPS*. Leicester, UK: BPS Publications.

Burgess, A.W. and Holmstrom, L.L. (1974) *Rape: Victims of crisis*. Bowie, MD: Brady Co.

Chambless, D.L. and Gillis, M.M. (1993) Cognitive therapy of anxiety disorders. *Journal of Consulting and Clinical Psychology*, **61**, 248–60.

Cheasty, M., Clare, A.W., and Colins, C. (1998) Relationship between sexual abuse in childhood and adult depression: A case controlled study. *British Medical Journal*, **316**, 198–201.

Clark, D.M., Salkovskis, P.M., and Chalkley, A.J. (1985) Respiratory control as a treatment for panic attacks. *Journal of Behavior Therapy and Experimental Psychiatry*, **16**, 23–30.

Clark, D.M., Salkovskis, P.M., Hackmann, A., Middleton, H., Anastasiades, P., and Gelder, M. (1994) A comparison of cognitive therapy, applied relaxation and imipramine in the treatment of panic disorder. *British Journal of Psychiatry*, **164**, 759–769.

Clarke, S. and Llewelyn, S. (1994) Personal constructs of survivors of child sexual abuse receiving cognitive analytic therapy. *British Journal of Medical Psychology*, **67**, 273–289.

Dreessen, L. and Arntz, A. (1998) The impact of personality disorders on treatment outcome of anxiety disorders: Best evidence synthesis. *Behaviour Research and Therapy*, **36**, 483–504.

Dunmore, E.C., Clark, D.M., and Ehlers, A. (1997) Cognitive factors in persistent versus recovered post-traumatic stress disorder after physical or sexual abuse: A pilot study. *Behavioral and Cognitive Psychotherapy*, **25**, 147–159.

Dunmore, E.C., Clark, D.M., and Ehlers, A. (1999) Cognitive factors involved in the onset and maintenance of post-traumatic stress disorder after physical or sexual assault. *Behaviour Research and Therapy*, **37**, 809–829.

Ehlers, A. and Stiel, R. (1995) Maintenance of intrusive memories in post traumatic stress disorder: A cognitive approach. *Behaviour Research and Therapy*, **23**, 217–249.

Everill, J. and Waller, G. (1995) Disclosure of sexual abuse and psychological adjustment in female undergraduates. *Child Abuse and Neglect*, **19**, 93–100.

Fairburn, C.G. (1981) A cognitive-behavioural approach to the management of bulimia. *Psychological Medicine*, **11**, 707–711.

Foa, E.B. and Rothbaum, B.O. (1992) Post-traumatic stress disorder: Clinical features and treatment. In R.D. Peters, R.J. McMahon, V.L. Quincy (eds) *Aggression and violence throughout the life span* (pp. 155–170). Newbury Park, CA: Sage Publications.

Foa, E.B., Rothbaum, B.O., Riggs, D.S., and Murdoch, T.B. (1991) Treatment of post-traumatic stress disorder in rape victims: A comparison between cognitive-behavioural procedures and counselling. *Journal of Consulting and Clinical Psychology*, **59**, 715–723.

Herman, J. and Hirschman, L. (1981) *Father–daughter incest*. Cambridge, MA: Harvard University Press.

Hollon, S.D., Shelton, R.C., and Davis, D.D. (1993) Cognitive therapy for depression: Conceptual issues and clinical efficacy. *Journal of Consulting and Clinical Psychology*, **61**, 270–275.

Janoff-Bulman, R. (1985) The aftermath of victimisation: Re-building shattered assumptions. In C.R. Figley (ed.) *Trauma and its wake: The study and treatment of post-traumatic stress disorder* (pp. 15–35). New York: Brunner and Mazel.

Jehu, D. (1988) *Beyond sexual abuse: Therapy with women who were victims in childhood*. Chichester, UK: Wiley.

Jehu, D. (1989a) Sexual dysfunction among women clients who were sexually abused in childhood. *Behavioural Psychotherapy*, **17**, 53–70.

Jehu, D. (1989b) Mood disturbances among women clients sexually abused in childhood: Prevalence, aetiology, treatment. *Journal of Interpersonal Violence*, **4**, 164–184.

Jehu, D. (1994) *Patients as victims: Sexual abuse in psychotherapy and counselling*. Chichester, UK: Wiley.

Kennerley, H. (1995) A schema questionnaire for survivors of childhood trauma: Preliminary findings. *International Cognitive Therapy Newsletter*, **9**(2), 1.

Kennerley, H. (1996) Cognitive therapy of dissociative symptoms associated with trauma. *British Journal of Clinical Psychology*, **35**, 325–340.

Kennerley, H., Whitehead, L., Butler, G., and Norris, R. (1998) *Recovery from childhood trauma: A therapy workbook*. Oxford: Oxuniprint.

Layden, M.A., Newman, C.F., Freeman, A., and Byers-Morse, S. (1993) *Cognitive therapy of borderline personality Disorder*. Needham Heights MA: Allyn and Bacon.

Leserman, J., Zhiming, L., Drossman, D.A., Toomey, T.C., Nachman, G., and Glogau, L. (1997) Impact of physical and sexual abuse on health status: Development of an abuse severity measure. *Psychosomatic Medicine*, **59**, 152–160.

McGinn, L.K. and Young, J.E. (1996) Schema focused therapy. In P.M. Salkovskis (ed.) *Frontiers of cognitive therapy* (pp. 182–287). New York: Guilford Press.

Marks, I., Lovell, K., Noshirvani, H., Livanou, M., and Thrasher, S. (1998) Treatment of post-traumatic stress disorder by exposure and/or cognitive restructuring: A controlled study. *Archives of General Psychiatry*, **55**, 317–325.

Mezey, G. and Taylor, P.J. (1988) Psychological reactions of women who have been raped: A descriptive and comparative study. *British Journal of Psychiatry*, **152**, 330–339.

Miller, J., Moellar, D., Kaufmann, A., DiVasto, P., Patnak, D., and Christy, J. (1978) Recidivism amongst sexual assault victims. *American Journal of Psychiatry*, **135**, 1103–1104.

Mills, N. and Williams, R. (1997) Cognitions are never enough: The use of 'body metaphor' in therapy with reference to Barnard and Teasdale's ICS model. *Clinical Psychology Forum*, **110**, 9–13.

Mullen, P.E., Martin, J.L., Anderson, J.C., Romans, S.E., and Herbison, G.P. (1993) Child sexual abuse and mental health in adult life. *British Journal of Psychiatry*, **163**, 721–732.

Padesky, C. (1993) Socratic questioning: Changing minds or guiding discovery. Keynote address delivered at the European Association of Behavioural and Cognitive Therapy, London.

Padesky, C. (1994) Schema change processes in cognitive therapy. *Clinical Psychology and Psychotherapy*, **1**, 267–278.

Padesky, C. (1996) Developing CT competency: Teaching and supervision models. In P.M. Salkovskis (ed.) *Frontiers of cognitive therapy* (pp. 266–292). New York: Guilford Press.

Power, M. (1997) Conscious and unconscious representations of meaning. In M.

Power and C.R. Brewin (eds) *The transformation of meaning in psychological therapies*. Chichester, UK: Wiley.

Pribor, E.F. and Dinwiddie, S.H. (1992) Psychiatric correlates of incest in childhood. *American Journal of Psychiatry*, **149**(1), 285–295.

Resnick, H.S., Kilpatrick, D.G., Dansley, B.S., Saunders, B.E., and Best, C.L. (1993) Prevalence of civilian trauma and PTSD in a representative national sample of women. *Journal of Consulting and Clinical Psychology*, **61**, 984–991.

Rodriguez, N., Ryan, S.W., van der Kemp, H., and Foy, D.W. (1997) Posttraumatic stress disorder in adult female survivors of childhood sexual abuse: A comparison study. *Journal of Consulting and Clinical Psychology*, **65**(1), 53–59.

Romans, S.E., Martin, J.L., Anderson, J.C., Herbison, G.P., and Mullen, P.E. (1995) Sexual abuse in childhood and deliberate self-harm. *American Journal of Psychiatry*, **152**(9), 1336–1342.

Rosen, J.C. (1997) Cognitive-behavioural body image therapy. In D. Garner and P.E. Garfinkle (eds) *Handbook of treatments for eating disorders* (2nd edn, pp. 188–201). New York: Guilford Press.

Safran, J.D. and Segal, Z.V. (1990) *Interpersonal process in cognitive therapy*. New York: Basic Books.

Salmon, P. and Caulderbank, S. (1995) The relationship of childhood sexual abuse to adult illness behaviour. *Journal of Psychosomatic Research*, **40**(3), 329–336.

Shea, M.T. (1993) Psychosocial treatment of personality disorder. *Journal of Personality Disorder*, **7**, 167–180.

Summit, R. (1983) The child sexual abuse accommodation syndrome. *Child Abuse and Neglect*, **7**, 177–193.

Teasdale, J. (1996) Clinically relevant theory: Integrating clinical insight with cognitive science. In P.M. Salkovskis (ed.) *Frontiers of cognitive therapy* (pp. 26–47). New York: Guilford Press.

Vanderlinden, J. (1993) *Dissociative experiences, trauma and hypnosis: Research findings and clinical applications in eating disorders*. Delft, Netherlands: Eburon.

Waller, G. and Smith, R. (1994) Sexual abuse and psychological disorders: The role of cognitive processes. *Behavioural and Cognitive Psychotherapy*, **22**, 299–314.

Waller, G., Quinton, S., and Watson, D. (1995) Dissociation and the processing of threat-related information. *Dissociation*, **8**, 84–90.

Williams, J.M.G., Watts, F.N., Macleod, C., and Mathews, A. (1997) *Cognitive psychology and emotional disorders* (2nd edn). Chichester, UK: Wiley.

Young, J.E. (1994) *Cognitive therapy for personality disorders: A schema focused approach* (2nd edn). Sarasota, FL: Professional Resources Press.

Young, J.E. and Brown, G. (1994) Young schema questionnaire. In J.E. Young *Cognitive therapy for personality disorders: A schema focused approach* (2nd edn). Sarasota, FL: Professional Resources Press.

Chapter 8

TREATMENT FOR THE PSYCHOSEXUAL IMPACT OF SEXUAL ASSAULT

Lynne Webster

This chapter reviews the treatments that can be offered to help people overcome the sexual problems and dysfunctions that might arise from the experience of sexual assault. The patient or client can be either male or female, but will generally be referred to as 'she' for brevity, as therapists are still more likely to be asked to treat females who have been assaulted than males, though the specific problems and needs of male patients will be considered. The case histories used to illustrate the types of problem encountered are composite accounts with significant details altered to protect confidentiality.

Although common sense predicts that the experience of being sexually assaulted is likely to cause sexual dysfunction, there has been relatively little research in this area compared with the rapidly growing evidence of the long-term harm that can be attributed to childhood sexual abuse. Research design is difficult, as gathering information from clinic populations is likely to overestimate levels of sexual dysfunction, given that only those people who are experiencing difficulties will be referred for help. Becker, Skinner, Abel, and Treacy (1982) tried to overcome this by advertising for subjects from a range of clinical and non-clinical sources. They interviewed a very mixed population of women who had experienced sexual assault or incest. Of the 22 women who had been raped, around 60% reported a fear of sex, arousal dysfunction, and desire dysfunction which they attributed to the impact of the assault.

This study suggests quite high levels of psychosexual morbidity in this group, but a comparison is needed with the background levels of sexual

The Trauma of Sexual Assault. Edited by Jenny Petrak and Barbara Hedge.
© 2002 John Wiley & Sons Ltd.

dysfunction in the general population. Meaningful data on this are hard to find, but reviews of general population surveys of sexual dysfunction (e.g., Spector and Carey, 1990) suggest that around 30% of women complain of low sexual desire, with a similar proportion of men reporting premature ejaculation. In a more systematic study, Becker, Skinner, Abel, and Cichon (1986) interviewed 372 sexual assault survivors and 99 women with no history of sexual assault. They again found that almost 60% of the survivors reported ongoing sexual dysfunctions, compared with under 20% of the non-assaulted women, and 71% of the survivors attributed their sexual problems to the experience of the assault.

It therefore seems that the available research tends to confirm the common sense hypothesis that sexual assault is associated with subsequent sexual dysfunction in a high proportion of women. But is this dysfunction temporary or long term? Burgess and Holmstrom (1979) conducted a longitudinal study of 81 adult rape survivors, interviewing them up to 6 years post-assault. They found that the sexual problems arising out of the assault seemed to be particularly enduring and were less susceptible to spontaneous remission than other symptoms such as depression and general anxiety. In the group that they studied, 37% of the women reported that their sexual function had returned to normal within months of the assault, 37% estimated that their recovery had taken a number of years, and 36% felt that they still had not recovered sexually. McCarthy (1990) also notes the potentially chronic nature of the sexual problems that can set in post-assault, and makes a plea that specific treatment should be offered for such problems as early as possible and not postponed until treatment for more generalized symptoms of trauma is completed.

THE SEXUAL DYSFUNCTIONS

These are classified in the *Diagnostic and statistical manual of mental disorders*, Version 4 (DSM-IV) (APA, 1994), and in *The ICD-10 classification of mental and behavioural disorders*, Version 10 (ICD-10) (WHO, 1992). Both systems give similar lists, based on problems with desire, arousal, orgasm, and sexual pain (see Table 8.1). From research findings and from observations in clinical practice, it is evident that the experience of sexual assault can lead to problems in any of these diagnostic categories, either singly or often in multiple combinations of difficulties. There are several possible underlying mechanisms for the development of sexual dysfunctions in these situations. To understand them, some knowledge of sexual anatomy and physiology is necessary, and for a more comprehensive account of this a good textbook is essential (e.g., Bancroft, 1989). However, the mechanism of how performance anxiety influences arousal

Table 8.1   DSM-IV sexual dysfunctions

Sexual desire disorders
   302.71 Hypoactive Sexual Desire Disorder
   302.79 Sexual Aversion Disorder

Sexual arousal disorders
   302.72 Female Sexual Arousal Disorder
   302.72 Male Erectile Disorder

Orgasmic disorders
   320.73 Female Orgasmic Disorder
   302.74 Male Orgasmic Disorder
   302.75 Premature Ejaculation

Sexual pain disorders
   302.76 Dyspareunia (not due to a general medical condition)
   306.76 Vaginismus (not due to a general medical condition)

can be summarized is shown in Figure 8.1. It is clear that the smooth operation of the system can be interrupted at many points. Desire is necessary for the initiation of sexual activity, so, if this is reduced or absent, the arousal circuit may never be activated. As soon as the physiological responses of arousal are triggered, this reaches awareness and may be negatively influenced and damped by cognitions. Instead of being able to focus on pleasurable sensations, the patient starts 'spectatoring' or monitoring their own responses. Attitudes, expectations, memories, and fears may be activated which make it impossible for arousal to continue to build towards the triggering of orgasm. Likewise, anticipatory fear of pain on penetration can lead to the involuntary vaginal muscle spasm of vaginismus, and negative associations between sexual activity and pain can lead to more generalized pain on intercourse (dyspareunia). Secondarily, the patient learns that attempts at sexual functioning post-assault are aversive rather than rewarding, and a cycle of avoidance can begin. Relationship factors provide a huge arena for possible complicating and perpetuating issues, with feelings of rejection and guilt on both sides. Eventually, couples and individuals may become entrenched in a habitually non-sexual lifestyle which becomes chronic and feels so safe for them that it is very difficult to move out of.

There are a number of typical negative thoughts and feelings that make it difficult to return to enjoyable sexual functioning after rape or sexual assault. Some victims feel confused and guilty about why they should have been singled out for attack, and begin to believe that their sexual attractiveness is a bad and dangerous aspect of themselves. This makes it difficult for a loving sexual partner to admire their appearance or express

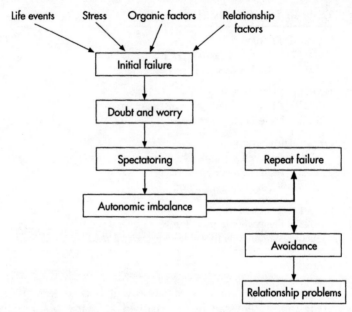

Figure 8.1   Performance anxiety.

desire without triggering these negative responses. In the case of men who have been sexually assaulted by other males, the victim may start to doubt his sexual identity and become confused about his sexual orientation. When someone has been subject to 'date rape' or 'acquaintance rape', it can be hard for them to regain trust in future potential sexual partners, as it may seem to them that everyone in their social environment is a potential attacker. All these attitudes need to be explored and checked against reality so they cannot form a permanent barrier to future sexual function.

The experience of sexual contact in a consensual situation after sexual assault can act as a trigger for distressing intrusive memories of the assault, and these can be so powerful and aversive that the couple cannot continue. Often, there are specific components of the sexual encounter, such as touching the breasts or genitalia during foreplay or the smell of sweat, aftershave, or semen, that are physical reminders of the attack. If these can be identified, the couple can learn either to avoid the trigger factors or become desensitized to them. A more subtle difficulty is the phenomenon of dissociation, a mental defence mechanism of emotional distancing that occurs at times of great stress and anxiety. This frequently occurs during an attack, so that the victim reports that it was 'as though it was happening to someone else' or 'as though it was happening in a film'. This dissociative sense of unreality can later recur during sexual activity, making it impossible for the patient to focus on intimacy, pleasurable sensations, and arousal. In a wider sense, the emotional numbing that occurs as part of the syndrome of post-traumatic stress can make it very difficult for the sufferer to sustain what might previously have been supportive and loving relationships.

ASSESSMENT

Surprisingly, there has been very little published about the assessment of sexual dysfunction in adults who have experienced sexual assault, compared with the much more extensive literature on the forensic aspects of interviewing and the assessment of sexually abused children. In practice, psychosexual therapists use modifications to their standard assessment schedules as appropriate to each case (Hawton, 1993).

It is obvious that patients presenting with sexual dysfunction after a sexual assault need careful and sensitive assessment. Unfortunately, many therapists, however experienced they may be in their own discipline, are not taught the basic skills of taking a sexual history. This requires a familiarity with sexual anatomy and physiology, along with the confidence to use sexual terminology without embarrassment (Webster, 1997). In making a full assessment, many or all of the areas in Table 8.2 will need to be explored, in addition to the details of the sexual assault.

It is important that the assessment is done with tact, sensitivity, and discretion. By the time the patient is referred for help with the sexual dysfunction, they have probably had to recount the history of the assault several times in great detail to the police and to other agencies. It can be unnecessarily distressing to require the patient to go over this again in detail at one sitting at the first assessment interview. It may be better to schedule a number of shorter assessment sessions, which allows the patient to unfold the history of her experiences in her own time, as she feels ready, and as it seems appropriate. It can also seem intrusive, prurient, and almost abusive for the therapist to probe for graphic details of the assault. These intimate details may be vitally relevant to the accurate assessment and therapy of the patient's sexual dysfunction, but, equally, it is the patient's privilege to disclose as much or as little of this as she wants to. It may be better to allow these details to emerge as therapy progresses and trust is built up, rather than leave the patient feeling that the history-taking has been a harrowing ordeal of reliving the assault. However, it is still important to obtain specific information about the assault, as sometimes the sexual dysfunction can be linked to

Table 8.2 A typical checklist of areas to explore in taking a sexual history

1. Details of the presenting problem
   —its nature, duration and development, along with any situational factors

2. Relationship history
   —with current and previous partners, including general relationship quality, separations, infidelities, areas of conflict, hopes, and fears

3. Sexual development and knowledge
   —source, extent, whether the person thinks he or she lacks information, and the therapist's assessment of level of sexual knowledge, details of puberty, menarche, menopause, masturbation, sexual orientation, past traumatic sexual experiences

4. Medical and surgical history
   —including past and current medications and contraception

5. Psychiatric history
   —including any previous therapy for sexual or relationship problems, assessment of any current psychiatric illness (e.g., depression, anxiety states)

6. Family history
   —including relationships with parents, parental relationship, family attitudes to sexuality, religious influences

7. Use of alcohol and drugs

8. Physical examination, if appropriate

this (e.g., the patient who showed sexual aversion towards her husband if she could smell alcohol on him, as her assailant had been drinking).

The checklist of areas to explore is very helpful in establishing a pre-morbid (i.e., pre-assault) level of sexual and relationship functioning. This is important in the formulation of realistic treatment goals. If a patient was primarily anorgasmic and suffered from sexual aversion before the assault, this would affect the possible outcome of therapy, compared with a patient whose previous experience of sex had been relaxed and enjoyable. Similarly, a patient in a relationship that has been unsatisfactory for many years may find it easier emotionally to attribute her sexual dysfunction entirely to the aftermath of a recent sexual assault rather than acknowledge the long-standing difficulties. Also, the experience of sexual assault can be a powerful trigger for the reactivation of distressing emotions connected with previous abusive experiences. Earlier encounters with childhood physical or sexual abuse and previous assaults including domestic violence can all affect the way in which a patient reacts and the sexual dysfunctions that they develop.

As regards the experience of the assault, it is useful to ask how this might have changed the way in which the patient sees herself, sexually. This question often leads into a discussion of feelings of guilt, self-reproach, dirtiness, defilement, and other negative emotions that can act as barriers to overcoming sexual dysfunction. Likewise, it is worth asking how the experience might have changed her view of current and/or potential future sexual partners, as this can start an exploration of problems with rejection and trust.

Patients are often referred for psychosexual therapy along with their partners, and this presents both challenges and opportunities for the therapist. It is good practice to offer the partner a separate interview as part of the assessment process, and this can be invaluable in allowing ventilation of thoughts and feelings that might be difficult to express in a couple interview. Partners often feel rage, helplessness, and grief about the assault, a powerful mixture of emotions that can get in the way of the progress of therapy unless they are acknowledged. They may also be torn between a wish to be supportive and unacceptable feelings that their partner has been defiled by the attack, along with unjustifiable guilt that they could not protect the partner. All these emotions are potentially explosive for a couple wishing to return to enjoyable sexual activity together.

Finally, it is vital to explore the tricky area of motivation for psychosexual therapy. It is not uncommon for patients to present at the clinic reluctantly, as their counsellor, their general practitioner, or their sexual partner has insisted that they go along to get help to 'sort out the sexual side of things'. The patient may be far from ready to tackle this, and the therapist's role may be to support the patient in allowing them to retain their sexual dysfunction for a while longer, until their emotional defences are stronger and they feel able to contemplate physical intimacy again. It has to be accepted that for some patients this may never resolve, and, despite our best attempts to offer appropriate psychosexual therapy, the patient chooses to withdraw from future sexual contacts and experiences. This is a pity, as the outcome of therapy is often good (Hawton, 1995), but the patient's ultimate choice in this must be respected.

THE TREATMENT PLAN

Ideally, outcome of the assessment process is an agreed formulation between the patient and the therapist regarding the origin and nature of the sexual dysfunction, along with a treatment plan. This is often not as clear-cut as it sounds, as patients may be suffering from a wide range of symptoms following a sexual assault, and it can be difficult for the psychosexual therapist to find and maintain a clear focus on the sexual problems when there are also symptoms of depression and post-traumatic stress that need treatment. In addition, patients may be in need of ongoing support through the legal process and through medical investigations and treatment. In the face of all this, the psychosexual therapist may be tempted to ask the patient to delay treatment for the sexual dysfunction until some of the other issues are resolved. This is probably reasonable in some cases, as the outcome of psychosexual therapy in patients who are deeply depressed is very poor, because they cannot summon the motivation or concentration to engage in a cognitive and behavioural treatment plan. However, as Burgess and Holmstrom (1979) pointed out, the sexual dysfunction can become chronic and entrenched if treatment is delayed. In particular, delaying treatment until the legal issues are resolved can subject the patient to a wait of several years in some cases. It is probably better for the psychosexual therapist to compromise, work alongside the other counsellors and agencies involved, and accept that progress will not be smooth because of unavoidable distractions and interruptions.

It sometimes emerges during the assessment or in the process of a cognitive and behavioural therapy, that the patient is troubled by a reactivation of emotions from earlier experiences of abuse, triggered by the more recent sexual assault. This need not necessarily be childhood sexual abuse, though it is easy to see why the re-experiencing of helplessness and fear in adult life would link strongly with that type of early experience. It could also be previous experiences of physical abuse, domestic violence, or unpleasant medical procedures that are recalled. Sometimes, these can be addressed through exploration within the psychosexual therapy, but if these factors are causing great difficulties, such as pervasive and lasting personality problems, a referral for a deeper and more lengthy psychodynamic, psychotherapeutic exploration may be indicated.

TREATMENT METHODS

As with assessment, there has been a lack of research and publication about specific treatment for sexual dysfunctions in patients who have been sexually assaulted, compared with the copious literature on helping people to overcome the effects of childhood sexual abuse. There is some useful overlap in this research, particularly in the area of treatment programmes for sexual dysfunction in patients with dissociative disorders (Ashton, 1995; Glantz and Himber, 1992). This is mainly de-signed for adult survivors of childhood sexual abuse, but is applicable to sexual assault victims who often develop symptoms of dissociation as a defence mechanism to help them survive the ordeal of the assault, and to distance themselves from emotional pain and distress afterwards. These treatment programmes use standard sex therapy techniques, but stress the importance of helping the patient to contact and utilize the part of herself that sees sexual expression as healthy and desirable. The partner is also involved in helping to avoid triggering flashbacks and bringing the patient back to the present when dissociating.

McCarthy (1990) outlines a useful cognitive-behavioural treatment strat-egy, which challenges the assumption that sexual dysfunction cannot be treated until the issues of previous sexual trauma are resolved, and stres-ses the importance of exploring the patient's cognitions that 'sex is a bad thing, that is not part of you as a person, and that sexuality is something done to you'. Again, this is designed more with early sexual trauma in mind, but is widely applicable.

In practice, psychosexual therapists use their standard techniques, as first outlined by Masters and Johnson (1970), updated to incorporate cognitive approaches (Hawton, 1985), and modified to be specific to the difficulties facing the individual patient and their partner.

TREATMENT FOR SPECIFIC DYSFUNCTIONS

Loss of Sexual Desire, Problems with Arousal and Anorgasmia

These dysfunctions are clearly interrelated, but can also occur separately from each other. In the assessment, it is important to ask about alcohol use and prescribed psychotropic drugs such as tranquillizers and antidepres-sants. In post-traumatic stress, it is extremely common for patients to self-medicate with alcohol for anxiety symptoms and more particularly for insomnia. This can soon reach a level where it affects sexual function, so advice and support regarding reduction of alcohol intake is sometimes the most effective strategy.

Most antidepressants affect sexual function (Baldwin, Thomas, and Birt-wistle, 1997), but the selective serotonin reuptake inhibitors (SSRIs) such as fluoxetine (Prozac) are particularly known for this. In some surveys, over 60% of patients on this type of drug experience loss of sexual drive, problems with arousal and delayed or absent orgasm. Unfortunately, it is not so easy to advise about this as it is with alcohol intake. SSRIs are the most effective drugs indicated in the treatment of post-traumatic stress disorder (PTSD), as well as being very efficient and otherwise well-tolerated antidepressants. These are therefore likely to be the medications of first choice for patients with PTSD or depression following sexual assault, and, although there are newer antidepressants available that spare sexual function (e.g., nefazodone and moclobemide), they are as yet relatively unproven for the syndrome of PTSD. It may be that treatment goals will need to be modified while the patient is on such medication, which will probably be for at least 6 months. However, it is often very reassuring to patients to know that their sexual dysfunction is at least partly due to a reversible effect of the medication that they need, rather than something more permanent.

In general, treatment for these dysfunctions usually relies on a modification of the standard sensate focus therapy, where couples are asked to do 'homework' sessions of non-demand pleasuring exercises, which help the patient to focus on pleasurable touch with their partner, progressing in a relaxed way to sexual arousal in the ensuing stages. This is highly effective in the treatment of arousal problems due to anxious cognitions, but may need to be supplemented with attention to the patient's general lifestyle. Some couples are exhausted by the demands of employment and childcare, even without the additional pressure of coping with the aftermath of a sexual assault, and these issues cannot be ignored. Another difficulty is that this therapy relies on a strong and cooperative couple bond, which may have been disrupted by the assault, so that relationship issues need attention before therapy can proceed. Sometimes, the focus may need to shift to more general couple therapy for a number of sessions to address this (see Case Example 8.1).

Case Example 8.1

Evelyn, a 27-year-old sales representative, was raped by a work colleague when they were away at a company conference. A group of delegates had gathered in her room to socialize after the bar had closed. When everyone else had left, Evelyn's manager stayed behind and, when she refused his sexual advances, he raped her. She called the conference centre staff immediately, the manager was arrested and subsequently convicted. Two years later, she was referred for help because of loss of libido, and on assessment it emerged that she and her husband Tony had not managed to return to any form of sexual contact since the incident. It also became clear that it was not Evelyn who was suffering from a sexual dysfunction, but Tony who was suffering from aversion to any sexual contact. They were successfully treated using a gradual programme of sensate focus therapy, but, before they could start this, they needed six sessions of more general couple therapy. During these sessions, Tony was able to express his anger and bitterness that Evelyn had gone to the conference against his wishes. She had been ambitious for promotion and he had been jealous because his own career was in a rut. Although he wanted to be supportive and sympathetic after the assault, he was struggling with unacceptable and inexpressible feelings that the attack was punishment for her independence, and he felt ashamed of these feelings. Because none of this had been discussed between them, the emotional stalemate was reflected in the lack of sexual contact. When they were able to talk about these issues in the relative safety and structure that the therapy sessions provided, they were able to move on to the behavioural programme.

For patients without a partner, a modification of Heiman and LoPiccolo's (1996) sexual growth programme can be offered. This is designed for anorgasmic women, but the exploration of sexual attitudes, bodily self-exploration, and self-pleasuring can be modified for reclaiming a positive sexual identity in both genders after sexual assault (see Case Example 8.2.).

Case Example 8.2

Joan, aged 55, worked part-time in a cake shop and spent most of her time caring for her husband who was brain damaged and partially paralysed after an industrial accident. They had had no sexual relationship for 10 years since the accident. Joan was attacked one afternoon when walking her dog on a secluded, local, country path. Her assailant forced her to perform oral sex, humiliated her in various ways, and raped her. He was never found. She was referred for help as she was determined that the assault was not going to blight her life. She wanted to work on making sex a positive part of her life again, as now she felt dirty, embarrassed, and distressed whenever sexual topics were mentioned at work or on the television. She was concerned that she might communicate this discomfort to her grandchildren, who had previously confided in her quite openly about their sexual worries. She knew it was not possible to enlist the help of her husband in the treatment, so she embarked on a modified sexual growth programme. Homework sessions included looking at her body, including her genitalia, and recording her thoughts and feelings for discussion. She was able to move on to self-exploration and self-pleasuring, setting the scene for sensuous enjoyment by using scented bath oils and candles. She was then able to view educational videos of couples doing sensate focus exercises, imagining herself in the female role. Using these techniques, she gradually reclaimed a sense of her sexuality being a healthy and pleasurable part of herself and her life.

Sexual Aversion

This is a phobic avoidance of sexual contact which goes beyond simple loss of interest or arousal, and shares many of the characteristics of other non-sexual phobias. The diagnostic criteria for PTSD include 'persistent avoidance of stimuli associated with the trauma and general numbing of responsiveness', with 'efforts to avoid thoughts, feelings or conversations associated with the trauma' (APA, 1994). When the traumatic event that triggered the PTSD is a sexual assault, it is quite likely that the avoidance component of the syndrome will centre around sexual activity, as this can bring back the feelings of fear and helplessness associated with the original event. This is sometimes so intense that the patient re-experiences the event as a flashback, and it is not surprising that it leads many patients to avoid sex in any form, even including television programmes and films with a sexual content.

Sexual aversion responds to the same cognitive and behavioural techniques used to treat the phobic avoidance component of post-traumatic stress, as outlined by Petrak (1996), with the emphasis on graded exposure to the feared situation, backed up by support from the therapist who helps the patient to modify their negative and fearful cognitions. The standard sensate focus programme for couples can be used in this way, but it relies on the co-operation of a sympathetic partner, who can put their feelings of rejection to one side, to participate (see Case Example 8.3.).

Case Example 8.3

When she was 16 years old and sexually inexperienced, Gemma had been raped by her uncle. She had been terrified of getting into trouble from her parents, so had told nobody about the incident. Now that she was 20 years old and nearing the end of her college course in Business Studies, she had been in a relationship with her partner Lee for almost a year. They were referred for help because each time they attempted intercourse, Gemma pushed Lee away just before penetration, and broke down screaming, shivering, and crying. She described how, when arousal occurred, she would feel a mounting anxiety, then see a pseudo-hallucination of her uncle standing beside the bed laughing at her. When Lee was able to understand the mechanism of dissociation, he no longer felt frightened and rejected by Gemma's behaviour, and was able to help her use relaxation techniques as part of a sensate focus programme. This enabled her to experience arousal without triggering anxiety and dissociation.

It is more difficult to organize graded exposure to sexual contact in a patient who is not in a relationship, but progress can still be made by using fantasy, written material, and videos. The patient can gradually work on becoming more comfortable with sexual expression through these means, with self-pleasuring exercises to help the patient reclaim their body and its sexual responses.

Vaginismus and Sexual Pain

Vaginismus is a reflex spasm of the muscles around the entrance to the vagina. The reflex can be set up by any painful stimulus in the genital area, so it is a fairly predictable consequence of sexual assault in some women. The spasm can be triggered by any attempt at penetration, including speculum examinations and the use of tampons, and may be set off by the anticipation of pain before the genital area is even touched. The spasm itself is painful, and further attempts at penetration are impossible or extremely painful while it is ongoing.

Treatment consists of explanation, reassurance, relaxation exercises, graded exposure to penetration, and modification of the patient's fearful cognitions. If the woman sustained any injury to her genital area at the time of the assault, she may be fearful that this has caused permanent internal damage, or that the injury is not properly healed. These fears are reinforced by the painful muscle spasm, and she may develop further fears that penetrative sex will exacerbate this by tearing the vagina. In these cases, it is very helpful to organize a gentle and reassuring vaginal examination, backed up by simple anatomical diagrams and explanations about the nature of vaginismic muscle spasm. It is often very useful for the partner to be present when this is explained, or to make sure the information includes them, as the partner can often share these fears that painful attempts at penetration are causing damage to the genital area. It is also important to emphasize the reflex nature of the spasm, as many patients and their partners believe that the inability to tolerate penetration is a purely psychological and almost wilful rejection of the partner. There is often much relief when the physical component of the spasm is explained, and this can be reinforced using some of the explanatory and self-help literature available (Goodwin and Agronin, 1997).

This physical component explains why counselling alone is often not enough in the treatment of vaginismus. Patients may work hard to gain an understanding of the fears and other feelings associated with the pain, but are then still left with vaginal muscles that go into a reflex spasm when touched. For this reason, relaxation training which includes specific exercises for the perineal muscles is used to help the woman regain control of that area. In addition, she is guided through a series of behavioural tasks, starting with exploration of the external genitalia and progressing to penetration with a graded range of objects. It is possible to do this programme with the patient's own fingers and tampons. Some prefer to use a graded set of vaginal trainers, which range from the size of a small tampon to that of an erect penis. These can be obtained by mail order as a set of five sizes (see 'Useful addresses'). The woman gains increasing confidence that her vagina can accommodate these increasing sizes comfortably and painlessly. She then needs to work on sharing the control of penetration with a partner. If she is not in a relationship, the programme cannot progress beyond this point, and further sessions may need to be scheduled flexibly in the future, when she may need help in establishing intercourse in a new relationship.

MALE VICTIMS OF SEXUAL ASSAULT

Until fairly recently, the problems of men who have been sexually assaulted have received little attention. It is now more generally acknowledged, thanks to the research and writings of authors such as Mezey and King (2000), that this neglected group has specific forms of presentation of their difficulties and specific needs.

As with women, much of the research has centred on the sexual adjustment in adult life of men who were sexually abused as children, and little information is available on the sexual problems that adult males experience after rape or sexual assault. Johnson and Schrier (1987) found that sexual dysfunction, including erectile difficulties, premature ejaculation, retarded ejaculation, and inhibited libido, were more common in men who had been sexually abused as adolescents. Interviews with male prisoners who had been sexually assaulted revealed that 58% of them subsequently had difficulties getting close to others (Struckman-Johnson, Struckman-Johnson, Rucker, Bumby, and Donaldson, 1996). Masters (1986) wrote case reports describing the sexual dysfunctions that occurred in three men who were sexually assaulted by women, and documented their progress in therapy towards regaining a sense of their masculinity and control.

Despite this paucity of data on men's sexual dysfunction after sexual assault, certain patterns of response have emerged from research (Mezey and King, 1989). In a review of the available literature, Coxell and King (1996) reported that confusion about sexual orientation was a common psychosexual consequence in men who had been assaulted by males, along with problems with erection and ejaculation (Myers, 1989).

There is no doubt that men find it generally more difficult to access helping agencies than women, and in this field it can be particularly daunting, as many of the services were set up with the needs of women in mind. Many sexual assaults on males take place in the context of homosexual contacts, which can make it doubly difficult for the victim to report the crime and feel they can legitimately seek therapeutic help (see Case Example 8.4).

Case Example 8.4

Sean was a 30-year-old homosexual man who had been in a settled relationship with his cohabitee Rob for 3 years. Despite Rob's possessiveness, Sean would occasionally rebel and seek clandestine, casual sexual encounters along the canal bank, a notorious local 'cruising' area for homosexual contacts. He always insisted on safer sex practices with these men, but not with Rob, as they had both been reassured by previous negative AIDS tests. On one of these evenings, Sean was set upon by three youths who beat him and robbed him. Finally, one of the youths subjected him to forced anal intercourse and taunted him that he had now been infected with AIDS. Sean cleaned himself up as best he could, and told no one about the attack, as he did not want his family, his employers, or his partner finding out that he had put himself in such a dangerous situation. He developed insomnia with nightmares and drank up to half a bottle of whisky each night to get to sleep. He became obsessively troubled about the possibility of AIDS, but was too fearful to be tested. He experienced erectile dysfunction with Rob, partly as a result of the alcohol intake and partly because of the AIDS phobia. Eventually, he confided in his general practitioner, who had always been discreet and sympathetic in the past. The GP arranged a screen for sexually transmitted diseases which was all clear, and prescribed antidepressant medication that enabled Sean to do without the alcohol. However, the sexual dysfunction remained, and, although he felt much better when he had unburdened himself of his guilty feelings to his GP, Sean refused to involve Rob in counselling, fearing disclosure would end the relationship. The GP then prescribed Viagra, which Sean used six times to enhance his erections. The resulting increase in confidence allowed him to re-establish a sexual relationship with Rob, despite the underlying problems of secrecy and fidelity in that relationship.

Self-medication with alcohol for symptoms of post-traumatic stress is even more common in men than in women, and can lead to destructive effects on sexual function and relationships, as do the patterns of emotional distancing and sexual avoidance that can be part of the syndrome.

The gender of the psychosexual therapist can be very important to the patient, with many women who have been sexually assaulted expressing a preference for a female therapist. In practice, male victims also seem to prefer working with a female psychosexual therapist, which fits with the research finding that these men have deep concerns about their masculinity which might be difficult to expose to another male. This does not mean that male psychosexual therapists cannot offer these patients successful treatment programmes, but that these sensitivities need to be respected and taken into account.

As with women, the techniques of cognitive and behavioural sex therapy can be used to good effect in these men (Becker and Skinner, 1983). This can now be supplemented by the judicious use of medication to enhance erections such as sildenafil (Viagra), which can be prescribed in the short term to boost confidence in men whose erectile dysfunction is being perpetuated by performance anxiety.

SPECIAL GROUPS

There are some groups of people who have undergone sexual trauma that need special consideration in the assessment and treatment of their psychosexual problems.

Victims of Torture

Sexual assault and rape is a common component of political and judicial torture in some regimes, with both men and women as victims. One study comparing male and female torture victims found that sexual torture was more common in women and that they were more likely than men to suffer sexual dysfunction as a consequence (Allodi and Stiasny, 1990), mainly in the form of sexual anxiety and avoidance. Other studies have demonstrated high levels of disturbance of sexual function in sexually tortured men, with effects on hormone balance (Lunde, Rasmussen, Wagner, and Lindholm, 1981), though it has been noted that the sexual aspects of torture are generally underreported, with researchers failing to ask about sexual dysfunction.

As regards treatment, this may present practical difficulties because of the need to work through interpreters in some refugee populations. Nevertheless, good outcomes have been reported in the reduction of sexual dysfunction in sexually tortured women, using non-verbal stress reduction techniques such as massage (Larsen and Paguadan-Lopez, 1987).

In some refugee populations, there may be numbers of women who have been raped as part of organized terror campaigns within a war situation. Often, there is excessive shame associated with this, and women may choose to keep quiet about their experiences rather than risk rejection within their culture. If such women are referred for problems with sexual dysfunction, it may be inappropriate to involve their sexual partner because of these justified fears.

Female Genital Mutilation (FGM)

This is a surgical procedure which varies in scope from the removal of the clitoris to a major excision of the entire labia and clitoris. The wound is then sewn up to leave a small orifice at the vaginal entrance. It is mostly performed in Muslim countries and traditional societies in North and sub-Saharan Africa, but it is estimated that, in immigrant and refugee populations in Britain, 10,000 girls risk undergoing this procedure, and in the USA about 168,000 women have had genital excision (Mackay, 2000). It is usually performed by female relatives with crude instruments and without anaesthetic. It is most commonly performed shortly before puberty, but some societies practise it in infancy or after childbirth.

There is no doubt that the procedure constitutes an assault on the girl involved, and it is illegal in many countries. Besides the short-term risks of haemorrhage and infection, there are long-term problems with pain on intercourse and reduced sexual responsiveness (WHO, 1995, 1996), along with symptoms of post-traumatic stress.

Any psychosexual therapist working in a large urban centre is likely to see women with sexual dysfunction because of FGM, and it is evident that they share many of the sexual problems of women who have been sexually assaulted. The excision can also cause distress to the male partner, who is often acutely aware that his wife finds intercourse painful and aversive.

Vulnerable Groups

People with learning disabilities, whether living in institutional care or in the community, are at increased risk of sexual exploitation. Their sex education is often poor, and they may lack the social power and assertiveness to resist coercive sexual advances (Craft, 1994). The psychosexual therapist may have a role both in the aftermath of sexual assault and in pre-emptive education, teaching the patient that they have rights over their own bodies and when it is safe and appropriate to choose to share sexual pleasure with another.

There is also a growing recognition of the prevalence of sexual exploitation of patients by doctors and therapists (Gabbard, 1989). This betrays the trust of the patient as the therapist exploits their professional power and authority to gain sexual gratification. The patients thus exploited are often already vulnerable and dependent. Although violent coercion is rarely used in this context, it is recognized that the sexual contact often constitutes an assault because the patient cannot give true consent. This is clear cut when the patient is mentally ill under the definition of the Mental Health Act, but it is also acknowledged by all professional regulatory bodies that any sexual contact between therapists and patients abuses the therapist's position of power and cannot be truly consensual. Afterwards, the patient is frequently left feeling betrayed and emotionally confused, and it can be very difficult for them to accept further professional help in overcoming their psychosexual problems given their lack of trust in therapists. Unfortunately, if the patient complains, this is often compounded by professionals who 'close ranks' and refuse to believe that a colleague could behave in such a way.

Drug-assisted Rape

The police have reported a growing problem with the covert use of powerful tranquillizing drugs (Slaughter, 2000). These are administered to an unsuspecting victim, usually when drinking in a social situation. They render the recipient semi-conscious and incapable of resisting unwanted sexual contact. Afterwards, although forensic tests show evidence of sexual intercourse, the victim may have only very vague and patchy recollections of the events that took place (Smith, 1999). This presents particular difficulties for both patient and therapist, as it can be even harder than usual for them to work towards the patient regaining a sense of sexual autonomy and self-determination.

Stalking and Sexual Harassment

British law now recognizes that psychological injury can be caused by the repeated intrusive harassment known as stalking, even though the perpetrator may never make physical contact with their victim (Mullen, Pathe, and Purcell, 2000). Likewise, the damaging effects of sexual harassment in the workplace are being increasingly acknowledged. The sense of defilement and intrusion described by the victims in these cases, using terms such as 'emotional rape', can be very similar to that described by assault survivors, and similar therapy is required to regain the sense of control over their own sexuality that is necessary for psychosexual recovery.

LEGAL ASPECTS

Therapists are sometimes asked to prepare reports for the courts regarding the effects of an assault on their client or patient. This is most often for the purposes of criminal injuries compensation, but can also be required in criminal or civil proceedings. It is not uncommon for the sexual dysfunction aspects of the case to be neglected, in favour of the physical injuries and non-sexual psychiatric or psychological effects on the victim. It is important to remember that the psychosexual disorders listed in Table 8.1 are usually recognized by the courts as psychiatric injuries worthy of compensation, if they are attributable to the aftermath of the assault. Sometimes, the patient will not spontaneously mention their sexual dysfunction at interview, as they can be reluctant to air these matters in front of their legal representatives, so it is the responsibility of the interviewer to make specific enquiries to ensure this aspect is not overlooked.

THERAPIST ISSUES

Unless a psychosexual therapist is working in a very specialist practice, patients who have been sexually assaulted will form a relatively small proportion of their caseload, along with the cases of general sexual dysfunction that are the majority of referrals. Nevertheless, these cases can be uniquely challenging and sometimes emotionally harrowing for the therapist. It goes without saying that the therapist should have access to adequate supervision, both in terms of quality and frequency (Ridley, 1996). Although the situation has improved, there are still some agencies that do not sufficiently support their employees' needs for supervision as part of their work contract, and some private practitioners who work in isolation from their peers. This is generally insupportable in psychosexual work, but even more so if work with survivors of sexual assault and rape is undertaken. Despite the challenges involved, psychosexual therapists who work with this group can be optimistic that sensitive and imaginative modifications of their standard sex therapy techniques will prove rewarding in helping their patients regain a positive experience of sexuality. Therapists without specific training in psychosexual work may wish to acquire skills in this area (see 'Useful addresses'), or may see ways in which their usual methods can be extended to help patients whose anxieties are affecting their sexual function after rape or sexual assault.

USEFUL ADDRESSES

Vaginal dilators for the treatment of vaginismus can be obtained from: Owen Mumford, Brook Hill, Woodstock, Oxford OX20 1TU (Tel.: 01993 812021).

Details of multidisciplinary psychosexual training courses and lists of accredited psychosexual therapists can be obtained by sending an s.a.e. to: The British Association for Sexual and Relationship Therapy PO Box 13686, London SW20 9ZH.

REFERENCES

Allodi, F. and Stiasny, S. (1990) Women as torture victims. *Canadian Journal of Psychiatry*, **35**, 144–148.

APA. (1994) *Diagnostic and statistical manual of mental disorders* (4th edn). Washington, DC: American Psychiatric Association.

Ashton, A.K. (1995) Structured sexual therapy with severely dissociative patients. *Journal of Sex and Marital Therapy*, **21**, 276–281.

Baldwin, D.S., Thomas, S.C., and Birtwistle, J. (1997) Effects of antidepressant drugs on sexual function. *International Journal of Psychiatry in Clinical Practice*, **1**, 47–58.

Bancroft, J. (1989) *Human sexuality and its problems*. Edinburgh: Churchill Livingstone.

Becker, J.V. and Skinner, L.J . (1983) Assessment and treatment of rape related sexual dysfunctions. *Clinical Psychologist*, **36**, 102–105.

Becker, J.V., Skinner, L.J., Abel, G.G., and Cichon, J. (1986) Level of postassault sexual functioning in rape and incest victims. *Archives of Sexual Behaviour*, **15**, 37–49.

Becker, J.V., Skinner, L.J., Abel, G.G., and Treacy, EC. (1982) Incidence and types of sexual dysfunctions in rape and incest victims. *Journal of Sex and Marital Therapy*, **8**, 65–74.

Burgess, A.W. and Holmstrom, L.L. (1979) Adaptive strategies and recovery from rape. *American Journal of Psychiatry*, **136**, 1278–1282.

Coxell, A.W. and King, M.B. (1996) Male victims of rape and sexual abuse. *Sexual and Marital Therapy*, **11**, 297–308.

Craft, A. (1994) Issues in sex education for people with learning disabilities in the United Kingdom. *Sexual and Marital Therapy*, **9**, 145–157.

Gabbard, G.O. (1989) *Sexual exploitation in professional relationships*. Washington: American Psychiatric Press.

Glantz, K. and Himber, K. (1992) Sex therapy with dissociative disorders: A protocol. *Journal of Sex and Marital Therapy*, **18**, 147–153.

Goodwin, A.J. and Agronin, M.E. (1997) *A woman's guide to overcoming sexual fear and pain*. Oakland, CA: New Harbinger Publications.

Hawton, K. (1985) Sex therapy: A practical guide. Oxford: Oxford University Press.

Hawton, K. (1993) Sexual dysfunctions. In: K., Hawton, PM., Salkovskis, J., Kirk, and D.M., Clark, (eds) *Cognitive behaviour therapy for psychiatric problems*. Oxford: Oxford Medical Publications.

Hawton, K. (1995) Treatment of sexual dysfunctions by sex therapy and other approaches. *British Journal of Psychiatry*, **167**, 307–314.

Heiman, J.R. and LoPiccolo, J. (1996) *Becoming orgasmic. A sexual and personal growth programme for women*. London: Piatkus.

Johnson, R.L. and Shrier, D. (1987). Past sexual victimization by females of male patients in an adolescent medicine clinic population. *American Journal of Psychiatry*, **144**, 650–652.

Larsen, H. and Paguadan-Lopez, J. (1987) Stress-tension reduction in the treatment of sexually tortured women—an exploratory study. *Journal of Sex and Marital Therapy*, **13**, 210–218.

Lunde, I., Rasmussen, O.V., Wagner, G., and Lindholm, J. (1981) Sexual and pituitary-testicular function in torture victims. *Archives of Sexual Behaviour*, **10**, 25–32.

McCarthy, B.W. (1990) Treating sexual dysfunction associated with prior sexual trauma. *Journal of Sex and Marital Therapy*, **16**, 142–146.

Mackay, J. (2000) *The Penguin atlas of human sexual behaviour*. London: Penguin Books.

Masters, W.H. (1986) Sexual dysfunction as an aftermath of sexual assault of men by women. Journal of Sex and Marital Therapy, **12**, 35–45.

Masters, W.H. and Johnson, V.E. (1970) *Human sexual inadequacy*. Boston: Little Brown.

Mezey, G. and King, M. (1989) The effects of sexual assault on men. A survey of 22 victims. *Psychological Medicine*, **19**, 205–209.

Mezey, G.C. and King, M.B. (2000) *Male Victims of sexual assault* (2nd edn). Oxford: Oxford Medical Publications.

Mullen, P.E., Pathe, M., and Purcell, R. (2000) *Stalkers and their victims*. Cambridge: Cambridge University Press.

Myers, M.F. (1989) Men sexually assaulted as adults and sexually abused as boys. *Archives of Sexual Behaviour*, **18**, 203–215.

Petrak, J. (1996) Current trends in the assessment and treatment of victims of sexual violence. *Sexual and Marital Therapy*, **11**, 37–45.

Ridley, J. (1996) Some thoughts on supervision. *Sexual and Marital Therapy*, **11**, 77–88.

Slaughter, L. (2000) Involvement of drugs in sexual assault. *The Journal of Reproductive Medicine*, **45**, 425–430.

Smith, K.M. (1999) Drugs used in acquaintance rape. *Journal of the American Pharmaceutical Association*, **39**, 519–525.

Spector, I.P. and Carey, M.P. (1990) Incidence and prevalence of the sexual dysfunctions: A critical review of the empirical literature. *Archives of Sexual Behaviour*, **19**, 389–408.

Struckman-Johnson, C.J., Struckman-Johnson, D., Rucker, L., Bumby, K., and Donaldson, S. (1996) Sexual coercion reported by men and women in prison. *Journal of Sex Research*, **33**, 67–76.

Webster, L. (1997) Psychosexual disorders minisymposium: Taking a sexual history. *The Diplomate*, **4**, 266–269.

WHO (1992) *The ICD-10 classification of mental and behavioural disorders: Clinical descriptions and diagnostic guidelines (CDDG)*. Geneva: World Health Organization.

WHO (1995) *Technical Working Group on Female Genital Mutilation*. Geneva: World Health Organization.

WHO (1996) *Joint WHO/UNFPA/UNICEF statement on female genital mutilation*. Geneva: World Health Organization.

Chapter 9

COPING WITH THE PHYSICAL IMPACT OF SEXUAL ASSAULT

Barbara Hedge

INTRODUCTION

The psychological impact of sexual assault can be considerable as indicated throughout this book. Justifiably, many texts deal only with the long-term impact of the sexual assault (i.e., post-traumatic stress syndrome). However, a sexual assault can also have severe physical consequences including death or injury; it can also increase the risk of a variety of health complaints. Prevalence surveys in community and hospital settings have found 43–46% of sexually assaulted women to have required some contact with medical services (Campbell *et al.*, 1999; Felhaus, Houry, and Kaminsky, 2000).

Physical violence is an attribute of many sexual assaults. Individuals can be left with cuts, bruises, scars, and physical trauma that results in urinary or faecal incontinence. Such injuries can leave a lasting memory of the assault.

Women who have been vaginally penetrated during a sexual assault may become pregnant. Both men and women who have been sexually assaulted have to consider the possibility of having contracted a sexually transmitted infection including HIV.

Any of these outcomes can increase the negative impact of the initial sexual assault and increase the risk of the assaulted person experiencing psychological problems. Many sexual health clinics and gynaecological services recognize the need for psychological support for people who have unwittingly become pregnant or acquired a sexually transmitted infection or HIV through a consenting sexual activity. When these

The Trauma of Sexual Assault. Edited by Jenny Petrak and Barbara Hedge.
© 2002 John Wiley & Sons Ltd.

events occur as the result of an unwanted sexual experience such as sexual assault, the overall stress experienced is likely to be even higher and make the ensuing problems even harder to deal with.

Consequently, assessment of the psychological impact of the sexual assault needs to include consideration of associated physical outcomes. Services need to make provision for their impact to be addressed. The management of comprehensive medical and psychological assessments can be difficult; some outcomes (e.g., a possible pregnancy or a potential HIV infection) may need immediate attention, at a time when the assaulted person may not be ready or able to make important decisions.

This chapter will consider the potential psychological and health sequelae of the physical outcomes of a sexual assault and suggest possible ways of alleviating their impact. It will also address some of the difficulties encountered in managing these while addressing the direct impact of the sexual assault.

PHYSICAL SEQUELAE OF SEXUAL ASSAULT

Physical Injury

The percentage of people suffering physical injury at the time of a sexual assault is reported to range between 30 and 80% (Koss, Koss, and Woodruff, 1991; Riggs, Houry, Long, Markovchick, and Feldhaus, 2000). Many people suffer acute trauma that will heal within a few weeks. Although the need for hospitalization is rare, a number will retain scars or resulting disabilities for years, some for life. A recent 4-year prospective study in an urban trauma centre in Cleveland, Ohio (Riggs et al., 2000) found that force had been used in 80% of sexual assaults. In 27% of these a weapon was present.

Many individuals who have been sexually assaulted experience widespread body trauma including cuts to the body, head, arms, and legs; some report multiple trauma or major fractures. Trauma have been reported to the mouth, the vagina, and the anus as well as general bruising or scratches caused by restraints, knives, or body blows. Injuries to the anorectal area can be produced by the insertion of blunt objects, fingers, hands, and other foreign bodies as well as by the penis (Chen, Davis, and Ott, 1986). Bottomley, Sadler, and Welch (1999) in a survey of a sexual assault clinic reported 23% of the sample to have genital injuries, 59% to have other physical injuries, and 11% to need further hospital care. Riggs et al. (2000) found evidence of general body trauma in 67% of their sample and specific genital trauma in 53%. Woodling and Kossoris (1981) found that half of all sexually assaulted persons who reported to a trauma centre had vaginal and perineal trauma. A study by Cartwright *et al.* (1987) found that around 15% of sexually assaulted women had significant vaginal tears of which 1% required surgical repair. Kinderman, Carsten, and Massen (1996) found the highest rate of injury in sexual assault to be in people over the age of 55 years. Biggs, Stermac, and Divinsky (1998) found that more women without than with prior sexual experience had visible genital injuries (65 vs. 25.8%).

Men who have been sexually assaulted frequently assume, and think that others assume, that men should be able to prevent themselves from being sexually assaulted. However, many men considered themselves to be in a life-threatening situation at the time of the sexual assault and reported that they submitted in a response to protect their lives (Hillman, O'Mara, Tomlinson, and Harris, 1991; Huckle, 1995; King, 1992). Often, men present for treatment with physical injuries and only later reveal that these were acquired during a sexual assault. Assumptions such as 'I was too weak to defend myself' can contribute to the underreporting of sexual assault in men when no physical injuries have been sustained.

The limited, reliable prevalence data we have regarding sexual assault, particularly on men, can lead to difficulties in the interpretation of surveys. Sorenson, Stein, Siegal, Golding, and Burnam (1987) in a large-scale epidemiological study found that women were more likely to be physically harmed during a sexual assault. Kaufman, DiVasto, Jackson, Voorhees, and Christy (1980) however, found that sexual assaults on men more frequently resulted in serious non-genital injuries than did those on women. This discrepancy may be explained by the fact that Kaufman and colleagues directly recruited some of his male sample from a trauma clinic where men identified the sexual assault following medical assessment of their physical injuries.

Medical Examination

In order to gather evidence about the assault and the assailant and to assess the harm caused to the assaulted person, a medical examination is usually conducted when a sexual assault is reported. The medical examination is necessarily directed at those parts of the body involved in the assault (i.e. the oral, anal, and genital areas). One function of the medical examination is to gather evidence that relates to the potential consequences of the assault such as pregnancy or acquired sexually transmitted diseases including HIV infection. Details of the requirements of the medical assessment are given by Petter and Whitehill (1998) for women and by Tomlinson and Harrison (1998) for men.

Investigation not only requires a medical examination but also requires information about past consenting sexual behaviours and an account of the assault including details such as whether ejaculation occurred, etc. To someone who has just experienced a sexual assault, and is still distressed, these details may appear irrelevant, trivial, or even a further assault (Parrot, 1991).

Pregnancy

Unprotected penetrative vaginal assault can result in pregnancy. Although the reported incidence of pregnancy following sexual assault is low, approximately 1–5% (Ledray, Lund, and Kiresuk, 1979; Koss *et al.*, 1991), it has to be considered. Bottomley *et al.* (1999) found 16% of females, reporting to a clinical service for sexual assault in the UK, to require emergency contraception.

The details of a woman's menstrual history and contraceptive practices, as well as details of the sexual act, need to be elicited to ascertain whether pregnancy is a possible outcome. It is not unknown for an assailant to wear a condom, maybe to prevent traces of bodily fluids that could lead to DNA profiling, or for a woman's request that she insert her diaphragm before intercourse to be granted. Such behaviours are not always revealed at first questioning as a woman may fear that they will be interpreted as her consenting to the sexual acts that followed.

Although pregnancy testing is recommended in most emergency care protocols for women who have been sexually assaulted, studies have found that this does not always follow. In the USA, the National Victims Centre reported (1992) that only 40% of women who had been sexually assaulted received a pregnancy test or prophylaxis. Smugar, Spina, and Merz (2000) surveyed the practice of providing emergency contraception to women who had been sexually assaulted. They found that some hospitals prohibited emergency contraceptives for cases of sexual assault and others only provided them when requested.

Sexually Transmitted Infections

The acquisition of sexually transmitted infections (STIs) such as chlamydia trichomatis, gonorrhea, herpes, or papilloma virus has to be considered. Although these infections can usually be treated successfully, they can have long-term negative consequences for health; papilloma virus that leads to genital warts is associated with cervical cancer, and chlamydia is associated with blocked fallopian tubes and possible infertility. Life threatening infections such as hepatitis B and C, and HIV (see below) can also be transmitted (Glaser, Hammerschlag, and McCormack, 1989). Current policy in the UK and in the USA (Centers for Disease Control, 1998; Clinical Effectiveness Group, 1999; Harrison and Murphy, 1999), is to offer all adults vaccination for hepatitis B. Unfortunately, no prophylactic vaccination is as yet available to protect against hepatitis C.

The risk of acquiring an STI is increased when sexual intercourse is traumatic. Even when no trauma is visible to the naked eye, micro-traumas are more common in assault when insufficient lubrication is present. When sexual assault is the first experience of sexual intercourse, this can be particularly risky. Anal intercourse is associated with more trauma than vaginal intercourse, even between consenting adults. Unconsenting anal penetration can result in major trauma and so increase the risk of STIs. Likewise, in postmenopausal women, a lack of lubrication can increase the risk of trauma. STIs can also be acquired through oral sex. Genital herpes can infect the oral cavity and gonorrhea in the mouth has also been reported.

There is little published data on the incidence of STIs following sexual assault. However, estimates have been made of 4–30% of women who have been raped acquiring a sexually transmitted disease during sexual assault (Forster, Pritard, Munday, and Goldmeier, 1986; Forster, Estreich, and Hooi, 1991; Koss and Heslet, 1992; Bottomley et al., 1999). A comparable figure of 18% has been reported in men (Hillman et al., 1991).

Swabs are usually taken during the medical examination to ascertain the presence of infection. As not all pathogens are detectable immediately following a sexual act, some tests may have to be repeated 2–12 weeks after the incident. As some STIs such as chlamydia trichomatis can remain asymptomatic, it is unlikely that a woman will request a screen. Routine screening needs to be a part of every assault screening programme.

Before the presence of an infection can be confirmed, an antimicrobial prophylaxis regime is increasingly provided. Rates of uptake of the offer of STI prophylaxis range from 26 to 90% (Bottomley et al., 1999; Ciancone, Wilson, Collette, and Gerson, 2000).

For treatable infections, examiners may suggest postponing the examination until the assaulted person is less traumatized. Protected sexual intercourse will be advised during this time to prevent the spread of any acquired infection to any consenting sexual partner.

AIDS

Another issue that requires immediate attention is the possibility that the sexual assault will result in the transmission of HIV infection. There may be a need to provide the results of an HIV test for compensation claims or court cases relating to the assault (Dyer, 2001).

It may also be possible to prevent the transmission of HIV with a course of anti-retroviral medications. Tests to determine a person's HIV status are based on the detection of antibodies that develop in response to infection. These are not immediately detectable. Thus, a continuing concern for those who have been sexually assaulted is the possibility of HIV infection. Reliable detection is usually possible 3–4 months after infection.

HIV infection which can lead to AIDS can be, and frequently is, transmitted sexually. Penetrative sexual acts between an infected person and another do not always lead to transmission of infection. It is twice as likely that HIV is transmitted from a man to a woman and anal sex is more risky than vaginal sex. The risk for HIV transmission following a single receptive penile–anal act is estimated to be 0.1–3.0% and for a single receptive penile–vaginal act 0.1–0.2% (Mastro and de Vincenzi, 1996), with an increased risk of transmission when sex is traumatic (Gostin *et al.*, 1994). It also seems possible that HIV can be passed through receptive oral sex (Schacker, Collier, Hughes, Shea, and Corey, 1996; Berrey and Shea, 1997). Again, there appears to be an increased incidence when the recipient has oral trauma. However, there have been few documented cases of HIV transmission consequent on sexual assault (Gostin *et al.*, 1994; Albert, Wahlberg, Leitner, Escanilla, and Uhlen, 1994; Murphy, Kitchen, Harris, and Forster, 1989).

Recently, great advances have been seen in the treatment of HIV. Combination therapies of anti-retrovirals can decrease the rate of people dying from HIV disease and increase the time people live with HIV (Wong *et al.*, 2000; Rogers, Sinka, Molesworth, Evans, and Allardice, 2000). However, the advances are not yet sufficient for medications to be seen as a cure. At best, they can be seen as allowing people to live with a chronic phase of HIV for some time. Unfortunately, HIV disease remains a fatal illness.

The prevention of HIV transmission therefore remains of paramount importance. Post-exposure prophylaxis has been shown to lower the risk of transmission of HIV by 79% following occupational exposure to HIV (Centers for Disease Control, 1995). However, there is limited evidence of the efficacy of such interventions following sexual assault. Notwithstanding, both in the USA and in France this has been the recommended standard practice for some time (Bamberger, Waldo, Gerberding, and

Katz, 1999; Centers for Disease Control, 1998; Bani-Sadr et al., 2001). Although there appears to be a general increase in this practice (Wilson, Mitchell, Bradbury, and Chavez, 1999), clinics in both the UK and the US vary widely in their practice (Glaser et al., 1989).

Current recommendations suggest that a course of medications be started within 72 hours. If the assailant is known, it may be possible to ascertain fairly quickly whether he is infected with HIV and so capable of transmitting infection. However, in many cases the assaulted person will not only have to make a decision of whether to start prophylactic medications with no knowledge of the assailant's HIV status, but will also have to accept that he or she will never know the assailant's HIV status. As the medications can have negative side effects, the decision of whether to continue with medications despite negative side effects or to stop in order to improve immediate quality of life has to be made in the absence of relevant information. The feasibility of offering HIV prophylaxis to people who had been sexually assaulted was assessed by Putz, Thomas, and Cowles (1996) and Weibe, Comay, McGregor, and Ducceschi (2000). Weibe and colleagues found that in the emergency department of a Canadian General Hospital, HIV prophylaxis was offered to all 258 people who were seen following a sexual assault. Of the 71 who accepted the offer of HIV prophylaxis, only eight completed the full 4 week trial and returned for the final clinic visit. Most of those accepting prophylaxis were at high risk of acquiring HIV. They had been assaulted by a person known to be HIV-positive, or by a man who has sex with men, or by a known injecting drug user. Men who had been assaulted were three times more likely, and those who had been anally raped were seven times more likely, to initiate post-exposure prophylaxis than women. Following these findings, the service changed its policy to offering HIV prophylaxis only to those at high risk. In the USA, the National Victims Centre (1992) reported that only 27% of women who had been sexually assaulted received information about the risk of HIV or an HIV antibody test. Putz et al. (1996) reported a higher level of completion of a prophylactic regimen. They found that 73% of individuals who received emergency care at a sexual assault treatment centre in Milwaukee reported completing the course of prophylactic medications. Various reasons were given for non-completion of treatment, a major reason cited being a misunderstanding of the need to continue. Similar results have been found in France (Bani-Sadr et al., 2001) with 62% of people remaining adherent to triple therapy after 4 weeks. Twenty-one per cent had already terminated the prophylaxis following negative HIV serology in the perpetrators.

Myles, Hirozawa, Katz, Kimmerling, and Bamberger (2000) report less uptake of the offer of HIV post-exposure prophylaxis in non-white and homeless women in San Francisco. This mirrors the uptake of anti-retroviral treatment in non-white people with HIV disease, (Moore, Stanton, Gopalan, and Chaisson, 1994; Palella *et al.*, 1998). The reasons behind this finding are unclear. However, they do not reflect the risk of transmission; non-white and homeless women are more likely to have been assaulted anally or vaginally than housed women. It could be that non-whites have more negative preconceptions about anti-retroviral drug treatments, or that they are less comfortable with taking preventative medicine. Alternatively, attempts make by health service professionals to engage people to partake of anti-retroviral prophylaxis may differ for whites and non-whites.

Weibe *et al.* (2000) noted that the clinic staff found it very difficult to engage the traumatized sexually assaulted persons in discussion about HIV prophylaxis, endorsing the assumption that people experience difficulties with difficult decision making when in a state of shock or distress.

PSYCHOLOGICAL SEQUELAE AND HEALTH PROBLEMS

Shock

One of the immediate emotions that frequently follows traumatic events such as a sexual assault is shock. When in shock, individuals may display symptoms of numbness and disbelief. They may appear dazed and confused and may experience dissociation and memory loss. Their ability to process cognitive information decreases and decision making is likely to be absent or ill thought through. Normal patterns of thoughts and behaviours can become disorganized and disrupted. All the above symptoms (considered in greater depth in Chapter 5) suggest an acute anxiety disorder (APA, 1994). It is at precisely this time that a number of issues that can have significant consequences for the future need to be addressed. First and foremost, there is a need to report the sexual assault and agree to a medical examination in order that evidence can be obtained that might be used to ascertain or prove the identity of the assailant. Second, the medical examination and clinical tests may reveal issues that require decisions and choices. It is crucial then that any state of shock is identified and that the assaulted person is given support in minimizing its impact. There is a need for access to crisis intervention services and further psychological support.

Physical Injury

Increased rates of enduring physical as well as mental health difficulties have been reported in people who have been sexually assaulted, even when little or no physical injury was sustained in the assault. The after-effects of physical trauma can encompass health, somatic, and psychological symptomatology. Sometimes, these are intricately related and not separable. However, for clarity, have they been considered separately in the following sections.

Somatic Complaints

It has been documented that people who have been sexually assaulted experience higher levels of chronic pelvic pain, premenstrual symptoms, stomach pains, nausea, loss of appetite, irritable bowel, and fibromyalgia (Koss and Heslet, 1992; Golding, 1999; Collett, Cordle, Steward, and Jagger, 1998; Ehlert, Heim, and Hellhamer, 1999). Other commonly reported symptoms are sleep disturbance, eating difficulties, headaches, and pelvic pain (Blanchard and Able, 1976; Norris and Feldman-Summers, 1981). These have been seen to persist for months and even years after the assault. All of these may be precipitated or maintained by psychological factors. Visible reminders of the sexual assault can have the effect of prolonging the negative experience of the event and postponing an adjustment to the sexual assault. Physicians who are not familiar with the association between somatic symptomatology and past sexual assault can find it difficult to diagnose the problem if they fail to elicit a complete history of the symptomatology.

Holmes, Resnick, and, Frampton (1998) reported 42.6% of individuals presenting at a follow-up to a sexual assault service to still report physical complaints. Continuing difficulties with sleep, appetite, and sexual functioning were common.

Men who assumed that they should have been able to defend themselves but did not, and later reflected on their response to the real or implied physical violence, have been found to experience psychological distress and low self-esteem (Perrot and Webber, 1996; Hillman et al., 1991; Mezey and King, 1989; and Huckle, 1995).

Sexual Dysfunction

A variety of sexual dysfunctions have been reported in people who have been sexually assaulted. These include fear of sex, arousal dysfunction, and decreased libido (Becker *et al.*, 1982; Ellis, Atkeson, and Calhoun, 1981) and are described in detail in Chapter 8.

Substance Misuse

There appears to be a complex relationship between serious alcohol and drug-related problems, selling sex for money, and sexual assault (Frank, Turner, Stewart, Jacob, and West, 1981; Burnam *et al.*, 1988). The direction of causation is unclear. Kilpatrick, Acierno, Resnick, Saunders, and Best (1997) conducted a longitudinal study in which they investigated substance use and violent assault in a group of women over a 2-year period. They found that initially the use of drugs, but not of alcohol, increased the probability of a woman receiving a further assault. Once a further assault had occurred, the probability of the woman abusing alcohol and drugs significantly increased even when a woman had no previous history of substance abuse or assault. Thus, there appears to be a cycle of increasing risk of substance abuse and assault.

Increased rates of alcohol abuse have also been reported following sexual assault. Frank *et al.* (1981) found 29% of women reporting excessive use of alcohol following sexual assault. Burnam *et al.* (1988), in a study of men, women and children who had been sexually assaulted, found 16% reporting alcohol abuse and 18% reporting drug abuse or dependence with the onset following the sexual assault. Later alcohol abuse was seen significantly more in men than women but no gender difference was found in drug abuse. Hankins, Skinner, Miller, Frayne, and Tripp (1999) reported alcohol abuse to be twice the rate in women who experienced military-related sexual assault.

Use of Medical Services

A number of studies have investigated the rate of use of general medical services by people who have experienced sexual assault. Phelps, Wallace, and, Waigandt (1989) found that people who had been sexually assaulted made 35% more visits to their physicians each year and viewed their health as poorer than did a control group of non-assaulted persons. The assaulted persons also reported more behaviours associated with long-term negative health outcomes such as increased smoking, alcohol and caffeine consumption. Kimmerling and Calhoun (1994) found that women who had been sexually assaulted continued to show an increased use of medical services, compared with a control group, 1 year after the assault when somatic symptoms were no longer elevated.

Koss (1988) assessed the relative impact of sexual assault, physical assault, and burglary on the use of medical services by women in the 2 years following the incident. All groups of women showed an increased use of medical services when compared with those experiencing no criminal events. Both the sexually and the physically assaulted showed higher rates of medical visits than did those who had experienced burglary; those who had been both sexually and physically assaulted had twice the rate of medical visits as did those experiencing no criminal event. A further report by Koss *et al.* (1991) found women who had been sexually assaulted contact physicians twice as often as other women with the greatest use of health care occurring 2 years after the sexual assault. Stein, Golding, Siegal, Burnam, and Sorenson (1988) reported that, when violence had been used in the sexual assault, the post-sexual assault functioning was better than when there was no violence. Although this finding may at first seem counter-intuitive, it could be that a woman is more easily able to attribute a sexual assault as an event outside her control when violence has been used. When there had been no violence, she may have been left questioning whether or not she could have prevented the sexual assault.

Medical Examination

To someone who has just experienced a sexual assault, the medical investigations may bring further distress (Parrot, 1991). Some authors (Williams and Holmes, 1981; Campbell, and Raja, 1999; Campbell *et al.*, 1999) have described the negative experiences encountered while receiving services provided to help with the initial sexual assault as a 'secondary victimization'. Women in the Campbell *et al.* (1999) study, particularly those who had experienced sexual assault by a non-stranger, reported finding hurtful comments from medical or legal service providers which indicated a lack of belief in their accounts or a suggestion that the case was not worth pursuing.

Pregnancy

Shock, anxiety, and fear are likely to follow the realization that a pregnancy has resulted from a sexual assault. The emotional impact may well continue at least until a decision is made on how to proceed. Termination of a pregnancy or continuation of the pregnancy with delivery of the baby is likely to have a profound psychological impact on a woman and significant others in her life.

Psychological Sequelae of Termination of Pregnancy

A number of studies suggest that the psychological distress experienced by women undergoing a termination of pregnancy can be affected by the attitudes and sensitivity of the medical and nursing staff providing the service. Although the research is not directly concerned with termination of pregnancy in those who have conceived through a sexual assault, it is relevant as not all care staff will be cognizant of the circumstances leading to each pregnancy.

Studies reviewing the psychological responses to women following termination of pregnancy find evidence that most women have as good or better psychological health, marital and interpersonal relationships as before the termination (Figa-Talamanca, 1982). Although these studies are not based on women who have been sexually assaulted, they are relevant in showing that the termination *per se* need not adversely affect the woman's mental health. However, ambivalence or negative attitudes to the termination do appear to contribute to a higher incidence of psychological problems (Belsey, Greer, Lai, Lewis, and Beard, 1977). Handy (1982) in a review of the distress associated with termination of pregnancy found that women who were ambivalent or distressed showed more psychological symptomatology when faced with unsympathetic service provision.

A number of studies (Osofsky and Osofsky, 1978; Jacobs, Garcia, Rickels, and Preucel, 1974) reported that when women expressed guilt about a termination then this recurred as a problem later. An Australian study (Quinn, 1980) noted that the stress induced by organizing a termination of pregnancy was frequently greater than that associated with the decision to have a termination. The importance of recognizing the effect of cumulative stressors on the woman at this time must be emphasized.

The importance of good social support in minimizing the negative effects of the termination has been demonstrated (Mosley, Follingsstad, Harley, and Heckel, 1981; Drower and Nash, 1978). Drower and Nash found that low social support was the most significant determinant of a poor response to a termination of pregnancy. When a partner or significant other was opposed to the termination, the woman experienced greater anxiety and depression. David, Rasmussen, and Holst (1981) report a higher rate of psychiatric admissions 3 months post-termination in those women who experienced less social support during their decision-making time and operative procedure. For younger women it seems that the parents' support is most important; for older women the partner's support is most important (Drower and Nash, 1978).

If a woman has had previous unprotected sex within that menstrual cycle, she may already be pregnant. The ambiguity of the paternity and the difficulties of proceeding with or terminating such a pregnancy need to be considered. This can be particularly problematic when a couple have experienced difficulties conceiving and a child is desired. Similarly, the potential difficulty of raising a child who could be the offspring of the assailant needs to be considered. Dunlop (1978) and Shusterman (1979) suggest that the characteristics of a termination of pregnancy associated with a poor outcome are:

- pressure in decision making;
- previous psychiatric condition;
- medical reasons for termination;
- anger on discovering the pregnancy;
- low intimacy with partner;
- dissatisfaction with the termination decision.

It is important that all these factors are considered in the assessment.

Sexually Transmitted Infections

Although the incidence of people acquiring an STI from a sexual assault is relatively low, in the range of 4 to 30%, within a genitourinary medicine clinic setting, a higher percentage of patients will disclose that their STI was acquired through a sexual assault.

High levels of psychological distress have been reported in people attending genitourinary medicine clinics (Ikkos, Fitzpatrick, Frost, and Nazeer, 1987; Catalan, Bradley, Gallway, and Hawton, 1981). Particular aspects of STIs appear to be associated with distress (Hedge, 1997). Responses to a diagnosis of genital herpes, a common recurrent and often painful infection, can include depression, anger, a desire to withdraw, and feelings of hopelessness (Drob, Loemer, and Lifshutz, 1985). The long-term sequelae of genital warts (i.e., an increased incidence of carcinoma of the cervix) can increase the distress of diagnosis.

The fear of transmitting an STI to a partner, and the fear of sexual rejection because of an infection, can affect sexual enjoyment and may negatively affect relationships. At a time when social support, especially from significant others, is of vital importance in coping with the sexual assault, the acquisition of an STI can have a devastating effect on a person's rate of recovery.

HIV Disease

Most people are these days aware of HIV and the long-term poor prognosis for those who become infected. A study by Baker, Burgess, Brickman, and Davis (1990) reported 26% of people who had been sexually assaulted to express concern that they may have acquired HIV. Infection can be accompanied by a flu-like illness. Thus, any such symptoms that follow a sexual assault are likely to increase stress and anxiety.

A recent feature of rape is an assailant who tells his victim that he or she will acquire HIV or AIDS as a consequence of the assault. Hillman *et al.* (1991) reported 57% of men who had been assaulted to report such a statement occurring during the assault. Whether or not the assailant was HIV-positive, and so in a position to transmit the infection, is generally not known. However, individuals experiencing this threat then have an additional concern for which the validity cannot immediately be established. Worrying about unpredictable outcomes can further increase the psychological trauma; increased anxiety states, panic attacks, obsessive compulsive disorder, and hypochondriasis can be experienced. If a person does contract HIV from an assault, they are then vulnerable to all the psychological sequelae that can arise from having HIV, a noncurable infection (Catalan, Burgess, and Klimes, 1995).

INTERVENTIONS

Decision Making

Possible sequelae of a sexual assault require a decision to be made by the assaulted person if adverse future outcomes are to be minimized. Women may have to consider the risk of a pregnancy resulting from the sexual assault, and both sexes are at risk of contracting an STI or HIV. Preventative behaviours taken soon after the sexual assault may be able to alter the outcomes.

Psychological models that aim to explain health behaviours frequently consider the decision-making process. Rational decision making has been linked to beliefs about the behaviour, its efficacy, social norms, etc. as in the Health Belief Model (Rosenstock, 1966; Becker and Maiman, 1975), the Theory of Reasoned Action (Fishbein and Ajzen, 1975), and the Theory of Planned Behaviour (Ajzen, 1985). It is very likely that these models could explain the reasoning of a health carer's internal dialogue when he or she offers a termination of pregnancy or prophylactic medications for sexually transmitted diseases or HIV infection.

However, the low explanatory value of such models in predicting actual behaviours suggests that people do not always engage in rational argument when making decisions. Leventhal (1970) suggested that the emotions generated by each of the possible alternatives influenced the final action taken. It is possible that following an emotive event, such as a sexual assault, undue weight will be given to an option that decreases the immediate negative emotions and that less rational thought will be given to the long-term consequences of the action chosen. Consequently, it is essential that, when people who have been sexually assaulted are required to make important decisions, the emotions associated with each of the available options are addressed, while a rational problem-solving approach is adopted.

The decision-making process has a number of stages. It is necessary to:

- gather evidence;
- weigh up advantages and disadvantages;
- explore the difficulties associated with making either decision;
- live with the decision made.

The support that a clinical psychologist or counsellor can provide for individuals making decisions, such as whether or not to continue with a pregnancy or to take HIV prophylactic medications, etc., are explored in the relevant sections.

Social Support

Good social support has been identified as a contributing factor to the adjustment of survivors of sexual assault (Burgess and Holmstrom, 1978; Kimerling and Calhoun, 1994). This is not surprising as research studies consistently report the protective effects that social support can have on the impact of stressful situations for many and diverse clinical samples (Cohen and Wills, 1985; Cohen and Smythe, 1985). The availability of post-assault social support has been shown to depend both on pre-assault variables and on factors relating to the assault. Generally, more violent sexual assaults are associated with better family support (Frank and Stewart, 1984). When the assaulted person is held responsible for the event or is unable to tell others, social support is necessarily limited and poor adjustment has been found (Cohen and Roth, 1987).

Statistics suggest that many relationships experience difficulties following a sexual assault. Crenshaw (1978) found that 50–80% of relationships broke up post-assault and Miller, Williams, and Bernstein (1982) reported increased communication difficulties post-assault. As social support is vital to adjustment, it could be that just when it is needed (e.g., when coping with an STI or a pregnancy resulting from the sexual assault), it decreases in availability. It is therefore important that psychological interventions aim to support the social network, especially the partner or the family, of the assaulted person in an attempt to maintain their available social support.

Medical Examination

The procedures required during a forensic medical examination are described in Chapter 11. The medical examination to determine the extent of trauma, and possible transmission of pathogens, will similarly require a detailed examination of those parts of the body involved in the assault (e.g., the genitals, anus, and the mouth). This examination can easily be construed as a further assault on the person as well as a reminder of the unwanted event (Campbell and Raja, 1999). The task is for the medical examiner to minimize further trauma during this necessary procedure. Similarly the interviewer needs to identify whether a person is in a state of shock, prioritize crucial issues, and develop sufficient rapport with the assaulted person to maximize the chance that he or she will return for further investigations. Assessment requires skilled, empathetic questioning.

It is important to ensure that all medical professionals who provide sexual assault services are aware of the effects that their behaviours and ways of approaching a person might be perceived or interpreted at this time. The medical examination and interview is not the place for judgements and moralization. If the health carers have doubts about the validity of a person's story, then this can be taken up discretely with the relevant professionals (e.g., police, psychologists, social workers). People who falsely report sexual assault have different psychological needs. Doubts may be misplaced; it is important that people are not further traumatized by the negative remarks of health carers.

Regular training of health carers can help them understand the needs of people who have been sexually assaulted and modify their behaviours accordingly (Campbell et al., 1999). Provision of training resources such as The Long Island College Hospital and Junior League of Brooklyn (1998) instructional video Restoring dignity: Frontline response to rape can alert health carers to people's psychological responses to medical investigations.

Pregnancy

One issue that needs to be prioritized for women is that of the possibility of pregnancy. To ascertain whether pregnancy is possible, the person needs to give an accurate description of the acts that occurred during the assault. Establishing whether vaginal penetration occurred (or did not) can eliminate inappropriate yet disturbing questioning and unnecessary investigations.

In order for appropriate examinations, clinical tests, and decisions about medications to be taken, it is crucial to know:

- the woman's reproductive status;
- the woman's contraceptive practices;
- the assailant's acts;
- the assailant's use of contraceptives;
- the date and time of the assault in comparison with the time of the discussion.

If from these there is a possibility of pregnancy, then it needs to be addressed. The Abortion Act does allow pregnancy following sexual assault to be terminated. However, not all women are at ease with termination even when conception is unwanted. Some view the foetus as innocent and feel protective towards it. They would experience feelings of guilt if they destroyed it. Feelings of guilt may also be evoked when individuals break their cultural society's traditional systems (Illsley and Hall, 1976). There can also be circumstances when the paternity of an unborn child could be that of a loved partner, and termination before paternity is established is unthinkable. It is therefore important to ascertain the background details of an assaulted person in order to assess the effect a termination might have.

The simplest termination procedure is that of emergency contraception or the 'morning-after pill'. This consists of a high-estrogen hormone (diethyl-stilbesterol) given for a few days. This prevents implantation of any foetus into the lining of the womb. It is reported to be 98% effective if taken in the 72 hours following sexual intercourse (Drife, 1993; Schein, 1999). Although the time of efficacy of this medication is widely publicised, its common name may not alert women, who have not immediately reported an assault, to the fact that they still have the option of taking it. Similarly, the 72 hours does mean that health carers have some time to establish the possibility of pregnancy before this option is no longer available.

Women who present too late for emergency contraception, or who are unable to make a decision at this time, do still have the option of a termination up to 24 weeks (Abortion Act, 1967; Human Fertilisation and

Embryology Act, 1990) if it is necessary to prevent some permanent injury to the physical or mental health of the pregnant woman. Up to 12 weeks, vacuum aspiration is the favoured method. During this procedure, the cervix is dilated and the placenta and foetus are dislodged and extracted. Later terminations usually induce an early labour and the birth of a dead foetus. This is a slightly more risky option to a woman's health than the 'morning-after pill' as the standard risks associated with a general anaesthetic—perforation, the risks of haemorrhage, rupture of the uterine wall, or cervical damage—are encountered (Gavey, Govan, Hodge, and Callander, 1972). However, the aim is to minimize the overall negative impact of the sexual assault and maximize the woman's overall quality of life following it. In some cases, it may be better to consider slowly the possibility of termination of pregnancy, rather than subject the woman to further trauma by an immediate medical intervention (Campbell and Raja, 1999).

Poor psychological response to a termination of pregnancy is seen when a woman is ambivalent or opposed to it. The clinic should aim to provide a setting in which no pressure or coercion is applied, where a woman and, when possible, her partner are allowed to explore the options of a termination or continuing with the pregnancy in a non-judgemental setting.

Pre-termination counselling aims to help a women (and her partner) make a decision she can live with and that does not increase psychological morbidity. There is a need for pre-termination counselling, especially when a woman shows ambivalence, or has little identifiable social support, or when she and her partner hold opposing attitudes to a termination of pregnancy. Pre-termination counselling aims to help a woman explore and come to a decision about how to cope with the pregnancy. It needs to provide a facility in which thoughts and feelings (e.g., guilt) can be expressed and where decisions can be made (Hare and Haywood, 1981; Ashton, 1980).

Rational theories of information-based decision making would suggest that pre-termination counselling adopt a problem-solving approach as detailed in Table 9.1. However, if, as described above (Leventhal, 1970), women make the decision about termination on the basis of their immediate emotional reactions, then a period for reflection is very important. This enables women to take time to consider the rational issues and not to feel pressurized by any counsellor.

Even though counsellors are bound to have their own views as to the best way forward for a woman, it is important that they are able to maintain a professional non-judgemental counselling role (i.e., help a woman to make an informed choice) and not attempt to bias her judgement. Some women, having lost their sense of control through the sexual assault, may

Table 9.1   Decision making for termination of pregnancy

Consider all the facts:
  Emotional
  Practical

List all the possible options:
  Continue with the pregnancy
  Keep the baby
  Have a termination of pregnancy

Consider the advantages and disadvantages of each option:
  Now
  In the future
  Practical considerations
Ensure that the worst as well as the best possible outcomes are considered:
  Beliefs and feelings
  Partner's view
  Effect on future partners/relationships

Weigh up all options:
  Make a provisional decision
Ensure understanding of effect of taking no decision:
  Taking no decision, amounts to a decision to continue with the pregnancy
Avoid procrastination:
  Final date for a 24-week termination

Reflect on decision and confirm:
  Aim to live with decision
  Live with decision

Provide support before and after the termination or during the continuing pregnancy.

be fearful of making any decision and unwilling to take responsibilities for own actions. They may view the counsellor as an expert and encourage him or her to make the decision for them. Rather than do this, it is important that the counsellor offer a woman the opportunity to address issues of control and low self-esteem. Such reasons make it important that suitably trained professionals (e.g., clinical psychologists or qualified counsellors) take on this task. Physicians, although specialists in the legal aspects of endorsing a termination of pregnancy, are rarely qualified to provide the sensitive yet focused support needed in this situation.

David *et al.* (1981) found that women who were experiencing difficulties with their relationship, or who were not in a relationship, were more likely to report psychological distress after a termination of pregnancy.

As the incidence of relationship break-up increases following sexual assault (Becker, Skinner, Abel, and Treacy 1982; Burgess and Holmstrom, 1979), it is important that both the assaulted woman and her partner are given support for their relationship as well as for the decision about the termination of pregnancy.

In order to increase social support to the assaulted woman, it can sometimes be useful to address the needs of her partner or parents. This may be particularly important in cultures and communities where an assaulted woman is seen as dirty or sinful, etc., even when no responsibility for the assault or ensuing pregnancy can be levied at her. For single women it is important to identify people who might be able to provide social support. The provision of a support group for women who have required a termination of pregnancy following sexual assault could prove useful for those who do not have an adequate support network. As the frequency of pregnancy following assault is relatively rare such a group may need to draw candidates from a wide area. Such a group can also provide support from role models who show that they have coped successfully with the negative outcomes of the assault. Alternatively, sexual assault self-help groups might usefully address the issue of what women can do if they become pregnant during an assault, as the thought of a possible pregnancy will have been entertained by many of the members.

Sexually Transmitted Infections

It has been well documented in this book that sexual assault carries significant mental health morbidity. Co-mordidity with an STI acquired during the sexual assault is likely to increase this morbidity, as STIs can themselves be associated with significant mental health problems (Hedge, 1997; Holmes, 1999).

The aims of psychological interventions with people who have acquired an STI are to:

- increase useful coping strategies;
- maintain adherence to medication regimens;
- reduce the possibility of somatic symptoms misattributed to the STI;
- reduce sexual and relationship difficulties.

Psychological interventions that help people to reduce the emotional and physical distress associated with the STI can be useful; for example, cognitive-behavioural strategies that increase perceptions of control of the situation such as positive thought control and decatastrophication can be

treatment of a rape induced psychophysiological cardiovascular disorder. *Behaviour Therapy*, **7**, 113–119.

Bottomley, C., Sadler, T., and Welch, J. (1999) Integrated clinical service for sexual assault victims in a genitourinary setting. *Sexually Transmitted Infections*, **75**, 116–119.

Burgess, A. and Holmstrom, L. (1978) Recovery from rape and prior life stress. *Research in Nursing and Health*, **1**, 165–174.

Burgess, A. and Holmstrom, L. (1979) Rape: Sexual disruption and recovery. *American Journal of Orthopsychiatry*, **49**, 648–657.

Burnam, M., Stein, J., Golding, J., Siegal, J., Sorenson, S., Forsythe, A., and Telles, C. (1988) Sexual assault and mental disorders in a community population. *Journal of Consulting and Clinical Psychology*, **56**, 843–850.

Campbell, R. and Bybee, D. (1997) Emergency medical services for rape victims: Detecting the cracks in service delivery. *Womens Health*, **3**, 75–101.

Campbell, R. and Raja, S. (1999) Secondary victimization of rape victims: Insights from mental health professionals who treat survivors of violence. *Violence and Victims*, **14**, 261–275.

Campbell, R., Sefl, T., Barnes, H., Ahrens, C., Wasco, S., and Zaragozo-Diesfeld, Y. (1999) Community services for rape survivors: Enhancing psychological well-being or increasing trauma? *Journal of Consulting and Clinical Psychology*, **67**, 847–858.

Catalan, J. (ed.) (1999) *Mental health and HIV infection: Psychological and psychiatric aspects*. London: UCL Press.

Catalan, J., Bradley, M., Gallwey, J., and Hawton, K. (1981) Sexual dysfunction and psychiatric morbidity in patients attending a clinic for sexually transmitted diseases. *British Journal of Psychiatry*, **138**, 292–296.

Catalan, J., Burgess, A., and Klimes, I. (1995) *Psychological medicine of HIV infection*. Oxford: Oxford Medical Publications.

Cartwright, P.S. and the Sexual Assault Study Group (1987) Factors that correlate with injury sustained by survivors of sexual assault. *Obstetrics and Gynaecology*, **70**, 44–46.

Centers for Disease Control. (1995) Case-control study of HIV seroconversion in healthcare workers after percutaneous exposure to HIV-infected blood—France, United Kingdom and United States, January 1988–August 1994. *Morbidity and Mortality Weekly Report*, **44**, 929–933.

Centers for Disease Control. (1998) Guidelines for treatment of sexually transmitted diseases. *Morbidity and Mortality Weekly Report*, **47**(RR1), 1–116.

Chen, Y., Davis, M., and Ott, D. (1986) Traumatic rectal hematoma following anal rape. *Annals of Emergency Medicine*, **15**, 122–124.

Ciancone, A., Wilson, C., Collette, R., and Gerson, L. (2000) Sexual assault nurse examiner programs in the United States. *Annals of Emergency Medicine*, **35**, 353–357.

Clinical Effectiveness Group. (1999) National guideline for the management of adult victims of sexual assault. *Sexually Transmitted Infections*, **75**(Suppl. 1), S82–S84.

Cohen, L. and Roth, S. (1987) The psychological aftermath of rape: Long-term effects and individual differences in recovery. *Journal of Social and Clinical Psychology*, **5**, 525–534.

Cohen, S. and Smythe, S. (1985) *Social support and health*. Orlando, FL: Academic Press.

Cohen, S. and Wills, T. (1985) Stress, social support and the buffering hypothesis. *Psychological Bulletin*, **98**, 310–357.

Collett, B., Cordle, C., Stewart, C., and Jagger, C. (1998) A comparative study of women with chronic pelvic pain, chronic nonpelvic pain, and those with no history of pain attending general practitioners. *British Journal of Obstetrics and Gynaecology*, **105**, 87–92.

Crenshaw, T. (1978) Counselling the family and friends. In S. Halper (ed.) *Rape: Helping the victim*. Oradell, NJ: Medical Economics Book Division.

David, H.P., Rasmussen, N.E., and Holst, E. (1981) Post-partum and post-abortion psychotic reactions. *Family Planning Perspectives*, **13**, 88–92.

Drife, O. (1993) Deregulating emergency contraception. *British Medical Journal*, **307**, 695–696.

Drob, S., Loemer, M., and Lifshutz, H. (1985) Genital herpes: The psychological consequences. *British Journal of Medical Psychology*, **58**, 307–315.

Drower, S.J. and Nash, E.S. (1978) Therapeutic abortion on psychiatric grounds: Part II, The continuing debate. *South African Medical Journal*, **16**, 643-647.

Dunlop, J.Z. (1978) Counselling patients requesting an abortion. *The Practitioner*, **220**, 847–852.

Dyer, C. (2001) Use of confidential HIV data helps convict former prisoner. *British Medical Journal*, **322**, 633.

Ehlert, U., Heim, C., and Hellhamer, D. (1999) Chronic pelvic pain as a somatoform disorder. *Psychotherapy and Psychosomatics*, **68**, 87–94.

Ellis, E., Atkeson, B., and Calhoun, K. (1981) Sexual dysfunction in victims of rape. *Women and Health*, **5**, 39–47.

Felhaus, K., Houry, D., and Kaminsky, R. (2000) Lifetime sexual assault prevalence rates and reporting practices in an emergency department population. *Annals of Emergency Medicine*, **36**, 23–27.

Figa-Talamanca, I. (1982) Abortion and mental health. In J. Hodgson (ed.) *Abortion and sterilization—medical and social aspects*. London: Academic Press.

Fishbein, M. and Ajzen, I. (1975) *Belief, attitude, attention and behaviour: An introduction to theory and research*. Reading, MA: Addison-Wesley.

Forster, G., Estreich, S., and Hooi, Y. (1991) Screening for STDs (Letter to the Editor). *Annals of Emergency Medicine*. **324**, 161–162.

Forster, G., Pritard, J., Munday, P., and Goldmeier, D. (1986) Incidence of sexually transmitted diseases in rape victims during 1984. *Genitourinary Medicine*, **62**, 267–269.

Frank, E. and Stewart, B. (1984) Depressive symptoms in rape victims: A revisit. *Journal of Affective Disorders*, **7**, 77–85.

Frank, E., Turner, S., Stewart, B., Jacob, J., and West, D. (1981) Past psychiatric symptoms and the response to sexual assault. *Comprehensive Psychiatry*, **22**, 479–487.

Gavey, M., Govan, A., Hodge, C., and Callander, R. (1972) *Gynaecology illustrated*. Edinburgh: Churchill Livingston.

Glaser, J., Hammerschlag, M., and McCormack, W. (1989) Epidemiology of sexually transmitted diseases in rape victims. *Review of Infectious Diseases*, **11**, 246–254.

Golding, J. (1999) Sexual assault history and headache: Five general population studies. *Journal of Nervous and Mental Diseases*, **187**, 624–629.

Gostin, L., Lazzarini, Z., Alexander, D., Brandt, A., Mayer, K., and Silverman, D. (1994) HIV testing, counselling, and prophylaxis after sexual assault. *Journal of the American Medical Association*, **271**, 1436–1444.

Green, J. and McCreaner, A. (eds) (1996) *Counselling in HIV infection and AIDS*. Oxford: Blackwell Science.

Handy, J.A. (1982) Psychological and social aspects of induced abortion. *British Journal of Clinical Psychology*, **21**, 29–42.

Hankins, C., Skinner, K., Miller, D., Frayne, S., and Tripp, T. (1999) Prevalence of depressive and alcohol abuse symptoms among women VA outpatients who report experiencing sexual assault while in the military. *Journal of Traumatic Stress*, **12**, 601–612.

Hare, M. and Haywood, J. (1981) Counselling of women seeking abortion. *Journal of Biosocial Science*, **13**, 269–273.

Harrison, J. and Murphy, S. (1999) A care package for managing female sexual assault in genitourinary medicine. *International Journal of STDs and AIDS*, **10**, 283–289.

Hedge, B. (1997) Sexually transmitted diseases. In A. Baum, S. Newman, J. Weinman, R. West, and C. McManus (eds) *Cambridge handbook of psychology, health and medicine*. Cambridge: Cambridge University Press.

Hedge, B. and Sherr, L. (1995) Psychological needs and HIV/AIDS. *Clinical Psychology and Psychotherapy*, **2**, 203–209.

Hillman, R., O'Mara, N., Tomlinson, D., and Harris, J. (1991) Adult male victims of sexual assault: An undiagnosed condition. *International Journal of STD & AIDS*, **2**, 22—24.

Holmes, M. (1999) Sexually transmitted infections in female rape victims. *AIDS Patient Care and Sexually Transmitted Diseases*, **13**, 703–708.

Holmes, M., Resnick, H., and Frampton, D. (1998) Follow-up of sexual assault victims. *American Journal of Obstetrics and Gynecology*, **179**, 336–342.

Huckle, P. (1995) Male rape victims referred to a forensic psychiatry service. *Medical Science and Law*, **35**, 187–192.

Ikkos, G., Fitzpatrick, R., Frost, D., and Nazeer, S. (1987) Psychological disturbance and illness behaviour in a clinic for sexually transmitted diseases. *British Journal of Medical Psychology*, **60**, 121–126.

Illsley, R. and Hall, M. (1976) Psychosocial aspects of abortion, a review of issues and needed research. *WHO Bulletin*, **53**, 83–105.

Jacobs, D., Garcia, C.R., Rickels, S.K., and Preucel, R.W. (1974) A prospective study of the psychological effects of therapeutic abortion. *Comparative Psychiatry*, **15**, 324–334.

Kaufman, A., DiVasto, P., Jackson, R., Voorhees, D., and Christy, J. (1980) Male rape victims: Noninstitutionalized assault. *American Journal of Psychiatry*, **137**, 221–223.

Kilpatrick, D., Acierno, R., Resnick, H., Saunders, B., and Best, C. (1997) A 2-year longitudinal analysis of the relationships between violent assault and substance use in women. *Journal of Consulting and Clinical Psychology*, **65**, 834–847.

Kimmerling, R. and Calhoun, K. (1994) Somatic symptoms, social support and treatment seeking among sexual assault victims. *Journal of Consulting and Clinical Psychology*, **62**, 333–340.

Kinderman, G., Carsten, P., and Massen, V. (1996) Ano-genital injuries in female victims of sexual assault. *Swiss Surgical*, **1**, 10–13.

King, M. (1992) Male sexual assault in the community. In G. Mezey and M. King (eds) *Male victims of sexual assault*. Oxford: Oxford University Press.

Koss, M. (1988) Criminal victimization among women: Impact on health status and medical services usage. Paper presented to the American Psychological Association, Atlanta.

Koss, M. and Heslet, L. (1992) Somatic consequences of violence against women. *Archives of Family Medicine*, **1**, 53–59.

Koss, M., Koss, P., and Woodruff, W. (1991) Deleterious effects of criminal victimization on women's health and medical utilization. *Archives of Internal Medicine*, **15**, 342–347.

Ledray, L., Lund, H., and Kiresuk, T. (1979) Impact of rape on victims and families: Treatment and research considerations. In D.K. Kjervik and I.M. Martinson (eds) *Women in stress: A nursing perspective*. New York: Appleton-Century Crofts.

Leventhal, H. (1970) Findings and theory in the study of fear communications. In: L. Berkowitz (ed.) *Advances in experimental social psychology* (Vol. 5). New York: Academic Press.

Ley, P. (1988) *Communicating with patients*. London: Chapman and Hall.

Mastro, T. and de Vincenzi, I. (1996) Probabilities of sexual HIV-1 transmission. *AIDS*, **10**(Suppl. A), S75–S82.

Meichenbaum, D. (1985) *Stress inoculation training*. New York: Pergamon Press.

Mezey, G. and King, M. (1989) The effects of sexual assault on men: A survey of 22 victims. *Psychological Medicine*, **19**, 205–209.

Miller, W., Williams, A., and Bernstein, M. (1982) The effects of rape on marital and sexual adjustment. *The American Journal of Family Therapy*. **10**, 51–58.

Moore, R., Stanton, D., Gopalan, R., and Chaisson, R. (1994) Racial differences in the use of drug therapy for HIV disease in an urban community. *New England Journal of Medicine*, **330**, 763–768.

Mosley, D.T., Follingsstad, D.R., Harley, H., and Heckel, R. (1981) Psychological factors that predict reaction to abortion. *Journal of Clinical Psychology*, **37**, 276–279.

Murphy, S., Kitchen, V., Harris, J., and Forster, S. (1989) Rape and subsequent seroconversion to HIV. *British Medical Journal*, **299**, 718.

Myles, J., Hirozawa, A., Katz, M., Kimmerling, R., and Bamberger, J. (2000) Post-exposure prophylaxis for HIV after sexual assault. *Journal of American Medical Association*, **284**, 1516–1518.

National Victims Centre. (1992) *Rape in America: A report to the nation*. Arlington, VA: National Victims Centre.

Norris, J. and Feldman-Summers, S. (1981) Factors related to the psychological impacts of rape on the victim. *Journal of Abnormal Psychology*, **90**, 562–567.

Osofsky, J. and Osofsky, H. (1978) Teenage pregnancy psychological considerations. *Clinical Obstetrics and Gynaecology*, **21**, 1161–1173.

Palella, F., Delaney, K., Moorman, A., Loveless, M., Fuhrer, J., Sutton, G., Aschman, D., and Holmberg, S. (1998) Declining morbidity and mortality among patients with advanced human immunodeficiency virus infection. *New England Journal of Medicine*, **338**, 853–860.

Parrot, A. (1991) Medical community response to acquaintance rape: Recommendations. In L. Bechhofer and A. Parrot (eds) *Acquaintance rape: The hidden victims*. New York: Wiley.

Perrot, S. and Webber, N. (1996) Attitudes towards male and female victims of sexual assault: Implications for services to the male victim. *Journal of Psychology and Human Sexuality*. **8**, 19–38.

Petter, L. and Whitehill, D. (1998) Management of female sexual assault. *American Family Physician*, **58**, 920–926.

Phelps, L., Wallace, D., and Waigandt, A. (1989) Impact of sexual assault: Post assault behaviour and health status. Paper presented to the Meeting of the American Psychological Association, New Orleans.

Putz, M., Thomas, B., and Cowles, K. (1996) Sexual assault victims' compliance with follow-up care at one sexual assault treatment centre. *Journal of Emergency Nursing*, **22**, 560–565.

Quinn, M. (1980) Decision making by single women seeking abortion. *New Zealand Nursing Forum*, **8**, 4–7.

Resnick, H., Acierno, R., Holmes, M, Dammeyer, M., and Kilpatrick, D. (2000) Emergency evaluation and intervention with female victims of rape and other violence. *Journal of Clinical Psychology*, **56**, 1317–1333.

Riggs, N., Houry, D., Long, G., Markovchick, V., and Feldhaus, K. (2000) Analysis of 1,076 cases of sexual assault. *Annals of Emergency Medicine*, **35**, 358–362.

Rogers, P., Sinka, K., Molesworth, A., Evans, B., and Allardice, G. (2000) Survival after diagnosis of AIDS among adults resident in the United Kingdom in the era of multiple therapies. *Communicable Diseases and Public Health*, **3**, 188–194.

Rosenstock, I. (1966) Why people use health services. *Millbank Memorial Fund Quarterly*, **44**, 94.

Salkovskis, P. and Warwick, H. (1986) Morbid preoccupation, health anxiety and reassurance: A cognitive-behavioural approach to hypochondriasis. *Behaviour Research and Therapy*, **24**, 597–602.

Schacker, T., Collier, A., Hughes, J., Shea, T., and Corey, L. (1996) Clinical and epidemiological features of primary HIV infection. *Annals of Internal Medicine*, **125**, 257–264.

Schein, A. (1999) Pregnancy prevention using emergency contraception: Efficacy, attitudes, and limitations to use. *Journal of Pediatric and Adolescent Gynaecology*, **12**, 3–9.

Selig, C. (2000) Sexual assault nurse examiner and sexual assault response team (SANE/SART) program. *Nursing Clinics in North America*, **35**, 311–319.

Shusterman, L.R. (1979) Predicting the psychological consequences of abortion. *Social Science and Medicine*, **96**, 683–689.

Smugar, S., Spina, B., and Merz, J. (2000) Informed consent for emergency contraception: Variability of hospital care of rape victims. *American Journal of Public Health*, **90**, 1372–1376.

Sorenson, S., Stein J., Siegal, J., Golding, J., and Burnam, M. (1987) The prevalence of adult sexual assault: The Los Angeles Epidemiological Catchment Area Project. *American Journal of Epidemiology*, **126**, 1154–1164.

Stein, J., Golding, J., Siegal, J., Burnam, M., and Sorenson, S. (1988) Long-term psychological sequelae of child sexual abuse: The Los Angeles Epidemiological Catchment Area study. In G. Wyatt and G. Powell (eds) *Lasting Effects of Child Sexual Abuse*. Newbury Park, CA: Sage Publications.

Tomlinson, D. and Harrison, J. (1998) The management of adult male victims of sexual assault in the GUM clinic: A practical guide. *International Journal of STD & AIDS*, **9**, 720–725.

Weibe, E., Comay, S., McGregor, M., and Ducceschi, S. (2000) Offering HIV prophylaxis to people who have been sexually assaulted: 16 months' experience in a sexual assault service. *Canadian Medical Association Journal*, **162**, 641–645.

Williams, J. and Holmes, K. (1981) *The Second Assault: Rape and Public Attitudes*. Westport, CT: Greenwood Press.

Wilson, S., Mitchell, C., Bradbury, D., and Chavez, J. (1999) Testing for HIV: Current practices in the academic Emergency Department. *American Journal of Emergency Medicine*, **17**, 354–356.

Wong, T., Chiasson, M., Reggy, A., Simonds, R., Heffess, J., and Loo, V. (2000) Antiviral therapy and declining AIDS mortality in New York City. *Journal of Urban Health*, **77**, 492–500.

Woodling, B.A. and Kossoris, P.D. (1981) Sexual misuse: Rape, molestation, and incest. *Pediatric Clinics of North America*, **28**, 481–499.

Chapter 10

INTERVENTIONS TO PREVENT RAPE AND SEXUAL ASSAULT

Christine A. Gidycz, Cindy L. Rich, and Nichole L. Marioni

The high frequency of sexual assault coupled with its serious consequences have led to an increasingly greater emphasis on prevention.
Federal mandates in the USA require that all colleges and universities
that receive federal funds provide some type of rape prevention
program to students (NASPA, 1994). While there has been an increased
emphasis on the evaluation of preventative efforts, the vast majority of
these evaluation studies have focused on college students. Additionally,
because at least 80% of all sexual assaults are perpetrated by acquaintances (Koss and Dinero, 1989), the published sexual assault evaluation
literature has emphasized the prevention of assaults by acquaintances.
Thus, the focus of this chapter will be on discussing issues relevant to
acquaintance sexual assault prevention in academic settings. Although
this area of research is in its infancy and the target populations have
been rather select, it still provides the foundation and impetus for
future efforts.

THEORETICAL MODELS UNDERLYING PROGRAM DEVELOPMENT

While early programs were primarily atheoretical in nature, current programming efforts have made a greater attempt to incorporate psychological theory into the development of programs both in terms of
structure and content. Specifically, many programs have incorporated
components of feminist theory either into the program's development
or implementation. These programs based on feminist theory have

The Trauma of Sexual Assault. Edited by Jenny Petrak and Barbara Hedge.
© 2002 John Wiley & Sons Ltd.

addressed the contention that rape is an issue of power, control, violence, and male dominance over women rather than a predominantly sexual issue. Social causes for rape, such as the socialization of women to be non-assertive and men to be dominant, have also been addressed. Programs designed from a feminist perspective commonly address sex-role stereotypes, rape myths, and societal constructs that are proposed to contribute to sexual assault (e.g., Frazier, Valtinson, and Candell, 1994; Breitenbecher and Gidycz, 1998).

Additionally, some male-only programs emphasize both a feminist and social norm theoretical approach. Proponents of such an approach contend that rape must be viewed as a severe act of sexual aggression that lies on a continuum of violence against women, and that these acts are common, normative, and supported by socialization. These programs suggest a feminist social change model for men and propose that effective programming must increase men's responsibility for sexual assault and attempt to encourage the examination of gender socialization that promotes or allows violence against women (Berkowitz, 2001; Mahlstedt and Corcoran, 1999). According to this model, men must take responsibility for preventing sexual violence by looking at their own potential for violence as well as by taking a stand against the violence of other men.

Models addressing issues of personal saliency have also been used to guide the development of prevention programs. These models, taken from the persuasion literature, are utilized in an attempt to increase the impact of a program's message. The Elaboration Likelihood Model (Petty and Cacioppo, 1986) has been the basis for a number of new evaluation studies on sexual assault prevention (Foubert and McEwen, 1998; Gilbert, Heesacker, and Gannon, 1991; Heppner, Neville, Smith, Kivlighan, and Gershuny, 1999). According to the Elaboration Likelihood Model, central route processing of a persuasive message occurs when the recipient of the message feels that the message has personal relevance, finds the quality and level of the message to be good and appropriate, is motivated to listen to the message, and engages in thinking about the message. When these characteristics are absent, the recipient of the message is theorized to engage in peripheral route processing, attending to peripheral cues such as 'attractiveness' or 'expertness' of the person giving the message rather than to its central content. According to the model, central route processing is hypothesized to lead to more stable attitude change and is more likely to influence actual behavior compared with peripheral route processing. Programs utilizing this model to guide their efforts have used several procedures to enhance central route processing including the use of role play, videos of rape survivors, interactive drama, and rape-scenario videos (Heppner, Good et al., 1995; Lonsway and Kothari, 2000; Rosenthal, Heesacker, and Neimeyer, 1995). The Health Belief Model

(Hochman, 1958) also addresses the issue of program saliency by increasing participants' perceptions both that they are vulnerable to an assault and that they can be successful in overcoming the threat.

Furthermore, researchers have also utilized components of social learning theory to guide their programming (Hanson and Gidycz, 1993; Lanier, Elliott, Martin, and Kapadia, 1998; Marx, Calhoun, Wilson, and Meyerson, 2001). These models have been used to design programs that specifically target cognitions that men hold that increase their likelihood to sexually assault women as well as to model appropriate behavior (Schewe and O'Donohue, 1996). Additionally, programs specifically targeting women have utilized lectures, discussions, and videotapes to define risky and safe dating behaviors and to model safe dating behaviors and assertive communication (Hanson and Gidycz, 1993; Breitenbecher and Gidycz, 1998). Some of these programs have specifically targeted women with assault histories (e.g., Marx *et al.*, 2001).

Overall, we view the growth of theoretically relevant programs as being quite positive. Early work in the area of program evaluation has been quite disappointing. We agree with others that taking a 'shotgun' approach to prevention, while well intentioned, is not likely to lead to long-term behavioral changes and is potentially an inefficient use of resources.

PROGRAMS TARGETING A MIXED-SEX AUDIENCE

The majority of published studies on sexual assault prevention are targeted at mixed-sex college student audiences. While, increasingly, the rationale for mixed-sex programming is being challenged, preferences for mixed-sex programs come from a number of factors, including multivariate models of sexual assault that focus on the characteristics of the perpetrator and victim, situational and societal factors, and sexual miscommunication. Some have suggested that both intent of the prospective perpetrator and resistance strategies of the prospective victim should be addressed by sexual assault prevention programs in a mixed-sex environment so that meaningful discussion or 'equality and respect between men and women can be encouraged' (Frazier *et al.*, 1994, p. 154). Holcomb, Sarvela, Sondag, and Holcomb (1993) also contend that mixed-sex programs might reduce the negative consequences of blame by addressing the shared responsibility for rape prevention by both men and women.

GOALS OF PROGRAMS

The primary goal of all mixed-sex programs is to prevent sexual assault by jointly exposing men and women to psychoeducational programming. The preponderance of these programs implicitly or explicitly promote goals that will both educate participants on personal, situational, and societal causes of rape while challenging prevailing myths and attitudes that are correlated with sexually aggressive behavior. Because the majority of programs use attitudes as their outcome measures, it must be construed that the primary goal of these programs is to change attitudes that are believed to be correlated with assault-related behavior change. Although early studies demonstrated significant relationships between negative rape-supportive beliefs and sexual assault (e.g., Muehlenhard and Linton, 1987), there is currently no evidence that changing these attitudes will reduce the incidence of sexual perpetration or sexual victimization. Therefore, in addition to facilitating attitude change, more current programs have also begun to use risk recognition and reduction models to guide program development. These programs use the modeling of assertive communication and responses as well as the perception and avoidance of risky behaviors and situations as program goals. Table 10.1 lists the goals of prevention and risk reduction programs as a function of the target audience. While program goals overlap in some instances, this table highlights the fact that some goals are most appropriately addressed to specific target audiences.

DESIGN OF MIXED-SEX PROGRAMS

Program Components

The majority of mixed-sex programs contain a number of common components that are designed to promote rape education, as well as attitude and behavior change among participants. Common program components include: (a) defining rape and sexual assault, (b) providing statistics on incidence and prevalence of sexual assault, (c) challenging sex-role stereotypes, (d) challenging prevailing rape myths, (e) discussing the effects of rape on victims, (f) discussing societal pressures and causes of rape, (g) discussing common attitudes and characteristics of victims and perpetrators, (h) promoting victim empathy, (i) teaching risk recognition, (j) identifying consent vs. coercion, (k) teaching safe dating behaviors, and (l) providing information about victim resources (e.g., Anderson et al., 1998; Dallager and Rosen, 1993; Ellis, O'Sullivan, and Sowards, 1992). Programs delivered this content in a number of ways, most of which

Table 10.1   Goals of prevention programs by target audience

Goals	Men's programs	Women's programs	Mixed-sex programs
Reduce the incidence of sexual victimization of women	✓		✓
Reduce the incidence of sexual perpetration by men	✓		✓
Reduce rape myths and beliefs	✓	✓	✓
Reduce acceptance of violence	✓	✓	✓
Reduce risky dating behaviors of men	✓		✓
Reduce risky dating behaviors of women		✓	✓
Reduce stereotypical beliefs about gender roles	✓	✓	✓
Reduce victim blame	✓	✓	✓
Increase rape knowledge	✓	✓	✓
Increase victim empathy	✓	✓	✓
Increase perpetrator blame		✓	✓
Clarify sexual consent vs. coercion	✓	✓	✓
Identify the characteristics of perpetrators		✓	✓
Identify risky situations		✓	✓
Educate participants about alcohol and rape	✓	✓	✓
Educate participants about date-rape drugs		✓	✓
Educate participants about rape after-effects	✓	✓	✓
Educate participants about rape resources		✓	✓
Educate men about bystander responsibility	✓		
Educate participants about societal inequality	✓	✓	✓
Acknowledge male victimization			✓
Explore opportunities for men to take social action to raise other men's awareness about the problem of sexual assault	✓		

included the use of didactic lectures. Other commonly used methods of persuasion frequently utilized in mix-sex programming includes the use of videos (e.g., Heppner, Humphrey *et al.*, 1995), interactive drama (e.g., Frazier *et al.*, 1994), vignettes (e.g., Rosenthal *et al.*, 1995), and the sharing of rape stories by victims (Ellis *et al.*, 1992; Lenihan, Rawlins, Eberly, Buckley, and Masters, 1992). The majority of mixed-sex programs were approximately 1 hour long and were conducted by mixed-sex facilitators who had varying degrees of prevention program training.

Program Evaluation

The efficacy of mixed-sex programs has primarily been evaluated by assessing attitude change utilizing a pre-test, intervention, post-test design conducted during one session. The most frequently used outcome measures were those designed to measure attitudes toward women, attitudes toward rape, and attitudes toward interpersonal violence. These studies have demonstrated mixed program effects on participants' attitude change, and questions have emerged concerning demand characteristics and the permanence of change using this research design. A number of studies using this methodology have demonstrated an immediate decrease in rape myth acceptance as a program effect. This change has primarily been measured by score changes on the Rape Myth Acceptance Scale (Burt, 1980) (e.g., Heppner, Good et al., 1995; Lenihan et al., 1992). However, in an effort to investigate the permanence of change, researchers have begun to institute follow-up sessions of varying lengths of time as part of their research design. A number of these follow-up sessions have demonstrated that attitude changes reported on the Rape Myth Acceptance Scale at post-test (immediately after an intervention) are no longer evidenced during a subsequent follow-up (Heppner, Humphrey et al., 1995). In one study (Heppner, Good et al., 1995), men demonstrated more of a rebound toward their pre-program attitudes than women at a 2-month follow-up. Research has also demonstrated a similar effect with the Attitudes Towards Rape-Revised Scale (Harrison, Downes, and Williams, 1991) such that these attitudes, while decreasing post-intervention, have been found to rebound at a 7-week follow-up (Anderson et al., 1998).

Attitudes toward women and interpersonal violence have also been investigated with mixed results. Rosenthal et al. (1995) and Dallager and Rosen (1993) found no changes on the Acceptance of Interpersonal Violence Scale (Burt, 1980) as an effect of program participation. Fisher (1986) found a desirable pre-, post-test change in The Attitudes Toward Women Scale for both men and women associated with program participation, however, Pinzone-Glover, Gidycz, and Jacobs (1998) found positive significant changes on this instrument only among male participants. Additionally, when confrontational strategies or empathy induction techniques were used with men, it appears that the potential for iatrogenic effects exists (Ellis et al., 1992; Fisher, 1986).

Behavioral intent has been recently used as an outcome measure to assess the efficacy of sexual assault prevention and risk reduction programs with mixed-sex audiences. Measures of behavioral intent have also been utilized to assess whether the Elaboration Likelihood Model is useful for understanding and predicting the changes that occur as a function of the intervention. After participating in a prevention program, participants were more likely to report that they intended to use more assertive resistance strategies, were more willing to volunteer time in prevention efforts, and were willing to pay increased fees to support these efforts (Lonsway and Kothari, 2000; Rosenthal et al., 1995). It is important to keep in mind that researchers were only measuring a participant's intent; in no study were any of the intended behaviors actually required to be carried out by participants or measured by the researchers. Only one study actually attempted to measure behavioral effects of a sexual assault prevention program with a mixed-sex audience and the results were disappointing; that is, the program was not found to have an effect on self-reported rates of sexual aggression or victimization among the participants during a 2-month follow-up period (Gidycz, *et al.*, 2001a).

Clearly, researchers have demonstrated mixed results on sexual assault prevention programs that were designed for mixed-sex audiences. Although a few programs have demonstrated some success in reducing negative or stereotypical attitudes towards women, results have been disappointing when collecting long-term follow-up data. In follow-up studies, attitude change has often rebounded to pre-intervention status and, in at least one program, this effect was especially demonstrated among male participants (Heppner, Good *et al.*, 1995). In addition, undesirable results have been reported in attempts to increase victim empathy among male participants (Fisher, 1986). Therefore, currently no prevention program for mixed-sex audiences has demonstrated long-term and significant attitude or behavior change among the program participants. We are concerned that in mixed-sex programs one sex may benefit at the expense of the other sex. Although it is easy to see that some goals of these programs overlap for the sexes, it is difficult to see how some goals that are appropriate for men (e.g., men taking responsibility for other men's behavior) can best be fostered with women also in the room. Furthermore, we believe that it is time to stop targeting attitude change when offering programs to women, given that there is ample data to suggest that neither attitudes towards rape or sex roles are correlated with victimization status in women (Koss and Dinero, 1989). For these reasons, we believe that further attention should be given to the development of single-sex programs.

PROGRAMS TARGETING MEN

Targeting men for sexual assault prevention is a relatively new, although potentially constructive endeavor. Recent work in this area generally has demonstrated growth in the theoretical foundation upon which programs are based, as well as improvements in method and design.

Berkowitz (2001) contends that men actually prefer all-male programs over mixed-sex programs. However, Berkowitz argues that many of the attitudes men express in favor of all-male workshops are attitudes and beliefs that need to be changed if men are to take responsibility for rape prevention; for example, men in programs indicate that they view gender dialogue as adversarial and find comfort in expressing men's complaints about women. We agree with Berkowitz that in all-male programs these attitudes and beliefs need to be brought out in the open so they can be challenged and changed. It seems likely that men would have a more difficult time honestly expressing feelings and attitudes when women are present.

DESIGN OF MEN'S PROGRAMS

Program Components

Most male-targeted prevention programs include similar components as mixed-sex programs. Some programs targeted only at men also focus on men taking responsibility for their own behavior and methods to confront sexually coercive behaviors in others. In addition, many programs incorporate other techniques or content, including: (a) videos or audiotapes of male or female sexual assault survivors discussing their experiences and videos designed to teach more effective sexual communication skills or appropriate definitions of sexual coercion, (b) panel discussions of survivors and significant others of survivors discussing the impact of sexual assault, (c) behavioral interventions requiring the generation of arguments convincing a sexually coercive man to change his behavior, (d) guided imagery of observing sexual coercion, and (e) theatrical vignettes of dating and assault situations.

In an integrative program, Berkowitz, Burkhart, and Bourg (1994) proposed a developmental model where he highlighted five strategies for change including: empathy induction, understanding conditions of consent, bystander interventions, resocialization, and cultural change. Therefore, the program focuses on change at both the individual and societal levels and encourages men to monitor and restrict the behavior of other men. Other programs targeted at men with a social change focus are also being developed on college campuses. Two of these programs are the Fraternity Violence Education Project (FVEP) at West Chester University of Pennsylvania (Mahlstedt and Corcoran, 1999), and the Mentors in Violence Prevention Project at Northeastern University (Boston, Massachusetts) (Katz, 1995). In both programs, peer educators are trained to become leaders and mentors and to challenge the inappropriate beliefs and behaviors of other men. The goals of these programs are to encourage men to view violence against women as a continuum of inappropriate but socially supported behaviors, to take personal responsibility for their behavior, and to actively work toward ending violence against women by challenging other men. Men in these programs present their message in the form of skits or workshops to fraternities, sports teams, and to students in the local schools.

Program Evaluation

As with mixed-sex programs, male-only programs typically focus on attitude change. The majority of male programs investigate attitudes regarding sexual assault, interpersonal violence, adversarial sexual beliefs, women, and gender roles, as well as their personal attraction to sexual aggression. Mixed results were found in comparing the attitudes of program vs. control participants on pre- and post-program attitudes. Generally, individuals participating in an intervention demonstrated more positive and egalitarian attitudes and less attraction to sexual aggression than those who did not participate (e.g., Foubert and Marriott, 1997; Heppner et al., 1999; Schewe and O'Donohue, 1996). Moreover, attitudes and attraction to sexual aggression typically improved after participation in a program compared with those beliefs demonstrated prior to the program (e.g., Earle, 1996; Gilbert et al., 1991, Heppner et al., 1999; Linz, Fuson, and Donnerstein, 1990). As documented in mixed-sex program evaluations, however, a rebound effect has been demonstrated in many all-male programs, such that, while attitudes seem to improve immediately following an intervention, longer term follow-up data suggested that attitudes declined in the direction of individuals' initial beliefs prior to the program (Foubert and Marriott, 1997; Heppner et al., 1999). Moreover, one study (Heppner et al., 1999), which used the longest follow-up period of any study (5 months), found three distinct response patterns to treatment. In addition to individuals who rebounded, there were individuals whose attitudes either simply improved or deteriorated. It is notable, also, that in certain studies no differences were found between program and control groups on attitudes (e.g., Berg, Lonsway, and Fitzgerald, 1999; Earle, 1996; Schewe and O'Donohue, 1993). However, some interventions have been found to be effective in decreasing victim blaming (e.g., Linz et al., 1990).

In an attempt to indirectly ascertain whether specific programs potentially lead to behavior changes, many studies incorporated various measures of assault-related behavioral intent, such as likelihood to rape, likelihood to use force, coercion, or alcohol to obtain sex, and likelihood to confront another person's sexual aggression. Mixed results have been found for assault-related behavioral intent. Individuals who participated in programs have been found to believe themselves less likely (Foubert and Marriott, 1997; Schewe and O'Donohue, 1993), equally likely (Foubert and McEwen, 1998), and in some instances more likely (Berg *et al.*, 1999) to engage in assault-related behaviors in comparison with the perceptions of individuals in control groups.

Studies that incorporated The Elaboration Likelihood Model tried to increase the saliency of the information that was provided in order to increase the likelihood that men's attitudes toward sexual assault and women would be effectively changed (Foubert and McEwen, 1998; Gilbert *et al.*, 1991; Heppner *et al.*, 1999). Moreover, they also evaluated whether the major components of The Elaboration Likelihood Model were in fact affected by the manner in which programming occurred. One study, which attempted to address the specific issue of personalizing information for a subgroup of participants, found that African American men who participated in a culturally relevant program were more cognitively involved in the program and in information processing than their counterparts who participated in a 'colorblind' or general program (Heppner *et al.*, 1999). Low numbers of participants, however, prevented the researchers from determining whether the African American participants in the culturally relevant program exhibited more attitude change than those in the colorblind program. Other studies using the Elaboration Likelihood Model in their programs found higher levels of motivation, ability, and favorability to be related to significant attitude change regarding rape, sex roles, sexual behavior, and violence, as well as participants' reported future likelihood to sexually assault (Foubert and McEwen, 1998; Gilbert *et al.*, 1991).

Overall, mixed support has been demonstrated for male-targeted sexual assault prevention programs. Interventions have generally generated decreased self-reported likelihood to sexually assault, positive changes in attitudes regarding sexual assault, women, and gender roles, and decreased victim blame and increased perpetrator blame in program participants compared with control group participants. However, undesirable results have generally been reported in attempts to increase victim empathy (Berg *et al.*, 1999; Schewe and O'Donohue, 1993). Thus, program design and outcome research for men are still in their infancy. Despite these obstacles, we believe that men must take responsibility for preventing rape and that models for rape prevention that are based on social norm and social change theories are most theoretically sound. We agree with Berkowitz (2001) that fears of embarrassment, the need to be politically correct, and concerns about judgments from women make it difficult for men to openly discuss their attitudes when women are present.

Unfortunately, the most theoretically sound programs such as the innovative prevention work of Mahlestdt and Corcoran (1999), Katz (1995) and Berkowitz *et al.* (1994) has limited published data on their effectiveness. However, Ohio University is conducting an evaluation study (funded by the Ohio Department of Health) of a male-only program based on a social change model of sexual assault prevention where outcome measures include a measure of self-reported sexual aggression. We believe that this study could potentially provide a model for other rape evaluation efforts with men.

PROGRAMS TARGETING WOMEN

A minority of studies that evaluated prevention programs specifically targeted women. Proponents of male-only and mixed-sex programs argue that programming that is only targeted at women may infer blame or transfer the responsibility of sexual assault prevention to women. Furthermore, because men most often perpetrate the crime of sexual assault, proponents suggest that prevention should be their responsibility and programming should be designed to include them (Frazier *et al.*, 1994). Conversely, Hanson and Gidycz (1993) stated that, 'Although men are always responsible for their acts of sexual aggression against women, ethical considerations suggest that methods need to be designed to educate women to lower their risk for victimization (p. 1046).' While we are waiting for effective male programs to be developed, programs that are designed to educate women about techniques and strategies to reduce their risk of sexual assault may be most beneficial to them. We agree with Schewe (in press) that it is inappropriate to share risk reduction messages in mixed-sex programs with men as it could provide potential rapists with information about what makes women more vulnerable to assault. While we believe that women-only programs are needed, it is clear, however, that they are more appropriately conceptualized as risk reduction or rape resistance interventions rather than 'true' prevention programs. It is also clear that these programs only address a part of what needs to be done to tackle the systemic problem of violence against women. Therefore, it is important that program facilitators address the issues of blame, responsibility, and the socialization of gender roles and sex roles in programs designed specifically for women. ·

DESIGN OF WOMEN'S PROGRAMS

Program Components

The format for women's programs generally consists of similar components as mixed-sex programs with an emphasis on information pertinent to women. In addition to standard information, these programs often contain: (a) provision of information about risk-reduction techniques, (b) information on rape after-effects, (c) teaching of assertive sexual communication and resistance behavior, and (d) the provision of information about victim assistance resources.

Recently, investigators have begun to target women with assault histories (Breitenbecher and Gidycz, 1998; Himelein, 1999; Marx et al., 2001). These women are considered to be at high risk of sexual assault, as data suggested that women with assault histories are between one and a half to two times more likely to be sexually assaulted than are women without assault histories (Gidycz, Hanson, and Layman, 1995). Programs targeting this population need to be particularly sensitive to issues of self-blame and issues of recovery.

Program Evaluation

All of the programs designed specifically for women focused on risk reduction and, therefore, used some type of evaluation to measure the reduction of risky behaviors or risk recognition. Hanson and Gidycz (1993) developed a scale to measures 'risky' dating behavior (i.e., alcohol use on a date) and found that women in the program group reported engaging in less risky behavior after the intervention than the control group women. Programs that have targeted high-risk women indicated that women who participated in the intervention reported greater self-efficacy compared with control participants for their perceived abilities to deal with a sexual assault situation (Marx et al., 2001). Program participants also reported that they intended to engage in less risky behaviors after the intervention (Himelein, 1999). However, some studies found no differences in risky dating behavior between control and program women when targeting college women in general (Breitenbecher and Scarce, 1999) and when targeting women who had experienced a sexual assault prior to the program (Breitenbecher and Gidycz, 1998). Cummings (1992) did not use a formal evaluation, but women reported feeling more assertive and confident after participating in a prevention program that contained a self-defense program.

Programs that have focused on the development of more assertive sexual communication have not been shown to have a beneficial effect on sexual communication (Breitenbecher and Gidycz, 1998; Hanson and Gidycz, 1993). The majority of women's programs, however, have demonstrated an increase in sexual assault knowledge at post-test (Breitenbecher and Scarce, 1999; Hanson and Gidycz, 1993; Himelein, 1999).

A few studies have evaluated whether their risk reduction program had an effect on the incidence of sexual assault among participants, utilizing a prospective design where rates of sexual victimization were assessed both before and after a risk-reduction program. Two studies indicated a reduction in sexual assault experiences among program participants (Hanson and Gidycz, 1993; Marx et al., 2001). In addition, Gidycz, et al. (2001), in a multi-site evaluation study, found that women who participated in their program did not differ from control group women with respect to the incidence of sexual assault during a 2-month follow-up period. However, women who experienced an assault between the pre-test and the 2-month follow-up demonstrated less chances of being revictimized at the 6-month follow-up. Although these studies are promising, two studies did not replicate these findings (Breitenbecher and Scarce, 1999; Breitenbecher and Gidycz, 1998). While it has been suggested that the evaluation studies with women's programs have been the most sophisticated (Yeater and O'Donahue, 1999), the results are still mixed. As discussed below, greater attention to theory in program development and systematic evaluation of these programs would be beneficial. Furthermore, the crucial task for programs targeting women is to be able to empower them without implying that they are to blame for sexual assaults. We view the teaching of self-defense skills as being an important mechanism for empowering women. However, while self-defense programs clearly exist on college campuses and in the community, they have not systematically been incorporated into risk reduction programs for women.

CRITIQUE OF SEXUAL ASSAULT PREVENTION EFFORTS AND RECOMMENDATIONS FOR FUTURE WORK

The Need for Systematic Development and Evaluation of Programs

The literature is replete with single investigations of specific programs that are rarely reassessed either in their existing or modified form. Although numerous researchers have called for the need to begin to understand what types of educational interventions are most effective for particular individuals (Schaeffer and Nelson, 1993) and to assess the critical components of these effective interventions (Schewe and O'Donohue, 1993; Yeater and O'Donohue, 1999), the existing literature cannot begin to address these issues. We believe that in order to accomplish this goal, a promising program (i.e., one that affects both attitudes and behaviors) has to be identified before we can begin to answer questions about the effectiveness of its particular components. Once a promising program is identified, multi-site testing of the program and replication of the results are essential.

We are currently involved in a federally funded project in collaboration with the University of Georgia. This multi-site project involves evaluating a program that is a modified version of a program developed by Gidycz and colleagues (Hanson and Gidycz, 1993; Gidycz et al., 2001). This evaluation project is a 2-year, longitudinal and multi-site study being conducted with sexual assault survivors at two college campuses with a variety of outcome measures, including measures of sexual victimization. Similarly, researchers investigating male programs are also beginning to systematically design and modify their programs based on evaluation information; for example, Foubert and Marriott (1996) designed a program for men which they first pilot-tested without formal evaluation, and have since replicated it with the addition of a control group (Foubert and Marriott, 1997; Foubert and McEwen, 1998), multiple experimental groups, and the evaluation of components of the Elaboration Likelihood Model. Across all three studies, the researchers have found similar and positive treatment effects. Programmatic work such as this will allow researchers in the field to begin to systematically evaluate critical components of rape prevention programs and allow us to begin to specify appropriate target audiences.

The Need for Increased Theoretically Driven Programming

A number of researchers have argued that prevention programming is atheoretical in nature (Yeater and O'Donohue, 1999; Heppner, Humphrey et al., 1995). While a number of programs espouse utilizing a feminist model or The Elaboration Likelihood Model to guide their interventions, it is often unclear how these models guide the development of the specific content of the programs. We agree with Yeater and O'Donohue (1999) that it 'often appears as if information is included in sexual assault prevention programs because it seems to make sense' (p. 751). Traditionally, programs have been based on identified empirical correlates of sexual victimization and aggression, and it is assumed that if one can change the correlates of sexual assault then one will reduce the incidence of sexual assault. This methodology is problematic, however, because undoubtedly there is no simple answer as to why sexual assault occurs. It is likely that it is the interaction between situational, personal, and social variables that contribute to the high rates of sexual violence. Without sound theoretical models to guide our efforts, it is difficult to identify realistic program goals and to select outcome measures that parallel our goals.

Marx *et al.* (2001) have developed a promising program for sexual assault survivors based on a risk recognition theoretical model. Their model is based upon empirical data that suggests that, while women possess an awareness of the general risk for sexual assault among other women, they tend to underestimate their own risk for sexual assault compared with their peers (Norris, Nurius, and Dimeff, 1996). Additionally, data suggested that women with a history of sexual assault may evidence poorer risk recognition skills than women without such histories (Wilson, Calhoun, and Bernat, 1999). Consistent with this model, a major component of their risk reduction efforts involves helping survivors to identify and cope with high-risk situations, and their outcome measures include measures that assess participants' abilities to recognize risk in a potentially sexually assaultive situation. This work is noteworthy because the content of the program is theoretically driven and the outcome measures allow for the assessment of whether the hypothesized theoretical processes underlie program efficacy.

Finally, we must continue to identify the causal variables associated with sexual assault and sexual victimization as this will allow us to further develop theoretically driven programs to address sexually exploitive behavior and to assess the processes that lead to change.

The Need to Address Populations in Addition to College Students

As stated at the outset, the vast majority of sexual assault prevention evaluation efforts have been conducted with college students. While they are certainly an appropriate target group, it remains unclear whether any of these efforts have the potential to be successful with other populations. Furthermore, it is difficult to actually document the extensiveness of rape primary prevention efforts with other populations in community or clinical settings, as the evaluation of such efforts are virtually non-existent. It is clear that community and clinical agencies often do not have the resources to evaluate their prevention efforts, while researchers in academic settings have an easily accessible population as well as readily available resources to assist with the evaluation processes. The obvious question is why do researchers and practitioners not collaborate to a greater extent? Because practitioners and researchers alike are working towards the ultimate goal of the prevention of sexual assault, collaboration and pooling of resources is absolutely essential.

It has been our experience that potential barriers to the forming of collaborative relationships exist including, on the practitioners' part, such factors as mistrust of researchers' motives, ethical concerns regarding the evaluation of human participants, lack of time to assist researchers with these efforts, and concerns about how the data may be used. Potential barriers on the part of researchers include the amount of time it takes to gain co-operation from settings outside the university, concerns about the integrity of the research design when input is obtained from a number of individuals outside the research community, and funding to compensate practitioners and staff for their collaboration. While these barriers seem to clearly exist, we believe that the evaluation of programs outside the university must begin to take place, that the results need to be effectively disseminated, and efforts need to be made to address these potential barriers to collaboration. Recent sexual assault risk reduction programs targeting sexual assault survivors would be particularly appropriate for community or clinical samples of rape survivors.

Crowell and Burgess (1996) recommended that federally funded research centers be developed that would serve to foster collaboration between researchers and practitioners. They suggested that these centers could also potentially move prevention-focused research away from simple outcome assessments that focus on atheoretical strategies toward theoretically derived models that could be experimentally tested in various populations. The Center for Disease Control funded The National Violence Against Women Research Center, whose mission is to foster collaborations among advocates, practitioners, policy makers, and researchers in order to most effectively help to prevent violence against women. Continued and increased federal efforts along these lines are clearly needed.

The Need to Address More Appropriate Outcome Measures

There are clearly a number of difficulties with the evaluation instruments typically utilized to assess program outcomes. Specifically, while there exist hundreds of attitudinal measures assessing such variables as sex-role stereotyping, rape-myth acceptance, acceptance of interpersonal violence, and rape empathy, a number of them have poor psychometric properties or are dated (Marioni, Gidycz, and Loh, 2001). Furthermore, it is often unclear how closely the outcome measures utilized parallel the program goals. It is imperative in conducting any outcome evaluation that the researchers evaluate the appropriateness of their outcome measures. Marioni et al. (2001) conducted a study with college men evaluating the psychometric properties of newer attitudinal, sex-role, and rape myth measures and found that a number of them evidenced sound psychometric properties. Table 10.2 includes a summary of these newer measures that were found to be psychometrically sound.

Table 10.2 Overview of new rape-related measures

Measure	Citation	Description	Reliability	Validity

Ambivalent Sexism Inventory	Glick and Fiske (1996)	22-item self-report on 5-point scale
		2 subscales
		  Hostile sexism
		  Benevolent sexism
		Higher scores indicate greater sexism regarding various beliefs that core differences between the genders exist
			Internal consistency $\alpha = 0.72$
			Test-retest (2-week) $r = 0.74^*$
				Significant correlations with 7 old and new sexism measures, $r = 0.52$ to 0.73^{**}

Modern Sexism Scale	Swim, Aikin, Hall, and Hunter (1995)	8-item self-report on 7-point scale Higher scores indicate greater covert sexism regarding traditional gender roles	Internal consistency $\alpha = 0.75$ Test-retest (2-weeks) $r = 0.68^*$	Significant correlations with 7 old and new sexism measures, $r = 0.42$ to 0.78^{**}
Neosexism Scale	Tougas, Brown, Beaton, and Joly (1995)	11-item self-report on 7-point scale Higher scores indicate greater covert sexism regarding social and political discrimination	Internal consistency $\alpha = 0.80$ Test-retest (2-week) $r = 0.65^*$	Significant correlations with 7 old and new sexism measures, $r = 0.70$ to 0.79^{**}
Old-fashioned Sexism scale	Swim, Aikin, Hall, and Hunter (1995)	5-item self-report on 7-point scale Higher scores indicate greater overt sexism regarding occupational, social, and political issues	Internal consistency $\alpha = 0.62$ Test-retest (2-week) $r = 0.39^*$	Significant correlations with 7 old and new sexism measures, $r = 0.58$ to 0.97^{**}
Hypergender Ideology Scale	Hamburger, Hogben, McGowan, and Dawson (1996)	57-item self-report on 6-point scale Higher scores indicate greater support for and identification with traditional gender roles	Internal consistency $\alpha = 0.95$ Test-retest (2-week) $r = 0.90^*$	Significant correlations with Bem Sex Role Inventory—Androgyny, $r = 0.37^{**}$, and Femininity, $r = 0.33^*$

Illinois Rape Myth Acceptance Scale	Payne, Lonsway, and Fitzgerald (1999)	45-item self-report on 7-point scale
		7 subscales
		  She asked for it
		  It wasn't really rape
		  He didn't mean to
		  She wanted it
		  She lied
		  Rape is no big deal
		  Rape is a deviant act
		Higher scores indicate greater rape myth acceptance
			Internal consistency $\alpha = 0.91$
			Test-retest (2-week) $r = 0.80^*$
				Significant correlations with Rape Myth Acceptance Scale, $r = 0.90^{**}$, and Attitudes Toward Rape Victims Scale, $r = 0.81^{**}$

$^* p < 0.01; ^{**} p < 0.001$

In some investigations, goals are not explicitly stated and, thus, it is difficult to judge the adequacy of the outcome measures that are utilized. In other instances, the goals are explicitly stated; however, the outcome evaluations do not allow for an adequate assessment of the program goals. For example, much of the research with male programming has proposed the goal of decreasing men's likelihood to perpetrate sexual assault. While there are a number of recent studies with women that have measured whether the risk reduction programs have an effect on rates of sexual victimization, only one study (Gidycz et al., 2001a) has measured sexually aggressive behavior in men post-intervention. While some programs assess behavioral intent, the evidence is lacking as to whether there is a relationship between behavioral intent and actual behavior. It is imperative that if one of the major goals of preventative interventions is to reduce rates of sexual aggression, then program evaluation efforts with men need to begin to document whether there are changes in rates of perpetration as a function of participation in programs.

Gidycz and colleagues (Gidycz et al., 2001a; Gidycz et al., 2001b; Hanson and Gidycz, 1993) have provided an evaluation model that could be used and extended in future rape evaluation efforts. In their rape prevention evaluation studies, they surveyed participants at the beginning of their studies and then randomly assigned them to either the program groups or the control group. Their key outcome measure in these evaluation studies was the Sexual Experiences Survey (Koss and Oros, 1982) which assessed self-reported experiences with sexual victimization (women) and aggression (men) in program and control participants. They assessed participants' histories of sexual aggression and victimization prior to program participation and during the follow-up periods. While their longest follow-up was conducted over a 6-month period, researchers could utilize the same methodology and obtain longer term follow-ups, supplement the information obtained from the Sexual Experiences Survey with legal or clinical reports of sexual assaults, and include some of the newer measures of rape myths and attitudes.

The Need to Target Interventions for Various Subgroups

The typical design of rape prevention evaluation efforts involves offering the various programs to general college student audiences. Typically, participants are recruited through introductory psychology classes and little attention is paid to the participants' histories of sexual aggression or victimization. This is potentially problematic in that Hanson and Gidycz (1993) found that a program offered to college women recruited through introductory psychology classes was found to be effective in reducing women's risk of sexual assaults if they did not have a history of sexual assault prior to participating in the program. However, for those women with assault histories, the program did not reduce their risk of sexual assault following participation in the program. These findings suggested that women with assault histories may need specialized programs or that programs designed for general women audiences need to be more sensitive to the fact that there will likely be a number of survivors in the audience.

While the vast majority of programs for men have not screened for assault histories, it seem likely that, consistent with the work with women, there may be some subgroups of men for whom these types of programs are ineffective. College and universities may be wasting valuable resources and time by offering a general program on sexual assault to all men who are recruited through psychology classes or other groups. Although it may be difficult to screen men for sexual assault histories given the legal and ethical implications, Gidycz *et al.* (2001a) found, utilizing the Sexual Experiences Survey (Koss and Oros, 1982), that approximately 20% of the male participants indicated that they had engaged in some kind of sexually coercive behavior from the age of 14 on until the beginning of their evaluation study. Furthermore, in addition to utilizing the Sexual Experience Survey, it is also possible to screen men on various correlates of sexual aggression (e.g., rape supportive attitudes, attitudes towards violence, dominant and controlling behavior with women), and then evaluate the effectiveness of existing programs as a function of these correlates. It seems likely that programming may not lead to the same reactions or responses among all participants, which suggests that the interaction between individuals' personalities and behaviors with various program components must also be addressed in future research. The work of Heppner and colleagues is noteworthy in that they were able to identify three patterns of attitude change in their study (Heppner *et al.*, 1999). The next logical step is to begin to identify how the individuals whose attitudes either deteriorated or rebounded during the follow-up period differed from those individuals who showed improvement in attitudes throughout the follow-up period as a function of the program. These types of investigation would allow us to begin to assess whether certain groups of men and women are in need of specialized programs.

The Need to Systematically Integrate Prevention and Risk Reduction Components into Treatment Protocols

Currently, there exist a number of treatment protocols for survivors of sexual assault including exposure treatments (e.g., Foa and Rothbaum,

1998a; Resick and Schnicke, 1993) and eye-movement desensitization and reprocessing (EMDR) (Shapiro, 1995). Concurrently, as evidenced in this chapter, there also exist a number of sexual assault prevention protocols that have been implemented and evaluated on college campuses throughout the USA. There is increasing evidence, however, that survivors of sexual assault may need specialized programs to decrease their risk for subsequent victimization. One cannot run a risk reduction program for women who have already been victimized and not address issues related to the negative impact associated with sexual assault. In fact, we believe that researchers conducting evaluation studies of sexual assault risk reduction protocols with sexual assault survivors must closely monitor the level of psychological symptoms as a function of their efforts. In our risk reduction program, issues of self-blame and other components of post-assault reactions are discussed in the groups. Similarly, it seems likely that treatment protocols addressing the post-rape symptoms are also addressing issues of revictimization; for example, Foa and Rothbaum (1998b) suggested that when conducting *in vivo* exposure therapy with sexual assault survivors that 'sexual assault victims must face the reality that their traumas may recur unpredictably' (p. 87). Foa and Rothbaum (1998b) suggested that the therapist may need to introduce discrimination training when necessary in order to help clients discriminate dangerous from safe situations. It seems imperative that, in addition to addressing whether their treatments are having an effect on post-rape psychological symptomatology, researchers conducting treatment interventions and clinicians also need to address the rates of sexual revictimization in their samples or clients. Clearly, one goal of treatment interventions is also to help increase the safety of women clients.

While the treatment and prevention efforts have really been separate lines of investigation in the literature, it is likely, as programs develop to prevent the sexual revictimization of women with assault histories, that the lines between treatment and prevention will become blurred. Clearly, components of risk reduction programs for women survivors of sexual assault could potentially be incorporated in a systematic manner into existing treatment protocols including such components as assertiveness training, problem-solving skills training, and exercises to help survivors identify and cope with potentially risky situations.

CONCLUSION

The number of published studies addressing the evaluation of sexual assault prevention and risk reduction programs are increasing. While it remains an empirical question as to which format is best, we believe for a number of reasons that programming that targets men and women separately is likely to be the most beneficial to participants. It is apparent that the goals of men and women's programs diverge in a number of respects, making it difficult to structure the content for mixed-sex programs. Although a number of mixed-sex programs have focused on rape-myth acceptance and sex-role attitudes and, thus, assessed these variables post-intervention as measures of program efficacy, the literature does not support a link between these types of attitude and the experience of being a victim for women (see Koss and Dinero, 1989). Thus, while challenging these attitudes seems to be an appropriate goal for men, we believe that programs for women need to help them to identify and cope with characteristics of sexually aggressive men and situations that are particularly risky. However, it is possible, after men and women participate in programs that are designed specifically for them, that joint programs which provide some opportunity to discuss these issues might be beneficial. Future evaluation efforts could clearly explore this issue.

We believe that we are at a point where we must begin to more systematically develop and evaluate programs. Long-term follow-up studies are needed with programs that are theoretically based and developed in a programmatic manner. Furthermore, multi-site studies are needed in order to obtain large enough samples to assess whether the programs are having an effect on rates of sexual aggression and victimization and to obtain diverse samples. The replication of results is clearly needed in order to begin to address program components that are associated with efficacy and the processes through which change is occurring. Furthermore, it is likely that programs for high-risk groups may be most beneficial and cost-effective. While college students have been the focus of evaluation interventions, we believe that many of the components of the reviewed programs could be utilized with community samples. Co-operation among researchers and practitioners is clearly needed in order to further evaluation efforts. By removing the barriers to collaboration between researchers and practitioners, the field of sexual assault prevention could move forward in an exponential manner.

REFERENCES

Anderson, L., Stoelb, M.P., Duggan, P., Hieger, B., Kling, K.H., and Payne, J.P. (1998) The effectiveness of two types of rape prevention programs in changing the rape-supportive attitudes of college students. *Journal of College Student Development*, **39**, 131–142.

Berg, D.R., Lonsway, K.A., and Fitzgerald, L.F. (1999) Rape prevention education for men: The effectiveness of empathy-induction techniques. *Journal of College Student Development*, **40**, 219–234.

Berkowitz, A. D. (2001) Applications of social norms theory to other health and social justice issues. In W.D. Perkins (ed.) *The social norms approach to prevention*. Manuscript submitted for publication.

Berkowitz, A.D., Burkhart, B.R., and Bourg, S.E. (1994) Research on college men and rape. In A. Berkowitz (ed.) *Men and rape: Theory, research, and prevention programs in higher education*. San Francisco: Jossey-Bass Publishers.

Breitenbecher, K.H. and Gidycz, C.A. (1998) An empirical evaluation of a program designed to reduce the risk of multiple sexual victimization. *Journal of Interpersonal Violence*, **13**, 472–488.

Breitenbecher, K.H. and Scarce, M. (1999) A longitudinal evaluation of the effectiveness of a sexual assault education program. *Journal of Interpersonal Violence*, **14**, 459–478.

Burt, M.R. (1980) Cultural myths and support for rape. *Journal of Personality and Social Psychology*, **38**, 217–230.

Crowell, N.A. and Burgess, A.W. (1996) *Understanding violence against women*. Washington, DC: National Academy Press.

Cummings, N. (1992) Self-defense training for college women. *Journal of American College Health*, **40**, 183–188.

Dallager, C. and Rosen, L.A. (1993) Effects of a human sexuality course on attitudes toward rape and violence. *Journal of Sex Education and Therapy*, **19**, 193–199.

Earle, J.P. (1996) Acquaintance rape workshops: Their effectiveness in changing the attitudes of first year college men. *National Association of Student Personnel Administrators*, **34**, 2–18.

Ellis, A.L., O'Sullivan, C.S., and Sowards, B.A. (1992) The impact of contemplated exposure to a survivor of rape on attitudes toward rape. *Journal of Applied Social Psychology*, **22**, 889–895.

Fisher, G.J. (1986) College student attitudes toward forcible date rape: Changes after taking a human sexuality course. *Journal of Sex Education and Therapy*, **12**, 42–46.

Foa, E.B. and Rothbaum, B.O. (1998a) *Treating the trauma of rape*. New York: Guilford Press.

Foa, E.B., and Rothbaum, B.O. (1998b) *Treating the trauma of rape: Cognitive-behavioral therapy for PTSD*. New York: Guilford Press.

Foubert, J.D. and McEwen, M.K. (1998) An all-male rape prevention peer education program: Decreasing fraternity men's behavioral intent to rape. *Journal of College Student Development*, **39**, 548–556.

Foubert, J.D. and Marriott, K.A. (1996) Overcoming men's defensiveness toward sexual assault programs: Learning to help survivors. *Journal of College Student Development*, **37**, 470–472.

Foubert, J.D. and Marriott, K.A. (1997) Effects of a sexual assault peer education program on men's belief in rape myths. *Sex Roles*, **36**, 259–268.

Frazier, P., Valtinson, G., and Candell, S. (1994) Evaluation of a coeducational interactive rape prevention program. *Journal of Counseling and Development*, **73**, 153–158.

Gidycz, C.A., Hanson, K,. and Layman, M.J. (1995) A prospective analysis of the relationship among sexual assault experiences: An extension of previous findings. *Psychology of Women Quarterly*, **19**, 124–131.

Gidycz, C.A., Layman, M.J., Rich, C.L., Crothers, M., Gylys, J., Matorin, A., and Jacobs, C.D. (2001) An evaluation of an acquaintance rape prevention program: Impact on attitudes and behavior. *Journal of Interpersonal Violence*, 1120–1138.

Gidycz, C.A., Lynn, S.J., Rich, C.L., Marioni, N.L., Loh, C., Blackwell, L.M., Stafford, J., and Fite, R. (2001) The evaluation of a risk reduction program: A multisite investigation. *Journal of Consulting and Clinical Psychology*, 1073–1078.

Gilbert, B.J., Heesacker, M., and Gannon, L.J. (1991) Changing the sexual aggression-supportive attitudes of men: A psychoeducational intervention. *Journal of Counseling Psychology*, **38**, 197–203.

Glick, P. and Fiske, S.T. (1996) The Ambivalent Sexism Inventory: Differentiating hostile and benevolent sexism. *Journal of Personality and Social Psychology*, **70**, 491–512.

Hamburger, M.E., Hogben, M., McGowan, S., and Dawson, L.J. (1996) Assessing hypergender ideologies: Development and initial validation of a gender-neutral measure of adherence to extreme gender-role beliefs. *Journal of Research in Personality*, **30**, 157–178.

Hanson, K.A. and Gidycz, C.A. (1993) Evaluation of a sexual assault prevention program. *Journal of Consulting and Clinical Psychology*, **61**, 1046–1052.

Harrison, P.F., Downes, J., and Williams, M.D. (1991) Date and acquaintance rape: Perceptions and attitude change strategies. *Journal of College Student Health*, **32**, 131–139.

Heppner, M.J., Good, G.E., Hillenbrand-Gunn, T.L., Hawkins, A.K., Hacquard, L.L., Nichols, R.K., DeBord, K.A., and Brock, K.J. (1995) Examining sex differences in altering attitudes about rape: A test of the Elaboration Likelihood Model. *Journal of Counseling and Development*, **73**, 640–647.

Heppner, M.J., Humphrey, C.F., Hillenbrand-Gunn, T.L., and DeBord, K.A. (1995) The differential effects of rape prevention programming on attitudes, behavior, and knowledge. *Journal of Counseling Psychology*, **42**, 508–518.

Heppner, M.J., Neville, H.A., Smith, K., Kivlighan, Jr, D.M., and Gershuny, B.S. (1999) Examining immediate and long-term efficacy of rape prevention programming with racially diverse college students. *Journal of Counseling Psychology*, **46**, 16–26.

Himelein, M.J. (1999) Acquaintance rape prevention with high-risk women: Identification and inoculation. *Journal of College Student Development*, **40**, 93–96.

Hochman, G.M. (1958) *Public participation in medical screening programs: A sociopsychological study* (Public Health Service, PHS Publication 572). Washington, DC: US Government Printing Office.

Holcomb, D.R., Sarvela, P.D., Sondag, K.A., and Holcomb, L.C.H. (1993) An evaluation of a mixed-gender date rape prevention workshop. *Journal of American College Health*, **41**, 159–164.

Katz, J. (1995) Reconstructing masculinity in the locker room: The mentors in violence prevention project. *The Harvard Education Review*, **65**, 163–174.

Koss, M.P. and Dinero, T.E. (1989) Discriminant analysis of risk factors for sexual victimization among a national sample of college women. *Journal of Consulting and Clinical Psychology*, **57**, 242–250.

Koss, M.P. and Oros, C.J. (1982) Sexual Experience Survey: A research instrument investigating sexual aggression and victimization. *Journal of Consulting and Clinical Psychology*, **50**, 455–557.

Lanier, C.A., Elliott, M.N., Martin, D.W., and Kapadia, A. (1998) Evaluation of an intervention to change attitudes toward date rape. *Journal of American College Health*, **46**, 177–180.

Lenihan, G.O., Rawlins, M.E., Eberly, C.G., Buckley, B., and Masters, B. (1992) Gender differences in rape supportive attitudes before and after a date rape education intervention. *Journal of College Student Development*, **33**, 331–338.

Linz, D., Fuson, I.A., and Donnerstein, E. (1990) Mitigating the negative effects of sexually violent mass communication through preexposure briefings. *Communication Research*, **17**, 641–674.

Lonsway, K.A. and Kothari, C. (2000) First year campus acquaintance rape education: Evaluating the impact of a mandatory intervention. *Psychology of Women Quarterly*, **24**, 220–232.

Mahlstedt, D. and Corcoran, C. (1999) Preventing dating violence. In S. Davis, M. Crawford, and J. Sebrechts (eds) *Coming into her own: Educational success in girls and women*. San Francisco: Jossey-Bass Publishers.

Marioni, N.L., Gidycz, C.A., and Loh, C. (2001) *Using new psychometric tools to predict sexual aggression in men*. Manuscript in preparation.

Marx, B.P., Calhoun, K.S., Wilson, A.E., and Meyerson, L.A. (2001) Sexual revictimization prevention: An outcome evaluation. *Journal of Consulting and Clinical Psychology*, 25–32.

Muehlenhard, C.I. and Linton, M.A. (1987) Date rape and sexual aggression in dating situations: Incidence and risk factors. *Journal of Counseling Psychology*, **34**, 186–196.

NASPA. (1994) *Complying with the final regulations: The Student Right to Know and Campus Security Act*. Washington, DC: National Association of Student Personnel Administrators.

Norris, J., Nurius, P., and Dimeff, L. (1996) Through her eyes: Factors affecting women's perception of resistance to acquaintance sexual aggression threat. *Psychology of Women Quarterly*, **20**, 123–145.

Payne, D.L, Lonsway, K.A., and Fitzgerald, L.F. (1999) Rape myth acceptance: Exploration of its structure and its measurement using the Illinois Rape Myth Acceptance Scale. *Journal of Research in Personality*, **33**, 27–68.

Petty, R.E. and Cacioppo, J.T. (1986) *Communication and persuasion: Central and peripheral routes to attitude change*. New York: Springer-Verlag.

Pinzone-Glover, H.A., Gidycz, C.A., and Jacobs, C. (1998) An acquaintance rape prevention program: Effects on attitudes toward women, rape-related attitudes, and perceptions of rape scenarios. *Psychology of Women Quarterly*, **22**, 605–621.

Resick, P.A. and Schnicke, M.K. (1993) *Cognitive processing therapy for rape victims: A treatment manual*. Newbury Park, CA: Sage Publications.

Rosenthal, E.H., Heesacker, M., and Neimeyer, G.J. (1995) Changing the rape-supportive attitudes of traditional and nontraditional male and female college students. *Journal of Counseling Psychology*, **42**, 1–7.

Schaeffer, A.M. and Nelson, E.S. (1993) Rape-supportive attitudes: Effects of on-campus residence and education. *Journal of College Student Development*, **34**, 175–179.

Schewe, P.A. (in press) Guidelines for developing rape prevention and risk reduction interventions. In P.A. Schewe (ed.) *Preventing violence in relationships: Interventions across the life span*. Washington, DC: APA Books.

Schewe, P.A. and O'Donohue, W. (1993) Sexual abuse prevention with high-risk males: The roles of victim empathy and rape myths. *Violence and Victims*, **8**, 339–351.

Schewe, P.A. and O'Donohue, W. (1996) Rape prevention with high-risk males: Short-term outcome of two interventions. *Archives of Sexual Behavior*, **25**, 455–471.

Shapiro, F. (1995) *Eye Movement Desensitization and Reprocessing: Basic principles, protocols, and procedures*. New York: Guilford Press.

Swim, J.K., Aikin, K.J., Hall, W.S., and Hunter, B.A. (1995) Sexism and racism: Old-fashioned and modern prejudices. *Journal of Personality and Social Psychology*, **68**, 199–214.

Tougas, F., Brown, R., Beaton, A.M., and Joly, S. (1995) Neosexism: Plus ça change, plus c'est pareil. *Personality and Social Psychology Bulletin*, **21**, 842–849.

Wilson, A.E., Calhoun, K.S., and Bernat, J.A. (1999) Risk recognition and trauma-related symptoms among sexually revictimized women. *Journal of Consulting and Clinical Psychology*, **67**, 705–710.

Yeater, E.A. and O'Donohue, W. (1999) Sexual assault prevention programs: Current issues, future directions, and the potential efficacy of interventions with women. *Clinical Psychology Review*, **19**, 739–771.

Chapter 11

LEGAL AND FORENSIC ISSUES

Deborah J. Rogers

The purpose of this chapter is to familiarize the reader with the forensic and legal processes pertinent to a sexual assault, the psychological impact of these processes on the assaulted person, and the implications for trauma aftercare. The chapter also contains a detailed discussion regarding 'false allegations' to assist the practitioner with providing psychological care for persons who make such allegations.

In this chapter the term 'sexual assault' includes penetration of the vagina or anus with a penis, digit, or inanimate object; insertion of a penis into the mouth; and other, non-penetrative sexual acts. Currently in England non-consensual penetration of the vagina or anus is legally defined as 'rape' which has a maximum penalty of life imprisonment; other penetrative sexual acts (e.g. fellatio) are combined with non-penetrative sexual acts (e.g., touching the breasts) under the umbrella of 'indecent assault', punishable by a maximum of 10 years imprisonment (Sexual Offences Act 1956, as amended by the Criminal Justice and Public Order Act 1994). Other jurisdictions (e.g., Victoria in Australia) have legislation in which fellatio is also considered as 'sexual intercourse' with the same maximum penalties as non-consensual penile penetration of the other body orifices (Crimes Act 1958). In Sweden the legal definition of 'sexual intercourse' is soon to be extended to encompass penetration by parts of the body other than a penis (Swedish Government Fact Sheet, 1999).

Official global statistics reveal that the number of sexual assaults committed each year is increasing (WHO, database, 2000). Even so, it is widely acknowledged that official databases are likely to underestimate the extent of the problem; various international studies have found that only 3–16% of women who recount non-consensual peno-vaginal or peno-anal penetration in self-report studies divulged the offence to the

The Trauma of Sexual Assault. Edited by Jenny Petrak and Barbara Hedge.
© 2002 John Wiley & Sons Ltd.

police or other authorities (MacDonald, 2000). The reasons for this reticence to report are personal and complex. Some complainants may be discouraged by the prospect of a further encroachment into the intimate areas of their body; others may be fearful of the actual legal process and the possibility of having to face their assailant in court; and some feel that they will be blamed or judged detrimentally if they disclose their ordeal (Anon., 2000).

For those who do disclose to the authorities, there are a number of forensic and legal processes that may be applicable to their particular case:

- collection of forensic evidence;
- documentation of injuries;
- the complainant's account of the incident;
- the trial.

These are discussed in detail below. Finally, false allegations are considered.

COLLECTION OF FORENSIC EVIDENCE

One of the fundamental principles guiding forensic science is that 'every contact leaves a trace'. This adage is particularly pertinent to a sexual assault, as there are many body fluids that can be transferred between individuals or deposited on objects or at the scene during a sexual act. These include:

  i semen;
 ii blood;
iii vaginal secretions;
 iv saliva;
  v faeces.

In addition, fibres from clothing, head and pubic hairs may be accidentally transferred between persons, or deposited at the location of the assault. Forensic analysis can also identify other substances that are material to an offence, such as lubricants (including that on condoms) and drugs.

The process of retrieving any forensic evidence requires that a complainant of a recent sexual assault undergoes a forensic medical assessment. In order to maximize the retrieval of forensic evidence, the forensic assessment should take place as soon as possible and complainants are advised not to eat, drink, wash any part of their body (including their mouths), or change their clothes until the relevant samples have been taken. Even when a complainant delays reporting for several weeks forensic material may still be retrievable on unwashed clothing or bedding.

Despite the apparent understanding that the forensic assessment is an important component to the investigation of the offence, many individuals remember the examination as a negative experience:

> The examination is the final straw. I know it has to be done, that it is part and parcel of reporting rape. Could it not be done with a little more compassion? More appreciation of what a woman has already undergone? I have had enough. All I want are my own clothes and to be left alone (Saward, 1991).

> In a soft voice he told me what had to be done. Swabs were taken from my mouth and vagina. He had to take a blood sample too. At this time I was numb. I had started out that morning with such high hopes and enthusiasm. Here I was, only one hundred minutes later, having my body probed in the most intimate way for a report. Even in my weakened state I knew that this was necessary, but it did not lessen the feeling of being dehumanised again (Nuttall, 1997).

> It is really, really intimidating ... They do basically everything. He had to take hairs out of my head and down below. He had to take saliva. These sort of things take a long time ... It was horrible. The whole lot of it was horrible (Temkin, 1996).

> They had to take hairs out and take swabs of the womb. They took blood tests and urine tests. I was there for about two hours while they did this ... the examination felt really awful. It made me feel even worse than I did before (Temkin, 1996).

A small group of women who reported rape in one English constabulary were questioned on their views of the medico-legal process (Temkin, 1996). Disturbingly, some of these complainants considered that the medical examination was almost as traumatic or more traumatic than the sexual act itself:

> The worst part of the whole thing was seeing that doctor. I can honestly say that it was almost worse than the rape itself ... Looking back on it now, I feel worse about that than I actually do about the rape itself. I don't know, but it really disturbed me ... I think that was more degrading and demoralising than the act itself. That was my experience anyway (Temkin, 1996).

> It was horrendous, it was like being raped all over again (Temkin, 1996).

Most concerning, from a practitioner's point of view, are the negative comments that have been made by complainants about the manner and attitude of the doctor who conducted the forensic assessment:

> He wasn't very sympathetic ... He asked me if I'd imagined it ... he just said 'Are you sure you didn't imagine this?' (Temkin, 1996).

> She was rushed all of the time. She kept saying that she didn't have much time, it was her day off, that it was a Sunday, that she was doing this as a favour ... She said 'This is a nice way to spend my Sunday afternoon isn't it?' That was a bit upsetting ... (Temkin, 1996).

Some female complainants have stated that they believe that a female doctor may have been more sympathetic to their distress:

> The examination was probably made worse because it was carried out by a man who I felt was cold and impersonal. I cannot believe that a woman examiner would have been as distant as he was, and a woman would have certainly been easier for me to accept under the circumstances (Nuttall, 1997).

Comments made by complainants demonstrate that some have felt that they have lost all rights of self-volition, both during the sexual assault and immediately thereafter, as they are guided by the investigating authorities towards a forensic assessment:

> I wanted to be in control. I didn't want anybody to control me at all and in that situation I felt that I was being controlled (Temkin, 1996).

Much has been done worldwide to address these and other criticisms levied at the forensic medical assessment; for example, most developed countries now have specifically designed facilities available for the examination of complainants of sexual offences that report to the authorities. An increasing number of such facilities are also directly accessible by persons who have been sexually assaulted but who do not want to report the incident at that stage. The specialist centres usually provide a waiting area, a private room for the examination and bathing facilities for the complainant to utilize after the examination. Some facilities have the benefit of special equipment, such as colposcopes (a microscope on wheels or on a limb attached to a wall, which have attachments that enable photo-documentation of genital injuries) and also allow complainants to return for tests for sexually transmitted infections. Although many such facilities are stocked with a change of clothing (e.g., unisex tracksuits in various sizes), it is often possible to arrange for some clean items of the complainant's clothing to be collected from his/her home should this be preferred.

From the investigation perspective, the use of designated complainant facilities ensures that there is no possibility of accidental transfer of material between the complainant and the suspect. Best practice dictates that complainant and suspect are transported in different vehicles, examined by different doctors, and dealt with by different police officers. When two or more complainants have been involved in the same incident, it is preferable that they are taken to different premises for their examinations and the same doctor does not examine them. Dedicated victim examination suites also mean that the complainant can be assured that she or he will not accidentally encounter her/his assailant.

In many countries the complainant will be accompanied to the suite by a specially trained police officer. If the allegation is reported in the area in which the offence took place, it is usually this police officer that obtains the statement and becomes the main conduit for communication between the police and the complainant. However, if the offence is to be investigated by the police in another area (i.e., the police area where it occurred), this may mean a different supporting police officer. Although both male and female officers are trained to fulfil these roles, one study has suggested that female complainants prefer a female officer (Jordan, 1998). In some centres full time crisis workers (with a health-care background) are present for the initial examination (Howitt, 1995). This resource enables the police to concentrate on the investigation of the case while still ensuring that immediate and ongoing emotional support is provided to the complainant.

Throughout the world various practitioners (doctors or nurses) are called upon to undertake the forensic assessment of a complainant of a sexual assault; for example, in the UK the role has historically been filled by a police surgeon (also called forensic medical examiners or force medical officers), the majority of whom also work as general practitioners. Elsewhere the assessment is undertaken by medical officers in a casualty department, forensic pathologists, gynaecologists, or, on occasions, any available doctor (Payne-James, 2000). Unfortunately, there is no internationally agreed definition of the knowledge, skills, and attitudes that these doctors should have for these sensitive assessments. Nonetheless, many countries are able to offer female complainants a female practitioner (Payne-James, 2000) and many specialist centres only recruit women for these posts. Training for these practitioners should be both theoretical and practical. Role playing using actors will address whether the practitioner has the appropriate skills and attitudes for the post. Participation in peer review groups and a commitment to professional development should also be prerequisites.

These consultations predominantly take place at night and at weekends. The complainant may be severely injured or psychologically traumatized. Practitioners can find their emotional equilibrium extremely tested by repeatedly dealing with such patients. In addition, the practitioners can experience friction at home when they are 'called out' or if they are too tired to participate in family life. They may also find themselves becoming suspicious of men and altering their behaviour to take account of the *modus operandi* of an assailant who is still 'at large'. The practitioners themselves need an avenue whereby they can express their feelings about such cases; peer support can provide this.

The forensic practitioner has an ethical duty to ensure that they obtain informed consent for each stage of the forensic medical assessment. The patient will be advised that they can stop the examination at any time they choose, despite having provided consent at the outset, without any ramifications. This returns autonomy to the complainant.

Complainants will have to be asked about relevant medical history; for example, if there is a complaint of vaginal bleeding, details of the normal menstrual cycle will be requested. In addition, some medical history may be elicited to determine appropriate aftercare, particularly in terms of the most suitable method of post-coital contraception. When obtaining informed consent, the complainant will be advised that the forensic practitioner is unable to guarantee confidentiality of the information obtained during the medical. Even in countries, such as England, where the medical notes are treated as third-party material and, in consequence, protected from automatic disclosure (BMA and Association of Police Surgeons, 1998), a judge (or other presiding officer of a court) can rule that the practitioner breach medical confidentiality if they feel that the information contained in the notes may be material to the case at trial. In England, orders are frequently made for the disclosure of any notes made by psychologists and psychiatrists even if the psychological assessment/ treatment preceded the alleged incident. When photo-documentation is to constitute part of the medical, the patient should be advised in advance of the means of storage and its potential uses; specific written consent should then be sought for this procedure.

The forensic practitioner should endeavour to accommodate requests made by the complainant that would make the assessment more acceptable to him/her; for example, the complainant may wish to defer the medical until a certain friend or relative can be present.

Attention to the urgent medical needs of the complainant (e.g., treatment of serious wounds) is paramount and takes precedence over all the other objectives of the forensic medical assessment. This principle accepts that certain medical interventions may diminish the chance of retrieving forensic evidence. All other aspects of medical care (e.g., the provision of emergency contraception and advice on sexually transmitted infections) will be addressed, as pertinent, during the medical. Further discussion around these issues, with the provision of written directions and advice, takes place at the end of the consultation. Although the forensic practitioner owes no legal duty of care to the complainant (*The Times*, 1999), most doctors perceive there to be an ethical obligation to also address the ongoing medical and psychological needs of the complainant during the assessment (Howitt and Rogers, 1996).

In recent years forensic practitioners have rejected the 'sample everything in case' philosophy for an evidence-based examination in which the emphasis is placed on respecting the examinee. The forensic assessment is tailored to the individual case; for example, if the complainant only describes being made to perform fellatio, there is no indication for the external genitalia to be examined. Similarly, forensic samples will only be requested when the assault is reported within the time limits for retrieval of spermatozoa from the site where ejaculation is believed to have occurred (i.e., 48 hours for the mouth). If the complainant is unclear as to what sexual acts took place during the assault (e.g., because of the effects of alcohol or drugs), consent will be sought for a comprehensive examination with sample collection from all body orifices. Plucking hair is painful and, fortunately, because of advances in forensic science techniques, most jurisdictions no longer require that plucked head or pubic hairs be obtained from the complainant.

In addition, the complainant should be consulted regarding the samples that can be retrieved in different ways; in some cases there is a 'best evidence' sample (e.g., cuttings of fingernails which are believed to have been contaminated by body fluids) and a 'second-best evidence' sample, which in this example would be obtained by scraping under the nails. These different options can be explained to the complainant who can then consider whether the intrusion is outweighed by the increased chance of obtaining forensic evidence from the contaminated area.

Forensic evidence is used to identify the assailant(s) and corroborate the complainant's account of the sexual acts that took place. The scientific analysis of areas of the body, or objects, believed to have been contaminated by body fluids is based on an identification of the particular body fluid (e.g., by the detection of spermatozoa), and obtaining a deoxyribonucleic acid (DNA) profile. Each individual's nuclear DNA pattern is unique (excluding identical twins) and can be determined from any of their body fluids or tissues (e.g., blood, semen, and hairs). A control DNA sample in the form of a buccal scrape or blood sample is obtained from the complainant to ensure that the DNA profile obtained from a specimen is not their own profile. It is also possible to compare fibres to identify if they originate from the same source.

Given the number of samples that are frequently obtained from a complainant following a recent sexual assault, it is disappointing that over half of the swabs submitted to the Metropolitan Police Forensic Science Laboratory had no detectable body fluids on them (Allard, 1997). This may be due to a number of factors that include delays between the incident and the medical examination, cleansing following the assault, poor sampling techniques, or lack of ejaculation. However, advances in forensic science mean that the number of samples yielding a positive result are likely to increase.

While the lack of forensic evidence to assist with identification of the assailant may not be particularly significant to a case where the complainant is able to name the suspect, in cases of stranger assault a lack of forensic evidence can seriously frustrate the investigation. Harris and Grace (1999) found that forensic testing established the identity of the assailant in only three of the thirteen stranger-rape cases that were considered in their study. This low detection rate meant that in relative terms the rapes committed by strangers during the period of the study were less likely than rapes committed by acquaintances or intimates to proceed to court (Harris and Grace, 1999).

Furthermore, a lack of forensic evidence can hamper the investigation in terms of corroboration of the sexual acts that have taken place. This is especially pertinent to those jurisdictions that require 'proof' of penile penetration of the vagina or anus in order to find a person guilty of a serious sexual offence (e.g., rape as defined by the Sexual Offences Act 1956), particularly as it is recognized that frequently no genital trauma is identified on gross visualization (Bowyer and Dalton, 1997).

DOCUMENTATION OF INJURIES

While obtaining the relevant forensic samples, as detailed above, the doctor will need to examine systematically all relevant body surfaces for tenderness, injuries, or other signs which may be relevant to the allegation. Forensic reference texts remind the doctor that 'Respect for the modesty of the examinee is essential. It should never be necessary for the patient to suffer the embarrassment of being naked; she should be covered as the examination progresses by an examination gown or sheet' (Howitt and Rogers, 1996).

On average, 60% of complainants of sexual assaults have no general injuries detectable at the forensic examination (Cartwright, 1986; Everett and Jimerson, 1977; Soules, Stewart, Brown, and Pollard, 1978). However, the absence of injuries does not negate the allegation as:

i The complainant may submit to the demands of her assailant(s) in response to expressed or perceived threats of physical harm.
ii The force used, or the resistance offered to that force, is insufficient to produce an injury.

iii Minor injuries, such as reddening and superficial abrasions, rapidly fade or heal without trace (Cartwright, 1986; Everett and Jimerson, 1977).

iv Some bruises can take up to 48 hours to become visible externally. Consequently, some practitioners advocate a re-examination of the complainant 2–3 days after the assault. This is particularly relevant if the complainant describes blunt trauma (punches, kicks, falls) as having occurred during the assault. This re-examination can be combined with the appointment for the obtaining of the statement, if the complainant prefers this.

v Some bruises will never be visible externally.

All injuries have to be documented precisely by the forensic practitioner. This entails measuring the dimensions of each injury and noting its site (measured if possible from a fixed, palpable bony point of the body). All of the body surfaces also have to be palpated and a note made of the site and approximate size of any tender areas identified. This painstaking examination and documentation can be stressful and arduous for the complainant.

Although photo-documentation of injuries may be beneficial to the presentation of the medical evidence in court (Harris and Grace, 1999), not all facilities have cameras on-site. Where such equipment is not available at the time of the examination, it is incumbent on the officer in the case, on the advice of the forensic practitioner, to decide whether to arrange for professional forensic photography of the injuries which necessitates a further appointment. Complainants often express a preference that the photographer is the same gender as himself or herself.

The genital and anal areas will need to be examined closely if the allegation suggests contact with either area has occurred during the assault. It is recognized that some complainants find it incredibly traumatic to disclose peno-anal penetration and others may be confused as to which orifice has been penetrated. Therefore, some practitioners will routinely seek permission to inspect the anal area whenever genital contact has been described.

Some centres routinely utilize a colposcope to facilitate genital and anal examination (Girardin, Faugno, Seneski, Slaughter, and Whelan, 1997). It is an excellent source of illumination and magnification (5–30×), the provision of which increases the likelihood of identifying a genital injury (Rogers and Newton, 2000). Although some commentators have expressed the opinion that 'colposcopy may be perceived as a stressful invasion of a woman who is already vulnerable' (Patel, Courtney, and Forster, 1993), it should be noted that, because of the instrument's focal length, it remains at a distance of approximately 30 cm from the area being inspected. When a colposcope is not available, the genital/anal area has to be examined at close proximity by the practitioner using a hand-held magnifying instrument.

Colposcopes can be fitted with facilities to make a permanent record of the genital/anal findings via an attached 35-mm camera, a Polaroid camera or a video recorder. Personal experience has found that reviewing the video with the complainant can more easily allay their fears of permanent damage than just verbal reassurance. However, such joint reviews would only be done if the complainant wished it.

On average, only a third of complainants of sexual assault examined without the use of a colposcope have detectable genital or anal injuries. Even when the specialist techniques described above are utilized, a number of the examinations will be normal (Slaughter, Brown, Crowley, and Peck, 1997). The reasons given for the lack of general injuries also apply to the genital and anal areas. Furthermore, the natural elasticity of the post-pubertal hymen and anus, and endogenous or exogenous lubricant (including saliva), help us appreciate why these areas may not be visibly injured even when a sexual assault has occurred.

Although not a publicised policy, there is evidence that in England and Wales discontinuation of a case prior to a trial, on the grounds of 'insufficient evidence', was more likely when there was no objective evidence of violence having occurred during the alleged assault (Harris and Grace, 1999). This demonstrates a regrettable failure on the part of some professionals to appreciate that both men and women may submit to sexual acts due to perceived or expressed threats by the assailant. (Knight, 1986; Lees, 1996).

THE COMPLAINANT'S ACCOUNT OF THE INCIDENT

Although the complainant will inevitably have described the incident to one or more police officers prior to the medical, some forensic practitioners require the complainant themselves to reiterate the details of the assault, in its entirety, to them. However, one UK support agency has commented how frustrating this could be for the complainant:

> For example, have you ever had to telephone a company to complain about something? Is it not better that, having explained your complaint to the first person you speak to, they take trouble to explain your dilemma to the appropriate person before putting you through? It saves you the frustration of having to go through all the details again. If that second person starts by saying 'Hello Dr Rogers, I believe you are calling about A, B, and C – is that correct?' you feel more confident about the level of service you can expect from them. We feel it is the same type of issue here.

What women need (and deserve) is a professional and informed service (Jones, pers. comm.).

Furthermore, differing accounts of an assault, albeit possibly due to the information not having been recorded verbatim, may be used in court in an attempt to discredit the evidence of the complainant.

Nonetheless, the forensic practitioner may need to ask specific questions about the incident to ensure that the appropriate samples are obtained. In addition, to prevent misinterpretation of the forensic results, the complainant will be asked about recent, relevant consensual sexual activity (e.g., vaginal intercourse in the 2 weeks preceding the medical). Where the forensic tests are positive, and there has been recent consensual sexual activity, it may be necessary to obtain a control DNA sample from the sexual partner to ensure that the results are not spuriously attributed to the assailant.

Recording of the actual deposition is ideally deferred until 1 or 2 days after the incident to allow recovery from the acute physical and psychological trauma. This is usually the domain of the investigating agencies, many of whom have specific training on how to retrieve the maximum amount of information from a complainant. Although it can take many hours to obtain a detailed statement, anecdotes suggest that complainants appreciate the importance of this information to the police investigation:

> The police required every small detail of the sex attack, but I found it difficult to put into words. Yet while feeling this way, I also knew that if I didn't give the police everything I could remember, I would be depriving them of their best chance of catching the man who had put me through this ordeal (Nuttall, 1997).

> We begin the statement. I don't object. I will do anything I can to get these men caught. I feel a bit sick reliving the actual rape, especially having to talk slowly so that it can be written down, but other than that it's OK. It's though it isn't me speaking. I'm still on remote control (Saward, 1991).

Despite reporting a serious sexual assault to the police, and (when relevant) undergoing a forensic medical assessment, the complainant is not obliged to continue to co-operate with police or to give evidence in court. There is only limited specific information available regarding why complainants withdraw an allegation (Harris and Grace, 1999) and the reasons are likely to be manyfold. Commentators have suggested that factors such as 'family and social pressures to avoid pursuing a case against someone who is well known to the victim and the courage and strength required to face her attacker in court, knowing that the evidence is her word against his and that in a criminal case the court is obliged to give the defendant the benefit of the doubt' can contribute to the low prosecution rate (Price, 1996). What is apparent is that withdrawal does not equate to the allegation being false (Aiken, Burgess, and Hazelwood, 1995; Harris and Grace, 1999).

THE TRIAL

Essentially, there are two types of legal system. The first, the adversarial system, is practised in most common-law countries including the USA, Australia, and the UK. In this system there are two 'opposing sides' referred to as prosecution and defence. In court the prosecution barrister presents the case against the defendant(s) and the defence barrister(s) (there may be more than one defence barrister if there is more than one defendant) refutes the allegation on behalf of his client. A legal dictionary describes how with this system the 'parties to a dispute and their representatives have the prime responsibility for finding and presenting evidence' (Curzon, 1993). However, it must be remembered that while the defendant is considered to be one 'party', thus allowing him or her to consult with his/her legal representatives both leading up to and during the trial, the Crown is the other 'party' and, hence, the complainant does not have this prerogative. This was identified as a deficiency in the recent Report of the Working Party on Rape to the United Kingdom Programme Action Committee of Soroptimist International (Soroptimist International, 1999). One of the conclusions of this report is that 'The complainant must have the opportunity to meet all the lawyers preparing and presenting the case for the Crown and discuss the case with them. Bar Council rules should be reviewed and amended.'

Even when a suspect is identified and charged soon after the assault the trial may not take place for several months. Although trial dates are fixed some months in advance, they may later be rescheduled to allow the defence or prosecution to address some additional information that has come to light. The anticipation of the court proceedings, compounded by a lack of information regarding the progress of the case, can be particularly distressing for the complainant (Temkin, 1999).

When at court, the adversarial system usually requires that the complainant is led through her/his statement by prosecuting council. This takes place in open court with the complainant standing or sitting in the witness box and with members of the public (which can include friends and family of the defendant) looking on. Some courts offer screens to ensure that the complainant cannot see the defendant. However, in such circumstances, to ensure a 'fair trial' the defendant may be allowed to see the complainant give evidence and be cross-examined, by means of a camera and a television. Furthermore, unless the defendant is in custody the complainant may encounter him/her in the court building.

Once the complainant finishes giving his/her account of the incident, the defence barrister(s) begin to cross-examine the complainant about the allegation. This cross-examination can sometimes be very aggressive and accusatory. The complainant usually remains in the witness stand until either she or he is released as a witness or the court rises for lunch or to adjourn for the day. However, if the complainant becomes visibly distressed, to the extent that she or he is unable to continue giving evidence, the trial judge may allow a short break in proceedings to enable the complainant to 'compose him or herself'. If the case is adjourned to the following day, the complainant is not allowed to discuss the case with anyone. As previously stated, the adversarial system allows for each defendant to be represented in court by their own barrister; this means that in cases where there are multiple assailants the complainant may have to endure several days of cross-examination by different barristers, repeatedly reiterating the details of the assault.

Under the adversarial system the defendant (via his barrister) 'can attack the complainant's credibility and mention her past criminal record or her bad reputation, knowing that he does not run the risk of being cross-examined as to his previous convictions or bad character since this is up to the discretion of the judge who rarely exercises the power' (Lees, 1996). This mode of questioning can have adverse effects on the complainant. Research conducted by Professor Sue Lees on the views of victims whose cases have proceeded to trial reveals that 'the majority of women found their experiences in court humiliating and distressing' (Lees, 1996). In particular, the women complained that they were limited to responding to questions posed by the barristers and 'not allowed to explain fully what had happened to them or how they felt during the rape.'

The second type of legal system is referred to as the inquisitorial system. Under this system, which is practised in some European countries, the judge searches for the facts, listens to witnesses, examines documents, and orders that evidence be taken, after which he makes further investigations if he considers them necessary (Curzon, 1993). In France (which operates under the inquisitorial system), the defendant's criminal record is read to the court prior to the trial.

There is no information as to whether this system is more supportive of the complainant. However, it is perceived that the inquisitorial system is more conducive to the presentation of non-partisan medical evidence.

In the adversarial system the guilt or innocence of the defendant is decided by a jury, consisting of 12 adults (male or female). In the inquisitorial system it is the judge who decides the outcome of the case. In the majority of cases at trial the defendant does not deny that sexual intercourse took place, instead they run the defence along the lines that the sexual acts were all consensual. As most such acts are unwitnessed, this leaves the jury or judge with the task of essentially deciding whose account they prefer.

Work by Suzanne Adler in England in the 1980s revealed the prejudices of jury members in this type of trial. Adler found that the cases most likely to end in a conviction were those where the complainant was sexually inexperienced, had a respectful lifestyle, was assaulted by a stranger, had sustained injuries while actively resisting her attacker, and promptly reported the offence to the police (Adler, 1987). Very few cases fulfil all these criteria. Even when the complainant has injuries, barristers will suggest that they resulted from 'vigorous' or 'overenthusiastic' sexual intercourse, and there is very little non-anecdotal information regarding the patterns of injuries sustained following consensual sexual acts to completely refute this suggestion.

Unfortunately, judges have also been shown to have prejudices which they reveal when summing up the case to the jury (Lees, 1996) and sentencing defendants:

> According to the judge the trauma that I have suffered is 'not so great'. He sentences Man 2 to five years for burglary and five years for rape, buggery and indecent assault. Man 3 receives five years for burglary and three for rape ... What did he say? No great trauma? A few trinkets and a video are roughly equal to being taken by force, put through the most revolting sexual acts, and left in total humiliation to discover whether two people you love are dead or alive (Saward, 1991).

This has led some commentators to call for judges to receive training on *inter alia* the effects of rape on the victims and the characteristics of rapists (Lees, 1996).

For those persons who do report the incident, the eventual conviction rate is low. A Home Office study found that only 6% of 483 cases of female rape that were reported to police in five constabularies in England and Wales during 1996 resulted in convictions for rape (Harris and Grace, 1999). Similar attrition rates have been noted in other countries (Craven, 1996).

FALSE ALLEGATIONS

There are undoubtedly occasions when a complainant will make an allegation of a sexual assault when no sexual assault has occurred (termed 'false allegation'). Not surprisingly, there is no accurate information regarding how frequently false allegations are made. Some commentators think that false allegations are exceptional whereas other authors report a 41–50% incidence (Kanin, 1994).

Between 1978 and 1987 Kanin studied the case files of 45 women who initially made an allegation of rape to the police, in a small metropolitan area in the USA's Midwest, but then later admitted that the allegation was false (Kanin, 1994). These cases amounted to 41% of the total rape cases that were reported to the police in that period. Kanin concluded that in each of these cases the false allegation appeared to serve one or more of three purposes. First, in 56% ($n = 27$) of the cases studied the false allegation provided an alibi; that is, 'a plausible explanation for some suddenly foreseen, unfortunate consequence of a consensual encounter, usually sexual, with a male acquaintance'; Aiken and colleagues refer to this category as 'sex stress situations' (Aiken *et al.*, 1995). An assailant was identified in approximately half of the 'sex stress situation' cases studied by Kanin. Kanin gives the following case example of this category:

A 16-year-old complainant, her girlfriend, and two male companions were having a drinking party at her home. She openly invited one of the males, a casual friend, to have sex with her. Later in the evening, two other male acquaintances dropped in and, in the presence of all, her sex partner 'bragged' that he had just had sex with her. She quickly ran out to another girlfriend's house and told her she had been raped. Soon her mother was called and the police were notified. Two days later, when confronted with the contradictory stories of her companions, she admitted that she had not been raped. Her charge was primarily motivated by an urgent desire to defuse what surely would be public information among friends at school the next day, her promiscuity.

Kanin's second proposed purpose is codified as 'revenge'. This apparently applied to 27% ($n = 12$) of the cases he studied. Kanin considered that the false allegation of rape was used in these cases as a means of retaliating against a rejecting male. In each of the cases the complainant named the 'rejecting' male as the suspect. One case example used to illustrate this category is:

A 16-year-old reported she was raped, and her boyfriend was charged. She later admitted that she was 'mad at him' because he was seeing another girl, and she 'wanted to get him into trouble'.

Kanin considered that in the remaining 18% ($n = 8$) of the cases he studied, the primary purpose of the false allegation was to gain attention and/or sympathy. A quoted case example for this category:

An unmarried female, age 41, was in post-divorce counselling, and she wanted more attention and sympathy from her counsellor because she 'liked him'. She fabricated a rape episode, and he took her to the police station and assisted her in making the charge. She could not back out since she would have to admit lying to him. She admitted the false allegation when she offered to be polygraphed.

The following example from the author's own practice also demonstrates this category:

The complainant and her boyfriend, along with a number of their friends, attempted to gain access to a nightclub. The complainant's boyfriend and the other friends were granted access but the complainant was refused entry as she appeared to the doormen to be intoxicated with alcohol. The complainant objected to being denied access and instigated an altercation with the doormen during which she sustained a number of minor injuries. She wandered around the local streets and then made her way home where her friends awaited her; they had left the nightclub when they realised that she was not going to be allowed to join them. She declared to the waiting, concerned crowd that she had been raped and her friends duly contacted the police. She gave the police a vague description of a stranger attack during which peno-vaginal penetration had occurred. She indicated the street on which the incident had occurred. The identified scene was well lit and overlooked by many local residents; it also happened to be the main street the police would use to access the local police station. The complainant underwent a comprehensive forensic medical examination in the early hours of the morning. At the time of the medical, she attributed all her injuries to the scuffle with the bouncers and said that none of them related to the rape. Later that morning, the complainant attended the police station and admitted that she had fabricated the allegation.

Kanin comments that as no one was specifically identified as the rapist in any of the cases that he included in the attention/sympathy category, this type of false allegations was 'socially harmless', by which he meant that such cases were unlikely to lead to a 'miscarriage of justice'. Aiken and colleagues refer to this category as the 'False Rape Allegation' defined as one in which all three components of the allegation (e.g., the act, the perpetrator, and the setting) are false and the complainant has a conscious understanding that they are false (Aiken *et al.*, 1995). They state that this category of complaint may serve financial motives (e.g., to claim 'victim compensation') in addition to the psychological needs for attention previously referred to. On occasions, descriptions of bizarre scenarios are purported to be supported by injuries which have been self-inflicted (McDowell and Hibler, 1987; Aiken *et al.*, 1995). Aiken and colleagues state that a fraudulent claim of rape could be interpreted as a form of manipulation of the criminal justice system, analogous to the way that patients with Munchausen's syndrome manipulate hospitals and doctors (Aiken *et al.*, 1995). Indeed, Gibbon has described a female with Munchausen's syndrome who presented complaining that she had been sexually assaulted (Gibbon, 1998).

Aiken and colleagues describe a further category of false allegation in which the complainant is 'psychotic and/or delusional'. In such cases claims of sexual assault may be made repeatedly.

Experts describe how complainants of false allegations may need help and support to address any psychological causes which have led to the allegation. However, in some countries criminal proceedings have been instigated against women who were considered to have wasted police time by making a false allegation of rape, which may lead to a fine, suspended sentence, or, exceptionally, imprisonment (Aiken *et al.*, 1995; Theilade and Thomsen, 1986). It is exceptional for such proceedings to be instigated in the UK.

SUMMARY

Complainants of sexual assaults, already physically and psychologically traumatized by the sexual violence that they have endured, may be further traumatized during the process of investigating the offence and any consequent legal proceedings. Dedicated 'sexual assault' centres, with free access for persons who wish to report the incident and those who do not, staffed by appropriately trained mental health professionals, psychologists and forensic practitioners, may be the way to minimize this trauma. Clearly, such centres need to be adequately funded to succeed.

REFERENCES

Adler, S. (1987) *Rape on trial*. London: Routledge and Kegan Paul.
Aiken, M., Burgess, A., and Hazelwood, R. (1995) False rape allegations. In R.

Hazelwood and A. Burgess (eds) *Practical aspects of rape investigations: A multidisciplinary approach* (pp. 292–293). New York: CRC Press.

Allard, J.E. (1997) The collection of data from findings in cases of sexual assault and the significance of spermatozoa on vaginal, anal and oral swabs. *Science and Justice*, 37(2), 99–108.

Anon. (2000) The day my life changed. *British Medical Journal*, 321, 1089

Bowyer, L. and Dalton, M. (1997) Female victims of rape and their genital injuries. *British Journal of Obstetrics and Gynaecology*, 104, 617–620.

BMA and Association of Police Surgeons. (1998) *Revised interim guidelines on confidentiality for police surgeons in England, Wales and Northern Ireland*. London: British Medical Association.

Cartwright, P. (1986) Reported sexual assault in Nashville-Davidson Country, Tennesee, 1980–1982. *American Journal of Obstetrics and Gynecology*, 154, 1064–1068.

Craven, S. (1996) Assessment of alleged rape victims—an unrewarding exercise. *South African Medical Journal*, 85, 237–238.

Curzon, L. (1993) *Dictionary of law*. London: Pitman Publishing.

Everett, R. and Jimerson, G. (1977) The rape victim: A review of 117 consecutive cases. *Obstetrics and Gynecology*, 50(1), 88–90.

Gibbon, K. (1998) Munchausen's syndrome presenting as an acute sexual assault. *Medical Science Law*, 38(3), 202–205.

Girardin, B., Faugno, D., Seneski, P., Slaughter, L., and Whelan, M. (1997) Care of the sexually assaulted patient. In *Color Atlas of Sexual Assault*. St Louis, MO: Mosby.

Harris, J. and Grace, S. (1999) *A question of evidence? Investigating and prosecuting rape in the 1990s* (Home Office Research Study 196). London: Home Office.

Howitt, J. (1995) Clinical forensic medicine services: London and Melbourne contrasted. *Journal of Clinical Forensic Medicine*, 2(1), 17–24.

Howitt, J. and Rogers, D. (1996) Adult sexual offences and related matters. In W. McLay (ed.) *Clinical Forensic Medicine* (pp. 193–218). London: Greenwich Medical Media.

Jordan, J. (1998) *Reporting rape: Women's experiences with the police, doctors and support agencies*. Wellington: Institute of Criminology, Victoria University.

Kanin, E. (1994) False rape allegations. *Archives of Sexual Behaviour*, 23(1), 81–92.

Knight, M. (1986) Rape—fact or fiction. False allegations of rape. *The Police Surgeon*, 30, 11–60.

Lees, S. (1996) *Carnal knowledge*. London: Penguin.

MacDonald, R. (2000) Time to talk about rape. *British Medical Journal*, 321, 1034–1035.

McDowell, C. and Hibler, N. (1987) False allegations. In R. Hazelwood and A. Burgess (eds) *Practical aspects of rape investigations: A multidisciplinary approach* (pp. 292–293). New York: Elsevier.

Nuttall, M. (1997) *It could have been you*. London: Virago Press.

Patel, H., Courtney, G., and Forster, G. (1993) Colposcopy and rape (letter). *American Journal of Obstetrics and Gynecology*, 168(4), 1334.

Payne-James, J. (2000) The history and development of clinical forensic medicine worldwide. In M. Stark (ed) *A physician's guide to clinical forensics*. Totowa, NJ: Humana Press.

Price, M. (1996) Assessment of alleged rape victims. *South African Medical Journal*, **86**(7), 842.

Rogers, D. and Newton, M. (2000) Sexual assault examination. In M. Stark (ed.) *A physician's guide to clinical forensics*. Totowa, NJ: Humana Press.

Saward, J. (1991) *Rape, my story*. London: Pan.

Slaughter, L., Brown, C., Crowley, S., and Peck, R. (1997) Patterns of genital injury in female sexual assault victims. *American Journal of Obstetrics and Gynecology*, **176**, 609–616.

Soroptimist International (1999) *Report of the Working Party on Rape*. United Kingdom Programme Action Committee of Soroptimist International.

Soules, M., Stewart, S., Brown, K., and Pollard, A. (1978) The spectrum of alleged rape. *Journal of Reproductive Medicine*, **20**(1), 33–39.

Swedish Government Fact Sheet (1999) *Violence against women*.

Temkin, J. (1996) Doctors, rape and criminal justice. *The Howard Journal of Criminal Justice*, **35**(1).

Temkin, J. (1999) Reporting rape in London: A qualitative study. *The Howard Journal of Criminal Justice*, **38**(1).

Theilade, P. and Thomsen, J. (1986) False allegations of rape. *The Police Surgeon*, **30**, 17–22.

The Times. (9 June 1999) Law report.

WHO. (2000) *Violence against women database*. Geneva: World Health Organization.

Chapter 12

THE IMPACT OF SEXUAL ASSAULT ON HEALTH-CARE WORKERS

Barbara Hedge

INTRODUCTION

The horrific stories of individuals who have been sexually assaulted are frequently difficult to listen to and may be deeply upsetting. How then do health-care workers manage to provide a high level of professional care on a long-term basis for people who have been sexually assaulted? Is there a high rate of burnout? Does this work lead to any lasting physical or psychological damage? Are there ways of managing sexual assault clinics that can minimize the negative impact on staff? These are a few of the questions that spring to mind when considering the difficulties faced by health carers working with people who have been sexually assaulted.

Although there are a number of accounts of individual health carers' experiences, the question of whether there are specific factors associated with working with sexual assault that may lead to high levels of distress remains unexplored. Koss and Harvey (1991) suggest that enhanced feelings of vulnerability occur in health carers when working with victims of brutal crime including sexual assault.

Few studies have investigated the impact on health carers of working with people who have been sexually assaulted, and even fewer have addressed the issue of managing the distress engendered in this setting. The cost to health services of staff who are sick or just absent can be enormous. If ways can be found to manage occupationally induced

The Trauma of Sexual Assault. Edited by Jenny Petrak and Barbara Hedge.
© 2002 John Wiley & Sons Ltd.

stress, it may directly benefit the health carers and indirectly, by reducing costs, benefit the organization and the clients.

This chapter provides a brief introduction to theories of stress and burnout. It then considers the general attributes of occupations, jobs, and people that might contribute to stress at work, particularly in a health-care setting, and reports on the few studies relating to disaster work. The difficulties of working with people who have been sexually assaulted and aspects of the work that might lead to elevated levels of stress and burnout are then considered. Finally, possible prevention strategies, interventions with those experiencing work-related distress, and the implications for the management of sexual assault services are addressed.

STRESS

In the psychological literature the term 'stress' is used to refer to a negative psychological state that develops as a consequence of a failure to cope. Lazarus and Folkman (1984) conceptualize coping as 'constantly changing cognitive and behavioural efforts to manage external and/or internal demands that are appraised as taxing or exceeding the resources of the person', and stress is said to occur when the perceived biological, psychological, and social resources available are not sufficient to meet the demands of the situation. Potential stressors can range from cataclysmic events and major life traumas to chronic strains and daily hassles.

It is well documented that stress, or a failure to cope, is frequently accompanied by emotional reactions of fear, anxiety, depression, and anger and by physiological changes that may increase the risk of illnesses such as cancer and cardiovascular disease (Steptoe, 1997). Stress can impair cognitive functioning, reducing efficiency by lowering levels of concentration and attention, or by altering a person's mood or motivation.

Lazarus and Folkman's model suggests that the costs and benefits of possible coping strategies are evaluated, and that the coping behaviour perceived as most advantageous is then adopted. There is evidence that the appraisal of the threat of the stressor can be 'buffered' by the availability and extent of the available social support system (Cohen and Wills, 1985), the individual's perceived control over the situation (Rotter, 1966), and the coping style employed (Lazarus and Folkman, 1984).

Social support can be understood as a belief in the availability of supportive social relationships that can be activated should the situation require (Dunkel-Schetter and Bennett, 1990). Studies by Payne (1979), Payne and

Fletcher (1983), and Janman, Jones, Payne, and Rick (1988) found social support to be an important variable in determining the amount of stress experienced in a work setting.

Perceived personal control is a major determinant of a person's response to stressors (Caplan, Cobb, French, van Harrison, and Pinneau, 1975; Fletcher, 1988). When individuals perceive that they can take effective action against stressors, they are less likely to experience stress than when they cannot. Authoritarian organizations that leave carers with little personal control over their physical, psychological, or social environment are likely to increase stress particularly where roles, power, or status in the organization are ambiguous, illogical, or unclear. Jones and Fletcher (1996) review a number of studies that provide evidence for the importance of control in an occupational setting as a predictor of health outcomes.

Lazarus and Folkman (1984) argue that individuals differ in their preferred style of coping. The use of denial or external coping aids such as alcohol or drugs can increase the level of stress experienced and has been found to be associated with increased levels of burnout (Bennett, Kelaher, and Ross, 1992). There is some evidence that problem-based coping is more effective when dealing with work-related problems than emotion-based coping (Anderson, 1977). However, it is likely that the style of coping that is most effective will vary with particular aspects of the work.

Payne (1979) proposed that a high level of occupational stress is best predicted by a combination of high demands, low control, and poor social support. There is widespread supportive evidence for this proposal, reviewed by Jones and Fletcher (1996). These findings lead us to expect that high levels of occupational stress will be a common occurrence in any health service in which staff experience high demands, low control, and poor social support. Even people who enjoy their work and find it inherently satisfying can experience work stress and leave their jobs because the stressors become too great and the support too weak.

Stressors are cumulative; so, even when stress related to work in a health-care setting is of primary concern, it needs to be viewed in the context of wider social stressors (e.g., everyday family life events and personal issues). The latter may contribute to the range seen in degree of stress experienced by different people in comparable health-care service settings.

This chapter next considers the stressful aspects of work, individual differences that might enable some people to cope better than others in stressful situations, and protective factors that may buffer some people from the impact of stressful work situations.

STRESSFUL ATTRIBUTES OF JOBS

Cooper (1983) identified six factors influencing stress at work:

- factors intrinsic to the job;
- role within the organization;
- career structures;
- work-based relationships;
- organizational structures and flexibility;
- pressures on family life resulting from work.

Factors Intrinsic to the Job

The demand factors associated with a particular job include the amount, quality, and variety of the tasks required, the timing of work (e.g., shift work or flexitime), and opportunities for personal control over work patterns. The suitability of a person for a job, their skills, training, and the available resources can, when insufficient, add to the demands of the job, or if excessive, exceed the demands of the job.

The actual nature of tasks intrinsic to certain jobs can increase the number of potential stressors. For health carers, issues—such as dealing with pain and loss, observing the outcome of sexual and physical assault, and listening to traumatic accounts that are intrinsic to work with people who have been sexually assaulted—may increase levels of stress.

Role within the Organization

The role of a person with respect to the role of others is important. Potential stressors are a lack of clarity or some ambiguity about a person's role and overlap or conflict with the roles of others.

Career Structures

Sources of stress can come with the career structure associated with a particular job. Failing to gain promotion or being promoted prematurely, dissatisfaction with pay, incongruency of status or pay with comparable staff, a lack of job security, and unpromising future prospects can all be stressors.

Work-based Relationships

Relationships with colleagues, supervisors, and subordinates can all be a source of stress or support. The amount of social support received can be a key factor in buffering the stress response.

Organizational Structures and Flexibility

Each workplace has a structure and an organizational hierarchy. These can vary in complexity and rigidity. Lines of accountability and responsibility to others and for others can affect the stress of a particular job. The organization and composition of teams, patterns of possible communication, teamworking, participation in decision making, and the potential for change can all contribute to the stress of a job.

Pressures on Family Life Resulting from Work

Stressors in the work setting (see above) can integrate or interact with pressures from outside work (e.g., home, social, and individual contexts). These may generate further stress. Factors affecting workplace stress are not unique to the health-care profession (Orton, 1996).

INDIVIDUAL DIFFERENCES AND STRESS

Individuals do not all cope equally well in stressful conditions. Differences can arise from genetic predeterminations, disposition, development, and learning experiences. Three variables that affect how people react to stressful environments have been widely investigated. These are Type A behaviour, locus of control, and dispositional or trait anxiety.

Friedman and Rosenman (1974) described the characteristic behaviours of people who they thought more prone to develop coronary heart disease as 'Type A behaviours'. Characteristics of Type A behaviours are high achievement, fast movements, hectic lifestyles, and hostility to those people or events that interfere with the ability to meet one's goals or achievements. There is supportive evidence of a relationship between Type A behaviours, stress, and coronary heart disease; Type A individuals are more likely to seek demanding situations and to overreact, and consequently to suffer more stress (Rosenman, 1996).

Rotter (1966) introduced the concept of 'locus of control'. This dimension reflects the beliefs that people have about control. Rotter describes 'Internals' as those at one extreme of the dimension, who believe that what happens to them is largely in their control, and 'Externals' as those at the other extreme, who believe that what happens to them is largely outside their control (i.e., in the hands of others or due to luck). The related concept of learned helplessness has been linked with depression (Seligman, 1975).

Dispositional or trait anxiety (i.e., a tendency to perceive the world as threatening) is likely to cause people to view the world this way even when it is not. In an occupational setting, people with high levels of trait anxiety may see more events as stressful than those who are low on trait anxiety. Those with low levels of trait anxiety and high levels of positive affect may be able to reduce the impact of work stressors (Watson and Pennebaker, 1989).

PROTECTIVE FACTORS

Social support appears to act as a 'buffer' to stress at work (Jones and Fletcher, 1996). It does not necessarily lower the stress experienced but it mediates the response in providing an additional resource for coping with the stressor (Payne, 1979). It has been suggested that social support is a coping mechanism that people can use when in a state of high stress (Thiots, 1986).

BURNOUT

The term burnout is used to characterize a syndrome that can develop when work-related stressors are not recognized and addressed. DSM-IV does not formally define burnout. It would best categorize it as an Axis I adjustment disorder (APA, 1994). Maslach and Jackson (1982) define burnout as a multi-dimensional process with the central constructs being emotional exhaustion, depersonalization, and a reduced sense of personal accomplishment that can render individuals unable to carry out their jobs effectively. In a health-care setting, emotional exhaustion is described as a lack of energy with a feeling that there are no longer sufficient emotional resources to support others. Depersonalization is a feeling of detachment and indifference that leads to patients and colleagues being treated as objects and their views ignored or disregarded. A reduced sense of personal accomplishment describes the feelings associated with negative self-evaluations, feelings of failure, feelings of dissatisfaction with professional competence, and a lack of satisfaction from work. Garden (1989) suggests that not all three constructs are necessary to define burnout and that emotional exhaustion alone is sufficient. He argues that a reduced sense of personal accomplishment and depersonalization are the consequence of certain work attracting certain personality types.

There is some commonality between burnout and depression. Emotional exhaustion is significantly related to depression (Meier, 1984; Firth, McIntee, McEwan, and Britton, 1986) when measured by the Maslach Burnout Inventory (Maslach, Jackson, and Leiter, 1996), and some individuals who fulfil the criteria for burnout may also fulfil those for depression. Generally, the context of the symptoms experienced in burnout is work-related and situation-specific (Warr, 1987). Cordes and Dougherty (1993) suggest that depersonalization (i.e., the negative and dehumanizing approach to patients and clients) is a coping resource adopted in response to emotional exhaustion. Leiter (1991) suggests that health carers are faced with unrealistic professional expectations, and, when other coping resources are not available, the clinical detachment and professional demeanour required in the professional setting can become exaggerated and serve as a protective factor.

Health carers are said to be particularly vulnerable to burnout (Maslach, 1982). However, not all health carers who report that their jobs are very stressful experience the severe symptoms described above. This chapter will therefore examine studies reporting stress in health-care workers as well as those that report on burnout.

STRESS IN HEALTH-CARE WORKERS

In the health-care system, the nature of the work might necessarily include a number of stressors such as breaking or receiving bad news, listening repeatedly to accounts of trauma, working with difficult patients or staff, and having to manage loss and grief. Common symptoms of stress that have been reported in health carers, associated cognitions, and the effects of these on the health-care setting are shown in Table 12.1. Not all symptoms are experienced by all individuals who are stressed, and symptoms frequently change over time; for example, initial feelings of anger with self-righteous beliefs may change to a depressive mood with beliefs of personal professional inadequacy when a person realizes that they are powerless to change the work stressors.

As well as affecting the primary health carer, a number of studies have shown that stress generated in the workplace can affect family

Table 12.1 Stress in health carers

Individual symptoms	Individual cognitions	Affect on health-care setting
Physical symptoms	About self	Absenteeism
Frequent bouts of minor	Overidentification with	Loss of skills
illness	patients	Neglect of duties
Headaches	Righteousness	Mistakes
Back pain	Inadequacy	
Gastrointestinal disorders	Intention to leave job	Staff turnover
Sleep difficulties		Inexperienced staff
	About the work	Loss of group
Mental health	Boredom	identity
Grief and sadness	Dissatisfaction	Waste of training
Hopelessness	Cynicism	
Depression		
Irritation and anger		
Impulsivity		
Inflexibility		
Consumptive behaviours		
Alcohol		
Drugs		
Caffeine		
Multiple sexual partners		
Many short relationships		

relationships and be associated with distress in other family members (Jackson and Maslach, 1982; Miller and Potter, 1982).

Many factors can affect the ability of a person to cope with a stressful job. These may include personal and motivational issues and characteristics of the work such as its nature and intensity, the length of time in this job, the proportion of the work spent in particular tasks, characteristics of the clients, the setting of the work, and the availability of support and resources.

Wall *et al.* (1997) found that, as well as factors associated with specific individuals, general factors appeared to affect the stress levels in health-care settings. They reported staff in larger institutions to have poorer mental health than in smaller ones; units varied in the number of staff above a threshold for a psychiatric diagnosis on the General Health Questionnaire from 17 to 33%. However, in an HIV setting, nurses experienced more stress in smaller units (Ullrich and FitzGerald, 1990). They hypothesized that relationships between staff and patients were able to become closer when a smaller team of staff cared for patients, but that this closeness increased the emotional intensity of the work. It is clearly the specific situation setting, rather than a single variable, that determines the amount of stress experienced by health carers. It has been suggested that such high rates of psychiatric caseness are to some extent due to self-selection factors in staff choosing to work in health care. The reasons that lead individuals to choose to work in health-care professions can result in them having unrealistically high expectations and high levels of self-criticism. These can interact with the lack of resources and the increasing demands from patients, commonly experienced in health services, to create depressive states that include a sense of failure and self-blame (Firth-Cozens, 1997).

Most studies of health professionals are cross-sectional in design. This makes it difficult to identify relationships between individual style, skills, contexts, stage of career, and age. However, it is clear that these variables are important in determining the levels of stress experienced.

Some studies have reported greater levels of work-related stress in females (Gross, 1997). However, in many studies gender is confounded with the job or with the person's role outside work. Hochschild (1989) and Roth (1995) note the inequalities between the sexes such as pay, career handicaps, care of the home, and childcare that may add to the stress experienced by women and make interpretation of study findings difficult.

A number of studies show that youth, inexperience, or not having the necessary skills to carry out the major tasks required by a job are associated with greater work-related stress than older age, skills, and experience (Handy, 1987; Bennett et al., 1992; Bellani, Furlani, Gnecchi, et al., 1996).

Cross-sectional studies of stress in nurses have frequently found high workload, lack of staff support, contact with critically ill patients, and the emotional demands of patients and relatives to be the main stressors (Gray-Toft and Anderson, 1985; Dewe, 1987; Guppy and Gutteridge, 1991).

High levels of staff stress have been reported by care workers in a number of fields including oncology, cystic fibrosis, and HIV units as well as direct access trauma teams. Ullrich and FitzGerald (1990) found age (younger), sex (female), profession (physicians rather than nurses) to be associated with higher levels of stress in an oncology unit.

Within health-care work, paramedics have high levels of early ill-health retirements and death that have been attributed to occupational stress (Hammer, Matthews, Lyons, and Johnson, 1986; Ambulance, 2000, 1990). Grigsby and McKnew (1988) and Miletich (1990) suggested that this is a consequence of the responsibility that paramedics take for human life or of working in difficult, dangerous, and potentially life-threatening incidents in a public and sometimes hostile setting, and that is an intrinsically stressful part of the work. However, Mitchell (1984), investigating stress in paramedics, found that, as in many other occupations, the organizational factors appear to be more important in generating high levels of stress than clinical factors. Questionnaire studies by James and Wright (1991) and Glendon and Glendon (1992) found the major sources of stress in ambulance work to be extrinsic to the job. An exploratory qualitative study by Sparrius (1992) found organizational stressors, specifically the design of the organization, the style of management, and the disciplinary system to be the highest reported causes of stress. This is not to say that responding to emergencies is not stressful. Within the types of emergency call received, Thompson and Suzuki (1991) identified the least frequent calls (i.e., those involving disaster incidents, children, and major fires) to be associated with most stress.

Another area of work that health professionals might have reported finding stressful is that concerned with child protection. Health carers may feel revulsion about what has happened to a child and powerless to stop such incidents. The incidence can bring up issues relating to their childhood or personal life. Youngson (1993) found that, in a sample of professionals working with children who had been ritually abused, 97% had experienced a deterioration in their emotional and physical health, 50% had difficulties with their partners, and 38% experienced sexual difficulties. Cresswell and Firth-Cozens (1999) found general stress levels in child protection workers to be higher than in general population studies, and rates of stress to be similar, around 27%, to those in other health professionals (Wall *et al.*, 1997). The tasks reported most stressful were court appearances, failure of the health and social services to work together, work overload, and poor management. The nature of the work was one of the least stressful tasks. It appears that aspects of the work that are amenable to change but that have not been changed are more stressful than the intrinsic nature of a difficult, and at times, harrowing job.

Symptoms reported by staff working in a number of stressful areas are frequently similar to those reported in post-traumatic stress disorder; for example, recurrent intrusive dreams, flashbacks, avoidance of the stressful stimuli (another trauma client), exaggerated fears that the problem will happen to them, emotional numbing and detachment. These have been described as vicarious traumatization or secondary traumatization (McCann and Pearlman, 1990).

Lesaca (1996) reported a study that compared the symptoms of post-traumatic stress disorder and depression experienced by therapists who provided counselling to individuals affected by the crash of a commercial airliner with therapists from the same mental health centre who did not participate. At 4 and 8 weeks the trauma counsellors reported more symptoms of post-traumatic stress disorder and depression than did the control therapists; at 12 weeks the only significantly increased symptom was avoidance behaviour.

Disasters

Studies reporting the effects on workers responding to disasters show the same factors to be important in determining the stress experienced. Weiss, Marmer, Metzler, and Ronfeldt (1995) identified levels of symptomatic distress in emergency service workers following the 1989 earthquake in the San Francisco Bay area to be predicted by degree of exposure to the critical incident. They found that adjustment, social support, years of experience on the job, and locus of control were associated with the levels of symptomatic distress experienced.

Hodgkinson and Shepherd (1994) found role-related difficulties and contact with their clients' distress to be associated with disaster-related distress in people giving support to two major disasters. Variability in helpers' responses was associated with coping style, prior life events, and previous experience of disaster work.

Sexual Assault

Ghahramanlou and Brodbeck (2000) investigated the psychological distress experienced by sexual assault trauma counsellors in the USA. They found that a personal trauma history and a younger counsellor age predicted high levels of self-reported psychological distress. These factors, plus a lower level of satisfaction with their counselling, predicted the intensity of what they termed 'secondary trauma' (i.e., an experience of psychological distress with symptoms similar to those of post-traumatic stress disorder).

Attribution theory (Jones and Davis, 1965) predicts that people will distance themselves from victims of misfortune and look for explanations of unfortunate events that will protect them from feelings of vulnerability to similar misfortunes. The belief in a just world suggests that individuals will look for an explanation of a criminal event that will allow them to believe that they are less vulnerable to the experience of a similar event than the victim of misfortune. For health carers this can be achieved by believing that an individual who is the victim of a crime did something or neglected something that may have contributed to his or her victimization (Symonds, 1975); for example, if the person who was sexually assaulted in some way deserved it, then I am safe as I do not deserve it. The generation of such beliefs can cause barriers in establishing a supportive relationship with a client and may lead health carers to attribute blame to the person who has been sexually assaulted. Warner (1978) reported emergency room staff to exhibit behaviours that reflected an uneasiness in dealing with people who had been raped. They appeared to be extremely busy, left the person who had been raped completely alone, related to her on an unemotional level, made premature evaluations and judgements, placed blame on her, and talked down to her. To get to know a person who has been sexually assaulted, and to find that the just-world hypothesis is not always true, can leave a health carer feeling very vulnerable.

Stereotypical myths about rape are prevalent (see Chapter 1), and it is important that health carers are aware of how these may affect their own approaches to this work, especially when they strengthen beliefs that allow them to distance themselves from their clients.

Although most women express a preference for a female clinician (Petrak, Skinner, and Claydon, 1995), there is evidence to suggest that, with training, men can be effective in the treatment of sexual assault (Resick, Jordan, Girelli, Hutter, and Marhoefer-Dvorak, 1989). However, there may be particular issues for male health carers who work with individuals who have been sexually assaulted. They may be especially concerned about the feelings and beliefs of their clients with respect to men. This may lead them to attempt to demonstrate compensatory and corrective experiences, in order to prove that men can be empathetic and trustworthy. Taking the role of a more than perfect man can increase the burden of sexual assault work (Koss and Harvey, 1991).

MANAGING AND PREVENTING WORK RELATED STRESS

To maintain a high quality of life with little stress requires a balance to be reached between the stressors that provide a stimulating environment, heighten arousal and prevent boredom, and the resources available to manage them. Since many stressors in health care are intrinsic to the work (e.g. sick patients) and constitute part of the attraction of the work, it may be counterproductive to eliminate them. Rather, as suggested by Ivancevich, Matteson, Freedman, and Phillips (1990), there is a need to identify and remove excessive stressors such as the intensity and chronicity of staff work patterns and to modify the work environment, and increase the resources available to health workers by changing and developing their cognitions, their coping skills, and their social support networks. Psychological support for individuals in distress may help where stress prevention has failed.

IMPLICATIONS FOR SERVICES FOR PEOPLE WHO HAVE BEEN SEXUALLY ASSAULTED

Employers have a legal duty to care for the physical, psychological, and social well being of their staff. In the UK, government policies make safeguarding the mental health of National Health Service employees a priority (Department of Health, 1998). When the intrinsic tasks of work are stressful, as in working with people who have been sexually assaulted, it is important that the work environment does not add to the stress experienced. Although work-related stress is consistently shown to be more related to the work environment than to characteristics of the individual workers, the majority of studies that attempt to minimize staff stress are aimed at helping individuals to cope with staff stress rather than to change the conditions that have been shown to generate stress (Reynolds and Briner, 1994; Cooper and Cartwright, 1994).

To manage and prevent work-related stress in sexual assault health carers, the issues outlined above need to be addressed. Unfortunately, there is a paucity of studies evaluating the efficacy of any practices set up to prevent high levels of stress in sexual assault health carers, and of interventions that aim to alleviate health carer distress. This section will, therefore, mainly make suggestions for interventions based on the apparent needs of sexual assault health carers and on findings from other areas of health care. Interventions can be:

- primary—changing the work environment to reduce the nature or number of stressors;
- secondary—helping staff to develop strategies to cope with the distress;
- remedial—treating the consequences of work-related stress.

Modifying the Work Environment

It is clear that the work environment, including health care, can be a major source of stress. Macks and Abrams (1992) suggest that many aspects of work—such as unclear definition or overlap of roles; insufficient available resources, a lack of staff development, education, or training; poor communication systems and appreciation mechanisms; inadequate provision of formal support; inefficient organizational structures, task planning and excessive work load—that can generate stress are amenable to change.

It is important that health carers have sufficient skills to enable them to carry out their roles when working with people who have been sexually assaulted and to recognize their limitations. Interventions by health carers who are underskilled can be detrimental to the individuals who come for support. The impact of working beyond a person's expertise can also significantly increase the stress experienced by that health carer. In the era of clinical governance and audit, it should be possible for staff strengths and weaknesses to be evaluated regularly and further relevant training to be provided where necessary. In the sexual assault clinic, continued staff training and education on sexual assault-related issues may be necessary to equip health carers with the appropriate skills (Kleiber, Gusy, Enzmann, and Beerlage, 1992).

Necessary professional health carer skills include the ability to show empathy to people while maintaining boundaries with clients. Without understanding and training, it is easy for professional boundaries to be lowered for people who seem to be in great need. A good therapeutic relationship does not blur the boundary between the professional relationship and friendship. Not only can this be bad for the client as he or she may then feel responsible for limiting the distress felt by the health carer, but blurring of roles can also lead a health carer to become emotionally involved with clients. The emotional burden that would be taken on would necessarily limit the input that a health carer could give, and could increase health carer stress which may lead to burnout.

Looking at the working of HIV units, Hortsman and McKusick (1986) and Bennett, Mitchie, and Kippax (1991) found that the intensity, rather than the total length of time spent working, was associated with levels of staff stress. In services for people who have been sexually assaulted it could be useful to vary the tasks performed and limiting the hours spent in direct involvement with clients. This could be achieved through the adoption of a policy of 'rotation' of sexual assault work with less stressful work (e.g., combining sexual assault work with general work within a genitourinary medicine clinic or gynaecological clinic).

As there are individual differences in suitability for stressful health-care work, staff selection is important. It can be useful to screen for those with higher levels of self-efficacy, an internal locus of control, and supportive social support networks outside the work situation. Many people are attracted to particular areas of work, such as sexual assault, because of an incident that has happened to themselves or to someone close.

However, it is important that they have come to terms with the incident sufficiently to be able to put the needs of clients first and to withstand trauma caused by hearing accounts of further sexual assaults.

Many work environments are not set up to minimize staff stress. However, as discussed earlier, it can be beneficial to clients and to health workers to minimize stress and burnout. Wherever possible, changes to the work environment should be attempted; simply viewing staff stress as an individual's unsuitability for the job will not prevent stress or burnout.

Making changes to the work environment has been shown to be most successful when the workers are involved, there is management commit-ment, and there is a supporting organizational culture (Murphy, 1999). Workers are able to contribute first-hand accounts of stressors; they have detailed knowledge of their jobs and have ideas for possible changes. Involving and empowering health carers to make changes has been shown to impart a sense of ownership, both for solving the problem and for implementing the proposed changes (President's Advisory Com-mission, 1998).

COPING SKILLS AND COGNITIONS

Lazarus and Folkman (1984) distinguishes between two types of coping: problem focused and emotional focused. The problem-focused approach is directed at managing or altering the problem and the emotional-focused approach is directed at regulating the emotional response evoked by the event.

It would seem likely that sexual assault care workers would need to use both. The former would be useful in making changes to the work environ-ment that might reduce the impact of the work, and the latter would be useful in helping workers cope with the emotional reactions generated by the work.

Using this model it would seem that the way sexual assault workers will deal with their jobs will depend on their understanding and interpretation of their work, the stresses experienced, the coping options they perceive as available, and on mediating factors such as the perceived availability of social support and the coping strategies they finally adopt.

STRESS MANAGEMENT TRAINING

The input of stress management training comes from the findings that relevant knowledge and appropriate skills will reduce the stressors of a job. Stress management training usually comprises a package of skills that can be useful to help individuals cope with the stressors encountered in a job. Training is usually given to groups of employees and would typically consist of six to twelve sessions. As most stress management training is tailored to fit an individual work setting and frequently does not evaluate separately distinctive aspects of the training programme, it can prove difficult to compare or evaluate the efficacy of a specific programme. A typical programme would include:

- relaxation;
- self-evaluation;
- goal setting;
- assertion skills;
- time management;
- problem solving;
- explanation of the model of stress;
- coping styles;
- role of social support;
- stress inoculation training.

Stress management training generally shows some impact on staff by increasing psychological mood, coping skills, and the access of social support (Kagan, Kagan, and Watson, 1995; Bunce and West, 1996).

PROFESSIONAL BOUNDARIES

When talking about intimate matters in a safe, confidential setting, it is easy for a close emotional involvement with clients to occur. Specific training aimed at increasing staff competence in expressing warmth and empathy while maintaining professional boundaries has been suggested to reduce emotional distress in people working with people with HIV disease (Bennett *et al.*, 1991).

SOCIAL SUPPORT NETWORKS

Increasing social support for health carers can help to buffer the stress engendered by the intrinsic tasks involved in working with people who have been sexually assaulted. This can be provided either formally or informally. As older, more experienced individuals cope better in stressful health-care settings, it can be useful to set up a support network that links the older, more experienced worker with younger, less experienced staff. Supervision arrangements, either individual or in groups that happen on a regular, frequent basis can fulfil this remit. Some workplaces set up mentoring networks. These can be useful as they pair individuals who have no lines of accountability or responsibility. This allows each individual to discuss issues openly without fear of reprisals from his or her line manager.

Informal social support can be a useful adjunct to any formal arrangements set up. However, this will not necessarily happen automatically. Organizing health carers into teams, having a workplace setting and a timetable that allows health carers to meet informally (e.g., a staff tea room or a refreshment break within a meeting) can increase the chances of supportive informal relationships being established.

Benefit may be gained from optimizing the opportunities for young staff to learn from those who are older and more experienced. This can be encouraged by increasing the opportunities for informal problem solving. On a more formal basis the provision of a staff support group can facilitate the exchange of information and coping strategies between experienced and inexperienced staff.

WORKPLACE COUNSELLING AND INDIVIDUAL PSYCHOLOGICAL SUPPORT

Good supervision can prevent a worker feeling isolated and solely responsible for cases. In addition, team meetings can foster an environment where sharing case reports can provide staff support on a regular basis. Dinoi and Brettler (1991) found such a team approach to enable staff in a haemophilia treatment centre develop staff support networks and reduce isolation and share coping styles.

Counselling in the workplace, specifically for work-related issues, has shown some benefit. Mitchie (1996) reported a short-term counselling intervention for health carers to increase mood and reduce the rates of absenteeism. Reynolds (1997) found that individual counselling which addressed the skills needed by health carers to deal with the difficulties they experienced proved beneficial. Although, as noted earlier in this chapter, the factors associated with stress in health care settings are not unique, Wykes and Whittington (1999) point out that what is unique to health carers is their self-image as carers of people. This can lead to a denial of stress experienced while caring, which can result in heightened distress if they perceive that they have lost control.

Maynard (1985) argues that during crisis interventions staff do not process and identify their own feelings in order to maintain effective interactions with clients. He suggests the use of support groups to allow staff a regular opportunity to identify and express and cope with their own feelings. Wade, Perlman, and Simon (1993) instigated staff support in an HIV setting by pairing groups of workers to form intense informal relationships to provide a buffer against stress.

Supervisors or staff support groups, for health carers working with people who have been sexually assaulted, need to have an understanding of how beliefs about causation, responsibility, and personal vulnerability are linked and how myths and stereotypes develop. Such knowledge would allow health carers to examine their own beliefs about sexual assault and their clients and could prevent some of the distancing behaviours described by Warner (1978).

The particular difficulties that male health carers may experience, when working with people who have been sexually assaulted (Koss and Harvey, 1991), suggest that supervision for men, or support groups, should specifically address responsibility and gender issues.

Individual counselling in psychiatric populations has been shown to help people who are depressed or anxious (Roth and Fonegy, 1996). It has also been shown to ameliorate distress in the workplace (Cooper and Sadri, 1991). Counselling health carers usually aims to lower levels of distress in those who are already distressed. It can be considered a useful remedial intervention when stress prevention measures have not proved sufficient. No standard format can be prescribed for counselling sexual assault health carers who are experiencing distress. It is useful if counsellors have an understanding of the factors that can contribute to the stress experienced in sexual assault work, as outlined in this chapter, in order to appreciate the number and level of stressors encountered by health carers. A full assessment of an individual health carer's problems, difficulties, beliefs, emotions, and behaviours can allow issues pertinent for them to be identified, and the appropriate counselling or psychological support to be implemented.

Although studies reporting the effects of counselling in the workplace generally show some improvement of the staff symptoms, there is rarely a comparison group or evaluation that enables studies to be compared. Hardy, Reynolds, Shapiro, and Barkham (1998) showed cognitive-behaviour therapy to be more effective than psychodynamic-interpersonal therapies in reducing work-related stress. Allison, Cooper, and Reynolds

(1987) found that counselling a group of Post Office workers resulted in a reduction of psychological symptoms and sickness, but failed to show less distress or increased job satisfaction.

SUMMARY AND RECOMMENDATIONS

Although it may not be possible to remove the prime stressors (i.e., people who have been sexually assaulted and who require care), it may be possible to lessen the stresses attached to that care. It is important that organizational stressors are not overlooked in services such as those for individuals who have been sexually assaulted. As demonstrated by studies in a number of fields ranging from HIV, ambulance, and child protection work, organizations can generate stress by failing to provide adequate resources and good communication systems. In addition, many jobs also generate intrinsic stressors that cannot be eliminated. It is clear that working with people who have been sexually assaulted can lead health carers to experience secondary traumatization (i.e., to feel increased vulnerability to sexual assault and violence). Provision of supervisory and support systems to prevent, rather than to deal with, secondary traumatization is required.

The intimacy and emotional intensity of sexual assault work makes it imperative that health carers are specifically trained for this work. A failure to use appropriate coping strategies, supervisory and social support, and to maintain professional boundaries can easily lead to high levels of distress and burnout.

Caring for carers requires resources, but these may prove less costly than the increased sickness rate and higher turnover of staff that can be a consequence of staff burnout. Although it is well documented that staff support can be beneficial to an organization, the public health-care systems in many countries are woefully neglectful in addressing the support needs of their staff.

REFERENCES

Allison, T., Cooper, C., and Reynolds, P. (1987) Stress counselling in the workplace—the Post Office experience. *The Psychologist*, **12**, 384–388.
Ambulance 2000. (1990) *Proposals for the future development of the Ambulance Service*. Ringwood, UK: Association of Chief Ambulance Officers.
Anderson, C. (1977) Locus of control, coping behaviours and performance in a stress setting: A longitudinal study. *Journal of Applied Psychology*, **62**, 44–61.

APA. (1994) *Diagnostic and statistical manual of mental disorders* (4th edn). Washington, DC: American Psychiatric Association.

Bellani, M., Furlani, F., Gnecchi, M., Pezzotta, P., Trotti, E., and Bellotti, G. (1996) Burnout and related factors among HIV/AIDS health care workers. *AIDS Care*, 8, 207–221.

Bennett, L., Kelaher, M., and Ross, M. (1992) Links between burnout and bereavement in HIV/AIDS professionals. Paper given at Quality of Life Satellite Symposium: VIII International Conference on AIDS, Amsterdam, 16 July 1992.

Bennett, L., Mitchie, P., and Kippax, S. (1991) Quantitative analysis of burn-out and its associated factors in AIDS nursing. *AIDS Care*, 3, 181–192.

Bunce, D. and West, M. (1996) Stress management and innovation at work. *Human Relations*, 49, 209–232.

Caplan, R., Cobb, S., French, J., Harrison, R., and van Pinneau, S. (1975) *Job demands and worker health*. Washington, DC: National Institute for Occupational Health and Safety.

Cohen, S. and Wills, T. (1985) Stress, social support and the buffering hypothesis. *Psychological Bulletin*, 98, 310–357.

Cooper, C. (1983) Identifying stressors at work: Recent research developments. *Journal of Psychosomatic Research*, 2, 369–376.

Cooper, C. and Cartwright, S. (1994) Stress management interventions in the workplace: Stress counselling and stress audits. *British Journal of Guidance and Counselling*, 22, 65–73.

Cooper, C. and Sadri, G. (1991) The impact of stress counselling at work. *Journal of Social Behaviour and Personality*, 6, 411–423.

Cordes, C. and Dougherty, T. (1993) A review and integration of research on job burn-out. *Academy of Management Review*, 18, 621–656.

Cresswell, T. and Firth-Cozens, J. (1999) Child protection workers. In: J. Firth-Cozens and R. Payne (eds) *Stress in health professionals*. Chichester, UK: Wiley.

Department of Health. (1998) *Our healthier nation: A contract for health* (Consultation Paper). London: Her Majesty's Stationery Office.

Dewe, P. (1987) Identifying the causes of nurses' stress: A survey of New Zealand nurses. *Work and Stress*, 1, 15–24.

Dinoi, R. and Brettler, D. (1991) The group process in the consultation to a comprehensive haemophilia treatment team: Reducing staff burnout relating to HIV. Poster presentation at IX International AIDS Conference, Florence, 16–21 June 1991.

Dunkel-Schetter, C. and Bennett, T. (1990) Differentiating the cognitive and behavioural aspects of social support. In B. Sarason, I. Sarason and G. Pierce (eds) *Social support: An international view*. New York: John Wiley.

Firth, H., McIntee, J., McEwan, P., and Britton, P. (1986) Burnout and professional depression: Related concepts? *Journal of Advanced Nursing*, 11, 633–641.

Firth-Cozens, J. (1997) Predicting stress in general practitioners: 10 year follow up postal survey. *British Medical Journal*, 315, 34–35.

Fletcher, B. (1988) The epidemiology of stress. In C. Cooper and R. Payne (eds) *Causes, coping and consequences of stress at work*. Chichester, UK: Wiley.

Friedman, M. and Rosenman, R. (1974) *Type A behaviour and your heart*. London: Wildwood House.

Garden, A. (1989) Burnout: The effect of psychological type on research findings. *Journal of Occupational Psychology*, **5**, 533–542.

Ghahramanlou, M. and Brodbeck, C. (2000) Predictors of secondary trauma in sexual assault counselors. *International Journal of Emergency Mental Health*, **2**, 229–240.

Glendon, A. and Glendon, S. (1992) Stress in ambulance staff. In E. Lovesey (ed.) *Contemporary ergonomics 1992: 'ergonomics for industry'* (Proceedings of the Ergonomics Society's 1992 Annual Conference). Birmingham: Taylor and Francis.

Gray-Toft, P. and Anderson, J. (1985) Organisational stress in the hospital: Development of a model for diagnosis and prediction. *Health Services Research*, **19**, 753–774.

Grigsby, D. and McKnew, M. (1988) Work-stress burnout among paramedics. *Psychological Reports*, **63**, 55–64.

Gross, E. (1997) Gender differences in physician stress: Why the discrepant findings? *Women and Health*, **26**, 1–14.

Guppy, A. and Gutteridge, T. (1991) Job satisfaction and occupational stress in UK general hospital nursing staff. *Work and Stress*, **5**, 315–323.

Hammer, J., Matthews, J., Lyons, J., and Johnson, N. (1986) Occupational stress within the paramedic profession: An initial report of stress levels compared to hospital employees. *Annals of Emergency Medicine*, **15**, 536–539.

Handy, J. (1987) Understanding stress in psychiatric nursing. Unpublished doctoral thesis, Lancaster University, Lancaster, UK.

Hardy, G., Reynolds, S., Shapiro, D., and Barkham, M. (1998) The comparison of cognitive-behavioural with psychodynamic-interpersonal therapy for the treatment of work difficulties associated with depression. Unpublished manuscript, University of Leeds, Leeds, UK.

Hochschild, A. (1989) *The second shift*. New York: Avon Books.

Hodgkinson, P. and Shepherd, M. (1994) The impact of disaster support work. *Journal of Trauma Stress*, **7**, 587–600.

Hortsman, W. and McKusick, L. (1986) The impact of AIDS on the physician. In L. McKusick (ed.) *What to do about AIDS*. Berkeley, CA: University of California Press.

Ivancevich, J., Matteson, M., Freedman, S., and Phillips, J. (1990) Worksite stress management interventions. *American Psychologist*, **45**, 252–261.

Jackson, S. and Maslach, C. (1982) After-effects of job related stress: Families as victims. *Journal of Occupational Behaviour*, **3**, 63–77.

James, A. and Wright, P. (1991) Occupational stress in the ambulance service. *Health Manpower Management*, **17**, 4.

Janman, K., Jones, G., Payne, R., and Rick, J. (1988) Clustering individuals as a way of dealing with multiple indicators in occupational health research. *Behavioural Medicine*, Spring, 17–29.

Jones, E. and Davis, K. (1965) From acts to dispositions: The attribution process in person perception. In L. Berkovitz (ed.) *Advances in experimental social psychology* (Vol. 2, pp. 219–266). New York: Academic Press.

Jones, F. and Fletcher, B. (1996) Job control and health. In M. Shabracq, J. Winnibust, and C. Cooper (eds) *Handbook of work and health psychology*. Chichester, UK: Wiley.

Kagan, N., Kagan, H., and Watson, M. (1995) Stress reduction in the workplace:

The effectiveness of psychoeducational programmes. *Journal of Counselling Psychology*, **42**, 71–78.

Kleiber, D., Gusy, B., Enzmann, D., and Beerlage, I. (1992) Causes and prevalence of stress and burnout among health care personnel in the field of AIDS. Amsterdam AIDS Conference, 19–24 July 1992.

Koss, M. and Harvey, M. (1991) *The rape victim: Clinical and community interventions*. Newbury Park, CA: Sage Publications.

Lazarus, R. and Folkman, S. (1984) *Stress, appraisal and coping*. New York: Springer-Verlag.

Leiter, M. (1991) The dream denied: Professional burnout and the constraints of human service organisations. *Canadian Psychology*, **32**, 547–555.

Lesaca, T. (1996) Symptoms of stress disorder and depression among trauma counselors after an airline disaster. *Psychiatric Service*, **47**, 424–426.

McCann, L. and Pearlman, L. (1990) Vicarious traumatization: A framework for understanding the psychological effects of working with victims. *Journal of Trauma and Stress*, **3**, 131–146.

Macks, J. and Abrams, D. (1992) Burnout among HIV/AIDS health care providers. In P. Volberding and M. Jacobson (eds) *AIDS clinical review*. New York: Marcel Decker.

Maslach, C. (1982) *Burnout: the cost of caring*. Englewood Cliffs, NJ: Prentice-Hall.

Maslach, C. and Jackson, S. (1982) Burn-out in health professions: A social psychological analysis. In G. Saunders and J. Suis (eds) *Social psychology of illness*. London: Lawrence Erlbaum.

Maslach C., Jackson, S., and Leiter, M. (1996) *Maslach burnout inventory, Manual (3rd edn)*. Palo Alto, CA: Consulting Psychologists Press.

Maynard, E. (1985) The intervener: Managing personal crises: Emotional first-aid. *Journal of Crisis Intervention*, **2**, 39–46.

Meier, S. (1984) The construct validity of burnout. *Human Relations*, **36**, 899–910.

Miletich, J. (1990) Police, firefighter and paramedic stress: An annotated bibliography. *Bibliographies and Indexes in Psychology* (Number 6). New York: Greenwood Press.

Miller, M. and Potter, R. (1982) Professional burnout among speech-language pathologists. *ASHA*, **24**, 177–181.

Mitchell, J. (1984) The 600 run limit. *Journal of Emergency Medical Services*, **9**, 52–54.

Mitchie, S. (1996) Reducing absenteeism by stress management: Evaluation of a stress counselling service. *Work and Stress*, **10**, 367–372.

Murphy, L. (1999) Organisational interventions to reduce stress in health care professionals. In J. Firth-Cozens and R. Payne (eds) *Stress in health professionals*. Chichester, UK: Wiley.

Orton, P. (1996) Stress in health care professionals. *British Journal of Health Care Management*, **2**, 91–94.

Payne, R. (1979) Demands, supports, constraints and psychological health. In C. Mackay and T. Cox (eds) *Response to stress: Occupational aspects*. London: IPC.

Payne, R. and Fletcher, B. (1983) Job demands, supports and constraints as predictors of psychological strain among schoolteachers. *Journal of Vocational Behaviour*, **22**, 136–147.

Petrak, J., Skinner, C., and Claydon, E. (1995) The prevalence of sexual assault in a genitourinary medicine clinic: Service implications. *Genitourinary Medicine*, **71**, 98–102.

President's Advisory Commission. (1998) *Quality first: Better health care for all Americans*. Washington, DC: Advisory Commission on Consumer Protection and Quality in the Health Care Industry.

Resick, P.A., Jordan, C.G., Girelli, S.A., Hutter, C.K., and Marhoefer-Dvorak, S. (1989) A comparative outcome study of behavioral group therapy for sexual assault victims. *Behavior Therapy*, **19**, 385–401.

Reynolds, S. (1997) Psychological well-being at work: Is prevention better than cure? *Journal of Psychosomatic Research*, **43**, 93–102.

Reynolds, S. and Briner, R. (1994) Stress management at work: With whom, for whom and to what ends? *British Journal of Guidance and Counselling*, **22**, 75–89.

Rosenman, R. (1996) Personality, behaviour patterns and heart disease. In C. Cooper (ed.) *Handbook of stress, medicine and health*. Boca Raton, FL: CRC Press.

Roth, A. and Fonegy, P. (1996) *What works for whom? A critical review of psychotherapy research*. New York: Guilford Press.

Roth, N. (1995) Structuring burnout: Interactions between HIV/AIDS health workers, their clients, organisations and society. In L. Bennett, D. Miller, and M. Ross (eds) *Health workers and AIDS: Research, interventions and current issues in burnout and response*. Reading, UK: Harwood Academic Press.

Rotter, J. (1966) Generalised expectancies for internal versus external control of reinforcement. *Psychological Monographs*, **80**, 1–28.

Seligman, M. (1975) *Helplessness*. San Francisco, CA: Freedman.

Sparrius, S. (1992) Occupational stressors among ambulance and rescue service workers. *South African Journal of Psychology*, **22**, 87–91.

Steptoe, A. (1997) Stress and disease. In A. Baum, S. Newman, J. Weinman, R. West, and C. McManus (eds) *Cambridge Handbook of Psychology, Health and Medicine*, Cambridge: Cambridge University Press.

Symonds, M. (1975) Victims of violence: Psychological effects and after effects. *American Journal of Psychoanalysis*, **36**, 27–34.

Thiots, P. (1986) Social support as coping assistance. *Journal of Consulting and Clinical Psychology*. **54**, 416–423.

Thompson, J. and Suzuki, I. (1991) Stress in ambulance workers. *Disaster Management*, **3**, 193–197.

Ullrich, A. and FitzGerald, P. (1990) Stress experienced by physicians and nurses in the cancer ward. *Social Science and Medicine*, **31**, 1013–1022.

Wade, K., Perlman, B., and Simon, E. (1993) Survival bonding: A response to stress and work with AIDS. *Social Work in Health Care*, **19**, 77–89.

Wall, T., Bolden, R., Borrill, C., Carter, A., Golya, D., Hardy, G., Haynes, Rick, J., Shapiro, D., and West, M. (1997) Minor psychiatric disorder in NHS Trust staff: Occupational and gender differences. *British Journal of Psychiatry*, **171**, 519–523.

Warner, C.G. (1978) The psychological reactions of victims and the response of attending personnel. In C.G. Warner, J. Koerper, D. Spaulding, and S. McDevitt (eds) *San Diego County protocol for the treatment of rape and sexual assault victims* (mimeo).

Warr, P. (1987) *Work, unemployment and mental health*. Oxford: Clarendon Press.

Watson, D. and Pennebaker, J. (1989) Health complaints, stress and distress:

Exploring the central role of negative affectivity. *Psychological Review*, 96, 234–254.

Weiss, D., Marmer, C., Metzler, T., and Ronfeldt, H. (1995) Predicting symptomatic distress in emergency services. *Journal of Consulting and Clinical Psychology*, 63, 361–368.

Wykes, T. and Whittington, R. (1999) Setting up a workplace counselling service. In J. Firth-Cozens and R. Payne (eds) *Stress in health professionals*. Chichester, UK: Wiley.

Youngson, S. (1993) Ritual abuse: Consequences for professionals. *Child Abuse Review*, 2, 251–262.

Chapter 13

SEXUAL AGGRESSION: RESEARCH, THEORIES, AND PRACTICE

Julia C. Houston

INTRODUCTION

Rape and sexual assault clearly have far-reaching consequences for both the individual survivor and for society as a whole. In order to reduce the risk of either initial or future offending, interventions to prevent sexual assault or treat offenders have to be informed by an understanding of the motivations behind this behaviour. This chapter provides an overview of the theoretical research into rape and sexual assault and explores the implications of this for clinical practice. The chapter focuses on male perpetrators of sexual aggression towards adult women. This is not to deny the potential extent of male victimization by women. The studies by Struckman-Johnson and Struckman-Johnson (1988, 1994) indicated that 16–24% of college males reported coercive sexual contact from a woman, the majority of which involved intercourse. However, as it is rare for female perpetrators to be reported, charged, or convicted, we know almost nothing about this population. The limited research on female perpetrators of sexual assault has focused on those who have abused children (Saradjian, 1998). The underreporting of male sexual assault is also generally acknowledged. Similarly, while there is an increasing body of work which explores the effects of this on the survivor (e.g., Rogers, 1997; Scarce, 1997), there is very little about the perpetrators.

The Trauma of Sexual Assault. Edited by Jenny Petrak and Barbara Hedge.
© 2002 John Wiley & Sons Ltd.

CHARACTERISTICS OF MEN WHO SEXUALLY AGGRESS

Numerous studies have explored the characteristics of men who have committed sexual assaults in an attempt to define this group and understand what differentiates them from men who have not offended. Since much of the research is based on convicted offenders in prison, who represent a small proportion of men who have behaved in a sexually aggressive way, the findings are, not suprisingly, limited. However, trends are beginning to emerge, and the work of Malamuth and colleagues in the USA with college students has particularly furthered our understanding of factors that contribute towards likelihood to rape (Malamuth, Heavey, and Linz, 1993). Relevant characteristics are outlined below.

Demographic Features

In many ways convicted rapists are very similar to other non-sexual offenders in prison, tending to be of low socio-economic status (Scully, 1990), disproportionately of non-European ethnicity (Grubin and Gunn, 1990), have an unstable employment history in unskilled work (Bard *et al.*, 1987), similar rates of contact with psychiatric services (Christie, Marshall, and Lanthier, 1979) and with lower levels of social competency than a community sample (Stermac and Quinsey, 1986).

Developmental Experiences

Most studies of sexual abuse in childhood have found higher rates among men who have gone on to offend against children, compared with those who have adult victims. However, these rates are still higher than for non-offenders. Carter, Prentky, Knight, Vanderveer, and Boucher (1987) reported that 23% of detained rapists had a history of sexual victimization. Studies have also found that rapists have experienced more physical violence in their families than other types of sex offenders (Marshall, Jones, Ward, Johnston, and Barbaree, 1991) and non-sex offenders (Leonard, 1993). There is evidence that, at least for the more repetitive and violent rapists, their experience of sexual abuse *plus* the quality of their parenting or caregiving is related to subsequent severity of sexual aggression (Prentky *et al.*, 1989). Prentky *et al.* (1989) used factor analysis to generate four significant constructs that related developmental experiences to both sexual and non-sexual aggression in adulthood. These were:

caregiver inconsistency, sexual deviation and abuse in the family, institutional history, and physical abuse and neglect. The former two factors were related to severity of sexual aggression, and the latter two were predictive of the severity of non-sexual aggression. The findings are consistent with the multivariate aetiological models of rape which include a developmental component (see p. 316). However, Polaschek, Ward and Hudson (1997) note that it is not yet clear what mediates the transition from an at-risk individual to an offender, and that there is still a need for a more consistent body of evidence to determine whether or how developmental antecedents can differentiate sexual offenders against adults from other sexual offenders, non-sexual offenders, and non-offenders.

Patterns of Sexual Arousal

There has been much research focusing on whether rapists show different patterns of sexual arousal to non-rapists. This has primarily been carried out using the penile plethysmograph (PPG), a physiological measure of sexual arousal which involves showing the subject visual and/or audio sexual stimuli and measuring erectile and other changes, such as galvanic skin response. Studies in the late 1970s and early 1980s found that convicted rapists responded more to rape scenes than to consenting sex. These studies suggested either that rapists may be motivated by deviant attraction to cues of non-consent or the use of force (Abel, Barlow, Blanchard, and Guild, 1977) or that they failed to inhibit erection, possibly due to less empathy for the woman (Quinsey, Chaplin, and Upfold, 1984). However, more recent studies have failed to replicate these results and found similar patterns of responding between groups, with lower responses to both sexual and non-sexual violence than to consenting sex (e.g., Blader and Marshall, 1989). This may reflect the high proportion of more violent and sadistic offenders in the earlier studies, and may in fact be consistent with the known heterogeneity of rapists, some of whom report being motivated by arousal to forced sex, while others convince themselves that their victims are consenting (see p. 309). In a more recent meta-analysis, Hall, Shondrick, and Hirschman (1993) concluded that deviant arousal may motivate some rapists, but that it is not specific to this group, and many non-rapists are also sexually aroused by depictions of forced sex. There is also increasing concern about the ethical and practical issues involved in using the PPG as a clinical and research method, such as the nature and origin of the stimulus material and reliability of the results.

Retrospective analysis of patterns of offending with men convicted of sexual assault often highlights the significance of coercive sexual fantasies, which both precede and post-date an assault. The association of sex and aggression in fantasy has been attributed to both violent pornography (Laws and Marshall, 1990) and to internal factors linked to early experiences (Prentky and Burgess, 1991). However, the presence of coercive sexual fantasies *per se* are not sufficient to define a rapist population, and are commonly reported by the male population in general (Leitenberg and Henning, 1995).

Personality Features

Studies comparing rapists with other offenders on measures of personality have generally failed to identify any defining characteristics, although these suggest that rapists are more similar to violent offenders than to other sex offenders (e.g., Langevin, Paitich, and Russon, 1985) Thus, both groups tend to score highly on scales indicating antisocial propensity, although data from the Minnesota Multiphasic Personality Inventory (MMPI) indicates that rapists also show features of hostility, impulsivity, irritability, avoidance of close involvements, poor social judgements, and conflict with authority. Blackburn (1993) therefore suggests that rapists are among the more personally deviant criminals and more likely to be found on testing to be secondary psychopaths (i.e., the more anxious, neurotic type).

More recent work on the personality attributes of sex offenders has focused on their limited capacity to develop intimacy and form attachments. There is evidence that sex offenders in general have problems in establishing intimacy with adult partners and experience loneliness as a consequence (Marshall, 1989). Seidman, Marshall, Hudson, and Robertson (1994) found that both child molesters and rapists suffered from intimacy deficits and were lonelier than other offender groups, and that lack of intimacy was a predictor of various indices of violence. Rapists and violent offenders have been found to have a more 'dismissing' attachment style than child molesters and other types of offenders (i.e., to be sceptical of the value of close relationships and blame others for their lack of intimacy: Hudson and Ward, 1997).

Attitudes towards Women and Rape Myths

The late 1980s and 1990s saw a greater emphasis on the contributing role of cognitive factors to the aetiology of rape and are comprehensively reviewed by Drieschner and Lange (1999). Because of the likelihood that the convicted rapist is not typical of the majority of (unconvicted) men who behave in a sexually aggressive way, studies have also been carried out with student or community samples. Two main measures have been used. The first of these asks the subject about their likelihood to rape (including forcing a woman to do something sexual) given that they could get away with it (LR measure). The second is a self-report measure of previous sexual aggression, such as the Sexual Experiences Survey (SES, Koss and Oros, 1982). Although there are limitations of both types of rape indicator, they do correlate both with each other and with other correlates of rape, and so have been seen as measuring a single underlying construct of 'rape proclivity' (Pollard, 1994).

Studies with samples from the general public have found that rape proclivity is associated with the extent to which force and coercion are regarded as acceptable in intimate relationships, the belief that sexual relationships are fundamentally exploitative, and the acceptance of 'rape myths' (such as women in certain situations being more likely to 'deserve' to be raped). Burt (1980) devised a set of scales that measure these beliefs and have been used widely in the research (e.g., Pollard, 1994). Rape proclivity is also associated with victim blame (Sundberg, Barbaree, and Marshall, 1991), a factor which has been shown to have the potential to disinhibit sexual arousal to forced sex. Studies have also suggested that macho attitudes may indirectly disinhibit rape (Mosher and Anderson, 1986).

The above studies indicate that men in the general population with high levels of rape proclivity have specific rape-supportive attitudes and beliefs, but, suprisingly, these attitudes have not been found in the studies of convicted rapists (e.g., Harmon, Owens, and Dewey, 1995). There is little evidence of attitudinal differences between convicted rapists, other types of convicted offenders, and non-offenders. Stermac, Segal, and Gillis (1990) suggest that this may partly be explained by the susceptibility of the self-report measures to socially desirable responding, which may be less of an issue in the large community samples where confidentiality is easier to guarantee. The failure to detect attitudinal differences does not therefore mean that they do not exist.

Perception of Women's Communications

Differences between convicted rapists and other offenders have been found with regard to their perception of women's communications. Fiske and Taylor (1991) describe generally how stereotypical ideas and prejudices can influence social perception and may lead to perceptual biases which then influence behaviour. Drieschner and Lange (1999) describe the three hypotheses which have suggested the way in which rapists may misperceive communications from women. The *overperception* hypothesis states that sexual aggressors tend to misperceive women's friendly behaviour as seductive and assertive behaviour as hostile. The *positivity bias* hypothesis suggests that, in ambiguous situations, rapists misperceive negative dismissive cues from women as positive and encouraging. Finally, the *suspicious schema* hypothesis states that rapists generally mistrust women's communications, independent of the type of affective cues that they give out. All three hypotheses have been supported empirically, with particularly strong evidence to suggest that rapists and men high in rape proclivity differ from other men in that they misperceive women's dismissive cues as encouraging (McDonel and McFall, 1991). Men higher in rape proclivity have also been found to perceive friendly and seductive women in videotaped heterosocial interactions as hostile (Malamuth and Brown, 1994). The clear differences between convicted rapists, other offenders, and non-offenders may be accounted for by the fact that performance tests of perceptual accuracy are less susceptible to social desirability than the self-report measures outlined above.

TYPOLOGIES OF RAPISTS

In recognition of the heterogeneity of men who commit rape, there have been attempts to classify such individuals into different types. One of the earliest typologies was that proposed by Groth and Birnbaum (1979), who distinguished between anger, power, and sadistic rapists. The authors suggest that these types can be differentiated by characteristics such as degree of physical force, mood, and nature of the assault. Thus the *anger rapist* is typically an individual whose behaviour is impulsive and their victim determined by availability. Their mood is one of anger, they may use more physical force than is required to achieve compliance although not necessarily use a weapon. Their motivation is one of retaliatory aggression. The *power rapist* is typically an individual whose assault is premeditated with previous rape fantasies. Their victim may be determined by vulnerability, and the assault may take place over a period of time, with the victim held captive. Such individuals use the degree of force necessary to control their victim, but may use a weapon as a threat. Their mood state is often one of anxiety, and they are motivated by using compensatory aggression to feel powerful. The *sadistic rapist* is the least common, probably accounting for about 5% of reported rapes. These individuals commit pre-planned assaults in a mood state of excitement and dissociation. They are sexually aroused by aggression and may commit ritualistic or degrading acts. Other authors have described features of the *impulsive* type of rapist (i.e., an individual whose lifestyle is characterized by antisocial behaviours in general, sexual assault being just one of these: Seghorn and Cohen, 1980)

The most recent attempt at the classification of rapists has been the empirically driven typology developed by Knight and Prentky (1990). This describes rapists, first, by their primary motivations: opportunistic, pervasively angry, sexual (sadistic or non-sadistic), and vindictive. A second discriminatory tier then classifies each type (except the pervasively angry) in terms of degree of social competency (high or low), leading to nine possible types in total. This typology is still being evaluated for reliability and validity. One of the issues for all classificatory systems is whether they can be helpful in informing clinical practice. Certainly the Knight and Prentky (1990) model is rather unwieldy, and may be less applicable to a broad range of rapists, including 'first offenders' (Barbaree, Seto, Serin, Amos, and Preston, 1994). It also questionable how useful the above typologies are in understanding rape within the context of a relationship or 'dating' situation (Humphreys and Herold, 1996).

THEORIES OF RAPE

The psychological literature has long been concerned with attempts to understand the aetiology of rape and sexual aggression. Historically, psychoanalytic and psychodynamic theories predominated until the mid to late 1970s, when feminist, evolutionary, biological, and behavioural perspectives started to emerge. One of the limitations of these 'single-factor' theories is the danger of oversimplifying and polarizing the issues, and current aetiological theories are multifactorial in nature. However, the works of the earlier theorists set the scene for such later developments and are outlined below.

Psychodynamic Theories

The earliest accounts of rape in the psychoanalytic literature interpreted women's accounts of rape and sexual abuse as fantasy, and saw male deviant sexual behaviour in adulthood as resulting from unresolved infantile sexual desires. Groth, Burgess, and Holmstrom (1977) suggested that sexual assault may occur when feelings of sexual or interpersonal inadequacy and unacknowledged homosexual tendencies interacted with aggression directed at the victim, who may be a substitute object for the mother. There has been little empirical support for psychodynamic theories and they have not had a significant impact on treatment developments.

Evolutionary Theories

Shields (1975) noted that evolutionary theories were the main explanations of gender differences until they were replaced by psychoanalytic theories in the 1930s. With the decline in popularity of psychodynamic approaches, Muelenhard, Harney, and Jones (1992) suggest that evolutionary theories are re-emerging as evolutionary psychology and sociobiological theories (Thornhill and Thornhill, 1992: Ellis, 1993). The essential premise of evolutionary theories is that behaviours, which facilitate the production of many offspring, are more likely to be favoured in natural selection. Such theories therefore assume a genetic basis to male sexual aggression and proclivity to rape. Ellis (1993) proposed a sociobiological theory of rape in which he sees rape as being motivated by two drives: the sex drive and the drive to possess and control. He suggests that, due to natural selection, men have a stronger sex drive than women and are therefore more motivated than women to use a variety of tactics, including force, to obtain sex with a variety of partners. Men learn tactics for obtaining sex (including alcohol, drugs, the use of deception, and physical force) more readily than women. He proposes a role for neurochemical influences (i.e., that exposure of the brain to testosterone and other androgens both increases sex drive and decreases sensitivity to punishment and others' suffering).

Ellis's (1993) evolutionary theory has been heavily criticised (Polaschek *et al.*, 1997). Critics note that much of Ellis's evidence comes from animal studies, and that cultural factors can account for other factors cited. By proposing a pure sexual motivation for rape, the theory ignores the heterogeneity of rapists, many of whom are motivated by aggression or dominance. Prentky (1985) argues that it is improbable that a single neurotransmitter is exclusively associated with sexual aggression, and that, even if such a relationship does exist, it is likely to be small and associated with violence in general (Hall, 1990).

Feminist Theories

Feminist theories of rape have made a major contribution to the way rape and its survivors are viewed in society and to research in this area. The psychodynamic and evolutionary approaches contain implicit elements of victim blaming and could be interpreted as viewing rape as behaviour for which men cannot be held responsible. Feminist theories emerging in the 1970s proposed a major shift in the conceptualization of rape, arguing that this was an act of violence rather than one of sex, and that fear of rape operated as a means of social control (Brownmiller, 1975). Rape is therefore viewed as predominantly driven by a generalized hostility towards women in the context of a society that favours men, rather than by a desire to be sexual. McCormick (1994) compares the two dominant feminist approaches. Radical feminists emphasize the dangers inherent in heterosexual relationships, viewing most such interactions as coercive and exploitative. Liberal feminists place a greater emphasis on the role of the patriarchal society rather than on men *per se*, and advocate removing the barriers imposed by such a society. Cross-cultural studies have examined the ways in which societies can be more or less 'rape-supportive'; for example, Sanday's (1981) study suggests that the incidence of rape in a given society is influenced by two factors: male dominance and the acceptance of interpersonal violence.

Feminist theories of rape set the scene for the increasing awareness of 'date rape' and sexual harassment, and later proponents of multivariate theories have acknowledged the significance of sociocultural influences (e.g., Marshall and Barbaree, 1990a, see p. 316). However, because of the focus on society in general, feminist theories alone cannot account for the heterogeneity of rapists and explain the differential impact of societal influences at the individual level (Polaschek *et al.*, 1997).

Behavioural Theories

Although feminist theories of rape drew awareness to the way in which rape is not always a sexual crime, the role of sexual arousal cannot be dismissed completely. Behavioural theories of rape have focused on the role of deviant sexual arousal, either in a positive response to perceived 'rape cues' or in a lack of the inhibitors which occur in most men. The most detailed behavioural theory is that proposed by Barbaree and Marshall (1991), who suggest six different models of the role of the offender's sexual arousal during rape. The *sexual preference model* suggests that some men may have a stable, trait-like preference for forced sex, which for those individuals is the most reinforcing type of sexual activity. Second, the *trait-inhibition of rape arousal model* suggests that, unlike most men, rapists do not experience inhibited sexual arousal in the combined presence of non-consent and knowledge that the women is in discomfort, fear, or pain. The third model, *state disinhibition of arousal*, is similar to the second, but refers to a lack of usual inhibition of sexual arousal in the presence of 'rape cues'. These are factors which increase an offender's antisocial motivation; for example, judging a woman to be responsible for the assault because of her clothing or for being alone in a remote area (Sundberg et al., 1991). The final three models suggest some type of interaction between sexual arousal and other emotions, either that other emotions augment the sexual response, or that rapists may have difficulty in voluntarily suppressing sexual arousal, or that they have a capacity to be both aggressive and sexually aroused at the same time. Polaschek et al. (1997) note that the strength of behavioural theories lies in their capacity to accommodate the heterogeneity of patterns of interaction between perceptions of victims and patterns of arousal which are evident in the analysis of individuals' offending. However, much of the evidence (particularly for the sexual preference model) is based on the phallometric studies outlined earlier, which have produced equivocal results. Socio-cultural and cognitive factors are largely neglected. It would seem that behavioural mechanisms might best be integrated into the multivariate theories if the broadest explanatory framework of rape is to be attempted.

Multivariate Theories

In addition to the theoretical criticisms of the single-factor theories outlined above, these theories appear frustratingly limiting when working clinically with men who commit sexual assaults, whose motivations appear to be varied and complex. There are three main multivariate theories for the aetiology of rape, which attempt to integrate separate factors into a comprehensive framework.

Malamuth's Confluence Model

Malamuth, et al. (1993) describe a multivariate model of sexual aggression in which several factors must converge in order for such behaviour to occur. Malamuth and colleagues describe six predictor variables of rape proclivity, with evidence that they interact in a synergistic way to increase the frequency of sexually aggressive acts when all six are present (see Figure 13.1). The variables are: sexual arousal to rape, dominance as a motive for sex, hostility towards women, attitudes facilitating aggression towards women, antisocial personality characteristics, and sexual experience as a measure of opportunity to aggress. They suggest that the predictor variables belong to two interacting pathways that lead to sexual aggression, *hostile masculinity* and *sexual promiscuity*. Childhood experiences contribute to the development of the first four predictors which make up the hostile masculinity pathway. Parental violence and physical/sexual abuse can lead to the development of antisocial attitudes

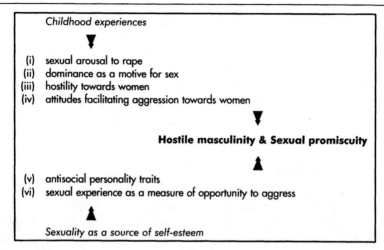

Figure 13.1 Malamuth *et al.* (1993) multivariate theory of rape: predictor variables of rape proclivity.

towards male/female relationships and personality features which make coercive behaviour more likely. The sexual promiscuity path reflects the overuse of sexuality as a source of self-esteem, and both increases the opportunity and the likelihood of using coercion in the pursuit of sexual conquest. Given the presence of the predictor variables, Malamuth *et al.* (1993) then identify three 'proximate causes' for an offence to occur: motivation to commit the aggressive act, reductions in internal and external inhibitions that usually prevent aggression, and opportunity (see Figure 13.2). There are clear similarities here with Finkelhor's (1984) four preconditions for child sexual abuse.

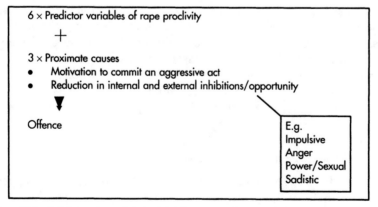

Figure 13.2 Malamuth *et al.* (1993) Multivariate theory of rape: proximate causes.

Malamuth and colleagues describe their pathways in very general terms, and Polaschek *et al.* (1997) suggest that the sexual promiscuity pathway in particular requires more theoretical underpinning, possibly linking to the research on intimacy deficits and attachment styles in men who sexually assault (Hudson and Ward, 1997). However, this is the only multivariate theory which has been empirically validated, both cross-sectionally and longitudinally on non-institutionalized populations.

Marshall and Barbaree's (1990a) Integrated Theory

Marshall and Barbaree's integrated theory emphasizes the role of early causal factors of sexual aggression, combined with later transient situational variables. They present evidence which suggests that poor parenting—particularly inconsistent, harsh physical discipline in the absence of warmth and accepting support—contributes to failure in the tasks of socialization, such as positive attitudes towards relationships and social controls with respect to sex and aggression. They argue that socially created inhibitors of the biological capacity to sexually aggress are crucial, particularly for males at puberty when there is a marked increase in hormonal activity. A vulnerable adolescent male may have poor social skills, particularly with respect to intimacy, negative attitudes, and a lack of distinction between sexuality and aggression. Such an individual may use the paternalistic culture, in which women and children are seen as objects to be used for the sexual satisfaction of males, to boost his sense of masculinity and self-esteem. The vulnerability factors then interact with more transient situational elements (such as intoxication, strong negative emotion, belief he will not be caught, presence of a potential victim) to determine the occurrence of sexual assault.

This integrated theory therefore takes into account the role of developmental, social-cognitive, biological and sociocultural factors in the aetiology of sexual assault, and allows for both the heterogeneity of sexually assaultative behaviour and the motivations of its perpetrators. There may be an overemphasis on the adolescent offender, but clinical experience suggests that most first-time adult offenders have experienced problems with sexual behaviour as a teenager, either in terms of a lack of relationship development or in promiscuity and rape supportive attitudes.

Hall and Hirschmann's (1991) quadripartite model

Hall and Hirschmann's (1991) quadripartite model of sexual aggression has four main components: sexual arousal, cognitions justifying sexual aggression, affective dyscontrol (particularly anger and hostility), and antisocial personality traits. These components serve both as motivational precursors which increase the probability of sexually aggressive behaviour occurring, and also to define subtypes of offenders, depending on which factor is most prominent. The critical component of this model is the offender's cognitive context; if the appraised benefits (e.g., sexual gratification, expression of anger) outweigh the appraised costs, (e.g., fear of being caught), then sexually aggressive behaviour is more likely to occur. Also relevant are the negative affective states of anger and hostility, identified by many authors as being facilitators in the early stages of the chain of events leading to sexual aggression (e.g., Quinsey, 1984). Hall and Hirschmann (1991) suggest a reciprocal relationship between these emotions and the normal inhibitors of sexually aggressive behaviour, such as victim empathy, guilt, and anxiety about consequences. Finally, as with the other proponents of multivariate models, the authors describe how negative, early developmental experiences increase the likely formation of antisocial attitudes and decrease the probability of adequate socialization.

Polaschek et al. (1997) suggest that the fourth personality component is described in very general terms, with its relationship to the other three factors not defined. Nonetheless, as with the other multivariate theories, Hall and Hirschmann's (1991) model is useful clinically as a framework with which to identify the relevant contributory factors to an individual's offending.

In conclusion, there are theoretical limitations with each of the single-factor and multivariate theories, not least that they all focus exclusively on sexual aggression perpetrated by males, albeit that men are by far the predominant perpetrators. The multivariate psychological theories have also been criticised by the feminist theorists for 'pathologizing' rapists, basing their evidence on men in prison or in treatment programmes (Muelenhard et al., 1992). Polaschek et al. (1997, p. 132) note that, as with other areas of theory development within psychology, there has been an absence of an integrated approach to theory building, which has resulted in 'the chaotic proliferation of theories at different levels, that often overlap but not infrequently seem to ignore each others' existence.' However, the multivariate theories all suggest the importance of adverse developmental experiences and the role of cognitive factors; the latter particularly informing treatment programmes. Although, at a theoretical level, delineation of the specific processes which mediate between vulnerability and offending may not yet be well defined, this can often be attempted at the clinical level with individual offenders. Indeed, when working clinically with individuals, it is often more productive to take an idiographic approach to understanding the meaning of their offending, such as the Personal Construct Psychology approach, which focuses on the way in which an individual construes the world (Kelly, 1955, 1991; Houston, 1998).

TREATMENT APPROACHES

It is important to understand why men sexually aggress in order to both prevent potential rapists offending and to reduce the risk of convicted rapists reoffending. Interventions aimed at rape prevention are addressed in Chapter 10, and so only the treatment of convicted sexual offenders will be addressed here. Throughout the 1980s and 1990s there was widespread development of treatment programmes for sexual offenders, most of these being cognitive-behavioural in orientation. There has been very public debate in the academic literature about the efficacy of such treatment. On the one hand, there are those authors who state that methodological inadequacies mean that it is not possible to determine whether treatment of sex offenders reduces recidivism (Furby, Weinrott, and Blackshaw, 1989; Quinsey, Harris, Rice, and Lalamiere, 1993). An equally vociferous reply has come from those who have argued that the 'perfect' experimental design is not possible with this population and that, despite methodological problems, there is evidence that comprehensive cognitive-behavioural programmes are associated with a reduction in recidivism for treated sex offenders (Marshall et al., 1991; Pithers, 1993). A recent meta-analysis of 12 studies, which did meet stringent research criteria, reported a small but robust treatment effect, with 19% of treated offenders and 27% of non-treated offenders reoffending at an average of 6.85 years follow-up (Hall, 1995).

One of the difficulties with the treatment literature is that the studies do not always differentiate between different types of sex offenders, and those that do generally report more encouraging results for child sex offenders and exhibitionists than for rapists (Marshall and Barbaree, 1990b). The numbers of sexual aggressors against adult women in the samples also tend to be much smaller than the numbers of child sex offenders. It is generally recognized both clinically and in the literature that it is more difficult to engage rapists in treatment and that they have higher drop out rates (Marshall, 1993). Nonetheless, following their review of treatment efficacy, Polaschek et al. (1997) concluded that

> Overall, despite the problems identified above, we believe that there are still grounds for cautious optimism with respect to whether treatment works with rapists ... substantial grounds exist for arguing that rapists do require a concerted research effort in order to parallel the gains made with child molesters (p. 134).

Treatment programmes are therefore fairly widely available for *convicted* sex offenders, including rapists. Typically, this consists of groups of about eight men who may have offended against adults or children or have committed 'non-contact' offences such as exhibitionism. Most groups tend to be cognitive-behavioural in orientation, with modules focusing on patterns and cycles of offending, distorted thinking, victim awareness, fantasy, and relapse prevention. The relapse prevention model developed in the field of addictions (Marlatt and Gordon, 1985) has been adapted for work with sex offenders (e.g., Pithers, 1990) and is now a major component of sex offender treatment. In the UK, sex offender treatment groups are run in a range of settings. There is a comprehensive Sex Offender Treatment Programme run in 25 English and Welsh prisons, which provides both a *core programme*, with the key elements as outlined above, and an *extended programme* for those who have additional needs, such as management of anger and other emotions (Mann and Thornton, 1998). Sex offender treatment groups are also run in the maximum secure hospitals (Perkins and Fisher, 1998), medium secure units and the community (Houston, Thomson, and Wragg, 1994, Craisatti, 1998), and by the Probation Service (Beckett, Beech, Fisher, and Fordham, 1994). Because of the smaller numbers of rapists and generally poorer outcome than for child sex offenders, many services are now developing treatment programmes specifically for this offender population. It is more difficult for *unconvicted* offenders who are concerned about their potential or actual behaviour to gain access to treatment. Community groups run by forensic mental health services do accept referrals of such individuals, but such referrals can raise complex ethical dilemmas regarding confidentiality. Clinical experience suggests that there is a fairly high dropout rate of unconvicted offenders from such groups.

IMPLICATIONS FOR CLINICAL PRACTICE

For a clinician, there are a number of differences between working with men who have committed sex offences and other types of offenders. There is always a specific victim who has been harmed, and this often raises strong emotions in the clinician that need to be acknowledged and dealt with in order to work effectively with the offender. It is therefore important for clinicians working with sex offenders to do so within a value framework that enables them to be clear about why they are working with this offender group. Based on the work of Salter (1988), Morrison (1994) outlines the essential components of such a value base:

1 sexual assault is always unacceptable and should be investigated as a crime;

2 sexual assault is damaging to the victim;
3 sexual assault results from an intention on the part of the offender to seek both sexual and emotional gratification from the victim;
4 sexual assault represents an abuse of power;
5 the overarching aim of intervention is to protect victims and potential victims;
6 intervention must be based on the offender taking full responsibility for the feelings, thoughts, and behaviour which support his offending (male sexual arousal is controllable);
7 where it is in the victim's interests, sex offenders should be prosecuted;
8 the goal of intervention is to ensure that sex offenders can control their behaviour so that they do not reoffend or sexually abuse others;
9 (*for men who have offended against children*) the management of offenders requires a co-ordinated response involving criminal justice and child protection agencies;
10 in the longer term, the prevention of sexual offences needs to address the sex role expectations of males in our society.

As well as having an explicit value stance, Salter (1988) also raises other differences for the clinician in working with this offender population. Unlike most other therapist/client relationships, confidentiality with sex offenders can never be total, and this needs to be overtly discussed with the individual. Because of the way in which sex offenders distort their beliefs to minimize or justify their offending (see below), it is also not appropriate to take what the offender says at face value, although many men are extremely convincing in maintaining their denial or version of events. More confrontation is therefore required to work with this client group than with others. However, it is important that this is done in a way which maintains rapport, rather than in a way which drives the offender into withdrawal and further denial. The clinician must therefore obtain the difficult balance between empathy and respect for the client vs. collusion with their justifications for their offences.

Clinical Features of Men Who Sexually Assault—Implications for Treatment

In the clinical setting, there are a number of common features observed in men who have committed sexual assaults. Many of these features reflect the way in which the offender has distorted his thinking in order to convince himself that his behaviour is less harmful. They therefore act as a type of psychological defence against the reality of sexual assault, enabling the individual to commit crime(s) which most people would find abhorrent. One of the aims of treatment is to enable the offender to identify and challenge his self-deceptions, thus contributing to a reduction in the risk of him further offending.

Denial and Minimization

There is a whole range of distorted thinking associated with offending (Salter, 1988). Some men show total denial of the offence (i.e., 'it wasn't me ... I wasn't there at the time ... I was wrongly identified'). Such men are very difficult to work with in the usual treatment groups as they do not admit to having committed any offence. However, because of the large numbers of men who show total denial, particularly in the prison system, specific treatment approaches are being developed for this population. These may address general criminogenic factors, such as impulsivity and empathy, or work at the 'what if' level, addressing hypothetical offence-related situations.

It is more common for men to admit to some aspect of the offending behaviour but to deny sexual intent or arousal; for example, a man who sexually assaults a woman in a crowded train may maintain that he 'accidentally' brushed against her, or a person convicted of indecent exposure in a park may maintain that he was stopping to urinate.

Men who admit to sexual assaults frequently deny full responsibility for their offending, trying to attribute some (or all) of this to their victim, or deny that their behaviour has been harmful. Most men seen at the point of assessment also considerably minimize the nature and extent of their offending, and try to give the impression that it 'just happened' or that the victim was exaggerating.

Justifications and Thinking Errors

What the academic and theoretical literature describes as 'rape myths' and 'rape-supportive attitudes' (Burt; 1980, Harmon et al., 1995) are identified and labelled in clinical practice as justifications, excuses, and thinking errors or cognitive distortions. The meanings behind the terms are the same, and all describe the ways in which many men who sexually assault distort their thinking in order to overcome their inhibitions or justify their behaviour. Common justifications and thinking errors shown by men who sexually assault include:

> she didn't physically resist therefore she must have enjoyed it
> women who dress like that don't mind men coming on to them
> I didn't physically hurt her ... it wasn't that bad
> I've got away with it once so I won't get caught another time

A large component of therapy offered by treatment groups includes identifying and challenging these justifications and thinking errors. One of the advantages of having mixed groups of sex offenders in treatment is that men who have not offended against adults may hold these beliefs with less intensity or not at all. Challenges from other male group members are much more likely to be effective than from the group leaders or from a single clinician. Treatment groups also explore an offender's general attitudes towards men, women, and children; again with the aim of identifying those that have contributed to later offending. Men who sexually assault women have often generalized their attitudes towards women with whom they have had negative experiences to include all women (i.e., 'women always get what they want').

Lack of Victim Empathy

Although the term 'victim' is usually not appropriate to use when working with survivors of sexual assault, it is used when working with offenders. When offenders begin treatment, many still considerably deny or minimize the harm they have caused, and there is a danger that using the term 'survivor' would reinforce this. Many men who assault women think of their victim solely as an 'object' for their own sexual gratification, or (as described above) convince themselves that their behaviour is not really harmful. For such individuals, it is important to increase both their intellectual and their emotional understanding of the consequences of their offending for their victims. This is done through giving information about the short- and long-term effects of sexual assault and, more importantly, through the use of role play and experiential tasks that are designed to have an emotional impact. There are, however, some types of sex offenders for whom it is inappropriate to participate in victim empathy work. For the sadistic type of offender, causing harm to the victim is part of the motivation for the assault. Material used effectively with non-sadistic offenders may be sexually arousing to those who are sadistic, fuel fantasy, and potentially increase the likelihood of future offending. These differences in the characteristics of sex offenders highlight the importance of a comprehensive initial assessment before the onset of treatment and is an example of one clinical implication of the theoretical typologies.

Case Example

Andrew was the youngest of three children. His father was frequently violent to both his mother and himself, and eventually left home when Andrew was 8 years old. His mother subsequently remarried. He was a large and clumsy child, and was subjected to emotional abuse and humiliation from his stepfather for not being a 'proper boy'. He found it hard to make friends and was bullied at school, leaving with no qualifications.

Andrew started to become sexually aware in his early teens and was attracted to girls but had little confidence. He found some hidden pornographic magazines at home and came to think that the use of these was easier than the thought of talking to girls in reality and developing relationships. A brief relationship in his late teens did not last long, and Andrew believed that this was because he was not 'man enough' to take the initiative in developing a sexual relationship. By his early 20s, Andrew was beginning to feel increasingly desperate about his lack of success in developing relationships. He started to fantasize about a young woman whom he regularly saw at a fairly isolated bus stop on his way to work, and, as she had smiled at him on a few occasions, he began to convince himself that she may be interested in a relationship. Over a period of weeks, his fantasies started to include an element of sexual assault, although at that time he did not conceptualize this as such. Looking back, he described how he convinced himself that if he approached her sexually she would comply. He had a belief that if he could behave in what he saw as a 'manly' way on this occasion, then this would make him feel better about himself and more likely to achieve success with relationships in the future. Andrew therefore planned his assault carefully, looking out for an opportunity when few other people were around. His plans were thwarted when the woman struggled and screamed during the assault, which had not been part of his fantasy. He panicked and ran off, and was apprehended shortly afterwards.

Andrew received a prison sentence and agreed to participate in a treatment group. During treatment he was able to identify the thinking errors which predated his offending, which included 'women expect men to be dominant sexually' and 'it's only rape if you force a woman into sex with a knife'. These beliefs enabled him to minimize the seriousness of his fantasies and behaviour and ultimately to justify this to himself. He talked about his own sense of inadequacy as a man and how this may have developed from his own childhood experiences. He came to see how distorted his thinking was (i.e., that by ultimately having intercourse this would transform his life). He struggled more with the acknowledgement that he had misperceived ordinary friendly behaviour from a woman as a 'come-on'. It was only through watching video material of a woman talking about the effect of sexual assault on her life and some experiential work in the group that he finally acknowledged the seriousness of his offence and its consequences for his victim. This also enabled him to recognize how his use of pornography had led him into a fantasy world, and the importance of controlling deviant sexual fantasies in future (i.e., those involving force or coercion).

Andrew continued to engage in a relapse prevention group in the community when he was released from prison. This focused on developing a personal

'Relapse Prevention Plan' to identify his most likely routes to relapse, high-risk moods and situations, and coping strategies to deal with them. This group also focused on developing his strengths and maintaining a non-offending lifestyle, incorporating elements to improve self-esteem and relationship skills. Andrew maintained voluntary contact with the group for 4 months after his licence ended, but then left to look for a full-time job. Five years on, he has not been charged with any further sexual offences.

CONCLUSIONS

Over the last three decades, theoretical research into rape and sexual assault has shifted in focus. The feminist theories moved both academia and society on from the victim-blaming stance of the early 1970s. Other single factor theories emphasize the importance of biological and evolutionary factors, and there is still a growing body of research into the role of cognitive factors in the aetiology of rape. However, it is the multivariate theories which have had most influence on treatment programmes, probably as they are more easily able to accommodate the heterogeneity of men seen in clinical practice. Therefore, although identifying and challenging distorted beliefs is a major component of treatment, other elements also need to be incorporated which target deficiencies in hetero-social skills and increase behavioural self-control. Some programmes also include a component which acknowledges the offender's own experiences of victimization, but only at a point in treatment when they have progressed enough for this not to be used as an excuse for their own offending. Because of the difficulties in engaging rapists in treatment and the less encouraging outcome than for sex offenders against children, it is also recognised that programmes need adapting to meet the specific needs of this offender group. This may involve an increased focus on the recognition and regulation of affect, more general cognitive skills training, or elements from programmes designed for violent offenders (Polaschek et al., 1997)

Finally, one of the difficulties in working with sexual offenders against adults, as compared with those who have offended against children, is that the distorted beliefs of the former group are more deeply embedded in the general culture. The recent use of discourse analysis with pairs of men and women, discussing a hypothetical rape incident, illustrates how rape myths are still perpetuating a rape-supportive culture in the UK (Doherty and Anderson, 1998). It is clearly important for survivors of sexual assault to be aware that distorted beliefs originate from the perpetrator and that they are not responsible for the assault. However, it is also important for society to acknowledge its own continuing role in reinforcing those beliefs, and that more could still be achieved to reduce this.

REFERENCES

Abel, G.G., Barlow, D.H., Blanchard, E.B., and Guild, D. (1977) The components of rapists' sexual arousal. *Archives of General Psychiatry*, **34**, 895–903.

Barbaree, H.E. and Marshall, W.L. (1991) The role of male sexual arousal in rape: Six models. *Journal of Consulting and Clinical Psychology*, **59**, 621–630.

Barbaree, H.E., Seto, M.C., Serin, R.C., Amos, N.L., and Preston, D.L. (1994) Comparisons between sexual and non-sexual rapist subtypes. *Criminal Justice and Behaviour*, **21**, 95–114.

Bard, L.A., Carter, D.L., Cerce, D.D., Knight, R.A., Rosenberg, R., and Schneider, B. (1987) A descriptive study of rapists and child molesters: Developmental, clinical and criminal characteristics. *Behavioural Sciences and the Law*, **5**, 203–220.

Beckett, R., Beech, A., Fisher, D., and Fordham, A.S. (1994) *Community based treatment for sex offenders: An evaluation of seven treatment programmes*. London: Home Office.

Blackburn, R. (1993) *The psychology of criminal conduct*. Chichester, UK: Wiley.

Blader, J.C. and Marshall, W.L. (1989) Is assessment of sexual arousal in rapists worthwhile? A critique of current methods and the development of a response compatibility approach. *Clinical Psychology Review*, **9**, 569–587.

Brownmiller, S. (1975) *Against our will: Men, women and rape*. New York: Simon and Schuster.

Burt, M.R. (1980) Cultural myths and support for rape. *Journal of Personality and Social Psychology*, **38**, 217–230.

Carter, D.L., Prentky, R.A., Knight, R.A. Vanderveer, P.L., and Boucher, R.J. (1987) Use of pornography in the criminal and developmental histories of sexual offenders. *Journal of Interpersonal Violence*, **2**, 196–211.

Christie, M.M., Marshall, W.L., and Lanthier, R.D. (1979) *A descriptive study of incarcerated rapists and child molesters* (Report to the Solicitor General of Canada) Leicester, UK: The British Psychological Society.

Craisatti, J. (1998) *Child sexual abusers: A community treatment approach*. Hove, UK: Psychology Press.

Doherty, K. and Anderson, I. (1998) Talking about rape: Perpetuating rape-supportive culture. *The Psychologist*, **11**(12), 583–588.

Drieschner, K. and Lange, A. (1999) A review of the cognitive factors in the etiology of rape: Theories, empirical studies and implications. *Clinical Psychology Review*, **19**(1), 57–77.

Ellis, L. (1993) Rape as a biosocial phenomenon. In G.C.N. Hall, R. Hirschmann, J.R. Graham, and M.S. Zaragoza, (eds) *Sexual aggression: Issues in etiology, assessment and treatment* (pp. 17–41) Washington, DC: Taylor and Francis.

Finkelhor, D. (1984) *Child sexual abuse: New theory and research*. New York: Free Press.

Fiske, S.T. and Taylor, S.E. (1991) *Social cognition* (2nd edn). New York: McGraw Hill.

Furby, L., Weinrott, M.R., and Blackshaw, L. (1989) Sex offender recidivism: A review. *Psychological Bulletin*, **105**, 3–30.

Groth, A.N. and Birnbaum, A.H. (1979) *Men who rape: The psychology of the offender*. New York: Plenum Press.

Groth, A.N., Burgess, A.W., and Holmstrom, L.L. (1977) Rape: Power, anger and sexuality. *American Journal of Psychiatry*, **134**, 1239–1243.

Grubin, D. and Gunn, J. (1990) *The imprisoned rapist and rape.* London: Institute of Psychiatry.

Hall, G.C.N. (1990) Prediction of sexual aggression. *Clinical Psychology Review*, **10**, 229–245.

Hall, G.C.N. (1995) Sex offender recidivism revisited: A meta-analysis of recent treatment studies. *Journal of Consulting and Clinical Psychology*, **63**, 802–809.

Hall, G.C.N. and Hirschmann, R. (1991) Towards a theory of sexual aggression: A quadripartite model. *Journal of Consulting and Clinical Psychology*, **59**, 662–669.

Hall, G.C.N., Shondrick, D.D., and Hirschman, R. (1993) The role of sexual arousal in sexually aggressive behavior: A meta analysis. *Journal of Consulting and Clinical Psychology*, **61**, 1091–1095.

Harmon, G.A., Owens, R.G., and Dewey, M.E. (1995) Rapists' versus non-rapists' attitudes towards women: A British study. *International Journal of Offender Therapy and Comparative Criminology*, **39**, 269–275.

Houston, J.C. (1998) *Making sense with offenders: Personal constructs, therapy and change.* Chichester, UK: Wiley.

Houston, J.C., Thomson, P., and Wragg, G. (1994) A survey of forensic psychologists' work with sex offenders. *Criminal Behaviour and Mental Health*, **4**, 118–129.

Hudson, S.M. and Ward, T. (1997) Intimacy, loneliness and attachment style in sexual offenders. *Journal of Interpersonal Violence*, **12**(3), 323–339.

Humphreys, T.P. and Herold, E. (1996) Date rape: A comparative analysis and integration of theory. *The Canadian Journal of Human Sexuality*, **5**(2), 69–82.

Kelly, G. (1955) *The psychology of personal constructs* (Vol. 1). London: Routledge.

Kelly, G. (1991) *The psychology of personal constructs* (Vol. 2). London: Routledge.

Knight, R.A. and Prentky, R.A. (1990) Classifying sexual offenders: The development and corroboration of taxonomic models. In W.L. Marshall, D.R. Laws, and H.E. Barbaree, (eds) *Handbook of sexual assault: Issues, theories and treatment of the offender* (pp. 23–52). New York: Plenum Press.

Koss, M.P. and Oros, C.J. (1982) Sexual experiences survey: A research instrument investigating sexual aggression and victimisation. *Journal of Consulting and Clinical Psychology*, **50**, 455–457.

Langevin, R., Paitich, D., and Russon, A.E. (1985) Are rapists sexually anomalous, aggressive or both? In R. Langevin, (ed.) *Erotic preference, gender identity and aggression.* Hillsdale, NJ: Lawrence Erlbaum.

Laws, D.R. and Marshall, W.L. (1990) A conditioning theory of the etiology and maintenance of deviant sexual preference and behaviour. In W.L. Marshall, D.R. Laws, and H.E. Barbaree, (eds) *Handbook of sexual assault: Issues, theories and treatment of the offender* (pp. 209–229). New York: Plenum Press.

Leitenberg, H. and Henning , K. (1995) Sexual fantasy. *Psychological Bulletin*, **117**, 469–496.

Leonard, R.A. (1993) The family backgrounds of serial rapists. *Issues in Criminological and Legal Psychology*, **19**, 9–18.

McCormick, N.B. (1994) *Sexual salvation: Affirming women's rights and pleasures.* Westport, CT: Praeger.

McDonel, E.C. and McFall, R.M. (1991) Construct validity of two hetero-social perception skill measures for assessing rape proclivity. *Violence and Victims*, **6**, 17–30.

Malamuth, N.M. and Brown, L.M. (1994) Sexually aggressive men's perception of women's communications: Testing three explanations. *Journal of Personality and Social Psychology*, **67**, 699–712.

Malamuth, N.M., Heavey, C.L., and Linz, D. (1993) Predicting men's antisocial behavior against women: The interaction model of sexual aggression. In G. Hall, R. Hirschman, J.R. Graham, and M.S. Zaragoza (eds) *Sexual aggression: Issues in etiology, assessment and treatment* (pp. 63–97). Washington, DC: Taylor and Francis.

Mann, R.E. and Thornton, D. (1998) The evolution of a multi-site sex offender treatment programme. In W.L. Marshall, Y.M. Fernandez, S.M. Hudson, and T. Ward (eds) *Sourcebook of treatment programmes for sexual offenders*. New York: Plenum Press.

Marlatt, G.A. and Gordon, J.R. (1985) *Relapse prevention: Maintenance strategies in the treatment of addictive behaviours*. New York: Guilford Press.

Marshall, W.L. (1989) Intimacy, loneliness and sexual offenders. *Behaviour, Research and Therapy*, **27**(5), 491–503.

Marshall, W.L. (1993) A revised approach to the treatment of men who sexually assault adult females. In G.C.N. Hall, R. Hirschmann, J.R. Graham, and M.S. Zaragoza (eds) *Sexual aggression: Issues in etiology, assessment and treatment* (pp. 143–165). Washington, DC: Taylor and Francis.

Marshall, W.L. and Barbaree, H.E. (1990a) An integrated theory of the etiology of sexual offending. In W.L. Marshall, D.R. Laws, and H.E. Barbaree (eds) *Handbook of sexual assault: Issues, theories and treatment of the offender* (pp. 257–275). New York: Plenum Press.

Marshall, W.L. and Barbaree, H.E. (1990b) Outcome of comprehensive cognitive-behavioural treatment programs. In W.L. Marshall, D.R. Laws, and H.E. Barbaree (eds) *Handbook of sexual assault: Issues, theories and treatment of the offender* (pp. 363–385). New York: Plenum Press.

Marshall, W.L., Jones, R.J., Ward, T., Johnston, P.W., and Barbaree, H.E. (1991) Treatment outcome with sex offenders. *Clinical Psychology Review*, **11**, 465–485.

Morrison, T. (1994) Context, constraints and considerations for practice. In T. Morrison, M. Erooga, and R.C. Beckett (eds) *Sexual offending against children: Assessment and treatment of male abusers* (pp. 25–54). London: Routledge.

Mosher, D.L. and Anderson, R.D. (1986) Macho personality, sexual aggression and reactions to guided imagery of realistic rape. *Journal of Research in Personality*, **20**, 77–94.

Muelenhard, C.L., Harney, P.A., and Jones, J.M. (1992) From 'victim-precipitated rape' to 'date rape': How far have we come? *Annual Review of Sex Research*, **3**, 219–253.

Perkins, D. and Fisher, D. (1998) Working with sexual offenders in psychiatric settings in England and Wales. In W.L. Marshall, Y.M. Fernandez, S.M. Hudson, and T. Ward (eds) *Sourcebook of treatment programmes for sexual offenders*. New York: Plenum Press.

Pithers, W.D. (1990) Relapse prevention with sexual aggressors: A method for maintaining therapeutic gains and enhancing external supervision. In W.L.

Marshall, D.R. Laws, and H.E. Barbaree (eds) *Handbook of sexual assault: Issues, theories and treatment of the offender* (pp. 343–362). New York: Plenum Press.

Pithers, W.D. (1993) Treatment of rapists: Reinterpretation of early outcome data and exploratory constructs to enhance treatment efficacy. In G.C.N. Hall, R. Hirschmann, J.R. Graham, and M.S. Zaragoza (eds) *Sexual aggression: Issues in etiology, assessment and treatment* (pp. 167–196) Washington, DC: Taylor and Francis.

Polaschek, D.L.L., Ward, T., and Hudson, S.M. (1997) Rape and rapists: Theory and treatment. *Clinical Psychology Review*, **17**(2), 117–144.

Pollard, P. (1994) Sexual violence against women: Characteristics of typical perpetrators. In J. Archer (ed.) *Male violence* (pp. 170–194) London: Routledge.

Prentky, R.A. (1985) The neurochemistry and neuroendocrinology of sexual aggression. In D.P. Farrington, and J. Gunn (eds) *Aggression and dangerousness* (pp. 7–55). New York: Wiley.

Prentky, R.A. and Burgess, A.W. (1991) Hypothetical biological substrates of a fantasy-based drive mechanism for repetitive sexual aggression. In A.W. Burgess (ed.) *Rape and sexual assault III* (pp. 235–256). New York: Garland Publishing.

Prentky, R.A., Knight, R.A., Sims-Knight, J.E., Straus, H., Rokous, F., and Cerce, D. (1989) Developmental antecedents of sexual aggression. *Development and Psychopathology*, **1**, 153–169.

Quinsey, V.L. (1984) Sexual aggression: Studies of offenders against women. In D. Weisstub (ed.) *Law and mental health: International perspectives* (Vol. 1, pp. 84–121). New York: Pergamon Press.

Quinsey, V.L., Chaplin, T.C., and Upfold, D. (1984) Sexual arousal to non-sexual violence and sadomasochistic themes among rapists and non-sex offenders. *Journal of Consulting and Clinical Psychology*, **52**, 651–657.

Quinsey, V.L., Harris, G.T., Rice, M.E., and Lalumiere, M.L. (1993) Assessing treatment efficacy in outcome studies of sex offenders. *Journal of Interpersonal Violence*, **8**, 512–523.

Rogers, P. (1997) Post traumatic stress disorder following male rape. *Journal of Mental Health*, **6**(1), 5–9.

Salter, A.C. (1988) *Treating child sex offenders and victims*. Newbury Park, CA: Sage Publications.

Sanday, P.R. (1981) The socio-cultural context of rape: A cross cultural study. *Journal of Social Issues*, **37**, 526–540.

Saradjian, J. (1998) *Women who sexually abuse children*. Chichester, UK: Wiley.

Scarce, M. (1997) *Male on male rape: The hidden toll of stigma and shame*. New York: Plenum Press.

Scully, D. (1990) *Understanding sexual violence: A study of convicted rapists*. Boston: Unwin Hyman.

Seghorn, T.K. and Cohen, M. (1980) The psychology of the rape assailant. In W.J. Curran, A.L. McGary, and C. Petty (eds) *Modern legal medicine, psychiatry and forensic science* (pp. 533–551). Philadelphia: Davis.

Seidman, B.T., Marshall, W.L., Hudson, S.M., and Robertson, P.J. (1994) An examination of intimacy and loneliness in sex offenders. *Journal of Interpersonal Violence*, **9**(4), 518–534.

Shields, S.A. (1975) Functionalism, Darwinism and the psychology of women: A study of social myth. *American Psychologist*, **30**, 739–754.

Stermac, L.E. and Quinsey, V.L. (1986) Social competence among rapists. *Behavioral Assessment*, **8**, 171–185.

Stermac, L.E., Segal, Z.V. and Gillis, R. (1990) Social and cultural factors in sexual assault. In W.L. Marshall, D.R. Laws, and H.E. Barbaree (eds) *Handbook of sexual assault: Issues, theories and treatment of the offender* (pp. 143–159). New York: Plenum Press.

Struckman-Johnson, C. and Struckman-Johnson, D. (1988) Forced sex on dates: It can happen to men, too. *Journal of Sex Research*, **24**, 234–241.

Struckman-Johnson, C. and Struckman-Johnson, D. (1994) Men pressured and forced into sexual experience. *Archives of Sexual Behaviour*, **23**, 93–114.

Sundberg, S.L., Barbaree, H.L., and Marshall, W.L. (1991) Victim blame and the disinhibition of sexual arousal to rape vignettes. *Violence and Victims*, **6**, 103–120.

Thornhill, R. and Thornhill, N.W. (1992) The evolutionary psychology of men's coercive sexuality. *Behavioural and Brain Sciences*, **15**, 363–421.

Chapter 14

THE FUTURE AGENDA FOR CARE AND RESEARCH

Jenny Petrak

INTRODUCTION

The consequences of sexual assault have a major impact on health and economic resources across the globe. The World Health Organization estimate that in industrialized countries rape and domestic violence account for 1 in every 5 healthy years of life lost to women aged 15–44 (Heise, Pitanguy, and Germain, 1994). Byrne, Resnick, Kilpatrick, Best, and Saunders (1999), using a broad definition of 'victimization' which included physical and sexual assault, found that these crimes significantly increase women's risk for socio-economic decline (e.g., unemployment, divorce, poverty). It therefore continues to be somewhat surprising that care, treatment, research, and prevention of violence against women and men does not appear to be high on the political agenda of the majority of countries, industrialized or otherwise. As we start the new millennium, many anti-rape programmes and community-based rape crisis organizations are experiencing dwindling resources and are struggling to survive. Social commentators emphasize the extent to which rape and sexual assault are ingrained within our social order and, perhaps, this contributes to a sense of inevitability regarding these crimes. However, only a few decades have passed since feminist activists called for the elimination of these crimes or at least '... a 24 hour truce during which there is no rape' (Dworkin, 1983). While essential statements set a tone for reform and incentive to action, it is likely that much more time, political action, and sustained reform is required to achieve such radical social and cultural change. Much has been learnt, however, over the past decades and translated into legal, medical, social reform, and clinical practice. Rape

The Trauma of Sexual Assault. Edited by Jenny Petrak and Barbara Hedge.

and sexual assault are less 'hidden crimes' than was once the case, although this may continue to be the case for men (see Chapter 3). Greater effort is made to encourage reporting to police and access to support. Public awareness of sexual assault and rape is high in developed countries, perhaps, partially stimulated by frequent reports in newspapers of controversial cases or issues, although sensationalist reporting can continue to perpetuate myths and stereotypes. An example of the latter are recent reports of using 'lie detector' tests with false complainants which emphasized, incorrectly, the high frequency of false allegations (*Independent*, 31 October 2000), and made no reference to the possibility that individuals making such allegations may require professional help themselves (see Chapter 11). Rape myths and stereotypes are pervasive and, as demonstrated in several chapters in this book, can influence both an individual's psychological response and how their social environment responds.

An evidence-based approach towards the physical and psychological care of survivors of sexual assault is emerging. Throughout this book an attempt has been made to draw together both the available evidence and general principles of therapy practice for individuals to apply in a variety of areas of clinical practice. As such it will hopefully be of relevance to both a range of professionals working directly with the care of those who have experienced sexual assault and those working 'indirectly' across a wider spectrum of services. The latter might well include any person working in any area of health and social services based on findings indicating high physical morbidity and use of medical services (Golding, Cooper, and George, 1997) and, in general, low reporting to police and rape support services by sexually traumatized individuals (Koss and Harvey, 1991).

Throughout this book, authors have highlighted areas related to the care, treatment, and prevention of sexual assault which require development and further research. This is recognition that this is not a static field but one that requires continued activism and research to ensure that complacency and acceptance do not become the dominating influences upon societal responses to rape. The aims of this concluding chapter are, thus, to pull together a number of future agendas for care and research of sexual assault. There is much left to do.

SERVICES AND THERAPY

The setting up of specialist centres combining forensic, medical, and psychological care following sexual assault is a relatively new initiative in the UK and, as such, their effectiveness will require evaluation. It is not clear that these centres will solve the problem of high attrition rates found in medical services in general (Holmes, Resnick, and Frampton, 1998). Volunteers who work within victim support schemes, usually in conjunction with the police, provide the majority of post-rape support in the UK. Services often employ a model of 'psychological debriefing' delivered by support workers who may lack comprehensive training in mental health and stress disorder diagnoses. Psychological debriefing following trauma, in general, has come under increasing criticism (Kenardy, 2000). A recent meta-analysis suggests that debriefing, defined in this review as a single-session intervention within 1 month or less of the trauma involving some form of emotional processing/ventilation by recollection of the traumatic event accompanied by normalization of emotional reactions, does not decrease the development of PTSD (Wessely, Rose, and Bisson, 2000). In some cases, debriefing may increase the likelihood of more problematic post-trauma responses leading the authors to conclude that compulsory debriefing should cease (Wessely *et al.*, 2000). The relevance of these findings to rape and sexual assault trauma is not clear. The high emotional distress observed post-assault may make it difficult for professionals not to respond, but it remains an important area of research regarding if, how, when, and by whom this should be provided. Training and ongoing supervision of 'front-line' staff (including police, forensic medical examiners, physicians, nurses, and support workers) in rape and sexual assault trauma seem like a bare minimum in order to facilitate assessment skills, increase non-judgemental responses, and prevent staff stress and burnout (see Chapter 12).

The mechanisms by which psychological debriefing might adversely affect recovery is unclear. It has been suggested that, while there will be great individual variation (e.g., personality, coping style, perception of the trauma as life-threatening, ongoing stressors) in response and recovery, psychological debriefing may simply be too brief an exposure, particularly in those individuals who are demonstrating high avoidance post-trauma (Kenardy, 2000). There is limited evidence that sustained early psychological intervention using CBT and prolonged exposure can result in a reduction in the likelihood of the onset of PTSD (Foa, Hearst-Ikeda, and Perry 1995; Bryant, Sackville, Dang, Moulds, and Guthrie, 1999). A new approach towards prevention of post-rape psychopathology using a hospital-based video intervention to reduce distress associated with forensic examination (Resnick, Acierno, Holmes, Kilpatrick, and Jager 1999) has also produced positive results but requires further research. While reducing distress associated with the forensic examination was achieved in Resnick *et al.*'s study, it remains to be seen whether this has an impact on other post-rape psychopathology. Clear recommendations are made in

Chapter 4 for the need for future research to attempt to identify the successful components of empirically validated psychological treatments in the aftermath of sexual assault. In addition, while there are a few studies documenting long-term psychological difficulties associated with a history of sexual assault (e.g., Kilpatrick, Saunders, Veronen, Best, and Von, 1987), there is a paucity of research examining whether the gains of psychological treatment are maintained and cause reduction in such symptoms. Few treatment studies address the question of which aspects of the treatment offered were more or less useful to participants, and this should also be considered in future research. A further requirement for future research will be to include treatment studies of male survivors of sexual assault, although a continued problem will be the difficulties that men have in identifying their needs and accessing health care in the first place.

Where services for sexual assault exist (statutory and voluntary), the focus of intervention is usually only directed towards the individual who has been sexually assaulted. There is a paucity of research on the impact of sexual assault on partners, family, and significant others, and it may be that their needs are not being adequately recognized or addressed. However, the negative response of others can be significant in terms of the development of post-rape psychopathology (e.g., Zoellner, Foa, and Brigidi, 1999). It is also, therefore, important that services also consider the impact on partners and others who may be experiencing difficulties which can interfere with adaptation on the part of the person who has been sexually assaulted.

REVICTIMIZATION AND PREVENTION

Several studies suggest that prior histories of sexual victimization increase the likelihood of revictimization (e.g., Koss and Dinero, 1989; Humphrey and White, 2000). Revictimization is also associated with higher post-assault psychopathology (see Chapter 6). While most treatment studies have focused exclusively on reducing post-rape psychopathology, the high rate of revictimization points clearly towards the need to enhance existing treatment approaches to include strategies that may reduce the risk of being revictimized. The question of which strategies (e.g., assertion training, training in recognizing potential high-risk situations, role play, and rehearsal of sexual scripts, interpersonal and negotiation skills) are more or less useful, and at what stage of therapy they could be introduced is an important area for research. Successful behavioural intervention strategies for prevention of sexually transmitted diseases (STDs) and HIV (e.g., Shain et al., 1999) may also provide relevant techniques to apply to the area of prevention of revictimization. The acceptability of such strategies to clients should also be investigated. It will be important that such interventions should make very clear that the responsibility for preventing rape and sexual assault does not rest solely on the actions of the survivor. Protective strategies aimed at individuals are only one aspect of sexual assault prevention, and the wider impact of rape attitudinal change programmes are also important areas for further research (see p. 341 and Chapter 10).

DRUG-ASSISTED RAPE AND SEXUAL ASSAULT

In the past few years, there has been increasing reports of drug-facilitated sexual assault using substances including flunitrazepam (Rohypnol), gamma-hydroxybutyrate (GHB), and ketamine (Smith, 1999; Slaughter, 2000; Schwartz, Milteer, and LeBeau, 2000). These substances (often used in conjunction with alcohol or slipped into complainants' drinks) are used by perpetrators of rape to commit sexual assault because they act rapidly, produce disinhibition, relaxation of muscles, confusion, and cause lasting anterograde amnesia for events occurring under the influence of the drug (Slaughter, 2000). Symptoms of these drugs may often seem to mimic alcohol intoxication, and their effects are certainly enhanced by alcohol. Such drugs become rapidly undetectable in blood and urine (within 72 hours) requiring the individual to report rape within a relatively short period after the rape has occurred for proof to be obtained. Typically, however, an individual will remain confused and unsure whether a rape has happened leading to a delay in reporting. In addition, an individual reporting sexual assault may be reluctant to have a toxicology test in case this identifies other substances that she may have taken, fearing her own arrest (Sturman, 2000). Individuals reporting sexual assault in the UK are not routinely tested for drugs (Sturman, 2000). Furthermore, as in the case of victims who are found to have high levels of alcohol, individuals may be considered unreliable witnesses resulting in a decreased likelihood that the case will proceed to court.

While studies from the USA support relatively widespread use of drug-facilitated sexual assault, there are to date few studies from other countries documenting the extent of this problem. Little is known about the psychological impact of drug-assisted sexual assault. Clinical experience suggests that men and women who suspect they may have been sexually assaulted while under the influence of these drugs may often experience distress at not remembering the event and may go to some length in an attempt to retrieve the memory or receive confirmation from some other source. Individuals may also experience flashbacks, limited recall of the event, or regain consciousness during the assault, causing high levels of distress. Whether or not an individual can remember the incident, 'being believed' remains an important component of recovery. Whether there is an effect upon the development of levels of PTSD and other psychopathology due to having no or limited memory (due to drug or alcohol intoxication) of the event is an area for future research. It is also important to study the neuropsychological profile of the effect of drugs used to facilitate rape. Such research may provide useful information to alert services (medical, legal, and otherwise) towards characteristic responses both during and post-intoxication. A recent report commissioned by the Home Office and Metropolitan Police in the UK on drug-assisted sexual assault recommends that expert evidence is given by a clinical psychologist as to what drug(s) may have been administered by describing the impact of the drug used upon the complainant. Such evidence might be used when no toxicological evidence is obtained (Sturman, 2000). It should not be assumed, however, that the majority of mental health professionals are any better informed than anyone else due to the newness of information in this area. There is a need for training in the impact of drug-assisted sexual assault across all legal, medical, and mental health professionals involved in the care of sexual assault. Finally, there is a call both in the USA and UK (e.g., 'The Roofies Foundation') that Rohypnol, which continues to be relatively easy to obtain on private prescription, should be banned. It is argued that more effective drugs now exist for its intended clinical use for anxiety and sleep disorder, and that Rohypnol is now better described as a substance of misuse, particularly due to being the most often reported drug used to facilitate rape. However, simply banning one class of drug used in sexual assault is unlikely to diminish the problem since other substances are readily available. There is clearly a need for continued research and understanding in this area, and a great need for an environment to be created to enable increased reporting of this crime.

MEDICAL CONCERNS

A further area of concern is the increasing use of prophylaxis medications post-rape (see Chapter 9). Adherence to post-exposure prophylaxis (PEP), administered for reducing risk of HIV infection post-sexual assault, is very low (Wiebe, Comay, McGregor, and Ducceschi 2000). It is not clear what the reasons for this might be, although there is some suggestion that those perceiving themselves to be at greater risk of acquiring HIV infection (e.g., men who had experienced rape by another male) were more likely to complete the treatment than those at lower risk. In the same study, it was also noted that service providers found it problematic to provide information on HIV prophylaxis to traumatized individuals (Wiebe *et al.*, 2000) which raises important questions regarding the ability to provide informed consent to such treatments. Few studies examining adherence to medical treatment and care post-sexual assault consider what is already know about disruption to functioning in the aftermath of trauma, which may well explain low uptake. Even less is known about adherence to other prophylactic medications (e.g., for preventing hepatitis) prescribed post-sexual assault.

Whether a greater prevalence of sexually transmitted diseases (STDs) including HIV is found in sexual offender populations compared with the general population is also not known. Some survivors of sexual assault understandably express resentment that assailants once apprehended do not experience mandatory testing for STDs and HIV. However, aside from criminal law and human rights issues, which are beyond the scope of this chapter, the argument against mandatory testing of assailants for infections include the length of time elapsed that most often occurs before an assailant is apprehended. A positive test result offers no information as to whether the assailant has infected the survivor or whether the survivor has acquired the infection elsewhere (Canadian Strategy on HIV/AIDS, 1998). There is obvious concern that widespread administration of medications post-sexual assault may further 'medicalize' distress and prolong psychopathology. This should also be considered in future research, in addition to establishing clear consensus guidelines on if, what, when, and how prophylaxis medications should be administered post-sexual assault. The cost of these medications also prohibit their availability in most developing countries and, thus, the vast majority of individuals experiencing rape will not receive any benefit. Lack of resources and inequalities in health care are an important and wider topic, beyond the scope of this book, but nevertheless provide the backdrop in which care for individuals who have been sexually assaulted may or may not happen. There is a continuing need for the implementation of international programmes which share skills developed countries have acquired in the care and treatment of individuals who have been sexually assaulted, within resource-poor settings.

TRAUMA RECOVERY

A majority of individuals will not make any contact with services post-sexual assault and future research should include evaluating differences in individual response and recovery and the capacity for seeking help. It remains unclear why some people develop persistent post-traumatic stress responses, and some more transitory conditions, while others may appear relatively unaffected by the traumatic event. Promising and relatively new areas of research include systematic investigation of cognitive factors which may maintain PTSD symptoms (e.g., Dunmore, Clark, and Ehlers, 1997; Dunmore, Clark, and Ehlers, 1999). Cognitive models of PTSD consider the contribution of guilt, shame, self-blame, mental planning (e.g., thinking of ways to escape) and/or mental defeat (e.g., feeling entirely at the mercy of the situation), the interpretation of symptoms, perceived negative response of others in the aftermath of the assault, and global negative beliefs about the assault, which may contribute to more persistent problems (Dunmore et al., 1997). The mechanisms by which these cognitive factors may contribute to PTSD directly include generating a sense of ongoing threat, and indirectly motivating both behavioural and cognitive strategies which impede recovery or affecting content of traumatic memories (Dunmore et al., 1999). Cognitive models of PTSD are also more likely to prove more directly relevant (and testable) to studies addressing therapy process and outcome following sexual assault, where research continues to be needed.

Although rarely addressed in the literature on post-rape psychological phenomena, cognitive models may also help explain how, for some survivors, self-appraisal of positive coping with a traumatic event may lead to perceptions of positive growth from the experience (McFarland and Alvaro, 2000). The few studies addressing the latter area emphasize that any positive outcome is not about being raped itself but relates to an individual's capacity in determining positive aspects of dealing with the trauma, such as increased self-worth (Veronen and Kilpatrick, 1983). Future research might also include questions that reflect that individuals may also have positive outcomes in coping with trauma, and may provide useful directions towards enhancing individuals' sense of motivation and mastery over such events.

CROSS-CULTURAL RESEARCH

Many studies now document the prevalence of sexual assault across different cultural and ethnic groups (Heise et al., 1994), but there are very few studies documenting post-sexual assault trauma across diverse groups. The impression given might suggest that mental health difficulties including PTSD are relatively universal phenomena in the aftermath of sexual assault. However, since the act of sexual assault is deeply embedded within prevailing social and cultural constructions, it is likely that this will also influence individual traumatic response; for example, Heise et al. (1994) comment on data documenting the high percentage of women becoming pregnant as a consequence of rape in countries in which abortion is illegal or where safe abortion services are not available, thus resulting in the woman experiencing the added trauma of having no choice but to bear the rapist's child. The consequences of rape in sub-cultures of, for example, Africa, Asia, and the Middle East, which place a high value on women's virginity, may also be particularly severe. If the rape is disclosed or found out, this can lead to women being ostracized by communities, if not also beaten, murdered, or driven to suicide because of the dishonour that rape has brought upon the family (Heise *et al.*, 1994). Clearly, in many instances the trauma is not going to be just about the rape itself but about the many potential negative outcomes determined by the cultural, social, and political milieu. The findings of cultural responses to rape and sexual assault are likely to be informative to many multi-cultural clinical settings in the West; for example, in one UK setting, low disclosure of sexual assault to family and friends and hence little available social support was found among a small number of South Asian women accessing clinic services following rape. Fears of reducing the opportunity for marriage and being ostracized by families were reasons for not disclosing the rape to others (Petrak, Doyle, Williams, Buchan, and Forster, 1997). Nevertheless, it should be noted that difficulties disclosing rape and sexual assault and achieving supportive responses are not limited to specific cultures, although the reasons given for non-disclosure may be different.

In general, research on the impact and treatment of sexual assault rarely includes issues such as gender, sexual orientation (see Chapter 3), and ethnicity when examining the psychological impact of sexual assault and treatment. Further cross-cultural research is essential in highlighting such issues and in contributing towards the development of culturally sensitive interventions for prevention and treatment of post-rape trauma. Models of response to trauma should also attempt to incorporate social and cultural factors to a greater extent than they currently do.

LEGAL REFORM AND TRAUMA

Considerable literature now points towards the need for legal reform both in terms of how complainants are dealt with by the police, medical examiners, courts, and legal systems in the aftermath of trauma (see Chapter 11) and in how rape and sexual assault are defined in law in various countries. For an in-depth understanding of these issues in the UK, readers are referred to the notable work of Sue Lees (1996). Among numerous recommendations for judicial reform, Lees (1996) makes particular recommendations for broadening the definition of rape beyond the current central focus on penetration. In clinical practice, it is clear that individuals experience many more acts of degradation constituting a sexual assault, which are as distressing, but which do not meet the current legal definition of rape in the UK (see Chapter 1). Lees (1996) also argues that the burden of proof placed on the person who is raped is far greater than for other crimes; for example, robbery victims do not need to prove that they resisted their assailant or 'consented' to be robbed. The interpretation of what constitutes 'consent' is central to the debate on legal reform regarding sexual offences. Offenders frequently shift the blame towards the complainant and argue they thought she/he had consented (Sturman, 2000). Sturman (2000) proposes that offenders should not be allowed to use this excuse, particularly where drugs and/or alcohol are used impairing a person's ability to consent. In general, he argues that police and legal services should adopt a much greater 'complainant-driven' approach enabling greater involvement of the complainant at all stages (Sturman, 2000).

Forensic medical exams are directed at finding physical evidence (e.g., bruises, cuts, semen, etc.) that a crime has occurred, and, unless such evidence is found, conviction of the assailant is rare. The rate of conviction for rape is decreasing in the UK while the number of reported rapes are increasing (Harris and Grace, 1999). The police and judicial system continue to mistakenly believe that women frequently make false allegations (Lees, 1996). Many cases are not brought forward to the prosecution service due to 'lack of evidence' and seemingly unreliable statements by complainants. Sturman (2000) recommends that the police should believe all rape complainants even if their account is confused and lacks credibility.

The symptoms of acute stress disorder (e.g., confusion, dissociation, and amnesia), and accumulating evidence documenting cognitive deficits associated with trauma in the weeks following rape (Jenkins, Langlais, Delis, and Cohen, 1998, 2000; Mechanic, Resick, and Griffin, 1998), suggest it should come as no surprise that statements taken post-sexual assault appear unreliable (and, see p. 335, regarding the further complications associated with drug-facilitated sexual assault). Stereotypical expectations of how an individual 'should' appear following rape and sexual assault continue to abound and are used in court to discredit sexual assault allegations. All of the above suggest the need for closer cooperation between those researching and providing care and treatment for the psychological aftermath of sexual assault and those involved in the judicial and legal system. Police and courts in the UK do not currently consider characteristic post-sexual assault psychopathology on behalf of complainants as evidence towards proving that a sexual assault has occurred (as occurs in other countries). In the UK, the psychological distress complainants have experienced is only used in determining sentencing once a conviction has been achieved, although, currently, there are moves towards including 'victim personal statements' of how the crime has affected their lives throughout the criminal justice process (Criminal Justice System, 2001). However, it might also be important that such statements are accompanied by expert evidence as to the psychological impact of the crime. At a bare minimum, training about the psychological effects of rape and sexual assault on the complainant, and how stereotypical views can prejudice the courts, should be provided for police, forensic medical examiners, lawyers, judges, and courts. There is much that the psychology of trauma could contribute towards this fraught area.

PREVENTION

The evaluation of a number of US-based rape and sexual assault prevention programmes are provided in Chapter 10. There is very little published research in this area in the UK, and little available information regarding the availability of rape prevention strategies within universities and colleges here (where many of the US programmes are centred). The attitude of faculty staff may in itself be a necessary area for change, as evidenced by a recent example reported to the author regarding a female student who informed her school tutor that her distress and disruption to her studies related to an incident following a campus-based party during which she reported being raped by a male student. She did not report the incident to the police because she had been drinking alcohol and did not think she would be believed. She reported the response of her college tutor to be 'you've been silly and shouldn't have drunk so much'. The college did not feel they could intervene with the male student even though his identity was known. The student reported that the fact that her school tutor was female, and she assumed a more supportive response, was additionally distressing. Again, the above example raises issues regarding stereotypical views of what constitutes consent after a person has consumed alcohol (see p. 335; Sturman, 2000). Many persons choose to consume alcohol and other drugs which does not mean automatically consenting to sexual intercourse.

There clearly is need to institute college and university campus-based rape awareness training for young men and women in the UK as described in Chapter 10. There have been, however, some laudable public awareness campaigns, notably the 'Zero Tolerance' campaign in Scotland. The Zero Tolerance Charitable Trust has particularly focused their campaign towards young people after publishing research demonstrating widespread tolerance of violence against women among younger age groups (Burton and Kitzinger, 1998). Over 2,000 young people (mostly aged between 14 and 21) participated in the survey, and findings revealed that one in two boys and one in three girls reported 'some circumstances when it was okay to hit a woman or force her to have sex' and over a third of the boys (36%) indicated 'they might personally force a woman to have sex' (Burton and Kitzinger, 1998). This research indicates that challenging rape-supportive beliefs should start early and be sustained in the education of young men and women. A review of the important components of such programmes is found in Chapter 10.

A major criticism of rape prevention messages has been that the focus has often been directed towards young women and in particular 'date-rape' and acquaintance aggression (Nurius, 2000). Nurius (2000) argues that such awareness does not necessarily lead to enhanced perception of future risk, due to the complexity of social-cognitive variables (e.g., peer norms, sense of personal invulnerability) involved that are likely to influence any given situation. She also argues that programmes creating too much generalized fear (e.g., training women to be wary of all men) are flawed, oversimplified, and can place too much emphasis on women detecting threat by men (Nurius, 2000). Clearly, there is much research required in this complex area but the point is made that it would be a mistake to concentrate our prevention efforts only towards women, not least because men may also experience sexual assault. Prevention efforts also need to be targeted towards potential and actual offenders (mostly men; but see Chapters 3 and 13) and also towards the situations and means by which sexual assault occurs. However, most importantly, the success of any such rape prevention strategies will require all our involvement and, as such, need to be multifaceted, sustained, and society-wide.

SUMMARY

The above merely provides a sample of the vast amount of work still required to continue to improve care, treatment, and policy in the area of rape and sexual assault. This is a field where researchers cannot ignore the influence of the dominant social and political climate of the time. Much has been gained, primarily from the action of feminist activists, clinicians, and researchers over the decades, and their efforts have meant that the care and treatment of sexual assault has improved greatly since the early 1970s. Such achievements are unfortunately not global, and, as conservative, social, and political climates gain prominence continued resource and commitment in places where good models of care and treatment are provided may not be sustained. As we enter a new millennium, the challenge to activists, clinicians, and researchers will be to continue to keep these crimes high on the political, care, and research agenda.

REFERENCES

Bryant, R.A., Sackville, T., Dang, S., Moulds, M., and Guthrie, R. (1999) Treating acute stress disorder: An evaluation of cognitive-behavior therapy and supportive counselling techniques. *American Journal of Psychiatry*, **156**, 1780–1786.

Burton, S. and Kitzinger, J. (1998) *Young people's attitudes towards violence, sex and relationships: A survey and focus group study* (Research Report 002). Edinburgh: The Zero Tolerance Trust.

Byrne, C.A., Resnick, H.S., Kilpatrick, D.G., Best, C.L., and Saunders, B.E. (1999) The socioeconomic impact of interpersonal violence on women. *Journal of Consulting and Clinical Psychology*, **67**, 362–366.

Canadian Strategy on HIV/AIDS. (1998) *HIV and sexual violence against women: A guide for counsellors working with women who are survivors of sexual violence.* Ottawa: Health Canada.

Criminal Justice System. (2001) *Criminal justice: The way ahead.* London: Her Majesty's Stationery Office.

Dunmore, E.C., Clark, D.M., and Ehlers, A. (1997) Cognitive factors in persistent versus recovered post-traumatic stress disorder after physical or sexual abuse: A pilot study. *Behavioral and Cognitive Psychotherapy*, **25**, 147–159.

Dunmore, E.C., Clark, D.M., and Ehlers, A. (1999) Cognitive factors involved in the onset and maintenance of post-traumatic stress disorder after physical or sexual assault. *Behaviour Research and Therapy*, **37**, 809–829.

Dworkin, A. (1983) I want a 24 hour truce during which there is no rape. Speech to the Midwest Men's Conference, Minneapolis, 15 October 1983.

Foa, E., Hearst-Ikeda, D., and Perry, K. (1995) Evaluation of a brief cognitive-behavioral program for the prevention of chronic PTSD in recent sexual assault victims. *Journal of Consulting and Clinical Psychology*, **6**, 948–955.

Golding, J.M., Cooper, M.L., and George, L.K. (1997) Sexual assault history and health perceptions: Seven general population studies. *Health Psychology*, **16**, 417–425.

Harris, J. and Grace, A. (1999) *A question of evidence? Investigating and prosecuting rape in the 1990s.* London: Home Office.

Heise, L., Pitanguy, J., and Germain, A. (1994) *Violence against women: The hidden health burden* (World Bank Discussion Paper No. 225). Washington, DC: World Bank.

Holmes, M., Resnick, H., and Frampton, D. (1998) Follow-up of sexual assault victims. *American Journal of Obstetrics and Gynecology*, **179**, 336–342.

Humphrey, J.A. and White, J.W. (2000) Women's vulnerability to sexual assault from adolescence to young adulthood. *Journal of Adolescent Health*, **27**, 419–424.

Jenkins, M.A., Langlais, P.J., Delis, D., and Cohen, R. (1998) Learning and memory in rape victims with posttraumatic stress disorder. *American Journal of Psychiatry*, **155**(2), 278–279.

Jenkins, M.A., Langlais, P.J., Delis, D., and Cohen, R. (2000) Attentional dysfunction associated with posttraumatic stress disorder among rape survivors. *Clinical Neuropsychologist*, **14**, 7–12.

Kilpatrick, D., Saunders, B., Veronen, L., Best, C., and Von, J. (1987) Criminal victimization: Lifetime prevalence, reporting to police, and psychological impact. *Crime and Delinquency*, **33**, 479–489.

Kenardy, J. (2000) The current status of psychological debriefing. *British Medical Journal*, **321**, 1032–1033.

Koss, M. and Dinero, T. (1989) Discriminant analysis of risk factors for sexual victimization among a national sample of college women. *Journal of Consulting and Clinical Psychology*, **57**, 242–250.

Koss, M. and Harvey, M. (1991) *The rape victim: Clinical and community interventions*. Newbury Park, CA: Sage Publications.

Lees, S. (1996) *Carnal knowledge. Rape on trial*. London: Hamish Hamilton.

McFarland, C. and Alvaro, C. (2000) The impact of motivation on temporal comparisons: Coping with traumatic events by perceiving personal growth. *Journal of Personality and Social Psychology*, **79**, 327–343.

Mechanic, M.B., Resick, P.A., and Griffin, M.G. (1998) A comparison of normal forgetting, psychopathology, and information-processing models of reported amnesia for recent sexual trauma. *Journal of Consulting and Clinical Psychology*, **66**, 948–957.

Nurius, P. (2000) Risk perception for acquaintance sexual aggression: A social-cognitive perspective. *Aggression and Violent Behavior*, **5**, 63–78.

Petrak, J., Doyle, A., Williams, L., Buchan, L., and Forster, G. (1997) The psychological impact of sexual assault: A study of female attenders of a sexual health psychology service. *Sexual and Marital Therapy*, **12**, 339–345.

Resnick, J., Acierno, R., Holmes, M., Kilpatrick, D.G., and Jager, N. (1999) Prevention of post-rape psychopathology: Preliminary findings of a controlled acute rape treatment study. *Journal of Anxiety Disorders*, **13**, 359–370.

Schwartz, R.H., Milteer, R., and LeBeau, M.A. (2000) Drug-facilitated sexual assault ('date rape'). *Southern Medical Journal*, **93**, 558–561.

Shain, R.N., Piper, J.M., Newton, E.R., Perdue, S.T., Ramos, R., Champion, J.D., and Guerra, F.A. (1999) A randomized, controlled trial of a behavioural intervention to prevent sexually transmitted disease amongst minority women. *New England Journal of Medicine*, **340**, 93–100.

Slaughter, L. (2000) Involvement of drugs in sexual assault. *Journal of Reproductive Medicine*, **45**, 425–430.

Smith, K.M. (1999) Drugs used in acquaintance rape. *Journal of the American Pharmaceutical Association*, **39**, 519–525.

Sturman, P. (2000) Drug assisted sexual assault: A study for the Home Office under The Police Research Award Scheme. London: Home Office.

Veronen, L. and Kilpatrick, D. (1983) Rape: A precursor of change. In E. Callahan, and K. McCluskey (eds) *Life-span developmental psychology: Non-normative life events* (pp. 167–191). New York: Academic Press.

Wessely, S., Rose, S., and Bisson, J. (2000) *Brief psychological interventions ('debriefing') for trauma-related symptoms and the prevention of post traumatic stress disorder* (*The Cochrane Library*, Issue 2). Oxford: Update Software.

Wiebe, E.R., Comay, S.E., McGregor, M., and Ducceschi, S. (2000) Offering HIV prophylaxis to people who have been sexually assaulted: 16 months' experience in a sexual assault service. *Canadian Medical Association Journal*, **162**, 641–645.

Zoellner, L., Foa, B., and Brigidi, B.D. (1999) Interpersonal friction and PTSD in female victims of sexual and nonsexual assault. *Journal of Traumatic Stress*, **12**, 689–700.

INDEX

The Wiley Series in

CLINICAL PSYCHOLOGY

Chris Barker, Nancy Pistrang and Robert Elliott	Research Methods in Clinical and Counselling Psychology
Graham C.L. Davey and Frank Tallis (Editors)	Worrying: Perspectives on Theory, Assessment and Treatment
Paul Dickens	Quality and Excellence in Human Services
Edgar Miller and Robin Morris	The Psychology of Dementia
Ronald Blackburn	The Psychology of Criminal Conduct: Theory, Research and Practice
Ian H. Gotlib and Constance L. Hammen	Psychological Aspects of Depression: Toward a Cognitive-Interpersonal Integration
Max Birchwood and Nicholas Tarrier (Editors)	Innovations in the Psychological Management of Schizophrenia: Assessment, Treatment and Services
Robert J. Edelmann	Anxiety: Theory, Research and Intervention in Clinical and Health Psychology
Alastair Agar (Editor)	Microcomputers and Clinical Psychology: Issues, Applications and Future Developments
Bob Remington (Editor)	The Challenge of Severe Mental Handicap: A Behaviour Analytic Approach
Colin A. Espie	The Psychological Treatment of Insomnia
David Peck and C.M. Shapiro (Editors)	Measuring Human Problems: A Practical Guide
Roger Baker (Editor)	Panic Disorder: Theory, Research and Therapy
Friedrich Försterling	Attribution Theory in Clinical Psychology
Anthony Lavender and Frank Holloway (Editors)	Community Care in Practice: Service for the Continuing Care Client
John Clements	Severe Learning Disability and Psychological Handicap

CPSIA information can be obtained at www.ICGtesting.com
Printed in the USA
LVOW091318140911

246208LV00001B/81/P